THE CHANGING WORKPLACE

DATE DUE

THE CHANGING WORKPLACE

RESHAPING CANADA'S INDUSTRIAL RELATIONS SYSTEM

Daniel Drache and Harry Glasbeek

James Lorimer & Company, Publishers
Toronto, 1992

James Lorimer & Company Ltd. acknowledges with thanks the support of the Canada Council, the Ontario Arts Council and the Ontario Publishing Centre in the development of writing and publishing in Canada.

Cover illustration: Ed McDormand

Canadian Cataloguing in Publication Data

Drache, Daniel, 1941-
    The Changing Workplace: Reshaping Canada's Industrial Relations System

ISBN 1-55028-405-3 (bound). ISBN 1-55028-404-5 (pbk.)

1. Canada - Economic conditions - 1945- .
2. Industrial relations - Canada. I. Glasbeek, H. J. II. Title.
HC115.D73 1992 330'.0071   C92-094856-X

James Lorimer & Company, Publishers
Egerton Ryerson Memorial Building
35 Britain Street
Toronto, Ontario
M5A 1R7

Printed and bound in Canada

CONTENTS

ACKNOWLEDGEMENTS

This book has benefited from the help of many people. While it is not possible to thank everyone who has been an enthusiastic supporter of this work, special mention must be made, however, of our students. They have been a receptive audience and have made many practical and critical suggestions on how better to integrate the concerns of political economy with the precepts and ideas of labour law. We were also fortunate to have had the research assistance of Ann Porter. She did much of the initial footwork. For this we are grateful. Principal funding for her assistance and this study came from a SSHRCC grant. Both Atkinson College and Osgoode Hall provided much-needed institutional support. In particular, release time provided by the Atkinson Leave Fellowship was most welcome. Along the way, a number of friends and colleagues discussed, criticized, read and reread the many drafts of different chapters and, even more importantly, pressured us to finish this work. Special acknowledgements are due to Andy Ranachan, Judy Fudge, John O'Grady, Gérard Boismenu, Michael Mandel, Reuben Hasson, Robert Cox, Robert Boyer, Pascal Petit, Daniel Latouche, Marjorie Cohen, Pat McDermott, Neil Brooks, Eric Tucker, Brian Bercusson and Sol Picciotto for their individual counsel. As well, Hazel Pollack who patiently typed the manuscript in its many different stages is owed a very special "thank you" by us. And special thanks is due to Diane Young and Cy Strom for their editorial vigilance. Finally, we are indebted to our respective families. *Grazie mille.* Needless to say, any faults that remain are our responsibility.

D.D.
H.G.
July 1992

The Seduction of a Misunderstood Past: Taking Stock

We are writing this book because we are afraid that Canadian workers are in danger of losing what they have won. They are faced with a revolution in work and employment conditions. The pervasive perception is that this revolution is driven by world-wide, impersonal economic forces and that there is no alternative but to accept this new global order as inevitable. Canadian workers are feeling the effects of these international pressures locally. They have to deal with them where they are, with such weapons as they have won over time. The historic resistance of workers to business's drive for profit and control over the workplace has spawned a particular form of institutional ordering. It is vital to understand the limits this order imposes on workers' ability to resist the invigorated attacks by employers. Hence, the purpose of this book is to provide a description and analysis of the structures and institutions of Canadian industrial relations.

The story we are about to tell details the way in which the schemes which make up the industrial relations system and their underlying ideology help business to attain its goals at the expense of workers. It is our thesis that, as long as workers remain confined within the existing régimes, they will be fighting with one hand tied behind their back.

Four major schemes constitute Canadian industrial relations: private sector collective bargaining, public sector collective bargaining, the common law institution of the contract of employment, and a number of minimum standards and human rights–type statutes which modify the market by different means and in different degrees. It is common to perceive these régimes as regulating discrete and unconnected capital-labour relationships. Yet, one of the keys to labour's weakness at a time of increasing globalization is that these schemes form an integrated whole. The more privileged workers have the advantage of collective bargaining, while the more marginal ones must rely on individual wage bargaining, supplemented by state intervention. But the achievements of the better-off workers are always restricted by the drag-down effect of the unorganized. There is a strong interaction between the operation of the various schemes.

Today, workers in all sectors are confronted by employer demands for concessions and by the state's attempts to attack the existing social net. As many of these attacks are attempts to erode existing collective bargaining rights and processes, trade unions will be at the forefront of the defence of *existing* rights. This is all the more so because the disparity between the better-protected workers and the ones at the periphery of the labour market has given the achievements of collective bargaining better standing than they deserve. The view that the existing collective bargaining institutions are an appropriate bulwark against employer and government assaults will be reinforced by the occasional breakthrough of well-placed unions who are engaged in these rearguard fights. This will support the argument that a defence of the existing system of collective bargaining, mildly reformed, is worthwhile. What this assessment downplays is that, all too frequently, this model of private and public sector collective bargaining, complemented by individual contract making and minimum standards of legislation, also has been repeatedly, and very successfully, used to *contain* workers' demands. In the present climate, the potential for positive reform is likely to be outweighed by the industrial relations system's restrictive features. Even with a sympathetic government in power, surface reforms — as opposed to a radical overhaul — of the system will mean that any benefits gained are likely to be offset rather quickly. Something very different is needed by way of institutional ordering if Canada's workers are to reap effective, meaningful and long-lasting benefits. This is the case we want to make.

In Chapter 1 we give an overview of how global pressures create local problems. As business reorients itself to deal with new forms of competition, there is a decline in investment in industries in which the better-protected jobs had been created in Canada. It was in these sectors that the most mature and modern of the institutions of industrial relations, statutory collective bargaining, had been the most effective. Workers' conditions and the trade unions' abilities to deal with employers are worsening rapidly despite their access to collective bargaining in these sectors. Further, the decline of manufacturing and resource industries has meant that the nature and composition of the workforce is changing dramatically. More women and young people are entering into the labour market, mostly in service sector industries where, historically, collective bargaining has played a minimal role. As unionization is diminishing in the traditional and older sectors, unions are seeking to get a foothold in the newly developing ones. The question is whether institutions and political practices developed in a different time can be adapted to the new circumstances. In large measure this depends on what the true nature of those institutions and organizations is and what they really did achieve in the past.

In Chapter 2, we show that the industrial relations mechanisms chosen by, and for, Canadian workers always have put serious limitations on workers' ability to make significant gains. Our argument is that, more so than in other advanced industrialized nations other than the United States, the structures and institutions which regulate bargaining between the state, capital and labour in Canada have caused workers to bargain about narrow economic matters. Workers and their trade unions have not been able to become partners, in any real sense of the word, in the industrial and economic planning of the nation. A consequence has been that Canadian workers, to a much greater degree than their European counterparts, have failed to embed advances made in respect of the social wage into the very fabric of the polity and turn them into political rights. Such workers' benefits in Europe are much more difficult to erode than are equivalent social welfare provisions in Canada. At the root of this socio-political backwardness is the fact that the Canadian economy always has remained an export-led growth economy.

In Chapter 3, we support this argument by offering an analysis of some of the more important outcomes of collective bargaining and the government interventions which have complemented it.

Next, we turn to a description of how the major industrial relations institution, statutorily controlled collective bargaining in the private sector, operates. The advent of this modern régime was a major step up from the industrial relations institutions which preceded it. It is perceived as a valuable tool by unions.

Our account of it emphasizes the fact that Canada has adopted an industrial relations system which emphasizes competitive capitalism and the attendant ideology of private property and contract. As a consequence of this, Canada has relied heavily on the maintenance of respect for law in labour relations practices. The quintessential function of legal ordering is to protect private property and contract ideals. This has helped ensure that, despite a commitment to a measure of Keynesianism, a mildly mediated form of competitive contractualism remains the chief characteristic of Canadian industrial relations. Workers have been forced to bargain *vis-à-vis* individual employers as individual competitive units, narrowing their orientation. What this has led to is a severely fragmented union movement. In addition, a wedge has been driven between the unionized and the non-unionized sectors. Under these conditions, the state has found it relatively easy to promote an economic kind of trade unionism, one geared largely towards wage bargaining. These developments have required a great deal of supervision and interference by the state and have built into the industrial relations régime a rigidity and a legalism which make it difficult for workers to develop and to pursue alternative visions. Collective bargaining, Canadian-style, comes with built-in controls and regulations, imposed and policed by the state.

In Chapters 4 and 5 the structure and functions of labour relations boards are examined; we highlight the ideology of competitive contractualism that pervades the decision making of these boards. This ideology is embedded in, and reinforced by, legal liberal pluralism. The legalism which pervades labour relations and infects trade union practices is underscored.

In Chapter 6 we turn to a discussion of the tightly controlled state regulation of the right to strike. The point is not that workers do not frequently seek to throw off the fetters put on their right to strike. They do. Our argument is that the formal, acknowledged starting position of the scheme is that the collective power of workers is to be severely curtailed and that legal means can be, and should be, used ruthlessly to this end, whereas capital is to retain an amazing amount of freedom. For trade unions to maintain their existing status, they must accept this starting position: strikes are not permitted during the term of an agreement even if workers believe that, in order to have an employer respect their existing rights, they should be able to stop production to force the employer to negotiate with them. Legally, unions are obliged to teach their members to accept these norms and enforce them on their members even when many trade unionists might prefer to do otherwise. This puts trade union leaders in a contradictory position: uphold the collective agreement but alienate the rank and file, or break the law and act in accordance with the apparent wishes of their members.

Chapter 7 focuses on what often is seen as one of the great benefits of collective bargaining: the grievance arbitration process. We believe that its benefits have been overrated and its disadvantages underestimated. Again, the point is not to deny that grievance arbitration has led to a good deal of amelioration of individual workers' conditions. It has. Employers are no longer as free to indulge their whims and caprices as they once were. Nonetheless, workers have gained little control over the daily work processes and, consequently, very little by way of an enhanced quality of working life. The grievance arbitration machinery has reinforced legalism and diminished the possibilities for militancy; trade unions have become preoccupied with grievance arbitration and have come to play the role of managers of discontent.

At this stage of the work, we turn to the plight of the majority of Canadian workers, the unorganized. They are not members of a trade union, and this leaves them outside the institution of collective bargaining.[1] It makes them dependent on the minimum-employment-standards legislation of the federal and provincial governments. Our emphasis is that it is precisely because workers have been unable to use their economic power to political ends that the conditions of the unorganized are, by advanced industrial nations' standards, unacceptable. The focus of the argument in Chapter 8 is that the state, when discharging its legitimation function, has been able to get away with the provision of relatively low minimum standards and conditions for the majority of Canadian workers. When a failure to meet with established liberal norms forces the state to interfere with the market — say, in respect of the inequitable treatment of women and of the especially poor occupational health and safety conditions which prevail in Canada — it largely mirrors the private ordering system. It has interfered on a fragmented, workplace-by-workplace basis. From the workers' point of view, such an approach is much less beneficial than one which envisages a nation-wide, universal régime. The outcomes show this in a stark way.

At this point, the role of the state should be manifest. The nature of the state's intervention is shaped by the requirement to increase Canadian competitiveness by supporting private employers' eagerness to discipline their workforces. To further bolster this view, we turn to a discussion of the state's more direct interference with collective bargaining in the private sector. In Chapter 9, we discuss governments' willingness to curb union rights whenever the public interest, as defined by governments, is said to demand it. We also examine the state's treatment of its own employees. Many of them have been granted the right to bargain collectively. This frequently gives the impression that private sector bargaining powers have been extended to them. This is not so; legally their power is much more limited. The thrust of this discussion will be to show that the state frequently has (ab)used its employees to demonstrate to private employers that they are justified in being tough with their own workers. Both the incidence and ferocity of direct interference with private collective bargaining and of attacks by the state on its own employees have accelerated in recent years.

The story we will have told by then is that Canadian employers and the state have been able to use the Canadian industrial relations system as a mechanism of adjustment. An export-led growth economy is a boom-and-bust economy. The vagaries of demand for Canada's primary resources induce employers and the state to dampen labour's aspirations and goals. The fragmented nature of labour and the continued emphasis on the value of anarchic competition have helped to create a political atmosphere of a special kind: one in which it is hard to resist the argument that competitive efficiency may require Canadian workers to lower their expectations. Thus it is that the corporate sectors have every reason to believe that it is legitimate to deal with the new competitive pressures on them by extracting more value for less pay. Unless fundamental changes are introduced, employers will continue to enjoy success in their enlistment of governments to help them erode workers' rights. Indeed, it has become even more difficult than it was for workers to tilt state action in their favour. The business classes' ability to get the state, rather than the rich, to pay for economic restructuring has been supported by the "legalization" of Canadian politics, which has become more pronounced with the advent of the Charter of Rights and Freedoms and the legal culture it has brought to prominence.[2]

While we cannot elaborate this argument in this book, it is our contention that during a period of sharpening class divisions, class and history have been removed more effectively from debate than before. The *Charter of Rights and Freedoms* and the general preoccupation with abstract kinds of constitutional reforms epitomize this kind of politics. Whether or not this was a conscious goal, the result is that meaningful participation by workers and popular-sector groups in everyday political struggles is becoming ever more attenuated. The legalization of politics ensures the fragmentation of issues. This makes it more difficult for workers to harmonize their struggles with those of the other popular sectors which also have much to lose from the ongoing economic restructuring.

At the site of production, the economic restructuring has both a physical and a political dimension. There is an increasing use of technology with the potential to transform workplace relationships. But, given Canada's starting point, employers are deploying the new technologies neither to enrich work nor to find new niches to give Canada trade advantages. Their primary goal is to use them (inasmuch as they do use them) to extract more surplus value from each worker. We devote Chapter 10 to assess what the introduction of radically new technologies is likely to mean for the Canadian workforce. While there will be some benefits for some workers, it is our conclusion that the way in which the technologies are deployed, particularly in the expanding service sectors, will lead to lessened employment opportunities generally and to more oppressive working conditions for many of those fortunate enough to retain their jobs.

We are conscious of the fact that, in describing these institutional and structural constraints, we will not have done justice to the way in which workers always have sought to resist the imposition of hardships. Workers never did swallow holus-bolus the ideology of collective bargaining with its emphasis on contractualism and consensus, and frequently have tried to change their world. But, nonetheless, it is our view that the logic of the existing institutions and structures has seriously limited workers' ability to act as an effective political force. This provides the focus for our final chapter.

Given the problems which labour always has had to face in Canada, how should it go about dealing with the brand-new conditions which are confronting it? The response we offer seeks to take into account the facts of industrial life. The workers' organizations derive their legitimacy and such powers as they do have from the existing institutional order and ideology. This imposes serious constraints. In particular, workers must be able to overcome their own isolation and be able to reach out to other popular-sector groupings. But they cannot be asked to take risks that will render them more vulnerable than they already are. We proffer a number of strategies which take account of these realities. While we hope that this will assist workers to resist better the hardships which the transformation of work is forcing on them, we do not provide a blueprint. Workers will develop their own, as they always have. Our idea is to make a contribution to their efforts.[3]

Global Pressures, Local Problems

There is a new order of capitalism.[1] Capital is more mobile than it ever has been before. This has been facilitated by the emergence of huge conglomerations of capital. Transnational corporations are supported by a frighteningly large transnational banking system.[2] They are backed by an array of legal institutions which promote the integration of activities of legally separate, but functionally integrated, economic entities in different parts of the world.[3] Business is no longer nation-bound.

At the same time, there has been an exponential increase in the variety of new technologies with extraordinary, innovative capacities. They give employers many more choices in deciding where to invest or whether or not to fragment the productive process to enable different components to be made in different parts of the world.[4] An instance of this is the European model of the Ford Escort, whose various parts at one point came from seventeen different countries.[5] Such decisions vitally affect the respective bargaining strength of employers and workers.

These developments have made it much easier for capital to transcend the boundaries, and to defeat the goals, of nation states. They have come at a time when many nation states are seeking to assert their sovereignty and independence for the first time. Much of the Third World, once a cheap source of labour and materials for capitalists supported by the colonizing states from which they originated, is now seeking to control its own economic destiny. These Third World countries want to process their own resources, create employment, develop domestic manufacturing to meet local demands and export to earn currency. An eager transnational banking sector has facilitated the borrowing of capital for these purposes. Third World countries have incurred huge debts as interest and inflation rates have escalated. As a consequence, they are under pressure to export as cheaply as possible to the advanced industrialized world and to import as little as possible from it.

These are some of the basic economic and political features that frame the restructuring of economies in advanced capitalist nations such as Canada. What impact will these pressures have in Canada?

The most highly mobile fragments of Canadian business will be under pressure to move to where they can obtain the best return. This is, after all, the logic of profit-driven economic activity. It will have consequences for growth and employment in Canada. At the same time, foreign producers will attempt to increase their share of sales of manufactured goods to Canadians. Canadian producers will also have to face augmented competition arising from the importation of goods made outside our borders by relatively low-paid workers employed by many of the enterprises which already have manufacturing plants in Canada.[6] As the *Harvard Business Review* noted: "The successful global competitor manages its business in various countries as a single system."[7] In comparative terms, Canada has been a high-wage economy; Canadian workers who are employed in sectors in which Canadian capital is mobile and/or challenged by foreign competition may have to face the choice of making concessions or accepting the loss of employment opportunities. The ability of Canadian labour to resist such pressures will depend on its capacity to reduce the threat of disinvestment and the unrestricted importation of cheap goods. This, in turn, will depend on its economic and political bargaining power. Labour will have to fight within a context that compounds its difficulties — namely, the principal focus of the Canadian economy: export-led growth.

Canada is an exporter of largely unprocessed mineral and forestry resources and commodities. In the long run, the new technologies will make many of the formerly high-priced resources, such as copper, lead and coal, less valuable than they were before. Moreover, many of the newly industrializing countries (whose resources were, in the not-so-distant past, not allowed to compete with those of the exploiting, advanced economic world of which Canada formed a part) are trying to obtain a larger share of the global market for these commodities.[8] Since Canadian investors in the resource sectors cannot easily engage in the same productive activities anywhere but where the resource is, the principal means by which they can remain profitable is by becoming more competitive locally — namely, by employing new technologies or by forcing workers to work harder, or both, thereby reducing the cost of labour. The ability of labour to deal with the difficulties created for it by these strategies will depend to a large extent on the existing strengths of its organizational structures and its ability to modify them if necessary.

In general terms, then, key sectors of the Canadian economy — the resource, mining and manufacturing industries — are likely to be the scene of sharp economic struggles. Workers who have relatively good job security will find this imperilled as employers seek (a) to slim their workforce to meet lessened demand, (b) to get more work out of each worker and (c) to employ labour-saving technology. There is already much evidence that these trends are changing into the dominant reality.

Slimming the Workforce

In the 1970s, the bottom fell out of the market for many of Canada's resources. Mining and forest industries began to shed their workforces wholesale. By the 1980s the toll was awesome. Overall, the forest industries lost approximately 30,000 jobs and mining saw its workforce cut by 20 percent. Thus, MacMillan Bloedel had nearly 21,000 employees in 1980; in 1986 it had just under 12,000. At the end of 1980, Inco, Canada's largest nickel operation, employed 18,000 at its Sudbury and Thompson plants. In 1986 it had 11,000 employees. Imperial Oil, Canada's biggest oil and gas company, had 17,000 employees in 1981. It is anticipated that, when the current downsizing of its workforce is completed, this company will employ fewer than 12,000 Canadians.[9] Inevitably, union membership (if not the incidence of unionization) has dropped in these sectors. The kinds of unions affected include leaders and pattern-setters, such as the United Steelworkers of America, the International Woodworkers, Canadian Pulp and Paper, as well as the fishing unions on both coasts.

In these economic sectors, dominated by the multinational assemblers, smokestack industries and their satellites, it is the globalization of production and the increased levels of competition, as well as slowing demand, that create problems for Canadian labour. For instance, Canada's U.S.-owned automobile producers face a particularly difficult future with world-wide competition from the many new entrants in the field: Japanese, South Korean, Mexican and Brazilian. They enjoy much lower labour costs than do producers in Canada, and many have at least as high a rate of productivity. Rubber, chemical and electrical industries also face a bleak future owing to the competition from imports from countries with labour costs ranging from 40 percent to 60 percent lower than those which prevail in Canada.[10]

Another threat to Canadian employment in the multinational assembly industries comes from the increased availability of low-wage areas to American and Canadian employers in these sectors. Whereas once there was a cost to capital to move a long way away from the markets (for example, to Southeast Asia), today it has become the fashion for American industrialists to move from the north of the United States to the American sun-belt states with their favourable labour laws and willingness to subsidize investment.[11] Increasingly, the sun-belt states themselves are coming under pressure as nearby Mexico has made itself available for low-cost investment on favourable terms. A large number of American firms are choosing to relocate on the Mexican side of the Texas border. By 1989, more than 1,700 large firms employing more than 400,000 workers had set up operations there. While Japanese corporations such as Sony, Sanyo and Toyota are there as well, so far the greatest number of firms are American.[12] This maquiladora phenomenon is part of a larger movement. American industrialists show a marked propensity for this kind of economic strategy. The study *The Global Factory* records that "more than one half of U.S. sales of certain products in textiles and electronics are assembled abroad."[13] Thousands of American firms have relocated in low-wage countries. This kind of movement will, in due course, be devastating to Canada, as American branch plants in Canada may well be the ones chosen to be closed down, their work contracted out to such cheap and readily available locations as Mexico, Puerto Rico, Guatemala, Sri Lanka, the Philippines, South Korea and Malaysia.[14] There are many examples of the temptations proffered by these corporate strategies. Esquire Industries Ltd. has established a plant in Sri Lanka where it began by employing 100 workers, planning to go to a workforce of 500, mostly women. Each worker produces twenty pair of Gloria Vanderbilt jeans per day. In 1983, each pair of jeans sold for about $40 in the United States. That is, each worker's output had a daily U.S. retail market value of $800. Each worker was paid $1.00 per day in Sri Lanka.[15] As American branch plants employ close to half the Canadian industrial workforce, if their American parents give in to this economic logic the results could be disastrous.

Not only American-owned capital may move out of Canada. Canadian employers also may seek to take advantage of cheaper foreign conditions to penetrate foreign markets. The threat of such disinvestment is a powerful bargaining tool and, indeed, actual disinvestment only needs to occur a few times to make the threat credible and effective. Even before the advent of the Canada-U.S. Free Trade Agreement, there was movement of capital out of the country by leading Canadian firms such as Dominion Textile, Dylex, Northern Telecom, Canadian Pacific and Noranda Mines. This made labour very anxious, even if it was hard to show that all such movement of capital led to the loss of productive activity in Canada.[16] Now that free trade is here, the loss of jobs — as firms relocate in the United States, or close altogether because of their inability to compete without tariff protections or other such subsidies — is fast becoming a flood.[17] Statistics Canada reports that 165,000 factory jobs had disappeared by 1989 — almost 8 percent of the total number of jobs in manufacturing.[18] This tendency can only worsen as the Americans draw Canada inextricably into a North American free trade agreement that includes Mexico. The intent is that Mexico will supply the cheap labour, while Canada will supply its cheap resources as the U.S. needs them. This latest development can only bode ill for Canada's employment prospects.

Extraction of More Value from Workers

Employers have been responding to the threat of increased competition by seeking to compete on wages.[19] There are many ways to do this. One that Canadian employers have adopted is the dismissal of workers on a scale which is unprecedented in modern times. It is important to note that the number of workers who are dismissed is not directly related to the decrease in demand. One of the features of the new economic situation is the abandonment of a post–World War II understanding (which we will detail below) between capital and labour. In its stead there has been something of a return to a mentality more consonant with the brute capitalism of an earlier era.

A consequence of mass dismissals, particularly in those sectors in which the lay-offs are taking place, is to lower resistance to demands made by employers on the workers they do continue to employ. This enables employers to extract more productive labour from each retained worker than they could obtain when trade unions were better able to mediate the more oppressive effects of scientific management. Falconbridge began the reduction of its workforce at its nickel mine in Sudbury in 1982. By 1986, according to its president, Bill James, "2,250 [were] doing the job of 4,000."[20] Employers are aided in this desire to get more value out of each worker by new technologies. In part, they can do so because the new machinery does speed up and rationalize work; in part, the mere possibility of the introduction of new technology, with its accompanying threat of job losses, makes workers more amenable to demands that they work harder for less.[21]

Deindustrialization

In addition, it is to be anticipated that, as part of this general economic restructuring in advanced capitalist nations threatened by new competition, there will be attempts to find new niches in the international marketplace. That is, these nations will seek to make use of their state of development to have their investors scale the peaks of high- (new-) technology industries and/or to have them exploit the possibilities of greater development of the service industries. The latter already constitute the fastest-growing sector of these economies. Thus, in Canada there has been an explosion of new jobs in service industries. For instance, in Ontario, between 1971 and 1981, 70 percent of all new additional jobs were created in business and personal services, trade, finance, insurance and real estate. On average, service-industry jobs pay 15 to 20 percent less than industrial jobs. Moreover, these are jobs in which female employment predominates. Clerical, service and sales occupations accounted for almost two-thirds of female employment growth, clerical occupations accounting for 40 percent of new jobs taken by women.[22] Many of the jobs are part-time.[23] Thus, employment growth is occurring precisely in those sectors in which unacceptably discriminatory low wages and gender ghettoization are to be found.[24] These changes are reflected in the transformed profile of unionization.

Changing Patterns of Unionization

Trade union membership increased sharply with the advent of contemporary bargaining near the end of World War II. It stood at 16.3 percent in 1940, and by 1950 it had risen dramatically to 30.3 percent. By 1971, trade union membership had increased to 33.6 percent. Since then it has risen steadily, but modestly. It actually reached 40 percent of the labour force in 1983, then dropped back to 37.7 percent by 1985 and settled at 36 percent by 1989.[25] But the maintenance of union membership at these levels masks some of the qualitative changes that are occurring as the economy restructures.

In recent times, there has been a diminution of membership in those very sectors that gave unions some justification for the belief that collective bargaining could achieve wage gains and better working conditions: the mining and mass-production assembly-line industries. Between 1971 and 1985, Canadian union membership fell by 4 percent in manufacturing, 3 percent in construction, transportation, communication and utilities, and 30 percent in mining.[26] This has had a sharp impact on many of Canada's leading private sector trade unions. While there has been an increase in the number of small unions, from thirty-seven unions representing 10,000 members in 1968 to ninety-one representing 38,000 members in 1990, some of the larger industrial unions' membership is stagnating or declining. The expansion of the Canadian Automobile Workers (CAW) into the non-automobile sectors has permitted it to continue to grow. Between 1982 and 1990 its membership rose from 121,000 to 167,000; many of those people do not work in Big Three assembly or supply plants, however. By contrast, the Steelworkers union membership has declined dramatically, falling from 197,000 in 1982 to 160,000 in 1990. Downward movements were also registered by the International Woodworkers of America (IWA), the International Machinists, and the Brotherhood of Carpenters and Electricians.[27]

This does not mean, of course, that these unions have become insignificant or that they are about to wither away. The density of unionization in their industries and, therefore, their solidarity still remain high. But the fact remains that what was the heart and soul of Canada's union movement has lost members. In addition, as we have seen, Canadian union membership has declined from a high of 40 percent of the workforce in 1983 to 36 percent in 1990 — that is, back to where it was fifteen years earlier. What is most important, however, is that Canadian unions are facing a crisis even though unions are increasing their efforts to unionize the unorganized. They are falling behind. Both the financial base and the bargaining leverage of Canada's private sector trade union movement is weakening.

Despite the diminished membership in the more traditional sectors and the difficulties of organizing the new workforce, a relatively large proportion of Canada's workers are members of unions, at least when a comparison is made with the precipitous decline of unionism in the United States. In large part, this is due to the fact that Canada has permitted public sector employees to unionize. Public servants were given the right to bargain collectively as a result of the large-scale labour and social reform movements which took off in the mid-1960s and lasted until the early 1970s. In addition, there has been some growth of union membership in the exploding private service sectors. The public and private service sectors now encompass more than three million employees. In short, the character of unionism, as well as the numerical strength of particular unions, is changing.

All of these enormous changes signify that a new set of bargaining relationships is evolving. Some of the old truths and values will have to be reconsidered.

The Need for a New Perspective

Labour needs to counter the reinvigorated attacks on its living standards and social role. It has to find ways to inhibit capital mobility and the increased bargaining power this gives employers. It has to reduce the ready availability to employers of cheap unorganized workers; its organizational efforts must be intensified and facilitated. Means must be developed to ensure that the new technologies, with their promise of more productive, safer and less alienating work, will be used to these ends rather than to shed jobs and further dilute the quality of working life. In addition, the social net will have to be widened to protect more people and enriched so that such dislocations as do occur do not lead to unacceptable impoverishment.

This is quite a shopping list. Does Canadian labour have the economic and political muscle to achieve anything like these results? Its organizational strength and potential are largely a reflection of the dominant industrial relations institution, collective bargaining. Are the existing institutional arrangements that secure labour's rights up to the task? Do they have within them the potential to modify their structure and organization to confront the new circumstances? We attempt to provide some answers to these crucial questions. We begin by examining the collective bargaining system that has played a major part in structuring labour relations in Canada.

Understanding the Post-War Compromise

Labour's Base: Canada's Collective Bargaining System

The modern collective bargaining system was introduced by the wartime regulation PC 1003 in 1944.[1] It gave trade unionism a new status and protections which added to its ability to prosper. In fact, it was a rather late adaptation of the 1935 U.S. *Wagner Act*.[2] The principal features of the Canadian scheme, as they eventually evolved, were these:[3]

1. Where the majority of workers in one workplace chose to be represented by a union, it was to be certified as the bargaining agent of these workers. The employer was required to recognize the union. This gave unions a new status in society and legitimated the trade union movement in a way it never had been before.

2. The employer was required to bargain with the union in good faith. This always was, and remains, a troublesome concept. The bottom line, however, was that an employer could no longer dip, or threaten to dip, into the reserve army of unemployed to defeat a recognized union's demands without first entering into serious negotiations with it.

3. If negotiations led to an impasse, the employer could exercise its right to lock out employees and the union could call on the workers to strike. The exercise of the right to strike thus was accepted as an appropriate way to resolve distributional problems.

4. Any agreement that was the outcome of negotiations was to be legally enforceable. This acceptance of the outcome of an exercise of collective rights by workers was another breakthrough. In due course, the logic of this enforceability was to come to mean that employers could not undermine trade unions by entering into individual arrangements with specific employees.

As the scheme matured, a system to resolve disputes during the life of a collective agreement evolved and became a central part of it. The parties were not allowed to lock out or strike during the life of a collective agreement. Formal grievance processes were established to deal with disputes about the administration and interpretation of the agreement. These processes imposed constraints on employers' power to act unilaterally in respect of the way work was to be done and the workforce deployed, at least to the extent that the collective agreement could be read as having imposed such limits. Workers no longer had to rely on industrial action to resist arbitrary and capricious employer decisions. As industrial action during the life of a collective agreement was illegal, the grievance mechanism came to be perceived as especially beneficial.[4]

All of these developments represented clear progress. Indeed, this new scheme of collective bargaining was a revolution of a kind. The state had acted positively to give workers more countervailing power than they had before and had granted unions new standing and respect. The promise for worker advancement was real. However, it has never realized its hoped-for potential.

The reasons for this failure are to be found in the way in which the scheme has been adapted to satisfy some overriding state objectives. In particular, Canada's modern collective bargaining régime was not all positive in its design. It could function in the way that has already been described, that is, as a *reformist* mechanism which encouraged changes in the organization and adaptation of the social relations of production because the pre-existing system of industrial relations was proving itself to be institutionally dysfunctional. To achieve this goal the scheme incorporated some features which might properly be characterized as *autonomist*, as well as reformist, in nature. It appeared to create institutions which were to have a discrete life, separate from the state, suited to the mediation and defusion of the more jarring features of class conflict. In this sense, it is appropriate to describe the new industrial relations mechanism as a device to legitimate, and to give effect to, the precepts of liberal democratic society. But there was another feature, one which was not noted as frequently. The new collective bargaining system also had a *coercive* aspect.[5]

All of this was well articulated by an influential early analyst and policy-maker. Mr. Justice Rand, noting that the scheme was designed to give workers more collective power than they had had before, argued that unions, having been granted a new privilege, had to assume responsibility for ensuring that workers did not abuse this privilege. That is, collective bargaining and strikes were still to be constrained. After welcoming the reformist aspects of the legislation, he wrote:

> I consider entirely equitable then that all employees should be required to shoulder their portion of the burden of expense for administering the law of their employment, the union contract; that they must take the burden along with the benefit.[6]

Starting from that principle he made an award in the specific case before him. It decreed that the union should hold a secret ballot under government supervision before it called a strike; that officers of the union be saddled with the responsibility to repudiate any strike not authorized in this manner; and that the union would be penalized for failure to abide by these rules. In short, the union was required to control its membership if it wished to preserve its standing and respect. Rand's notion that, if unions did not restrain workers who overstepped the tightly drawn boundaries of the new scheme of privilege for unionism governments should and would, has never been abandoned. As Rand put it, this imposition of restraints was warranted because statutory collective bargaining had given so much more freedom to collectivism than it had been accorded before. But, of course, if the restrictions are many and they are invoked often and easily, there is a real question as to how much more freedom has been given to workers and their unions, regardless of the formal structure.

The remainder of this chapter deals with the complex interplay between the reformist/autonomist and coercive features of Canada's system of industrial relations. It is our claim that, overall, the positive, reformist and autonomist aspects have been less significant than the negative, restrictive features embedded in the régime. To support this proposition it is necessary to put the role which collective bargaining has been assigned in Canada into a larger context.

The Post-War Accords

After World War II, pressures to reform collective bargaining insti-tutions and to grant labour a new standing were felt throughout

Western Europe, the United States and Canada. Each nation state responded to these pressures in a manner which suited its macro-economic strategy. The approaches adopted varied a good deal because of the differing specific economic circumstances which each country had to face. But, as the *régulation* theorists have demonstrated,[7] there was a common understanding in the immediate post-war period to the effect that labour had to be given a new place at the political and economic bargaining tables.

Régulation in Western Europe

While each Western European nation developed its own strategies, the reform of collective bargaining institutions was seen by all as crucial to the attainment of the political and economic stability which Keynesian demand policies were expected to achieve. Broadly speaking, in Western European countries collective bargaining reforms were instituted both at the micro-level, that is, in respect of workplace relations, and at the macro-level, that is, in respect of the relationships between unions and the state. One of the most important common features of the new arrangements was that workers in the mass-production industries were offered contracts of indefinite duration at wage rates sufficiently high to sustain consumer demand. The notion was that this would promote the expansion of mass-production industries. Workers not engaged in these sectors were provided with a social wage which allowed them to participate in the mass-consumption economy. Individual employers were no longer to maximize profits at all costs, particularly they were not to browbeat workers into low-wage, low-benefits situations. The incentive for employers was that the state would help them conquer domestic markets. To obtain labour's co-operation it was necessary for certain benefits to be bestowed on all workers, regardless of the bargaining strength that any one group of workers might have *vis-à-vis* their particular employer. Accordingly, the state undertook to provide greater support to labour, such as assistance to help displaced workers retrain, to facilitate early retirement on relatively generous terms, and so forth. Sometimes the state entrenched these guarantees directly. Sometimes workers were given a greater institutional participatory role to help them obtain the protections that the model promised. A rich variety of state-mandated and privately negotiated industrial democracy schemes evolved.[8]

As far as wages were concerned, they were partly to be administered and partly to be left to competitive bargaining. The flow-on effect to the more poorly placed sectors was sought to be ensured by having national bargaining occur on a regular basis. The intent was to provide some benefits to the unorganized as well as to the organized.

Initially these kinds of policies were successful in linking mass production to mass consumption. Until the late 1960s, increases in wages approximated the rise in productivity.[9] But then, the entente began to break down.

There were many reasons for this. Most importantly, workers, feeling that they were shielded from downward pressures on wages and conditions, got bolder and bolder. Employers began to see the system as putting a real squeeze on their profit-making ability. In addition, some of the compromises did not turn out to be as attractive, or as useful, as some of the workers had anticipated. This was particularly so in respect of the amount of control over production which workers had hoped to gain through the various models of industrial democracy that had been developed. The heightened tensions caused employers and employees, for quite different reasons, to abandon the post-war compromise.[10] It is fair to say that the golden post-war era of Western European accommodation was over by the mid-to-late 1960s. By the eighties, wage flexibility no longer was understood to mean the maintenance of close links between mass consumption and productivity growth. Rather, economists were stressing the need to create a new bargaining process which would lead to less inflation proofing of benefits. In addition, they were urging that corporations be given greater powers to dismiss and discipline workers.[11]

The effects of this unravelling are now being exacerbated as the economic pressures of a fiercely new kind of competitive world are being felt: wage structures, guarantees of job security and the contents of the social wage are all being fiercely attacked in Western Europe, just as they are here. Yet it is important to note that the growth rate of wages in many Western European countries in the middle 1980s was almost twice the rate enjoyed in the United States. It is readily acknowledged that, to keep their wage growth higher, there has been a trade-off in these Western European countries. They created fewer jobs than the United States and Canada during this period. (But it is also clear that the greatest number of jobs created

Table 2.1

The Fordist Growth Model
Wages and Productivity Rise Together
1960–1973
(annual % change)

	France	U.K.	Italy	Germany
Productivity, per capita	4.9	2.9	5.6	4.2
Real wages	5.0	3.3	6.5	5.3

Breaking Down The Fordist Compromise
Wages Lag Behind Productivity Growth
1975–1987
(annual % change)

	France	U.K.	Italy	Germany
Productivity, per capita	2.2	2.2	2.1	2.2
Real wages	1.3	1.5	2.3	1.4

Real Unit Labour Costs Decline[1]
(1981=100)

	1960	1973	1981	1989
Eur 8[2]	95.5	97.1	100	93.5

1. Real per capita labour costs divided by productivity (GDP over total employment).
2. The European Community excluding Greece, Spain, Portugal and Ireland.

Unemployment Rate Soars

	1973	1979	1982	1989
Eur 9[3]	2.4	5.2	9.3	10.1

3.The European Community excluding Greece, Spain and Portugal.

Source: Robert Boyer, *La fléxibilité du travail en Europe* (Paris: La Découverte, 1986), Table 2, p. 29; OECD, *Economies in Transition* (Paris: OECD, 1985), Table 2.4, p. 35; CEE, *European Economy*, Annual Report 1988-89 Preparing for 1992 No. 38, November 1988, adapted from Table 22, p. 42, and Table 7, p. 21.

in the United States and in Canada have put the new employees at the bottom end of the wage scale.) On the other hand, those people who have lost their jobs in Europe have had the benefit of the relatively good income replacement schemes that are part and parcel of their richer social security safety nets.[12] Thus, while the impetus to increase wage competition to meet the pressures generated by the globalization of production is being felt in Western Europe, it has not been allowed to hold as much sway as in the United States and Canada. Moreover, what does, and will continue to, help European workers is the now pervasive and hard-to-challenge rhetoric in their countries which acknowledges labour's legitimated role as a real partner in economic decision making, and the guaranteed nature of some of the workplace rights and social entitlements established in the immediate post-war period. This is not to say that European workers are not in peril. Concrete proof of this was to be found in the attempts to create a Bill of Rights to guarantee European Community (EC) workers the maintenance of their social net in preparation for "1992" — Europe's very special version of a liberalized trading bloc. What workers won was minimal, a clear indication of the weakening position of European labour.[13]

The Post-War Accord in the United States

When the war ended, there was no impetus for the United States to restructure its economy, at least not to the degree it was felt it had to be done in Europe. There was no need to help domestic producers to conquer the domestic market, as this was already in hand;[14] externally, the competitive advantage which American capital enjoyed throughout the world was very real. In that context no new *political* concessions had to be made to labour. Indeed, the central institution remained collective bargaining as practised under the 1935 *Wagner Act*. But while the 1947 Taft-Hartley amendments put some tough limits on recently won union rights, they did not prevent some developments that favoured workers from taking place.[15]

A consensus was built on the basis of the economic strength of America's major corporations. This did give America's labouring classes material gains. Piore and Sabel have shown that the new consensus was based on informal productivity agreements entered into by America's industrial unions and its leading corporations in key consumer and capital goods industries, such as automobiles and steel.[16] The aim of these agreements was to create industrial peace, to increase output and efficiency and to expand consumer purchasing power by placing upward pressure on wages. The initiative for productivity agreements came from the president of General Motors who, in 1948, established the principle that the annual wage increase in the automobile industry would equal the 3 percent annual improvement factor for productivity (calculated on the basis of the long-term rate of productivity increases), plus an amount to adjust for any increases in the cost-of-living index.[17]

As these increases became part of the base on which the next productivity and cost-of-living increases would be calculated, there was a seemingly irresistible upward pressure on wages in these key industries. Moreover, pattern bargaining evolved. Some of the gains made in the leading enterprises in these dominant industrial sectors flowed on to the workers in the less well-placed firms in those sectors. This kind of intra-industry pattern bargaining continued into the seventies, although it was becoming rarer and rarer. Thus, in the 1960s, such an agreement was concluded in trucking and transport, covering close to a million teamsters. As late as 1973, an agreement of this kind was concluded in the steel industry. More recently, these linkages have all but disappeared.[18]

Piore has argued that the consensus also had an inter-industry effect. As productivity agreements were reached in the key sectors of the economy there was a flow-on effect to the rubber, aerospace, copper and farm equipment industries, and others.[19]

But this American entente was never anything but fragile. There were always a great number of workers and employers who did not participate. In particular, as the result of the diluting amendments to the *Wagner Act* in the late 1940s, so-called right to work laws had been enacted by many Southern states, effectively preventing unionization. Moreover, large numbers of black Americans migrated from the South to the industrial cities of the northeast in the 1960s. There they added to the pool of unorganized and unskilled workers. The U.S. social security system never provided an adequate protection for these excluded people. The potential for undermining the existing capital/labour accord was always there.[20]

In addition, the consensus, with its flow-on effects, was vulnerable to attack because the state never had made it an explicit part of its overall economic strategy. Rather, it was the result of an understanding reached between private sector employers and major industrial unions. As American employers came under competitive challenge, they sought to undermine the consensus which had made wages "sticky." By the early-to-mid-1970s, under the combined pressure of double-digit inflation, two oil shocks and the legacy of the war in Vietnam, the American post-war accord had collapsed. American organized labour had made economic progress without ever becoming a partner in a capital-state-labour accord as some of its counterparts in European settings had done to varying degrees. American labour was not granted, nor did it win, the legitimation for the right to use *economic* power for *social and political* purposes. When it pursued political goals, it had to present itself, in Piore's words, "as a spearhead of a broad, progressive coalition."[21] It never became more than an active lobbying force. Thus, now that American capital is under attack and is restructuring, American labour is at an institutional and structural disadvantage. This is also true in Canada, albeit for different reasons.

Canada: The Weakest Keynesian Link

After World War II, Canada was not devastated, as Europe was. There was no need for a wholesale economic restructuring of the kind required in European countries and, therefore, no equivalent pressure to reach anything like the new, sophisticated neo-Keynesian compromises concluded in Europe. On the other hand, post-war Canada was not in the dominant economic position in which the United States found itself. It still had not conquered its domestic markets, nor was it confident about its manufacturing industries' ability to compete in foreign markets. Its economy always had relied on export-led growth strategies.[22] Thus, the problem which confronted Canadian policy-makers was how to adapt the *Wagner Act* model (which it had accepted), with its reformist, autonomist features and the upward pressure on wages its early days seemed to promise, to the requirements posited by the overriding logic of an export-led growth economy based on price competition, low-cost resources and cheap component parts largely destined for the American market. The story of how this was done is a central theme of this study.[23]

Like governments everywhere, Canadian decision-makers could, and did, accept the idea that unions be given more power. But they could not afford the logic of a centralized collective bargaining scheme with upward pressure on wages in an economy with a small industrial sector, inefficient by international standards and labour intensive in the main. A growth model was developed which set out to respond to the expectations that arose from the ashes of the Depression and the promises of a new order made to workers during the war. The 1945 Speech from the Throne declared that

> a national minimum of social security and human welfare should be advanced as rapidly as possible. Such a national minimum contemplates useful employment for all who are willing to work; standards of nutrition and housing adequate to ensure the health of the whole population; and social insurance against privation resulting from unemployment, from accident, from the death of the breadwinner, from ill-health and from old age.[24]

At the same time, however, the policy-makers also declared that there would be a continuation of resource-based strategies.

The model which evolved was posited on four pillars.[25] Three of these were compatible with Keynesian notions: (1) the maintenance of private investment and capital stock; (2) the maintenance of private consumption expenditures; and (3) the maintenance of government expenditures. The fourth pillar was the maintenance of the export of resources, the very antithesis of the Keynesian notions of demand and supply control. Keynesian strategies do not depend on trade as the primary means by which to promote growth. Rather, the idea is to have as many goods and services as possible produced domestically by ensuring high enough wage levels to create a strong demand for locally produced goods and services. By contrast, export-led growth policies are posited on a different macro-economic mix. They depend on fostering the willingness in foreign and domestic entrepreneurs to invest their capital and technological know-how in the commodities-exporting country. Development relies on being able to attract both the technology and capital to support high levels of growth. As ideal types, these two competing strategies were bound to clash and vie for dominance in post-war Canada. In practice, both might be modified so as to create something of a functioning amalgam. In Canada, the compromise that emerged established export-led growth as the dominant macro-economic policy at the expense of Keynesianism.

An export-led growth strategy requires the state to assist its resource sectors with direct financial subsidies and with the provision of infrastructural support, such as the public underwriting of highways (for example, the Trans-Canada Highway), railways, ports, navigable waterways (for example, the St. Lawrence Seaway) and pipelines (for example, the Trans-Canada Pipeline).[26] At the same time, the state has to maintain a good investment environment if its goal to develop viable domestic manufacturing sectors is to be achieved. Stability in production, and competitive wage rates and labour markets, become major, if not overriding, considerations for policy-makers. Income policies which guarantee workers a steadily increasing share of the national income are antithetical to these objectives.

Innis and others have pointed out what is problematic about this strategy.[27] There is no compelling reason why the profits earned by selling resources will lead to investment in domestic manufacturing. In fact, the raw materials exported are likely to be processed elsewhere and be imported as finished products into Canada. Right from the start, this created a conundrum for governments anxious to promote industrial development. The solution they hit upon was innovative for its time.

The late-nineteenth-century National Policy was meant to create infant Canadian industries by deepening the domestic market. Tariff barriers were erected to ensure that Canadian manufacturing would be protected from the harmful effects of foreign competition. But, as Innis found, this stratagem backfired. Foreign investors who wished to have access to Canada's market were forced to come and hide behind these tariff barriers. This pattern has held sway until the present. It has led to an anti-competitive, non-innovative manufacturing sector, one whose individual members far too often are integrated into a foreign parent's world-wide operation. The prevalence of branch-plant manufacturing has led to the costly importation of goods by these branch plants; frequently, they have been unwilling to compete in markets already serviced by the parents' affiliates.

The result is that much of the manufacturing sector that has developed is neither Canadian nor competitive. As late as 1978, foreign-owned firms accounted for 72 percent of all imports into Canada. Foreign-owned firms had a ratio of imports to sales of 22.4 percent, a ratio which was five times as high as that which Canadian-owned firms maintained between imports and sales.[28] In fact, much of the manufacturing sector cannot be meaningfully regulated or controlled by Canadian policy-makers who want to address inflation or anti-competitive practices.[29] Thus governments inevitably look to industrial relations practices and labour markets — policy instruments within their reach — to foster competitiveness.

The effects of this macro-economic strategy on bargaining rights have put Canada's unions under constant pressure. The dynamic of an open economy forces governments to come down heavily on labour and to use both market and non-market forces to hold down wage costs. This is so because in an export-led economy there is the persistent threat of inflationary price movements that inevitably result from the volatile swings of the business cycle. When Canada's commodities are in high demand, the economy will boom. The effect of this boom will be fuelled by government spending of the revenues generated by resource selling and tariff collection. This will keep the boom going after it has run its natural course. Inflation is built into the economy. Consumer demand will continue the pressure for imports; this leads to trade-balance difficulties. Currency value and interest rates come under pressure. All of this is aggravated by the prevalence of branch plants. Dividends flow out of the country as branch plants send profits back to their parent organizations. The effect of this is frequently worse than it might be because they often pay their accounts to their parents in foreign currency. These intra-firm debts arise because the branches are often forced to buy their supplies from their parent companies. Letourneau found that the major source of inflationary pressures experienced in Canada during the 1970s was the practice of non-competitive importing by branch-plant operations. He went on to demonstrate that more than 40 percent of Canada's inflation had its origins outside Canada.[30] In this climate, stability in production and, most importantly, competitive wage rates become major, if not overriding, considerations for policy-makers. Incomes policies that guarantee workers a steadily increasing share of the national income are antithetical to these objectives.

This sketch furthers our understanding as to why any Keynesian-type measures which did evolve could not have been permitted to act as a national wage-setting mechanism of a Keynesian kind. It also offers an insight into why Keynesian-type measures came later to Canada than to Europe and why, when they did come, they were much less rich than were the European variants. The commitment to a fully fledged Keynesian welfare scheme was never very deep.[31] Welfare measures were enacted piecemeal and begrudgingly by governments.[32]

The years prior to 1945 saw the beginnings of an unemployment insurance scheme, and there was a federally funded pension scheme. All provinces already had established workers' compensation régimes. Some relatively puny welfare programs for single and deserted mothers had been put into place. In the 1950s a somewhat restricted, but universal, old age security plan was put on the statute books, as well as one for permanently disabled people; some aid was proffered to those who were unemployed but who were not eligible for unemployment insurance benefits. The development of a universal general assistance plan was now under way. In the 1960s, a comprehensive health care system was added to this list of programs, and the Canada and Quebec pension plans (the CPP and QPP) were put in place. The general assistance plan, which came to be called the Canadian Assistance Plan, was improved in its benefits and in its coverage, gradually becoming universalized.[33] The Social Planning Council of Metropolitan Toronto has noted, however, that it was not until the early 1970s that it could be said that "an institutional welfare state existed in Canada. [Only by then was] Government spending on income security and social services ... tied to the level of unemployment, the aging of the population, the educational requirements of the young, and the medical needs of an industrial society, [and] a vast array of non-discretionary universal social programmes ... an accepted part of Canadian life."[34] But the existence of the programs was one thing, their generosity quite another.

Throughout the post-war era, Canada has kept its minimum wage levels, unemployment insurance benefits and transfer payments to the poor at low levels compared to other advanced industrialized nations. In 1983, Canada ranked thirteenth in a list of eighteen comparable countries in terms of social spending of this kind. Other open economies showed much more largesse. The Netherlands ranked first, Belgium third, Denmark seventh and Ireland ninth in respect of this kind of spending.[35]

These kinds of figures reflect the fact, as Julia O'Conner says, that Canada's liberal welfare state has had "a limited preventive and redistributive orientation."[36] It is "designed to compensate for market imperfections while remaining compatible with the basic principles of market organization."[37] This insight is central to the development of an understanding of how limited Canada's post-war acceptance of Fordism in the *régulation* sense was. From this vantage point, Canada's new statutory collective bargaining régime could not have

Table 2.2
Social Transfers in Eighteen OECD Countries — 1983

Rank		As % of GDP
1.	Netherlands	28.8
2.	France	26.0
3.	Belgium	22.9
4.	Austria	20.1
5.	Italy	19.9
6.	Sweden	18.5
7.	Denmark	17.8
8.	Germany	17.0
9.	Ireland	16.2
10.	Norway	15.5
11.	United Kingdom	13.7
12.	Switzerland	13.5
13.	Canada	12.4
14.	United States	11.9
15.	Japan	11.3
16.	Australia	10.7
17.	Finland	10.2
18.	New Zealand	9.9

Source: Adapted from Julia O'Conner, "Welfare Expenditure and Policy Orientation in Canada in Comparative Perspective," *Canadian Review of Sociology and Anthropology* 26:1 (1989): 131.

been expected to act as a national wage-setting mechanism of a neo-Keynesian kind.

Collective Bargaining Yields

In the Canadian scheme, only well-placed workers in the traded sectors have done well, and then only when conditions permitted. Workers who find themselves in sectors that are not central to the staple-led growth economy do poorly, whether they are organized or not. The regional inequalities and fragmented labour markets typical of Canada's market-driven economy have been perpetuated.[38] In short, the flow-on effects which might have been anticipated if the collective bargaining system actually had been used to implement modern Keynesian policies were not present.[39]

Table 2.3
Trends in Real Labour Compensation and Output
Per Hour, 1961–1973 and 1973–1984
(average annual rate of change)

	1961–1973		1978–1984	
	Real compensation	Output per hour	Real compensation	Output per hour
Food	3.3	3.3	1.9	1.4
Beverage	3.6	5.6	2.7	-1.2
Tobacco	4.6	5.4	3.5	1.5
Rubber	2.7	4.3	1.8	3.9
Plastic	2.6	8.5	1.2	2.2
Leather	2.4	2.0	1.1	3.9
Textiles	2.9	6.9	1.8	5.0
Clothing	2.6	2.0	0.5	2.9
Wood	4.0	2.8	2.2	5.0
Furniture	2.7	4.4	1.1	-0.4
Paper	3.1	2.4	2.2	0.2
Printing & publishing	2.4	1.6	1.4	2.1
Primary metal	2.9	3.4	2.7	1.0
Fabricated metal	2.6	3.8	1.1	1.0
Machinery	2.5	3.0	1.0	1.4
Transportation equipment	2.7	7.8	1.5	2.6
Electrical equipment	2.1	4.8	1.9	6.9
Mineral prod.	3.4	5.1	1.6	0.2
Petroleum & coal	3.7	6.8	2.9	-0.2
Chemicals	2.6	5.4	1.8	3.1
Other mfg.	2.4	3.6	1.3	1.7
Total mfg.	3.5	4.5	1.8	3.0

Note: Changes in real compensation calculated as changes in nominal compensation minus the CPI.

Source: *Aggregate Productivity Measures*, cat. 15-204, June 1989, Statistics Canada, and *Quarterly Economic Review*, Annual Reference Tables, June 1988, Department of Finance.

Indeed, for long periods at a time, even workers in some of the more heavily unionized sectors in Canada were unable to make wage gains that matched productivity gains. Ostry and Zaidi have shown that, between 1950 and 1968, workers' wages in the manufacturing sector rose by 58 percent, while productivity grew by over 97 percent.[40] Zohar made similar findings in respect of the period 1970–1977.[41] He found that sporadic outbursts of militancy and localized strikes had surprisingly little overall impact on the ratio between productivity and wage growth. While a number of workers did succeed in besting productivity growth in some specific industries for brief periods, real wage growth lagged behind increases in output, in the aggregate.

Another measure of the inability of collective bargaining to ensure a steady increase in wages for all of Canada's workers is the aggregate share of the national income which goes to labour. In 1987 it was 67.2 percent.[42] This was only marginally more than the share going to labour in 1967 when the Woods Task Force calculated labour's share of the national income to be 66.7 percent. In 1949, when collective bargaining in its modern form had just taken off, labour's share was 63.2 percent.[43] But it would be wrong to imply that there never have been any impressive upward movements. Labour has occasionally made some large advances. From the late 1960s through the mid-1970s, labour's share hovered around 72 percent of the national income, before it began to diminish. A similar slide is occurring at the moment. Between 1982 and 1988, real wages declined by 0.6 percent nation-wide.[44] Statistics Canada has shown that for the eleven-year period, 1976–1987, increases in wages outperformed growth in productivity in only three years. Between 1983 and 1988, wage-earners lost ground in every year. This five-year losing span is the longest recorded since 1976.

What all of these figures comparing wages and productivity growth and recording labour's share of national income suggest is that labour's ability to hold its ground, let alone improve its position, is not guaranteed by the system. To the contrary, the collective bargaining system, the most pro-labour industrial mechanism established thus far, has left labour with powers that ensure that its gains go up and down with the ups and downs of an open economy. However, it is true that *some* gains are made by *some* of those workers who engage in collective bargaining.

Table 2.4
Growth of Real Labour
Income per Hour Worked
and of GDP per Hour Worked (%)

Year	Labour income per hour	GDP per hour	Difference
1976	7.6	5.8	1.8
1977	1.3	1.7	-0.4
1978	-3.2	0.1	-3.3
1979	-0.5	-0.3	-0.2
1980	1.4	0.2	1.2
1981	2.5	2.4	0.1
1982	0.8	0.6	0.2
1983	-2.5	2.1	-4.6
1984	1.1	3.7	-2.6
1985	0.5	1.1	-0.6
1986	0.0	0.3	-0.3
1987	1.4	1.6	-0.2

Source: Statistics Canada, Historical Labour Force Statistics, Cat. 71201; Statistics Canada, National Income and Expenditure Accounts, Cat. 13201, 13531.

Thus, in the late 1940s and early 1950s, when demands for Canada's resource exports were very high, real gains were made in the mining and construction sectors. In the middle and late 1960s, after enduring a downturn, macro-economic conditions gave workers another boost. A combination of factors — which included the devaluation of the Canadian dollar, the conclusion of the Auto Pact, an increase in the demand for Canadian oil and sales of Canadian wheat to the USSR — enabled large numbers of workers, this time in a greater number of sectors, to catch up and to improve their position. These much more widely spread gains continued on into the 1970s, buoyed by rising prices for Canada's energy exports. This throws some light on the aggregate figures presented earlier.

The uneven distributive effect of collective bargaining means that better-positioned workers do make real gains. Typically, this is the case in mining, construction and automobile and other large-assembly manufacturing. Other segments of the economy, whether unionized or not, make few advances, and indeed may go backwards. Characteristically, these are the labour-intensive industries, such as textiles, shoes, furniture, and those which produce for local or regional markets. It is now understandable why some workers believe that collective bargaining has the capacity to offer economic and other kinds of progressive advances. But a more reflective evaluation of the nature of collective bargaining reveals that even well-placed workers have faced difficulties which are likely to deepen.

Keynesian Objectives versus the Imperatives of Export-Led Growth

A chronic difficulty with the stop-and-go fortunes that Canadian labour enjoys is that, when some workers do manage to ride the back of a resource boom, their gains are likely to be huge in percentage terms because of the low baseline established during more stagnant times. Then, when the boom falters, governments become very uneasy. At the behest of employers who want to protect the profits they made during the good times, courts and administrators of the scheme begin to emphasize the coercive, rather than the autonomist and reformist, features of the industrial relations system. Whenever possible, strikes are condemned as illegal. The help of unions is sought to restrain workers; the unions are reminded of their responsibilities under the scheme. The reminders are not all that subtle. There are threats that unions may lose their standing if they do not discipline their members; often damages have to be paid, and fines and other criminal sanctions may be imposed as well.

This goes some way towards explaining some of the rather dramatic shifts in government moods and attitudes which occur with great regularity and which have marked post-war state-labour relations. For instance, during the 1960s, militant workers, eager to strike before the economy lost all of its heat, were seen as a threat to stability. To employers, this threat connoted interruptions in production and an erosion of accumulated profits as workers asserted themselves. Alarmed administrators of the régime, as well as employers, relied on the punitive elements of collective bargaining to restore what they deemed to be the rightful order. This did not work in the economic and political climate of the middle to late 1960s. Indeed, overt repression created a dangerous backlash.

Policy-makers, therefore, sought to co-opt unions and workers into accepting the need for stability and restraint by offering them new procedural rights. This was the principal recommendation of both the Carrothers Commission and the Woods Task Force, major public inquiries set up in response to the militancy of the 1960s after some of the cruder attempts at repression had failed. What this new approach recognized was that recalcitrant employers were finding it far too easy to have courts and labour relations boards apply the coercive features of the collective bargaining scheme.[45] The danger was that a rarely referred-to iron fist of repression might be found inside the much-propagandized velvet glove of industrial relations. The think-tank people feared that this might lead workers to reject the legitimacy of the collective bargaining régime. Consequently, both commissions recommended that new protections should be given to unions. The idea was to bolster the belief that Canada did accept the right of workers to use collective power, despite the behaviour of some employers, labour relations boards and courts. But, at the same time, both commissions endorsed the notion, so clearly proclaimed at the very beginning by Justice Rand, that unions had a central disciplinary role to play in the working of the system.[46] That is, they believed there was a need to reinforce the autonomous and reformist aspects of the scheme, while the coercive features were to be more cloaked, more hidden from view. The message given to unions and workers was that workers, on occasion, were to be allowed to exercise their privilege to use concerted economic power. But, because it was a privilege, it should never be abused.

In this way, labour did win some reforms, and the status of collective bargaining as a pivotal wage-setting mechanism was reaffirmed. It is to be noted, however, that trade union pressures were not the only, or perhaps the most important, reason for collective bargaining reforms offered by governments. In particular, a good deal of the reformist mood must be attributed to the revolution in politics in Quebec. The social democratic reforms in Quebec frequently spilled over into other jurisdictions.[47] In addition, there was the larger political environment: Prague 1968, Paris 1968 and the civil rights and anti-war struggles in the United States. Given all these reformist pressures and shop-floor militancy, it is surprising how small the gains offered to labour were.

The late sixties and early seventies, however, did produce a further boost to the legitimacy of collective bargaining as an institution. First Quebec, and then Ottawa, reversed their long-time opposition to extending collective bargaining to the public sector. By

1973, public servants had been given the right to bargain collectively in all jurisdictions in Canada.[48] The legal nature of those bargaining rights differed greatly in different public sectors and from jurisdiction to jurisdiction. This will be discussed in some detail in Chapter 9. Here it suffices to note that, on the face of it, public service workers were given analogous rights to those won by workers in the private sector. Given the aura of progressivity which once again attended collective bargaining, this was seen as a great leap forward. But just as workers with collective bargaining rights in the private sector had had their demands contained, governments, as employers, always retained the ability to constrain the impact of collective bargaining by public sector employees.

Precisely because the activities of employers in the state sectors are explicitly political, governments have had no problem in justifying the fashioning of even more severe restraints on their employees' unions and their bargaining rights than those which have been imposed in the private sector. There is no question that, in public sector bargaining, the coercive elements have been more important than the reformist ones. Governments feel little, if any, inhibition when they deny their employees the right to strike and when they restrain their wages. Indeed, often they have done so explicitly as a means to stiffen the backbone of private sector employers.

Although the reforms of collective bargaining have been many, both in the private and public sectors, from a labour perspective they have been limited in scope. The institution of collective bargaining and reforms to it have not served to make labour a true partner in national decision making. The régime has not acted as a Keynesian national incomes scheme. Its defenders argue that this is not a failure. Collective bargaining is to be a relatively autonomous scheme designed to offset the grosser imbalances between employers and employees. In this sense it is not unlike the minimum-standards legislation which governments enact to redress the worst effects of unfettered profit making. The difference is that collective bargaining is to achieve this by giving countervailing power to workers so that they themselves can rectify the problem, rather than have governments do it for them. This is its conceptual attraction: the results are not mandated by regulators but rather by an impartial, if slightly modified, market.[49] The state reinforces this perception of the system by purporting to be a mere facilitator, promoting the objective of fairer, voluntary settlements. From this perspective, collective bargaining outcomes cannot be faulted for failing to yield benefits that spread evenly through the economy, nor for the state's failure to create a bountiful social welfare system. The institution of collective bargaining is only a subset of a whole series of national capital-labour adjustment mechanisms, and cannot be asked to bear the freight which would be carried by a central incomes plan.

But this image of a relatively autonomous, discrete collective bargaining system is something of a deception. As we have seen, the environment in which collective bargaining takes place is structured by macro-economic policies, and, therefore, so are its outcomes. Export-led growth strategies have functioned as a different kind of a national plan, a non-Fordist one. What has happened is that, over time, without any overt, conscious attempts to make it so, collective bargaining has become a useful tool in the maintenance of the wage discipline so necessary to an economy that seeks to attract investment capital by competing on wages. This has been made possible because collective bargaining is first and foremost an economic instrument. It emphasizes the advancement of workers' job rights at their own place of employment. The organizational form this has spawned is ill suited to advance direct, co-ordinated participation by workers in the political sphere. Indeed, the state can actually change the rules of collective bargaining when its outcomes threaten its macro-economic policies, without much fear of political reprisal. It does so increasingly often. In this way, collective bargaining *has* become a means of national planning, if not overtly so. But the hidden way in which it operates leaves open the theoretical possibility that it could be used in a different way.

Reform-minded governments could use the reasoning and ideology which underlie this national-planning-by-stealth to achieve positive results for labour. A labour-sympathetic government could purport to leave the outcomes of collective bargaining free to be decided by the parties, as the legislation mandates, while restructuring the environment and social network in which it is to take place. Any gains made by well-placed workers would then be an add-on to a now elevated plateau of rights for all workers. In theory, nothing would have changed; collective bargaining would still be conducted with ostensible autonomy, at least as much as it is now. Only the results would be different. To get to this position, however, will require the establishment of a government which is willing and able to enlist the support of trade unions — which have been formed, and are mentally bound, by the parameters of the competitive collective bargaining scheme — for strategies which may require them to re-form and reorganize themselves.

The Questions to Be Addressed

What does this simplified version of a very complex story denote?

Workers are facing serious threats posed by the globalization of production. Their armoury is limited inasmuch as they must rely on the forms and powers spawned by the industrial relations mechanism which has sponsored their formation and growth — namely, collective bargaining. It has been our argument that, when evaluated from the perspective of what existed prior to 1944, or from the point of view of the majority of Canadian workers who do not have any collective bargaining rights as yet, there are many positive features in the scheme. Understandably, this leads trade unionists to emphasize these positive aspects (the autonomist and reformist features of the system, as we have called them). But the fact is that the scheme has left employers and governments with a larger number of weapons. In the era of globalization of production the danger is that these restrictive features will be relied on with ever more telling effect.

Two successive Mulroney governments have launched attacks in support of the employers' position at the bargaining table. These governments have promoted liberalized trade, which posits a more brutish, unregulated political economy. As we have seen, the Canadian collective bargaining régime provides a useful framework for the pursuit of this kind of agenda.

The following chapters discuss some of the particular characteristics of collective bargaining which can be used, and are being used, to restrain labour. Specifically, the emphasis will be on those features which impose legal limits on the unions' ability to act collectively, and which promote attitudes inimical to the furthering of broader class action and consciousness. Our purpose is twofold. First, we want to show that collective bargaining is nowhere near as autonomous as its proponents believe. Governments interfere directly with its workings. Its reformist possibilities exist; its restrictive characteristics are equally real and are frequently exploited. Second, we want to examine critically the possibilities for procedurally reformed collective bargaining as a means to deal with the harmful effects of a growth model in which trade plays an increasingly central role. A smoother, more union-friendly collective bargaining (but which is essentially unchanged) is not capable of doing the job. The point of attack should be the growth model. The issue is political, not narrowly economic or technical.

Unionization and Union Power: Two Different Things

The Apparent Potential of Trade Union Power

Canada has a relatively high incidence of unionization. This is particularly true when it is compared to the level of contemporary American unionization. In 1989, 36 percent of Canada's workforce was unionized; in the United States less than 18 percent of workers belonged to unions. The idea that unions are powerful economic actors in Canada is given an additional boost by the fact that a large amount of regularly recurring collective bargaining takes place. It involves a very large number of people in the workforce, larger than the number of people unionized.[1] This is because unions are given exclusive bargaining agency. They frequently negotiate on behalf of both union and non-union members who work for the same employer. Despite the recent declines in membership noted in Chapter 2, as much as 50 percent of the workforce is covered by the terms of collective agreements.[2]

Another fact which leads to the impression that trade unions are significant actors is that there has been an immense growth in the number of public sector workers who have become union members and who bargain directly with government agencies. At the same time, there has been much job shedding in the smokestack, resource, construction and transportation industries. This has taken its toll on membership numbers in those sectors.[3] But there has been union growth in one area of the private economy, the service sectors. In British Columbia and Ontario, for instance, service sector certification increased from 16 to 36 percent of total union certifications between 1971 and 1985.[4] The result of all of this is that, out of the top seventeen unions, seven are either public sector unions or private sector service-industry unions, including the three largest in the land.

All of this suggests that trade unionism, particularly in the public sectors, has given workers a great deal of countervailing power.

Table 3.1
Membership of Unions with Membership
Exceeding 50,000
1986–1989
(Membership in 1000s)

	1986	1987	1988	1989
Canadian Union of Public Employees	304.3	330.0	342.0	356.0
National Union of Provincial Government Employees	254.3	278.5	292.3	297.2
Public Service Alliance of Canada	182.0	179.9	175.7	171.9
United Steelworkers of America	160.0	160.0	160.0	160.0
United Food and Commercial Workers	156.0	160.0	170.0	170.0
Canadian Automobile Workers	140.0	143.0	143.0	160.4
Fédération des affaires sociales	93.0	93.0	96.5	94.6
Teamsters	91.5	91.5	91.5	100.0
Fédération des enseignantes	75.0	75.0	75.0	75.0
Carpenters	68.0	66.0	66.0	62.0
Service Employees International	70.0	70.0	70.0	75.0
International Brotherhood of Electrical Workers	68.6	68.6	64.6	64.6
Canadian Paperworkers Union	57.0	57.0	69.0	69.0
Machinists	58.6	58.6	58.5	58.4
Syndicat des fonctionnaires	44.0	44.0	40.0	40.0
Labourers' International	46.7	46.7	46.7	48.4
International Woodworkers of America	48.0	48.0	45.0	50.0

Source: Labour Canada, *Directory of Labour Organizations in Canada*, October 1989 (Ottawa: Supply and Services, 1989), pp. XV–XVII.

There is a widely held perception, therefore, that workers are capable of meeting their employers head-on, as equals, and that collective bargaining must be paying handsome dividends. This is not the whole story, however.

Collective bargaining is now a mature system and the benefits which have been obtained by even well-placed workers often are surprisingly meagre — surprising to those who share the perception that the regularity of bargaining and the density of unionization must be yielding good results.

Some Outcomes of Collective Bargaining

Labour Canada compiles a comprehensive and authoritative data bank on collective bargaining outcomes for large-sized unionized firms in the private sector. It provides a good indication of how much progress the labour movement has made when it has been able to use collective bargaining to the fullest extent. Many of the agreements are the result of long-established bargaining relationships where, it is reasonable to assume, some of the better results yielded for workers by the Canadian labour relations system are to be found.[5]

It has already been noted that, even for the unionized sectors, wage gains are uneven and not constant. The question to be addressed now is how well-placed trade unions have fared in four areas of bargaining, other than wages, which are of singular significance to them.

First, in a country which suffers a continuous upward push on prices, it is important for workers to seek protection against inflation. Second, in an economy subject to boom-bust conditions, there will be a great need to develop defences against lay-offs as employers respond to the ever-varying market conditions. Third, given the low commitment to social welfare programs by governments, private collective bargaining should be a primary means to improve social entitlements which, by contrast, European workers have largely won through direct participation in the political system. Fourth, collective bargaining should be expected to be used to enhance workers' control over their jobs.

Indeed, those who acclaim the system argue that it is the gains on these and similar fronts that have given workers a new place in civil society.[6] But our reading of the data questions the validity of this claim. On each of these important matters, trade unions have done relatively poorly.

1. Defences against the Rising Cost of Living

For trade unionists, the best way to combat inflation is to include a cost-of-living clause (COLA) in the collective agreement. A COLA is a kind of insurance policy that automatically compensates workers when inflation begins to erode their salary base. While, increasingly, inflation has been a real problem in Canada, the data recorded in 1990 show that 72 percent of all agreements covering 500 or more employees did *not* provide any protection against inflation at all. The picture worsens when employees in smaller employment settings, who are not in as good a bargaining position, are included. As an indication, 73 percent of collective agreements covering 200 or more employees in the federal jurisdiction had no COLA provision of any kind.[7] Most employees are in even smaller — and, usually, less well-placed — bargaining units.

Nor can it be assumed that workers who have succeeded in negotiating a COLA clause are fully safeguarded against inflation. The protection afforded by COLA provisions differs markedly amongst the relatively few workers who have it.[8] Of those few workers (less than 30 percent) in major collective agreements who enjoyed the benefit of a COLA clause, 57 percent had clauses that went into effect as soon as the cost of living went up; 40 percent had to wait some time for this to happen. Even some of the protected people, then, do not do very well.

The amount of protection against inflation that is negotiated is even weaker when inflation is not anticipated to become a serious problem at the time of bargaining. Thus, in 1973, when the cost of living was beginning to rise dramatically, only 17.8 percent of agreements covering 500 or more employees contained COLA clauses; in 1976, as the inflationary push continued, this figure rose to 45.9 percent. The reason for this is found in the logic of collective bargaining. To get a COLA clause, unions may have to give up something on another front. During a period of low inflation, they will be reluctant to make this sacrifice. Such a period existed around 1981. Workers were being asked to make concessions; inflation proofing was not on the agenda because it was a luxury in the circumstances. By the middle 1980s there was something of a recovery and inflation was a problem again. By 1986, only 44.7 percent of agreements had a COLA clause.[9] Workers continue to fight hard for improved COLAs,[10] but this can be expected to diminish as inflation is squeezed out of the economy.

2. Defences against Job Insecurity

Given the historic volatility of the Canadian economy and the persistently high unemployment rates, it should have been expected that workers would use whatever power they have to make breakthroughs to improve their job security. We begin by noting that collective bargaining Canadian-style has provided employees with increased protection against capricious, authoritarian action by employers who want to exercise disciplinary powers.[11] The question is: how have workers done in respect of much-needed protection against *economic* lay-offs?

Lay-off provisions

As of April 1990, 5.5 percent of agreements covering 500 employees or more required notice of forty-four days or more to be given to employees before they were to be laid off. A rather alarming 13.6 percent of the major agreements required only one to five days of notice to be given, and a dramatic 47.9 percent required *no* notice to be given at all. Presumably, those workers are entitled only to the notice that the law prescribes for all workers, unionized or not. From this perspective alone, Canadian unions apparently have gained little protection against employers intent on slimming their workforces. But the picture is more nuanced than that.

Collective agreements often set out a recall procedure to deal with laid-off employees. The 1990 data tabulation does not provide this information, but the 1985 one did. Roughly 74 percent of agreements covering 500 or more employees had recall provisions in 1985. Most commonly, they required the employer to take the seniority and productive qualifications of the laid-off workers into account. That is, "seniority, plus other factors," rather than "straight seniority," was the most common criterion. This is good evidence of the fact that employers have been able to ensure that their control over workplace decisions remains extensive. Workers ought to remind policy-makers of this when employers complain that their ability to manage efficiently is undermined by union-created rigidities.

One of the ways workers seek to counter the employer's predisposition to reduce its workforce during slack periods is by bargaining for a provision mandating an equitable redistribution of work between *all* the workers during slow times, rather than permitting the employer to resort to drastic lay-offs for some. Remarkably, the data published in 1990 show that only 6.7 percent of major Canadian agreements had provisions for job sharing, while 1.1 percent provided that there should be consultation about it; a staggering 92.2 percent had no reference to this possibility at all. The idea that work sharing is a useful (albeit partial) answer to the endemic problem of lay-offs is not much better developed in the well-organized sectors than it is in the unorganized ones.

Another way in which workers might seek to cushion the blow of job separation is to bargain to have the employer pay them relatively generous compensation if they are to be laid off. This helps them survive for a while longer and gives them more time to find another acceptable job. It also makes it more expensive for employers to get rid of employees. This may cause employers to think of other ways to reduce costs when they hit a market problem. Job security would be enhanced. Not surprisingly, trade unions have made efforts to win these kinds of protection.

Supplementary unemployment benefits
When employees are temporarily laid off or permanently separated from their job they become entitled to unemployment insurance benefits. Now, as these government-supplied unemployment insurance benefits are relatively low in Canada, a requirement in a collective agreement that an employer supplement such benefits would improve the workers' job security and, if terminated, their market position. But the data recorded in April 1990 reveal that only 3.7 percent of collective agreements involving 500 workers or more had provisions for such a supplementary unemployment benefit (SUB) plan, although another 9.8 percent had provision for such a plan in combination with a severance pay plan. In Canada, then, even employers who have to deal with large unions are able to socialize labour costs which they themselves ought to bear. This gives them the flexibility to resolve the ups and downs of a wide-open economy at the expense of their workforce.

Notice for mass dismissals
Notice provisions found in collective agreements regarding mass lay-offs are frequently no more generous than those found in legislation that applies universally. Most jurisdictions have statutes which require that termination notice be given when a large number of employees are to be laid off simultaneously, whether unionized or not. For instance, at the federal level and in Ontario, if more than 500 workers are to be laid off, they are to be given sixteen weeks'

notice.[12] Governments have sought to ensure that employers will be forced to bear some of the cost of large-scale dislocations. Indeed, some legislative schemes, such as the one in Ontario, require that employers who are planning a mass lay-off must notify the minister of labour. The minister can then require the employer to co-operate during the period of prescribed notice with the ministry's attempt to find alternative work for the separated employees.

People with collective agreements tend to rely on government provisions rather than on any they have bargained for because it is rare for their agreements to provide them with better notice rights. It is true, of course, that unions have helped establish these legislative standards, both by their collective bargaining efforts and by their involvement in more direct political activities. But we should not be too impressed.

If employers characterize the mass lay-off as a temporary one, employees will have a right to be recalled when the employer decides it needs them. The employer has no duty to pay them anything. While laid off, workers will have to rely on unemployment insurance benefits, plus any supplementary benefits for the lucky few who are entitled to them. It says something about the bargaining power of Canadian trade unions that they have accepted this compromise. The employer has been left free to respond to the vagaries of the market without incurring direct costs. Government and the affected workers bear the burden.

Obviously, what unions want is a good deal more advance warning and the right to be involved in any planning which affects the size of the workforce. They need access to managerial information in order to influence these important decisions. The CAW and the Steelworkers have recently made some impressive gains in this sphere. But most trade unions are not in a position to win this kind of protection at the bargaining table. What is needed is the kind of government intervention which has been commonplace in Europe for some time.

France, Germany and the Netherlands have adjustment-planning programs which kick in if a factory is to close. This kind of legislation requires employers to negotiate with unions in a unionized plant and with a committee of elected workers in a non-unionized setting. In France, for instance, *comités d'entreprises* — workers' representatives at the factory level — can react when there is a crisis and lay-offs are imminent. Such a committee can investigate the economic conditions and the social plan of the enterprise. If it is not satisfied with the company's response, it can appeal to a judge to delay the notice period. As well, it can ask for the advice of outside experts, including accountants. Similar provisions exist in other countries, including Italy and Germany.[13]

However embryonic Canada's legislative requirements for notice of mass dismissal may be, they are a good indication of how governments can change the outcome of collective bargaining while leaving the parties alone. By engaging in these market-adjustment policies, governments have made it less necessary for trade unions to make compromises on issues such as wages, something that they might otherwise have to do to win a measure of protection against lay-offs. The setting of floors by the state in any one area has manifest impact on bargaining outcomes in other spheres. This is well understood in Keynesian-minded countries where schemes like the ones described above are devised to induce employers into long-term planning. On the one hand, this helps governments to protect employees from the effects of the ups and downs of the business cycle. On the other hand, it makes management more efficient.

Severance pay
An additional protection for workers who are about to be terminated would be a provision in a collective agreement for a payment of a lump sum over and above notice pay. Trade unions can advance two supporting reasons for demanding severance pay of this kind. The first is that workers who have invested a good deal of their life in a business are entitled to a return on this investment, in addition to their contractual right to wages and termination pay. The second, and related, argument is that employers should bear a larger share of the cost for putting long-time employees back onto the labour market. In Canada, both arguments have been made at the bargaining table with limited success.

According to the data published in 1990, 45.1 percent of the major collective agreements covering 500 employees or more had severance pay plans. A surprisingly high 41.4 percent did not. This does not say much for the unions' bargaining power around this issue.

Given the need for this kind of job security provision in a high-unemployment economy, workers have had to rely on legislative intervention by the state. It was in this context that, in the early eighties, severance pay legislation was enacted by the federal and Ontario governments.[14] Unions played a significant role in pressuring governments to pass these laws. Their arguments were supported by the plight of the increasing number of unionized and non-unionized workers laid off during a deepening recession. These workers had lost their jobs without any safeguards to help soften their landing. Electorally sensitive governments had to take action.

In Ontario, the policy of the legislative reform was to reward employees for long service. To obtain severance pay, workers have to have completed five years of service. Fifty or more workers must have been displaced in a period of six months as a result of a permanent discontinuance of part, or all, of a business. If the business had a payroll of more than $2.5 million, a terminated employee who had five years of service would be entitled to the standard severance pay benefit. This is one week of pay for every year of service, up to a maximum of twenty-six weeks. The many qualifications and technical hurdles to surmount make this a very meagre benefit scheme.[15]

The policy underlying the federal system is directed at making the employer pay a greater share of labour-market adjustment costs. As a result, long-standing service is not a prerequisite. Any terminated employee who had twelve months of service is entitled to severance pay. However, the benefit available is poor: a minimum of five days' wages, or two days of wages for every year worked, whichever is the greater.[16]

Given the inability of most trade unions to win adequate severance pay packages, which would make employers more careful and workers better protected, the legislated route seems to be the most promising avenue of attack. But it will require a conscious effort by labour-supporting governments to utilize the policy justifications for severance pay benefits to the fullest extent.

Contracting-out provisions
The danger presented to employment security by an employer's ability to contract out bargaining-unit work to outside contractors is acute. While it has been a long-standing practice, employers increasingly began to look to contracting out during the 1980s as a means by which to reduce trade union bargaining power.[17] The residual ability to contract out tips the power balance further towards employers when negotiations commence. Moreover, if an employer has the right to contract out bargaining-unit work, it can more easily approach its workforce during the life of a collective agreement in order to obtain concessions from it. Even though the employer cannot lock out its workers during this period in order to persuade them to accept

changes in their conditions of work, an implicit threat to contract out bargaining-unit work may pressure a union into opening up the agreement for renegotiation. Yet, as of April 1990, the data indicated that over 60.6 percent of collective agreements covering 500 employees or more gave workers *no* protection at all against contracting out. This is astonishing because it is accepted arbitral law that, in the absence of a specific provision to the contrary, an employer is entitled to contract out bargaining-unit work.[18] For workers, this is a scary situation; the new economic circumstances have increased incentives for employers to use more and more non-union labour at ever lower rates.[19]

Technological change provisions
The introduction of new technology and methods has major implications for the quality of worklife and job security of workers. Employers want greater control over the job and pay structure. They are looking at ways to slash payrolls and increase productivity by having workers work not only smarter, but also harder (see Chapter 10). Management is pressing for more flexibility and the elimination of restrictive work rules. Again, the record shows that workers in the best collective bargaining situations have achieved very little protection against these significant threats to their working conditions.

In 1990, Labour Canada documented that 47.4 percent of collective agreements covering 500 or more employees required either advance notice to, or consultation with, employees prior to the introduction of technological changes. A startling 84 percent of these agreements did not contain any provision requiring the establishment of a joint labour-management committee to monitor the introduction of technological changes. Only 8.9 percent of the major agreements required that employees be given notice of the fact that any newly introduced technology would lead to lay-offs; 22.4 percent provided for some income guarantee should this be necessitated, while 5.5 percent referred to a relocation allowance. Only 8.6 percent gave workers a specific right of retraining, while 25.7 percent made some reference to the possibility of it. An amazing 45.4 percent of agreements had no provision whatsoever dealing with technological change.

This appalling lack of protection at a time when everyone is talking about the need for technological restructuring has led unions to make it a more important bargaining issue.[20] Woods and Kumar have noted this increasing demand for better job security provisions.[21] Governments have had to step in to deal with the apparent inability of so many trade unions to win much on this front. Apart from any social consciousness that they might have, governments feel the need to interfere because they want to promote the deployment of new technologies to improve Canada's productivity. Yet, thus far, Canadian governments have not done very much to see to it that workers are not harmed by the introduction of new technologies.

Provisions of a similar kind are found in the labour legislation of Saskatchewan and Manitoba, and in the federal government's *Canada Labour Code*. They provide that, where a collective agreement is silent on the issue of technological change, an employer planning a change that is likely to affect a significant number of employees must notify the union of its intent. If the labour relations board agrees that the collective agreement is silent on the issue and that the proposed change is a technological one and will affect a significant number of workers — both very contentious issues — it may rule that the trade union be allowed to use its collective muscle during the life of the collective agreement to settle any dispute, a most unusual right. Thus far, this right has proven very difficult to exercise. Not only are there technical legal difficulties, but by the time workers are faced with the demand to adjust to the new technologies, they often are not in a very good position to take a militant stance.[22]

3. Improvement to the Social Benefits Package

Hours of work
The issues of how many hours must be worked and how many hours of paid work must be provided are central to all bargaining. Struggles over these relate directly to job and income security. For an employer, these issues are the key to the amount of surplus value it can get out of each employee and to the flexibility it can build into its productive activities. For employees, the converse is true: how much labour must they do? how much control over the work process are they to have? The question of how many hours workers must work also determines the quality of their non-working life. The length of the work-week affects the time left for leisure. It is for this reason that collective bargaining provisions that deal with work time are considered in this discussion of the social benefits package.

Many industrial relations experts implicitly tend to exaggerate the gains made on this front. For instance, Craig has suggested that

Canadian unions have managed to win "more leisure time in a highly-paced stressful society.... The forty hour week has also had an impact on government setting standard hours per week and establishing regulations concerning overtime for non-union workers."[23] Indeed, it is true that, based on the 1990 tabulations, 62.3 percent of collective agreements covering 500 or more employees provided that the work-week was to be from 37 1/2 to 40 hours long, that these hours were to be spread over a five-day work-week and that any extra hours were to be paid at a premium. But these bare facts do not tell the whole story.

First, any provision in a collective agreement stipulating a 40- or 37 1/2-hours "ordinary" work-week is not a firm guarantee that, in any one week, employees will be provided with those hours of *paid* work. In the absence of any provision to the contrary, the specification of the ordinary hours of work in a collective agreement leaves the employer free to reduce the number of hours of work for which employees are to be paid. Further, the employer also is left free to lay off *some* of the employees while others remain obliged to work the full complement of ordinary hours specified in the agreement. Unless unions specifically win a right to a guaranteed number of paid working hours, then, the employer is left with the prerogative to manipulate its workforce as it sees fit.[24]

The sad fact is that Canada's unionized workers rarely obtain a specific provision in a collective agreement that will guarantee them a number of paid hours each and every week. Employers often complain about the rigid work practices that powerful unions have imposed on them, a complaint which is made ever more shrilly as the globalization of production makes its impact felt. The truth is that, in respect of determining the number of hours of paid work to be made available, employers have retained great flexibility. On the other side of the coin is the fact that workers do not have much control at all over the hours they work.

Workers rarely win an absolute right to leisure time. Just as the usual clause relating to the ordinary hours of work does not mean that employees are guaranteed a specific number of paid hours, it also does not mean that there is a maximum number of hours beyond which workers cannot be compelled to work. Only 7 percent of collective agreements covering 500 or more employees specifically provide that overtime will be voluntary. Another 22.8 percent provide that workers may refuse to work overtime in some circumstances. In

70.2 percent of agreements, then, overtime *must* be worked when the employer requires it. This coercive stipulation has been mediated somewhat. Arbitrators have held that workers may refuse overtime when they can offer a good reason. What constitutes a good reason is not always clear. In one case, a worker's refusal to work overtime in order to attend his wedding celebration — which had been planned for many months — was held to have been justified. But a worker who had planned to attend a motorcycle event on a particular weekend, and who had already paid a deposit to the event's organizers, was found not to have been entitled to refuse the employer's request to work overtime on that weekend. The employer's right to punish him for this "unreasonable" refusal was upheld.[25] Employers, however, do have to respect seniority clauses that speak to the allocation of overtime. This means that if the agreement requires it, they must allot overtime on the basis of seniority. The point bears repetition: collective bargaining has yielded results which favour employer managerial flexibility over workers' job, income and quality of work-life rights.

The system, then, has not given unions sufficient bargaining leverage to do well on hours of work. A labour-sympathetic government should take the position that the standard work-week for all employees should be limited to forty hours, and that overtime must be limited and purely voluntary. In a traditionally high-unemployment country, now going through a severe crisis, this would make a valuable contribution to job creation and worker autonomy. The market needs to be trumped.

Paid vacations
Paid vacation time is yet another measure of the advances made in work and social life. In many European countries, four weeks' vacation after one year of employment is guaranteed to all employees, whether unionized or not.[26] In Canada, this is the exception, not the rule. To earn four weeks' vacation, 35.7 percent of collective agreements that cover 500 or more employees required a minimum of six to nine years of service; 17.7 percent required a minimum of ten years of service; 4.5 percent required a minimum of eleven to fourteen years of service; and 2.5 percent required a minimum of fifteen years of service.These major collective agreements entitled only 6.5 percent of workers to four weeks' vacation after one year of employment. A full 93.5 percent of those Canadian workers in the best

bargaining position are not entitled to a benefit available to all workers in countries such as France, Germany, Sweden and Australia.

Most organized workers in Canada do not do much better than the non-unionized sectors who are forced to rely on minimum-standards legislation for their right to paid vacation. The legislative benefits are limited. To get three weeks' vacation, workers need to work for one year in Saskatchewan, four years in Manitoba, five years in British Columbia, six years if they are covered by federal legislation and ten years if they work in Quebec.[27]

Parental leave
Workers have a justifiable claim to be compensated by employers for time lost in giving birth or caring for newborn children. After all, the family is the private means of the reproduction of labour. The absence of any requirement to provide compensation is of great benefit to the employing classes. Until very recently, Canadian unions had been singularly unsuccessful in making advances in this respect. In part, this is explicable by the fact that the largest and most active bargaining units in the mass-production industries were male dominated. As more women enter the workforce and more of them become unionized, there is an impetus for invigorated bargaining efforts on this front. One giant push in this direction was given by a consciousness-raising strike conducted by the Canadian Union of Postal Workers, which led to a provision for paid maternity leave in 1981.[28] Unions are now more sensitive to the issue. But, in large part, the past failure to provide adequately for parental leave was due to the highly fragmented nature of collective bargaining.

By 1990, 29 percent of major collective agreements still did not make any provision for maternity leave at all, even without pay, while 32 percent did provide that there be some pay while female employees were on maternity leave. Only 1.5 percent undertook to pay women 100 percent of their salary while on leave for seventeen weeks. Even these relatively few agreements which did allow for paid maternity leave, then, left much of the costs to be borne by employees.

Canadian workers, therefore, have had to turn to the state. Two things are necessary to provide them with useful parental (contrast unpaid maternity) leave rights. First, they must be able to take time off without losing their right to return to their job. Second, they must be paid during their temporary absence. Every jurisdiction has acted to meet the first requirement. Employees will be entitled to parental leave for a specified period without affecting their job rights.

In all but two jurisdictions they must have been employed for a prescribed amount of time before a woman can demand leave.[29] The most common period of entitlement has been seventeen weeks.[30] An interesting aside is that this is not just a *benefit* for a mother-to-be. An employer can insist that a pregnant woman take leave, whether she wants to or not, if it makes a reasonable judgement that she cannot perform her job because of her pregnancy. This is particularly important because an employee does not have a right to be paid while enjoying this legislative right to leave.[31]

To be paid, an employee must rely on the federal government's Unemployment Insurance Act (UIA). Twenty weeks of service is required to qualify. The benefits do not cover the wage loss in full, however: they are two-thirds of normal pay, up to a maximum. Recently, the period for which they can be paid unemployment benefits was extended to forty-one weeks. Some of the paid time off may be taken by either parent; the decision of how to share it is theirs. This kind of paid leave is also available for adoptive parents.

To be able to take full advantage of these newly extended unemployment insurance benefits, the employees must be entitled to leave their employment during the whole of the period for which the benefits are available. Ontario and Quebec have altered their parental leave provisions to increase the period of leave they allow without pay, so that qualifying parents can take advantage of the newly granted Unemployment Insurance Act benefits. Until all jurisdictions do so, the entitlement to paid parental leave will vary throughout Canada.

While some progress has been made on this front, Canadian workers, especially women, continue to bear much of the material cost of bearing children.[32] Government intervention is posited on the basis that people who take parental leave should be treated no differently than other unemployed people even though, by definition, they are still employed. The decision to have children is still constrained by the discipline of labour markets, which are largely controlled by employers. To underscore that point, it is noteworthy that only 3.8 percent of agreements covering 500 or more employees made some provision for daycare. Thus far, the state has not responded positively to this problem. Having the autonomy to make decisions about reproduction is an index of the quality of life. Unions understand this and are confronting the issue better than before.[33] Government intervention is needed to make employers pay more of their share of this social cost.

Retirement income

Most collective agreements have provisions for a retirement income plan into which either the employer alone or the employer and employee both make contributions. In addition, all persons in the paid workforce are enrolled in the Canada/Quebec Pension Plan schemes (CPP/QPP). Further, all Canadians who have been resident in Canada from the age of eighteen are entitled to the benefits of the federal government's Old Age Security scheme (OAS).

On average, negotiated retirement schemes, known as employer-sponsored plans, provide 32 percent of the retirement income received by the employees covered by them. In 1987, this worked out to $7,734 per pension beneficiary, with a low of $1,470 and a high of $16,201.[34] As could be expected, male averages, at $9,110, are much higher than female averages, at $5,372. These amounts are so miserly that, for most elderly Canadians covered by privately negotiated pension plans, the publicly provided benefits of CPP/QPP/OAS are vital components of their retirement income.

Two factors give rise to these disappointing results. First, for workers to get the maximum return on the contributions made on their behalf and by them, they need to be employed by one employer for their whole working life. This is so because a plan is devised for one employer at a time, and contributions and benefits are rarely portable. Second, hardly any private sector unions have been able to win inflation proofing for their pension benefits. This means that the value of whatever retirement income to which workers eventually do become entitled erodes very quickly.

Inevitably, there has been much pressure to compel greater portability and inflation proofing of employer-sponsored plans. The impoverishment of elderly Canadians has come to be seen as a national shame. Legislative measures are being sought to guarantee the benefits that even the best-placed workers and their unions have been unable to force out of their employers.[35] (See Chapter 8 for a more detailed discussion.)

4. Worker participatory rights

As soon as a union and an employer bargain about terms and conditions of work, workers are participating in making decisions about their lives. The question is, how much participation does that entail? In Canada, there are no formal structures which enable unions or employees to participate in the management of firms or industries as a matter of right. Unions must win rights to participate at each and every bargaining table at which they sit. Workers, as individuals, play little part in making the decisions that affect their daily lives.[36]

It is true that once a collective agreement has been struck in Canada, dozens and dozens of decisions are made every day, in which workers and their representatives participate directly. But this kind of participation does not mean that workers have won participatory *rights*. The crunch comes when an employer insists on how work is to be done, or by whom it is to be done, or in what manner an employee ought to behave on or away from the job. In Canada, the employer is entitled to have its orders carried out, even if they appear to offend some provisions of the ruling collective agreement. The employee's only "right" of reply in such a case is to initiate a process to vindicate her claim that the employer has acted in violation of the agreement. This process is highly dilatory, technical and legalistic in nature. The union frequently becomes a mediator between employer and employee, while the employee is all too often reduced to the status of an alienated bystander. This is a primitive form of worker participation, one which continues to let an employer act unilaterally in the first instance. It fosters hierarchical arrangements, rather than participation between equals.

Reasons for the Relative Inefficacy of Collective Bargaining

The reduction of competition among workers is vital to the success of trade unions. The larger trade union membership is, and the more densely organized any industrial sector becomes, the greater the unions' leverage ought to be as they get closer to the attainment of a regulated labour market. However, data on the outcomes of collective agreements that we have presented are persuasive evidence that, in Canada, the relatively high incidence and density of trade unionism have not led to all that much enhancement of workers' economic power. Nor has the interplay of the private sphere of collective bargaining and the public one of government intervention in the market been as positive as it might have been, in spite of its potential. There are two major reasons for these shortfalls: first, the highly decentralized, factory-by-factory design of Canadian collective bargaining which leaves governments relatively free to pursue their own agendas, and second, the enormous fluctuations in legal rights between provinces.

Factory-by-Factory Bargaining

A central conceptual building block of Canada's statutory régime is that collective bargaining should lead to only a minor modification of an ideal competitive labour market. The monopolies that workers are allowed to create are to be very restricted ones. They are to extend to only one employment site at a time. For small locals this presents serious bargaining problems. Small groups of workers, bargaining on their own, do not have much leverage. Even for large locals the dynamics may be the same when they confront highly integrated multinational enterprises. For instance, the workers represented by a Steelworkers local during a bitter and lengthy dispute at a Radio Shack location in Barrie got some administrative and strike fund support from the parent union organization. But they could not call on fellow union members to engage in supporting strikes against Radio Shack's transnational parent and affiliates. Barrie's local Radio Shack operation was not so handicapped.[37]

Close adherence to the competitive model is a barrier to the effective government intervention required to redress problems that cannot be overcome by bargaining with one employer at a time. The ideological baggage attached to the competitive model's bargaining system has persuaded governments that the market can be left to fix its own difficulties if the more extreme imbalances that have caused it to malfunction have been corrected.

As we already have noted, in a scheme designed to consolidate and perpetuate market pre-eminence, there is little flow-through from the unionized sector to the unorganized one. Nor are these modifications of the market meant to upgrade social security norms; rather, social security is supposed to conform to market-efficiency criteria. The gender gap in women's earnings and the poor record in improving health and safety norms are powerful indicators of the extent to which this institutional design inhibits the amelioration of the plight of the weak.

Women's earnings

The gap between male and female wage rates in Canada has been among the widest in the Western world. A 1980 OECD report on women revealed that Canada was the only country where the earning situation of women actually worsened between 1968 and 1977.[38] By way of comparison, female hourly earnings had climbed to 85 percent of male hourly earnings in France and Sweden by 1977. This marked a significant closing of the gender gap which had existed in those countries in 1968. The wage gaps largely reflect job ghettoization. The position remains grave, as women are over-represented in the service sectors and are actually losing ground in manufacturing, professional and technical employment.[39]

This ghettoization is the result of, and has perpetuated socially constructed undervaluation of women's work. This problem cannot be addressed meaningfully on an employer-by-employer basis. Until mid-1980, this was the only mechanism on offer. Inevitably, this has meant that the supposed logic of the market, a logic which created much of the problem in the first place, still plays a significant role. There is evidence that this is hindering legislative attempts to tackle the problem. In 1988, Statistics Canada reported that, despite much governmental intervention at all levels, women still earned only 66 percent of what men earned, an improvement of less than 4 percent over ten years.[40] Collective bargaining and the legislative intervention associated with it are inherently incapable of meeting the challenge.[41]

Workers' health and safety

A similar picture emerges in respect of occupational health and safety. Canada has one of the worst workplace health and safety records amongst the OECD countries.[42] Each year, 800 fatalities are caused by work accidents, and close to a million injuries, half of which are debilitating, are recorded. They occur at a rate of one every twenty-two seconds of the working week. In addition, every year an estimated 10,000 people die earlier than they otherwise would have from occupationally related diseases.[43]

This appalling record exists side by side with elaborate legislative schemes which provide for standard-setting and inspections by the state. But the standards set are low, inspections rare, and enforcement pusillanimous. The reason for this is that governments administer their schemes with an abiding respect for the employers' investment needs. Profitability and productivity are considered of great importance when standards are set. As the adequacy of standards is judged principally by what employers say, employers exercise a great deal of control over what level of safety is to prevail. Much of the daily administration and application of these inevitably poor health and safety standards has been left to an internal responsibility system. Governments have created joint health and safety committees to monitor the workplace. These committees have been given nothing but recommendatory power. Inevitably this makes for poor results.

Variations in the Degree of Collective Bargaining Power

Collective bargaining law is different in detail in each jurisdiction. Some of these differences are important and some are not. The net effect is a checkerboard of collective bargaining rights. The specificity of collective bargaining law requires different organizational and political responses in each jurisdiction. Moreover, the legal collective bargaining rights are not constant in any one province. Governments frequently change the rules of the game.

In the early seventies, British Columbia was the most reform-minded jurisdiction in Canada.[44] Later, as conditions and governments changed radically in British Columbia, there was a marked retrenchment of collective bargaining rights.[45] Quebec also had a progressive period. It led the way in the 1960s when it established public sector bargaining rights and again, later, when it enacted anti-scab legislation.[46] Since then, however, it has cut down on public sector rights and the anti-scab legislation has come under pressure from some business organizations.

Recent changes to the laws in Saskatchewan[47] and Ontario[48] permit an employer to force unions to take a vote amongst the employees on the last offer made to the union by the employer, potentially overriding a trade union's stance and, thereby, affecting its bargaining position. In Alberta, recent decisions by the Labour Relations Board permit unionized employers in the construction industry to establish formally separate, but actually connected, corporations which do not hire trade union members. These new entities are permitted to bid competitively on jobs against the unionized enterprises with which they are affiliated.[49] This has had considerable impact on trade unionists' collective bargaining power in the construction sectors.

All of this makes it abundantly clear that it is misleading to treat collective bargaining in the private sectors as if it were an autonomous institution, left alone by the state. At any one time, collective bargaining law reflects electoral and economic strategic needs. The terrain of struggle is changed periodically by the local government of the day, which may be sympathetic to union pressure, but more often than not sets out to satisfy an agenda it shares with business. Sometimes, then, governments reinforce the autonomous and reformist aspects of collective bargaining mildly; sometimes they strengthen its restrictive and coercive aspects a bit. The changes are never fundamental. They never bring into question the basic concept that collective bargaining should depart as little as possible from the paradigm of the competitive, atomized market.

The very fact that the manipulation of the collective bargaining régime has become a legitimate policy tool of governments affords governments an opportunity to refashion it to achieve lasting gains for workers. But it will require a trenchant approach, one which is designed to cut through the limitations imposed by a market model. If this is not done, reforms which facilitate union organization and do, in fact, make collective bargaining a little easier, while welcome, can readily be reversed. The British Columbia experience evidences this all too well. Without such a radical approach, nothing will have been done to counter the immense thrust of export-led growth strategies.

As was shown in Chapter 2, the ability of workers to use collective bargaining positively has always been constrained by the larger economic environment. The factory-by-factory collective bargaining model has not given workers sufficient leverage to counter the effects of the economic decisions mandated by governments' reliance on resource-led growth. The reforms they have won have made it easier for them to bargain locally, but not to become partners at the central decision-making tables. It is this which has to change.

From the mid-seventies onwards, governments have been emboldened to use their well-established right to shape collective bargaining to serve what they term "the public's needs." The dominant view has been that public welfare is best served by increasing trade liberalization; that is, the market is to have its way. Here the significance of the fact that collective bargaining has never been envisaged to be a denial of the values and assumptions of a free enterprise model becomes manifest. Conservative-minded governments find it plausible to claim that some of the positive aspects of collective bargaining may be taken away if they unnecessarily obstruct the furthering of these competitive goals. When this is done it is always done on the basis that collective bargaining rights should be suspended temporarily only, and that the régime should stay in place. In this context, trade unions that resist these roll-backs and demand a return to "full" collective bargaining rights are fighting to retain the model in its more positive form, rather than to change it radically.

The Lack of Political Power of Trade Unions

Of course, trade unions and their officials feel committed to the betterment of the lot of all workers, unionized or not. Moreover, they have a real stake in making sure that there is no reserve army of unemployed and underpaid people reducing their leverage. Not surprisingly, they participate in electoral and special-interest politics. Further, labour organizations participate in many tripartite bodies, along with employers and government officials. But they come to these decision-making bodies without any real clout.

When Ottawa proposed to formalize existing instances of corporatist organization into something of a European model of institutional relations in the seventies, many unionists rebelled against the leadership of the Canadian Labour Congress (CLC), which seemed to be ready to enter into such an arrangement.[50] The perceived problem lay in the fact that the Canadian Labour Congress, Canada's principal trade union central, has no authority over the rank and file or over its affiliated unions when it comes to negotiations with the government. It is not much more than a front organization for lobbying, and an arbiter of disputes between its members. In addition to this lack of any credible threat when sitting at the decision-making table, central union movement leaders cannot guarantee that their affiliated members will abide by any agreement they make. From the perspective of developing a mature corporatist model, this is a serious weakness. It is in this context that Panitch has suggested that the Canadian labour movement has not been sufficiently centralized to "justify resorting to corporatism as a means of integration for capital and the state."[51] A major contributing factor to this problem is the lack of a national collective bargaining scheme.

Canadian labour is organized on a regional and provincial basis because each province is responsible for setting the standards and norms in its jurisdiction. The decentralized nature of the labour movement and Canada's system of industrial relations is a result of the 1948 decision by the federal government to return labour relations regulation to provincial jurisdiction. Pentland characterized this move as "a giant step backward," leading to "the reversion to the jungle-type relations of industrial relations" of an earlier period.[52] His concern was that intransigent employers, who might have little presence on the national stage, would have a disproportionate amount of power in the provincial setting. Their influence on local governments was likely to be great, whereas national unions would have more power *vis-à-vis* a central government.

This emphasis on localism and the resulting provincialization of labour movements has meant that, in practice, in the absence of a unified treatment of labour relations, Canada's system of industrial relations has privileged local labour markets at the expense of a national one. It is primarily this factor that has prevented the institution of collective bargaining from spreading wage gains evenly throughout the economy. It has no way to make any real impact on pre-existing labour market disparities.[53]

While the emphasis on localism has indeed been costly for Canada's trade union movement, at the sub-national level it has supported a high degree of trade union militancy. For instance, British Columbia and Quebec have been centres of mass upheavals. (See Chapter 6.) No doubt, Operation Solidarity and the formation and the struggles of the Common Front have had symbolic and psychological effects on the way politics are viewed throughout the nation. But, as important as this is, there was never much possibility that the uprisings would lead to nation-wide organization. The fragmentation of the working classes' principal agents militates against this. Important here is the fact that different relations to export-led growth in each of the regions throws up different needs and agendas.

Localized trade unions must respond to the specificity of their situation, rather than to any overall national strategy. As a consequence, branches of the same union may require different organization and use different tactics. In addition, they will have to respond to different collective bargaining rules which, in turn, reflect local politics. Thus, it is not surprising that Canada should continue to experience a large amount of regional, rather than national, class conflict.[54]

There is a potentially positive side to the regionalization of Canadian politics. While Pentland was right in pointing out that local employers might have a disproportionate amount of influence with local governments, it is also true that given Canada's working class and populist history, it is probable that parties sympathetic to working people will win power from time to time. When this happens, such governments can restrict themselves to making it easier for unions to grow and expand on a factory-by-factory basis. Alternatively, they can create a floor of rights external to the bargaining system to serve as a launching pad for further bargaining. The former is merely a reformist and reversible set of measures. The latter would be a warning shot that the existing competitive model is no longer to be the core instrument by which to regulate capital-labour relationships. It would be the beginning of a recognition that different economic and political strategies exist which do not accept the idea that a largely unmediated market is the primary responsibility for the creation of welfare.

This scenario seemed to have become a realistic one with the election of the NDP government in Ontario. This is not the first time that a social democratic government has been elected in Canada. But, in the small provinces, even if they had seen the need for it, it would have been extremely difficult for these governments to restructure their economies. This explains why their approach to collective bargaining was merely reformist. Ontario, Canada's industrial heartland and the most populous province, presents a different opportunity. It is possible for an Ontario government to lead a restructuring of Canada's economy. Its economic influence is enormous, and could be enhanced through co-operation with NDP governments in Saskatchewan and British Columbia. But it would have required a good deal of vision and courage for the Rae government to undertake fundamental change rather than simply to reform and streamline the collective bargaining system.

Understandably, perhaps, it is facing the challenge. In its labour law reform proposals, all it has done is to make the organization and certification processes a little more responsive to union needs, and offer some more organizational potential for part-time workers. In respect of bargaining power, it has offered a somewhat feeble set of anti-scab provisions, some improved protections for striking workers, and the right to have agreements imposed by the labour relations board in certain kinds of impasse situations. In the key area of management prerogatives, particularly in respect of the right to contract out, to impose technological change, to exercise disciplinary powers and the like, very little is to be done.[55]

One of the reasons why it may be difficult for NDP governments to do as much as they should is that many trade unionists and politicians in the NDP share the conventional view that a reformed collective bargaining system is all that is required to yield satisfactory outcomes for workers. They see private, voluntary agreement making, supported by a government-guaranteed right to strike, as a public good. From this perspective, all that stands in the way of progress are the rulings and decisions of labour boards and arbitrators that make union formation and collective bargaining difficult. Reform is all that is necessary. And because when even mild reforms are offered, they are met with vehement opposition, the reformers tend to believe that they are doing something truly positive, even radical.

This misses an important point. Such a reformed system would still be one in which control would be exercised over (1) the kind of unions that can participate in the scheme; (2) the bargaining power that unions ought to have; (3) the scope and extent of strike rights; and (4), more tangentially, the extent of control by workers over their daily working lives. Real control over the reformed scheme still would be exercised by administrators and arbitrators who consider themselves to be above the fray, zealous guardians of a truly consensual system who help attain objectives on which capital and labour agree. The acceptance of this portrayal of collective bargaining has always stood in the way of fundamental change. In large measure, labour's containment has been achieved by the success with which collective bargaining has been characterized as an institution based on, and furthering, a liberal pluralist ideology. It is this feature of the industrial relations scheme which must be confronted. To this end, the way in which collective bargaining rules have evolved and have been administered is the focus of the next chapters. It is a first and necessary step on the way to appreciating that this model of collective bargaining, no matter how kindly it is administered, embeds political and economic fragmentation.

Labour Relations Boards I: Moulding the Contours of the System

The Neutral Look

Labour relations boards are the expert agencies chosen to administer, protect and promote collective bargaining.[1] They structure the conditions in which collective bargaining is to take place. Yet, boards are perceived, and indeed see themselves, as being above the fray. They are characterized as facilitators, favouring neither employers nor unions.

Their expertise and evenhanded approach is assured by staffing them with neutral members who are appointed by the state and who enjoy the respect of the labour relations community, and with a number of employer and union representatives. Not only do these people bring experience and knowledge to the tasks at hand, but they can be counted on to share the ideology and goals which underpin the collective bargaining scheme they have been asked to administer. This gives both the scheme and the administrative agencies legitimacy in the eyes of the major protagonists. Further, it is claimed that boards are particularly suited to their task. The argument is that, because of the backgrounds of their personnel, their expertise and their deep understanding of the parties' needs, they can deal with issues quickly, objectively and relatively cheaply.[2]

From their inception, boards have been required to strike a series of delicate balances. Necessarily they have been left with a great deal of discretionary power. Collective bargaining takes place in a market setting with highly volatile employer-employee relationships. Boards are to promote workers' collective power. But because this power might make the consequences of work disruptions graver, they also have been assigned the task of achieving a measure of stability in capital-labour relations. Their task is even more complicated than it might appear at first blush because they are also there to safeguard the rights of individuals in the system. The last point weighs heavily with them. Indeed, they always have been careful to ensure that employees are truly exercising autonomous choices when deciding what union, if any, should represent them. This has been done by monitoring the behaviour of unions, employees and employers.

The conduct of unions and employees has to be regulated because, once a majority of a group of workers in an appropriate bargaining unit have freely and democratically chosen a particular trade union as their bargaining agent, that bargaining agent has the *exclusive* right to represent all workers in that unit, including those who actively opposed it. It is essentially an opt-in system, which requires evidence that a majority of workers have signed, and paid for, a membership card. The conduct of employers also must be regulated to prevent them from unduly influencing their employees to vote against unionization, or to vote for a union that favours the employer. As will be shown, this continued concern for the protection of individual freedoms and rights has significant impacts — some of which are unintended — on the collective bargaining possibilities of workers. In particular, this strong adherence to liberal precepts requires that there be as much regard for the rights of *employers* as individuals as there is for *employees* as individuals. This leads to upside-down effects because the scheme initially set out to protect individual employees from employers who had the power to deny them their freedom of choice.

Legal Ordering — Some Fundamental Premises of Labour Relations Boards

Protection of Old-Fashioned Individualism

For workers, a trade union is a means by which to promote their economic and social solidarity. It is an initial assertion of shared class interest. For the purposes of common law, however, a trade union is no more than an association of workers who have entered into contracts with each other for the purpose of restraining their own, and other people's, trading rights. They want to impede free trade in labour power. The restraint arises, then, from the fact that they seek to create a relative monopoly of workers. In legal terms, they contract with each other to fix the price of their labour.[3]

From this perspective, a trade union is constituted by a series of contracts, with identical terms, concluded between each of the members of that association that wants to characterize itself as a union. The terms of these contracts are found in the constitution or the by-laws of the union. This constitution contains the union's stated objectives, as well as the rules and procedures which it will follow to administer its affairs. This contract-based notion of what a trade union is continues to guide labour relations boards in their legal regulation of unions. A group of workers that claims to have formed a union must show a labour relations board to which it applies for recognition for bargaining purposes that its members have entered into a series of private contracts with each other on identical terms. In practical terms, a good deal of technical know-how is needed to deal with these requirements, a formidable obstacle for lay people.[4]

The boards require evidence that all of the employees who sign up with a union truly want to be represented by it and constitute a majority of the employees in the suggested bargaining unit. Further, boards need to be persuaded that the applying union intends to participate fully in the kind of collective bargaining which they favour. The requirements, therefore, are the following:

1. There is evidence that a majority of the relevant employees have signed a membership card and paid a token amount of money by way of initiation dues ($1.00 to $1.50). The union must prove to the board's satisfaction that its constitution gives all employees in the bargaining unit the right to belong to it. This is important because a certified trade union might succeed in having a security clause included in an ensuing collective agreement providing that an individual will not have the right to remain employed unless union membership is obtained or maintained. If a certified union that wins such a security clause has by-laws that preclude some current employees from becoming union members, its certification may lead to the denial of their right to employment.

To overcome this difficult evidentiary problem, boards, from early on in their history, deemed all members of a proposed bargaining unit eligible to belong to an applicant trade union unless they were faced with clear evidence to the contrary. This policy of favouring the collective over the individual was controversial but, eventually, became the accepted norm.[5]

2. The union's eligibility clauses do not discriminate in a manner proscribed by human rights laws.[6]

3. The employer has played no part in the establishment or creation of the union. This requirement stems from the real fear that employers, having become aware that some of their workers want to organize or to form an antagonistic union, might manipulate workers into belonging to a union that is not interested in diminishing the employer's power in any way.[7]

4. The trade union's constitutional objectives include the regulation of terms and conditions of employment. Positively, this means that a labour relations board can disqualify unions which do not truly represent workers' interests. An applicant trade union which merely states that its objectives are to create harmonious relationships, to better the quality of services of the employer and/or to make the place of employment more agreeable is not considered a trade union for the purposes of collective bargaining.[8] Negatively, it means that the boards have been left with a rationale enabling them to disqualify unions that might want to use their collective power to create a different kind of economic order than the one posited by the collective bargaining statute.

Promotion of Modern Collectivism

To avoid the hurdles presented by these requirements, the easiest thing for workers to do is to ask an existing union to organize them. The parent-to-be will be asked to set up a local and to apply for certification as the bargaining agent for the workers who have sought the help of the established union. This strategy of reaching out to existing unions is actively encouraged by the practices of the administrative agencies. Once a labour relations board has recognized a union as a bona fide one for collective bargaining purposes, it will accept the credentials of any local of that union without further question. This eliminates the need to draft a constitution, to hold meetings to have it ratified and to appoint officers. Indeed, this flexibility is typical of the practices developed by the boards.

To give effect to their explicit twin policies of promoting trade unionism and of safeguarding individual rights, the boards have created an elaborate web of legalistic procedural rules. Participants in the process have come to rely on these rules. An aura of legally mandated fairness, precision and predictability has been created. Boards have developed "standard unit" criteria to help them decide how, and by whom, workers should be represented in bargaining. For the most part, they seem to apply these criteria without paying any overt attention to the external world. The routine of union certification constitutes the bulk of their administrative work and, in the overwhelming majority of cases, they perform it with apparent straightforwardness, evenhandedly applying the rules they have fashioned. Such inconsistencies as do occur more often than not can be attributed to the fact that different boards, acting at different times, resolve the tension between individualism and collectivism somewhat differently. The variations can be said to flow, therefore, from subjective factors which affect all decision-makers, rather than from systematic manipulation. Yet, this is too sanguine a view.

The fact is that the legal rules and practices that have evolved, like all legal rules and practices, are expressions of political will. In the labour relations sphere, the rules are shaped by the ups and downs of Canada's business cycles and by a lack of a genuine commitment to a national industrial strategy. Collective bargaining is meant to be only a modification of the anarchic competitive-market model, not a rejection of it. Boards have understood this fundamental fact very well and have used their discretionary powers to reflect this vision of the scheme. The ways in which boards have dealt with the routine questions support this assertion. We will address this directly in the next chapter. Here, we concentrate on the kinds of situations which require boards to be explicit about their loyalty to this agenda.

Because these situations do not occur frequently, they could be explained away as a "wilderness of single instances." But the reality is that boards have sometimes used their residual powers instrumentally either to satisfy a particular government's immediate needs or to follow what a board's personnel perceive to be the dominant political wisdom. In some much rarer cases, governments have overridden labour relations boards' decisions directly. This undermines the boards' much-prized and oft-asserted autonomy. This kind of intervention is aberrational, but it serves as a useful reminder to the boards that their ultimate role is to pursue state aims. Of course, state goals are not formulated all that explicitly or precisely. This gives the boards a good deal of leeway. But there is an overall sense of what the state's macro-economic objectives are and boards do, in fact, promote them. If they stray they will be brought into line pretty smartly.

Labour Relations Boards — Lifting the Veil a Little

Overriding a Labour Relations Board — the Michelin Bill

Some time ago the Nova Scotia government inveigled the multinational Michelin tire company to invest in the province. Michelin established two plants. In due course, the workers at these plants asked a union to initiate an organizational drive. The union failed to sign up the majority of employees at the plant where it sought to be certified as the bargaining agent. It alleged that unfair labour practices committed by Michelin had prevented it from obtaining a majority and thus went forward with its application, seeking automatic certification as a remedy. As it was to turn out, the Nova Scotia Labour Relations Board did not certify the applying union. But, even before the issue was resolved by the Board, Michelin had taken steps to ensure that it would not have to face this kind of aggravation again. It used its economic clout to convince politicians to change the norms.

The province passed legislation which specified that if an employer has two plants in geographically distinct areas within the province, a majority of the total number of employees at both plants have to be signed up by an applicant trade union in order for it to be granted certification *vis-à-vis* that employer.[9] At the time this legislation was passed, it was clear that these new rules could apply only to Michelin's operations in Nova Scotia. The Nova Scotia government was rewarded for its efforts. Michelin has established a third plant in the province. None of its employees are represented by a union, nor are they likely to be in the immediate future. The new legislative barriers are so effective that two organizing drives at Michelin by the energetic and well-run Canadian Automobile Workers, in 1983 and in 1987, also ended in failure.

The Michelin legislation attracted widespread attention. Proponents of the extant collective bargaining system have a stake in the maintenance of the perception that the state is, and should act as, a neutral agent. To them, overt intervention, such as that of the Nova Scotia government, is anathema.[10] This is so because it belies the conventional assumption of labour relations that neither the government nor its agency have any interest in controlling the strength of particular parties or in achieving specific outcomes. Boards get their legitimacy from devising practices and applying them in a routine manner. Their appearance of neutrality is reinforced by their purported indifference to the outcomes of bargaining. The whole idea is to emphasize the voluntaristic features of collective bargaining. Largely this has been achieved by the insistence of labour relations boards that it is their policy to ensure that workers should be left alone to decide whether or not to unionize and how to bargain. It is their success in portraying themselves in this way that has made it justifiable to argue that boards are mere facilitators who should be given free rein to effectuate the policies necessary to the promotion of collective bargaining. But, if they should come to be seen as being controlled by governments who may have a clear interest in manipulating outcomes at certain times, their independence and prestige and, ultimately, the legitimacy of the scheme they administer, will be put at risk.[11]

Of course, Canadian legislatures only rarely feel the need to intervene with Michelin-type bills. More often than not the objectives of the administrative agencies and governments are compatible. On the few occasions when they get out of kilter, the boards are well placed to divine what a government's wishes are and to give them effect.

Some Decisions in a Changed British Columbia

In 1973, a large reform movement resulted in the passing of the British Columbia *Labour Code*. This was hailed as the most pro-collective bargaining and pro-union legislation in Canada.[12] Yet the British Columbia Labour Relations Board, while still administering this self-same *Labour Code* in the 1980s, made some remarkably anti-union decisions. They reflected the well-known government hostility to unionism that then prevailed in British Columbia.

In one case it was determined that, despite the well-established practice of the B.C. Board to the contrary, a union had to win a majority at two plants of one employer to be certified as the bargaining agent. That is, the British Columbia Labour Relations Board, without legislative intervention, reached the same result as that reached in Nova Scotia when the Michelin Bill was passed there. In yet another case, the Board denied its own practices. In the past, the Board had helped a trade union win bargaining rights when an employer set up a new plant in the same geographical area. If the union could show that a majority of the aggregate of employees were members of that union, regardless of whether or not it had signed up anyone in the new plant, certification was automatically extended to the second plant. The British Columbia Board reversed itself. This made unionization more difficult and union-busting easier.[13]

Giving the Government a Helping Hand — the Post Office

When, in 1982, the Post Office ceased to exist as a department and its functions were taken over by a Crown agency, the Canada Post Corporation (CPC), the statute which established the CPC provided that the pre-existing certified bargaining agents would continue to represent the previously designated bargaining units. There were many of these, and all parties knew that in due course there would have to be a rearrangement. In 1985, as the government was making it clear that it wanted the postal services to be leaner and meaner and that it saw the unions, particularly the Canadian Union of Postal Workers (CUPW), as obstacles, the CPC brought an application for a global review. In particular, it argued that because it needed to run an integrated service, it wanted an all-encompassing operational unit to cover members of the Canadian Union of Postal Workers, the Letters Carriers' Union of Canada (LCUC) and the Canadian Postmasters' and Assistants' Association. The Canada Labour Relations Board granted the employer's wish over the objections of the unions. It was explicit as to why it did this:

> The Corporation, always under the scrutiny of the public and politicians, has been, and continues to be, under enormous pressures to improve service and balance its books. Our decision, by providing needed flexibility to the Corporation, should better permit it to deal with these pressures.[14]

To serve the government and the CPC in this way, the Board had to override the express wishes of the unions who had long-established, separate bargaining rights which they wanted to maintain. The forced amalgamation between LCUC and CUPW was bound to lead to bitter disputes which the CPC (and the government, not too hidden in the shadows) could exploit to further its aims of "flexibility." The CUPW won the vote to become the sole bargaining agent, as it had slightly more members than did the LCUC. The leadership of the LCUC was not happy with the result. As a consequence, postal workers' unions got busy, tearing each other apart, bringing their complaints against each other before a Board that itself had set the stage for their internecine warfare.[15] While it is true that the Board had had to make a decision, the one it made favoured an employer, so closely related to the government, to such an extent that it is difficult not to think of it as a repudiation of the argument that administrative labour agencies are merely impartial facilitators.

Bank Workers: A Test for Labour Relations Boards

Sometimes the rules promulgated by the labour relations administrative agencies are overtaken by events. If the outcomes they generate create discontent, their legitimacy may be jeopardized. In these circumstances they are likely to use their vast discretionary powers to adapt their practices, all the time protesting that they are not changing their basic approach. Such efforts will be aimed at achieving more acceptable results while maintaining an air of neutrality. The dictates of the rule of law by which they claim to be bound, however, create rigidities, often making the task of adaptation a difficult one. The organizational drives at Canada's banks provide a case in point.[16]

The banks are federally chartered institutions. This means that it is plausible to characterize their branches all over the country as part and parcel of one large, integrated organization, rather than a set of discrete employment sites. Thus it was that when bank workers employed at local branches had organized themselves into local unions and asked the Canada Labour Relations Board to certify their union, it seemed natural for the Board to accept the banks' argument that no single branch was to be treated as *the* employer. The Board, therefore, ruled that for a trade union to be certified as the bargaining agent for bank workers, it had to demonstrate that it had signed up a majority of the employees of *all* of the branches of any one bank.[17] This made organization all but impossible. Canadian banks remained union-free. This approach could be defended, at least in legal circles, by arguing that the Board was acting within the normal bounds of labour relations board practices in defining the term "employer" as it did. After all, an autonomous, neutral facilitating body should not be second-guessed.

But, eventually, this effective denial of rights to bank workers put the federal administrative agency in an untenable position. This was so because the poor conditions of employment of the largely unorganized female banking workforce came to the attention of a public whose level of consciousness about the denial of rights to women in *all* spheres was increasing sharply. The treatment of working women became a major political and social issue.

It was in this context that a small group of gutsy women in British Columbia — the Service, Office and Retail Workers' Union of Canada (SORWUC) — sought to organize a single branch of a bank.[18] They signed up a majority of the employees at that branch and made an application for certification. The Canada Labour Relations Board now reversed its previous approach. It established a rule that bank workers could organize on a branch-by-branch basis. Each branch of a bank was to be treated as a separate employer, rather than a dependent component of a larger whole.[19] By this redefinition of the word *employer*, the Board was able to say that it still was adhering to its existing general practice of allowing workers to organize on an employer-by-employer basis. The trick was transparent, but necessary. A recognition of a changed political climate had caused the Board to promote the bank workers' right to organize more directly. As it turned out, its flexible use of its discretion was not to yield the desired effect.

It quickly became clear that to organize on a branch-by-branch basis was an impossibility for spontaneously created unions, such as SORWUC, which had very few resources. It obtained certifications at a mere 6 of the 1,824 Canadian Imperial Bank of Commerce (CIBC) branches. Overall, it managed to organize only 26 of the thousands of branches operated by the six major banks. In 1978, it left the struggle to others.[20] More established trade unions, such as CUPE and the Steelworkers, realizing the potential rewards of organizing a large number of bank employees, fought each other for the right to unionize these workers now that the law had become more favourable to unionization. But they had not reckoned on the banks' intransigence. It is relatively easy, given that organization is to be done on a branch-by-branch basis, for banks to intimidate workers into quiescence. The banks have proved themselves all too willing to avail themselves of bully-like tactics. They have been assisted in their tactics by the fundamental premises of labour relations boards. Here we refer to a conceptual point raised earlier; its importance can now be concretized: labour relations agencies are wedded to a liberal ideology which signifies that, even in administering a collectivist scheme, the rights of individuals are to be accorded as much respect as possible. Indeed, all individuals, regardless of their wealth or power, should be treated as equally as it is possible to do, given social and legal restraints.

Employers are individuals. Like all other individuals, they have the right to deal with their property as they see fit. As the business is the employer's property, employers are entitled to control the internal mail systems they have set up to conduct their business. Therefore, they can deny the use of those internal mail systems to employees who might want to contact their colleagues for the purpose of unionization. The denial of this means of access to organizers makes it more difficult for workers to unionize than it should be. But it is legal. It was so held by the Canada Labour Relations Board when a CIBC branch, faced by an organizational drive, denied its would-be union employees access to notice boards and the internal memorandum system.[21] Similarly, because their business is their property to do with as they see fit, individual employers have the right to transfer employees from one department to another, or from one branch to another to increase efficiency, unless there is a specific contractual provision to the contrary. In the absence of a collective agreement, there rarely is. Employers also can fire employees whose conduct they deem to be harmful to their enterprise.

These legally established property rights make it difficult for workers to organize when they have good reason to believe that their employer is antagonistic to unions. This is so even though the labour relations boards have developed remedies to help workers and union organizers after the fact. While the law and its administrators have put some constraints on the rights of employers to act as untrammelled property-owners, the profoundly anti-union banks have been able to use their legally implied managerial rights to discourage trade union organization. More dramatically, pillars of the banking community, such as the Bank of Montreal and the CIBC, have exceeded the bounds of legality on many occasions.[22] While they have been ordered to make amends for their misconduct, this has not helped very much: while the intimidation is going on, workers cannot be sure that a favourable finding will be made, or that an appropriate remedy will be provided — eventually.

In addition, employers, like all other individuals, are entitled to express their opinions. Again, while some controls are imposed by labour relations boards on this right of free speech, clever anti-union employers are in a good position to discourage unionization. They can chill the atmosphere.

All of this has meant that unions seeking to organize banks on a branch-by-branch basis have encountered difficulties.[23] The problems have been so serious that the embarrassed administrative agency, desirous of being seen as a supporter and promoter of trade unionism, has had to change its practices once again.

In the *National Bank of Canada* case, the Canada Labour Relations Board adopted a "cluster" approach. This permits employees working in a number of a bank's branches located in a particular region to constitute one bargaining unit. All they have to show is that the work done at this cluster of branches is so tightly integrated as to be fairly characterized as the business of one "employer." The Board's residual discretionary power is now being used, in a different way, to achieve a desired outcome: the unionization of more bank workers.[24] But they have not solved their problem yet. How is a Board to determine which branches in which region are sufficiently integrated to be designated an appropriate bargaining unit? Trade union success depends on the way in which employers structure their business organization. Most of the cards have been left in the hands of hostile employers who can easily reorganize if they wish to do so. The anti-unionism of the banks and other financial institutions may well lead them to do this. Their past actions speak for themselves. After ten years of attempted organization in the banking sectors, less than 3 percent of the workforce had been organized.[25]

Promoting Unions That Share the Prevailing Ideology
There is nothing remarkable about the fact that state agencies such as labour relations boards should support existing power relations. Understandably, therefore, boards do not see themselves as doing anything untoward when they shape their rules and practices in accordance with newly emerging dominant strains of development. In this sense, they are something of a window through which a glimpse can be obtained of the state's changing perception as to how labour relations are to be constructed and conducted.

The story of how left-wing militants and communists were removed from power in trade unions in the late 1940s and 1950s is well documented.[26] In Canada, the best-known examples are provided by the assault on the Canadian Seamen's Union (CSU) led by the governments, employers and the Seafarers International Union (SIU), and by the Steelworkers' efforts to oust Mine Mill.[27] The labour relations boards played their part in this political realignment of trade unions: they hid behind the façade of applying existing rules. What they did was to use their power to define a trade union for the purpose of collective bargaining to disqualify left-wing and anti-American unions.[28] In the Mine Mill cases, they redefined successor right rules to achieve their purpose.[29] Precisely at the same time as trade unionism was being legitimated, its ideological construction was taking place with the boards' help. While these examples must seem ancient history, they demonstrate that these labour agencies played a crucial role in the creation of a terrain of struggle which favoured a specific polity and particular economic-growth model. This has had a lasting impact.

The boards were able to act in this instrumental way without losing legitimacy. After all, their decisions were in step with what was presented as the incontrovertible political consensus of the times.[30] This dominant belief system had been internalized by the members of the boards. Many of them were probably quite unconscious of the instrumentality of their decisions. They felt, and had little trouble convincing others, that they were using their residual powers neutrally. This kind of manipulative power is still possessed by labour relations agencies.

A more recent manifestation of its use took place when an incumbent United Steelworkers of America local was challenged by a national union, CAIMAW, at Trail and Kimberley in British Columbia. CAIMAW had been successful in signing up a majority of employees at a large plant, despite some flagrantly unfair labour practices by the employer.[31] Indeed, it is clear from a reading of the facts, as set out by the British Columbia Labour Relations Board, that the employer's unfair labour practices were meant to benefit the Steelworkers. When CAIMAW presented an application to the British Columbia Board asking that it be certified as the bargaining agent instead of the Steelworkers, it was able to show that it had signed up a majority of employees in the unit. The Board held, however, that the signing-up period had taken just under four months, and that any signatures which were more than three months old constituted only "equivocal" evidence of membership. Such "old" membership evidence could not be relied upon because people might have changed their mind since signing up. To substantiate its holding, the Board was able to point to an existing policy it had promulgated to the effect that membership evidence should not be older than three months. The Board thus was able to defend its decision by reference to a policy it had established to permit the free wishes of the employees to triumph.

However, there are other ways to test the employees' true wishes than rigid reliance on arbitrary time lines. Indeed, the totally inflexible application of the Board's own rule was a startling departure from the past practices of that same Board. It had frequently used its discretion to rely on "old" membership evidence where it thought it safe to do so. Further, if the Board had been really concerned as to whether or not the proffered membership cards rcflected the employees' wishes, it could have ordered a supervised vote rather than reject CAIMAW's application outright. The fact that it did not do this indicates that the Board had an agenda which was probably influenced by the same kinds of views held by boards when the Mine Mill was attacked some twenty-five years earlier by the Steelworkers.[32] The Board's rejection of CAIMAW's application on technical grounds meant that CAIMAW was legally barred from applying for certification for a long time.[33] This allowed the Steelworkers to solidify their position.

These kinds of happenings have become more rare. After the initial convulsions, the system is no longer confronted by explicitly left-wing unionism. The associated fights between American "internationals" and Canadian unions are becoming less and less significant. The celebrated divorce of the automobile workers, leading to the formation of the Canadian Automobile Workers' union, is but the most vivid and dramatic example of a clear trend.[34] Canadian unions are searching for independence, and American union membership has declined in Canada.

The Illusion of Neutrality

These struggles and the role the boards played in them, as well as the Michelin Bill story, that of the B.C. Labour Relations Board, the Post Office and the bank workers' cases, all show that the labour administrative agencies are not mere facilitators, disinterested as to the nature of the participants or the outcomes they are likely to produce. In each of these circumstances they have shown themselves to be willing to pursue clear (albeit often unarticulated) policy goals. This suggests that even when they are not dealing with obviously politicized issues, they are relying on rules which are not neutral in origin or are applying them in ways which have a built-in bias.

Yet, to much of the world, including many of the savvy participants in the scheme, the personnel of the labour relations boards are seen as relatively impartial functionaries. The administration of collective bargaining has been given an aura of precision. But even the most routinely applied rules do have a general focus. They are aimed at the maintenance of as much employer power as is consonant with the promotion of *some* trade unionism and *some* collective worker power. While this rather open-ended characterization of how they perceive their role does not mandate specific results in any one case, it does suggest that there is a particular mindset which governs day-to-day decision making.

Labour Relations Boards II: Designing the Nuts and Bolts to Fit the System

Labour relations boards are typical of agencies that are created to implement government policies. They do not examine their navel every day to see whether or not they are abiding by the mandate given them by the legislature, even though they have been provided only with the skeleton of a framework for decision making. They use their residual discretionary powers to handle particular problems and to put flesh on the bare bones of the scheme. They make innumerable decisions in respect of certain categories of cases that crop up on a recurring basis. Consistency is strived for, and certainty emerges. This provides reliable guidelines for participants and the public at large and, over time, makes boards look like neutral administrators of a set of acceptable rules. But, on closer scrutiny, the practices which they have developed do reveal some preferences and values that are seldom articulated.

The Designation of the Bargaining Unit

To start the bargaining game, a union must have been chosen to represent employees at a particular place of employment. To be certified, it must first sign up a majority of employees who belong to the bargaining unit to be represented by the union. It is for a labour relations board to determine what constitutes an appropriate bargaining unit for such collective bargaining. The way in which this discretionary power to designate is exercised has a significant impact on the union's bargaining leverage. Canada's labour relations boards have developed a routinized way of dealing with the difficult task of designating an appropriate bargaining unit.[1]

Standard Bargaining Units

Typically, a standard unit may be constituted by all the production workers in a plant, all of the office, clerical and technical workers in a firm, or all of the sales personnel. Frequently, clerical workers who work in the plant, such as inventory clerks in a warehouse, may be included in the production unit. Similarly, the sole maintenance worker in an office may be included in the office unit, or salespeople may be included in production or office units. In recent times, special technical workers' units have evolved. Where there is more than one plant, a decision has to be made as to the extent of the integration of the work performed at the various locales to determine whether the employees should be in one unit or in separate ones. Special, but very clear, guidelines have been developed to determine whether casual and part-time workers and students ought to be kept distinct or made part of the standard units. Craft workers who have developed historic monopolies have been permitted to form standard units.[2] All in all, the standard-unit approach to the designation of bargaining units gives the practices of boards a look of neutral facilitation.

Units have become standard ones because boards have determined that certain commonly found groupings share a "community of interest." The following kinds of factors are taken into account to determine whether or not a community of interest exists: the employees' hours of work and other major terms of employment, such as earnings and benefits; geographic proximity and frequency of contact between workers; continuity or integration of production; the level of common supervision and the relationship of any proposed unit to the administrative organization of the employer.[3] In addition, the board examines the wishes of the employees who belong to the bargaining unit. All but the last of these variables fall within managerial control.

The variety and generality of factors means that a good deal of flexibility is built into standard-unit determination, even though this is hidden from view because so many cases seem unproblematic. The boards make their determinations on a case-by-case basis and the criteria used to give the "community-of-interest" concept life permit them to tailor bargaining units. This is not to suggest that boards engage in pure ad hocery; to the contrary. The flexibility built into their practices has at least two identifiable goals in addition to the overriding one of promoting workable bargaining agencies. First, these state agencies want to maintain the employers' ability to manage as they see fit, and second, they seek to enhance the maintenance of stability in production — all within the context of giving workers more bargaining power. These assertions need to be supported.

In one case, a board, having said that its function was to support strong trade unionism, was frank enough to point out that "a [bargaining] structure is needed which is conducive to voluntary settlements without strikes and will minimize the disruptive effects of the latter when they do occur."[4] That is, trade unions should have the potential to conduct a meaningful, legal strike against particular employers, but not one which might have an unduly adverse effect on other economic actors. Boards are in a position to decide how that balance should be struck.

Similar considerations arise when boards determine the extent to which they will take the rights and beliefs of individual employees into account. After all, in a liberal democratic society, employees have a justifiable claim to have their special occupational, religious, political, cultural and occupational concerns honoured. But this sensitivity to individualism has had to be limited. As one board put it rather candidly, exaggerated respect for individual desires might "result in an unnecessary fragmentation or atomization of the employees. Thus, an employer faced with the possibility of lengthy, protracted, and expensive bargaining and the further possibility of judicial disputes among multiple bargaining groups represented by one or more trade unions may find it impossible to carry on a viable and meaningful collective bargaining relationship."[5]

In short, unions must not be too strong lest they cause too much havoc, nor too small lest their proliferation lead to instability in production and so harm the employer's bargaining position. The agencies are very conscious of these goals when they deal with what they deem to be essential public services. Thus, in the 1988 *Canada Post Corporation* decision (see Chapter 4), the Canada Labour Relations Board declared that jurisprudence was unequivocal on the point: boards were to guard against "the latent potential which (fragmentation of bargaining units) would have for competitive bargaining and sequential shutdown of the essential service."[6]

It is rare to find boards articulate their motives so explicitly when they deal with private sector certifications. Moreover, it would be wrong to assert on the basis of such statements that boards are solely concerned with the maintenance of employer bargaining power and industrial stability. After all, their *raison d'être* requires the promotion of effective trade unionism. Further, the liberal ideology which pervades the scheme demands that boards resolve conflicts between workers by paying homage to their particular needs whenever possible. The traffic, then, is not all one way. There may be larger units or more fragmentation than particular employers might want. But, in the end, boards tend to produce certification rulings that contain the consequences of disputes as much as possible and enhance stability for individual employers.[7]

Industry-Wide Agreements: Enhancing Stability

The fragmentation of bargaining which inheres in the scheme does not always suit the purposes of employers or those of policy-makers. When it does not, boards prove themselves flexible. Industry-wide bargaining schemes evolved in the automobile industry as a result of deals struck between the U.S. car manufacturers and the United Automobile Workers (UAW). This suited the oligopolistic automotive industry.[8] This development was not hindered by labour relations boards on either side of the border. Yet, while this large modification was allowed, the underlying legal model was not brought into serious question.

In the same vein, bargaining in the construction industry was restructured in the 1970s. Craft unions, through their monopoly over essential skills needed by the construction industries, were able to get a good agreement from the worst-placed employers.[9] This put them in a position to bargain more successfully with other employers who otherwise might have put up a more vigorous fight. These employers found it hard to obtain the labour they needed at prices their particular market power might have commanded because their rivals were in production while they were still bargaining. Overall, this put craft workers in construction in a good position to take advantage of building booms. This was particularly noticeable around 1974, when construction workers made huge monetary gains and were widely regarded as the fuel which fanned the fires of inflation which the federal government sought to put out with its Anti-Inflation Board (AIB) legislation in 1975.[10] The need to stabilize bargaining in the construction industry was not a new idea. The difficulty of unbalanced power relations (read: employer disadvantage) can be measured by the number of reports on industrial relations in the construction sectors.[11] Atomized, free collective bargaining was perceived as a recipe for chaos. The alternative was to create monopolies for employers to counteract the monopolies of craft unions even though this threatened to undermine the spirit of competition between investors. Nonetheless, this was precisely the route chosen in British Columbia, Ontario and Saskatchewan when these provinces legislated regional and province-wide bargaining.

These new construction industry schemes permit employers to form trade unions. An agreement by such an employer's union with a workers' union provides for regional employment conditions and pay structures covering the jurisdictional domain of that trade union. This has put an effective end to competition between employers on wages. It also has limited the ability of employees to pit one employer against another. For the trade unions, the increased stability and legitimation of their existing jurisdictional rights has made this a not unattractive compromise, as they do not have to fight as hard as before to retain control over their membership.[12]

In Ontario, these changes in bargaining structures lowered the rate of wage increases during a period of mild expansion. In Saskatchewan, where construction boom conditions existed during the same period, wage settlements did increase, despite the new bargaining structures. Rose and Wetzel, who studied the impact of the new province-wide bargaining structures on outcomes, concluded that the construction unions have lost some of their power wherever particularly favourable conditions have not intervened. In this regard, they point to the relative decrease in strike frequency in the two provinces.[13]

In a similar vein, Anne Forrest has shown that, while boards are willing to live with voluntarily created nation-wide or industry-wide bargaining units as long as this suits employers, they will respond favourably to employers' demands to change these bargaining structures. She studied the Canadian meat-packing industry. It had had a national bargaining scheme since 1947. This had suited both the union and the employers. The latter were content with the situation because they enjoyed an oligopolistic position. They could readily pass wage costs on to consumers. The certainty and stability so obtained was beneficial to them.

More recently, the restructuring of the American meat-packing industry and the generally much lower demand for meat have put the employers under fierce competitive pressure. They have felt the need to compete on wages. As part of this strategy — which has led to massive disruptions, exemplified by the infamous Gainers strike —

they have demanded a return to localized bargaining under provincial jurisdiction. The union, seeing the danger of fragmentation, insisted on what it thought was its long-established right of nation-wide bargaining. A labour relations board declared that it had never had such a right.[14] All that it had had was friendly permission to bargain nationally for as long as the employers continued to give their consent. The board, therefore, held that the employers were entitled, as a matter of law, to demand that bargaining take place on a province-by-province or local-by-local basis.[15]

There have been other departures from the fragmented standard-unit designations that have not been so obviously favourable to employers. Writing in 1985, the former chair of the Ontario Labour Relations Board, George Adams, identified an increasing preference for employer-wide (that is, multi-employer) bargaining units in several jurisdictions.[16] But, in fact, this phenomenon remains uncharacteristic of the Canadian collective bargaining scene. Up to 1986, only 8 percent of collective agreements in Canada were negotiated in multi-employer settings. Further, at least one commentator has suggested that, after enjoying an upsurge, multi-employer bargaining may be on the decline again.[17] The general picture, then, remains that of a huge number of workers engaged in discrete negotiations, legally and institutionally separated from one another.[18] This makes the manipulation engaged in by the legislatures and by the boards in the automobile, construction and meat-packing industries all the more remarkable.

Deciding Who Are Managerial Employees

Managers have been excluded from bargaining units by the governing statutes. This leaves many managerial people in an awkward situation. While they do have supervisory functions, they are also employees and, like all other employees, have a need for more bargaining power.

The principal rationale given for excluding managerial employees from standard bargaining units is the same as that offered for the exclusion of confidential employees, another statutorily exempted category of workers. Since collective bargaining is an adversarial process, the employer should not have its representatives placed in a situation where they might identify with the employer's opponent, the union. Another related rationale is offered by boards. There is a need to protect the employer's right to direct productive activities.

Boards, then, accept the employers' premise that hierarchical management is efficient management. Thus, justifying the need for the managerial exclusion, the Chair of the British Columbia Board, Weiler, wrote:

> For the more efficient operation of the enterprise, the employers establish a hierarchy in which some people at the top have the authority to direct the efforts of those nearer the bottom.... The British Columbia Legislature, following the path of all other labour legislation in North America, has decided that in the tug of these two competing forces, management must be assigned to the side of the employer.[19]

The labour relations boards have devised tests to reflect these related approaches when deciding whether or not an employee is a managerial employee. People become managers if they have "effective control or authority"; if they have the power to hire, fire or discipline; if they are policy-makers rather than policy-implementers.

The routine application of such criteria leads to surprising results. In an industrial setting, a foreman is usually excluded from the production unit; in a craft setting, a non-working foreman is considered to be managerial. These definitions of management by the boards are hard to square with the ones used by business analysts. It is inconceivable that a foreman would ever be found on a managerial chart produced by General Motors. Yet, labour relations boards accept that it is natural to exclude anyone with a modicum of decision-making power from the standard unit.[20] The fact that so many relatively low-level supervisors may be excluded from bargaining units leaves available a pool of workers who can be asked to do production work during a strike, thereby lessening the impact of the strike. Whether or not this has been a conscious goal of the boards, it has been a real disadvantage to unions.

It is true, however, that increasingly boards recognize the need for low-level managers to have collective bargaining rights because, often, they are clearly in no better position than many powerless employees are. Overall, there seems to be a growing tendency for supervisors who do not have the right to hire and fire, though they may have the power to recommend that discipline be imposed on other workers,[21] to be given bargaining rights. A contributing factor to this development is that the new technologies make many managers' tasks more like those of hourly workers than those of traditional managers. If nothing else, this movement underscores the willingness of the state agencies to adapt their practices to accommodate the employers' changed organizational needs resulting from the new production realities.

The Promotion of Trade Unionism versus the Protection of Employer Rights

Employers who want to oppose trade unionism can do so at two points: first, when workers seek to form a trade union — that is, during the organization period leading to the application for certification; second, after trade unions have been certified. From the inception of the collective bargaining scheme it was understood that there would be many employers who would exploit any opportunity which existed at either stage to avoid having to bargain with a union representing their workers. Labour relations boards have devised elaborate rules and practices to deal with these kinds of problems.

Employer Interference with Trade Union Formation — Unfair Labour Practices

Workers who want to unionize have every reason to fear reprisals when their employer is known to be opposed to unionism. In this kind of setting it is quite possible that an employer will use its disciplining power to move activists around or even to dismiss them. To discourage employers from interfering with union formation in this manner, individuals and unions have been given the right to complain to the labour relations board.

The labour relations boards have devised tests to find whether the employer's motive for disciplining or discharging an employee was tainted by anti-union motivation. Individuals and unions are aided by the fact that boards impose on the employer the duty of showing that the discipline or discharge was not motivated by anti-union animus. This reversal of the normal burden of proof makes it clear that boards treat trade unionism as something of a public good. This is reinforced by the sanctions they have devised to deal with offenders. Once a board finds that an unfair labour practice has been committed, it may fully reinstate a fired worker; it also may force the employer to apologize and/or to notify all the workers in the bargaining unit that it has committed an unfair labour practice and that it will not impede unionization again.

These remedies ought to act as powerful deterrents to employers who are bent on stopping unionization of their workplace. Often they do; but often they do not. In any one case there is no certainty that a labour relations board will find that an employer has acted out of anti-union motivation. The nub of the problem is that employers make disciplinary decisions all the time in the day-to-day running of their enterprise. In this context, they are armed with readily available arguments to persuade boards that the imposition of discipline during an organizational drive was not an anti-union tactic. Experience has taught workers and unions that there is a high degree of uncertainty as to whether or not boards will protect them from harassment. On the other side of the fence, an employer may well calculate that its discipline of an employee will not be adjudged to be a violation by a board. The uncertainty of board judgements encourages employers to take risks and to act in an anti-union way. Meanwhile, unions know that the promotion of trade unionism is not the sole goal of labour relations boards: they also support the rights of individuals, whether they be employees or employers. Even though an employer cannot use its power to intimidate, coerce or harass workers in order to deny their statutory right to belong to a union, the employer must be left free to exercise its rights as a citizen.

As we have seen, these rights include the right to use its private property as it sees fit. One major consequence of this is that no employer is under an obligation to let workers organize during working hours or to permit trade union officials onto its property to organize. This has significant consequences.

Unions and their organizers who obtain the employer's permission to come onto its premises to organize cannot use such permission for different purposes. In particular, they cannot come in to talk politics with the workers, as officials of the Steelworkers found out when they sought support for the NDP during a by-election. They wanted to canvass their members on the job during non-working time — that is, to lobby them where they are most easily contacted and approachable. The employer kicked the canvassers out. When the union complained that the employer had committed an unfair labour practice by not letting it exercise its right to talk with its members, the board found for the employer.[22] By contrast, employers cannot be stopped from talking politics to their workers at their place of work during working hours. During the free trade election of 1988, employers often told their workers — at the workplace — that, while they would not instruct them how to vote, a vote against the free trade agreement might very well lead to the loss of their jobs. No legal rule forbade this kind of politicking. This is a neat illustration of how the collective bargaining régime, and the labour relations boards which administer it, maintain the separation between the political and the economic spheres. This dovetails nicely with the precepts of liberalism which, when dominant, make class politics so difficult. More mundanely, but no less importantly, the willingness of the boards to defend the property rights of employers has a profound impact on workers' abilities to carry on successful organizational drives.

An employer's permission is needed to contact the employees at work. Canvassing and/or posting of notices cannot be done without employer approval. In a situation where the employees suspect that their employer will object to unionization, they will not seek this approval until they have a solid core of support for unionization. This means that they have to contact unionists who are willing to organize them and meet with them outside working hours. Meetings have to be arranged, rooms hired. This imposes organizational and financial costs. As well, the necessity of secrecy is likely to heighten the workers' anxiety; an atmosphere of fear may be created. It may dissuade many people from forming a union if they perceive unionization as neither normal nor respectable.

Another element of the respect accorded to employers as individuals is their right to free speech. They are free to tell their workers that it would be a fatal mistake for them to join a union. The employers, of course, cannot simply say anything they choose. Liberal democracy always puts limits on free speech. Lines are drawn by the labour relations boards. It will always be difficult to know when the bright line to be drawn by a labour relations agency will have been crossed.

In one case a union complained about a workplace newsletter containing a report of a speech made by the employer elsewhere. The employer had discussed an organizational structure which would exclude the possibility of a union presence. The union argued that letting workers know that their manager was thinking along these lines had had an adverse impact on its organizational efforts. Its claim was dismissed. The board held that the mere expression of an employer's views did not constitute unacceptable interference with union organization.[23] In another case, it looked as if the union had the requisite number of employees signed up to warrant certification. During a lunch break, a petition opposing certification was circulated. Enough people signed it to throw the issue of membership in doubt, but the union persisted in its application for certification. It asked the labour relations board to ignore the dissidents' petition and to certify the union without holding a vote. In support of its claim, the union argued that the employer had interfered unduly with its organizational efforts: a plant manager had made a speech urging the employees to give careful consideration to the meaning of the certification of a union and indicating his personal disappointment that so many workers had found it advisable to join a union. In this context, the union claimed, the dissidents' petition did not reflect the true wishes of the employees. The board held that the plant manager's address was neither intimidating nor coercive, but was a fair expression of his opinion. The signatories to the petition, therefore, were held to have expressed their genuine feelings when they said that they were no longer willing to stand by their signing of membership pledges. The union thus did not have the requisite number of members to warrant certification and was forced to go through a representation vote.[24]

In yet another "free speech" case, an employer was found to have overstepped the bounds of propriety when the chief manager called all the employees involved in an organizational drive into the main cafeteria. He told them that they did not have to attend and that they could leave the room before he addressed them on the undesirability of trade unionism. He offered to turn his back while they left. But none of the employees left, because standing next to the chief manager on the podium were other managers keeping an eye on the audience. This was held to have constituted an illegal exercise of speech rights by the employer.[25]

In sum, the boards have been very conscious of the need to fashion remedies to deal with anti-union employers. They have done so with care and with the purpose of enhancing trade union formation based on the exercise of free choice by workers. However, it remains possible — indeed, relatively easy — for stiff-necked employers to exploit the rights that they have been accorded as individuals and property owners to resist organizational efforts.

Protecting Certified Trade Unions

Several mechanisms help unions survive once they have been certified. First, a trade union is free from challenge to its status by another union or by anti-union workers until there is an open period — that is, a period when no negotiations are taking place and no collective agreement is in existence. Second, once a trade union is certified and it enters into collective bargaining, it is legislatively entitled to some security of tenure or it may bargain for provisions giving such a guarantee. At the very least, these may provide unions with an automatic dues check-off. They then are guaranteed a flow of funds without having to contact the workers to collect any outstanding dues. This makes belonging to a trade union, and/or paying dues to it, a matter of routine. A security provision may go further, however, and include a requirement that every member of the bargaining unit be, and remain, a member of that union. This, of course, is much desired by trade unions. Many bargain successfully for such closed shops. The legalization of this practice is a vast advance for unions over what they were, and are, entitled to at common law. Third, the legislation provides that, when a trade union which has been given bargaining rights *vis-à-vis* one employer has this status imperilled because that employer has merged with, or has been bought by, another entrepreneur, it shall have a right to claim successor rights. If it can show that the enterprise has not really changed its character, a board may confirm its continued status as the bargaining agent. These are not easy requirements to meet. In these times of mergers and takeovers, these issues frequently are contested. Highly technical battles are fought before the boards, and unions often lose their rights. Nonetheless, the existence of this statutory provision is further evidence of the legislative intent to protect trade union rights.[26]

In this section, however, we do not discuss these important security-enhancing provisions. Rather, we concentrate on the practices developed by labour relations boards to protect unions from bargaining tactics used by hard-nosed employers who want to rid themselves of an existing trade union.

Good-faith bargaining

A central aspect of modern collective bargaining law is that an employer is compelled to bargain in good faith with the union which has been certified as the bargaining agent. Significantly, this does not mean that there is an obligation to conclude an agreement with that trade union; rather, the requirement is that the parties make reasonable efforts to reach an agreement. The potential tension is clear. If the employer is not required to enter into a collective agreement, at what point can its failure to do so be called an act of *bad* faith?

Over time, labour relations boards have spelled out their understanding of what bargaining in good faith encompasses. Two major strands are discernible in the jurisprudence.[27] The first is that the duty to bargain in good faith should be interpreted so as to teach the employer and the trade union the value of collective bargaining. It is thought that this will lead to the development of a harmonious relationship even if, from time to time, the parties resort to economic warfare. In the frequently cited words of one of the gurus of labour relations law, the hope and belief is that the parties will develop "lilliputian bonds," bonds of mutual interdependence.[28] The second, and related, strand is that the bargaining process should accept and promote the legitimation of a trade union which has been certified. The pursuit of these policy aims presents boards with many difficulties.

Because an employer does not have to conclude an agreement with a trade union, labour relations boards must accept that employers might engage in hard bargaining, provided that they are truly bargaining. So-called surface bargaining is bad-faith bargaining. If an employer takes a position at the beginning of the bargaining process and never shows any movement at all, it is likely to be held to have bargained in bad faith.[29] The same will be true if a board finds that the employer's offer was one that no self-respecting union could accept, such as increasing the employer's right to exercise disciplinary powers beyond what it had when there was no union.[30] Similarly, if the employer's tactics, whatever they be, can be characterized as having as their goal the alienation of employees from their certified trade union, a board might find the employer to have acted in bad faith.[31]

Manifestly, in making these judgement calls, boards exercise discretionary powers. It is not to be doubted that the boards, given their function, are pro–collective bargaining and, therefore, favour the spread of unionism. This is why they have developed sanctions to deal with employers whose bargaining tactics thwart these goals. But it is questionable just how effective the boards' remedies are. While boards have been willing to fashion imaginative remedies in cases in which a breach of good faith has occurred, the overall results are disappointing. This disjunction between stated aspiration and actual achievement reflects a phenomenon that is typical of liberal democracies. An administrative agency, established to pursue empowering objectives, is inhibited from enforcing its own policy norms as well as it might by the political and economic context of the day. The difficulty that labour boards have experienced in deterring rogue employers from busting certified trade unions is a striking illustration of this phenomenon.

Rogue employers in a changing economic environment
It was not until the 1970s that boards were given powers to fashion remedies to enforce the good-faith bargaining requirement. Once they got them, they took the bit between their teeth. They were actively reformist until the early 1980s. During that relatively progressive period, boards leaned heavily on rogue employers who, by their negotiation practices, indicated that they were unwilling to accept the public policy commitment to collective bargaining. Frequently, such employers took a tough negotiating stance after they already had committed unfair labour practices during an organization drive. Boards tried to stamp this out. A dramatic instance is provided by the decision in a case which arose in Barrie, Ontario, in 1979.

The Radio Shack case:
In the *Radio Shack* case,[32] a subsidiary of a large American multinational employer had unlawfully interfered with the employees' initial organization drive. It intimidated and dismissed people; the Steelworkers, the union leading the organizational drive, was, in due course, certified, even though it did not have the requisite number of membership signatures. The bad faith bargaining complaint which the union eventually brought cried out for strong action by a board.

During the organizational drive the employer had not only dismissed pro-union employees, but had given indications that, should there be a union, the company might move to the West. The employer had made available T-shirts with the logo "We're company finks and proud of it" to its anti-union employees during the organization drive. It refused to follow an order of the Ontario Labour Relations Board to reinstate dismissed employees. When bargaining began, it did not provide the union with necessary information it requested, such as job classifications, seniority lists, wage rates and details of fringe-benefits plans. It claimed to be protecting the privacy of its employees, and wrote to each employee that the demand for a union shop was anti–civil libertarian. At the bargaining table, the employer made proposals intended to foil standard union activities. For instance, it asked that penalties imposed by the employer for disciplinary reasons were not to be subjected to arbitral review. Rarely will employers show their arrogance and anti-unionism so overtly.

All of this made it very easy for the Board to take a firm stand in fashioning remedies. The Ontario Labour Relations Board already had used its power to certify the union, although a majority of employees were not shown to have applied for union membership. It had done so because the atmosphere had been irreversibly chilled by the employer's anti-union tactics. Now the Board also found that the employer's subsequent negotiation tactics amounted to bad-faith bargaining. By way of remedy, the Board forced the employer to pay the extra costs incurred by the union as a result of the employer's tactics, which had made negotiations a farce. The employer also was ordered to pay damages equivalent to the employees' losses resulting from their inability to conclude an agreement because of its unlawful tactics. The parties were ordered to continue to bargain in good faith and, eventually, an agreement was concluded.

The decision was much heralded. Forcing employers to recognize the legitimacy of certified trade unions in these path-breaking ways was seen as an indication of the Board's earnestness in promoting collective bargaining. It is dubious, however, whether the Board's much-applauded remedies served to educate bloody-minded employers.

The usual dilatoriness of board proceedings took its toll. By the time the Board had fashioned its pro-union remedies, the bargaining unit at Radio Shack had shrunk to half its size. This left the workers in a weakened position *vis-à-vis* their employer. In 1985, the same unit of workers, bargaining for its second collective agreement, was unable to settle with the employer. Workers had to go through a bitter six-month strike. In Ontario, the law provided that workers on legal strike retain their right to be reinstated should they want to return to work within the first six months of the strike. After that point they lost this right and, perhaps, the right to their job.

At the end of six months, therefore, the Steelworkers local at Radio Shack was forced to accept the employer's last offer, which it had already rejected. Now, however, Radio Shack took an unprecedented step and removed this offer from the table. In its stead it proposed conditions which were even less generous. By any standard, this should have been seen as an attempt to break the union. The union certainly saw it this way and complained to the Ontario Labour Relations Board of bad-faith bargaining.

On this occasion, the Labour Relations Board, which had been so imaginative in fashioning pro-union remedies for the same two parties in 1980, denied the local's claim.[33] This time the employer had been cleverer. It had bargained hard, but its conduct had not been gross enough to characterize it as mere "surface bargaining." Despite the notoriety of the employer's behaviour and the ensuing bitter strike, the Board rejected the plausible conclusion that Radio Shack was trying to smash a legitimate trade union by its extraordinary bargaining tactic of removing a firm offer from the table. The Board made a contentious legal finding when it held that this was merely a case of tough bargaining. Whatever the merits of the legal posture, what is clear is that it was retreating from its pro-union stance in the first *Radio Shack* decision.[34] Of course, this was not acknowledged by the Board. We are left to speculate as to why this new approach was taken.

In part, it may be that the Board instinctively felt that its neutrality would be impaired if it did not show that, while it remained in favour of unionism, it understood the need to buttress managerial prerogatives from too much erosion. In part, the Board may have been influenced by the perceptibly changing economic and political climate. By the mid-1980s, employers were demanding greater managerial and market freedoms, demands which clearly resonated with politicians. It would be disingenuous to pretend that board members were unaware of or unaffected by these changing attitudes. This was probably the key to the 1985 decision. Other noteworthy decisions in "good-faith" bargaining cases illustrate this search for a new balance.

The Eaton's case:
Canada's giant retailer, Eaton's, always has been a vehemently anti-union employer. In 1985, the Retail, Wholesale and Department Stores Union (RWDSU) succeeded in organizing a small number of Eaton's southern Ontario branches. When negotiations began, the employer refused to accept proposals to match even the most minimal of seniority provisions found in modern collective agreements. Indeed, it continued to argue for the retention of its right to promote, demote and lay off in the same way as it had always done. It refused

to accept that outcomes of more than thirty-five years of grievance arbitration in major industries should become part of the daily work relationships at Eaton's. No self-respecting trade union could accept these proposals. The union complained to the administrative agency that Eaton's anti-union behaviour was an indication of unwillingness to enter into a collective agreement. It also argued that Eaton's insistence that it be allowed to bargain separately with each of fourteen different bargaining units was further explicit evidence of bad faith.

The Ontario Labour Relations Board upheld Eaton's bargaining stance *in toto*. By its holding, it showed that it accepted the reasonableness of Eaton's organizational structure and of its employee deployment as decisive criteria. Yet, to use this fragmented structure as a proper basis for *bargaining* denied the reality of the situation. After all, the workers in each of the fourteen separate units were represented by the same trade union officials at the bargaining table. Further, the union sought to have the terms of any collective agreement it might obtain apply to all of them in the same way. The decision by the Board to accept the employer's fragmented bargaining strategy caused innumerable delays which, eventually, led to the union's total defeat.

In this case, the Board took a legal, minimalist approach. Each of the hard-nosed employer's proposals, and its insistence on treating each unit as a separate entity, could be characterized as tough, but lawfully justified, bargaining. It was a surprising result nonetheless. According to their established practices, boards assess an employer's motives by looking at the context in which the alleged bad-faith bargaining acts occurred. This was done in the first *Radio Shack* decision (of which the supporters of labour relations agencies as neutral facilitators are very proud). From this perspective, Eaton's neanderthal stand on seniority provisions, and its arrogant claim to the right to preserve its pre-union managerial rights, should have revealed the real purpose underlying its extraordinary insistence on splintered bargaining. It should have been seen for what it was: a clear attempt at breaking the union. There was further supporting evidence for this, as Eaton's had used every trick in the book to stop unionization in the first place. Only the Board's unusual decision to de-contextualize each of the events permitted it to make the decision that Eaton's had bargained in good faith.

As a result, the RWDSU had no alternative but to call a strike. After six months, with no end in sight, the union feared that its members would lose their jobs. The workers were forced to go back to work on terms totally unacceptable to them. Given the failure of the strike, Eaton's was able to manipulate disaffected workers into applying for decertification. This application was successful.

The Westroc case:

Westroc, an Ontario employer, had locked out its employees.[35] A lock-out is defined as a temporary interruption of production to persuade workers to accept the conditions that the employer wants to impose. It is the equivalent of a strike. Both are tactics to break an impasse to reach a collective agreement. They are not to be used, of course, to end collective bargaining relationships. Thus, all of Canada's labour relations boards have held that the duty to bargain in good faith persists during a strike or lock-out. An employer cannot use a lock-out to smash a union. This principle was undermined by the *Westroc* decision.

When Westroc locked out its employees, it hired scab labour. Its productivity was not interrupted at all. The union argued that this was not a normal lock-out, one aimed at persuading workers to come back on terms favourable to the employer. Rather, it was an attempt to break the union, a goal which would make an otherwise legal lock-out illegal. The union asked the Ontario Labour Relations Board to make a ruling to that effect. The Board refused. It held that an employer was entitled to hire scab labour during a lock-out. This decision raised questions about that Board's commitment to the promotion of good-faith bargaining — one of whose purposes is to protect the status of certified unions.[36]

The Paccar case:

Similar doubts were raised by a 1989 Supreme Court of Canada decision upholding a ruling of the British Columbia Industrial Relations Council.[37] The question was whether an employer was acting in bad faith when, after reaching an impasse in the negotiations with the union, it gave notice of termination of the old collective agreement and entered into a series of separate contracts with individual members of the bargaining unit. Normally, employers cannot enter into private contracts with individuals, as this undermines the position of the trade union as a bargaining agent and erodes the very protection sought in the requirement to bargain in good faith. In most jurisdictions, therefore, there is a statutory provision which freezes the conditions of any collective agreement while negotiations are going on between the employer and the union. No changes in individuals' working conditions can be imposed unilaterally by the employer.

But in British Columbia there is no such provision. In the *Paccar* case the employer saw the loophole and drove its cart through it. After negotiating for a while, it gave notice that it wished to terminate the collective agreement as that agreement permitted. It then proposed to change the terms and conditions of work for individual employees. The union complained that this undermined its position and amounted to bad-faith bargaining. The labour relations agency dismissed this complaint. On appeal, the Supreme Court of Canada upheld the ruling that this was not bad-faith bargaining by the employer because it was still possible for the employer and the union to continue to bargain. As with the *Eaton's* decision, this was a legally plausible holding, but a totally unrealistic one. As a result of this decision, unions in British Columbia have a new burden. They must bargain for language which will not give an employer a way out of its obligation to respect a union's rights. In British Columbia, therefore, the good-faith bargaining protection embedded in the legislation has been diluted by acceptance of the Board's restrictive reading of the law. Decisions similar to *Paccar* have been handed down in Saskatchewan and Alberta.[38]

The other side of the coin: some wins for unions
The decisions do not all run one way, of course. The boards still do protect trade unions from much outrageous employer behaviour. If it were not so, the collective bargaining scheme would fall into disrepute and the administrative agencies would lose their prized reputation as neutral facilitators.

In a number of cases employers have entered into negotiations to produce a collective agreement without telling the union that they were intending to close or partially close their enterprise. This made the negotiations a sham and the unions, having reached an agreement and subsequently having lost part (or all) of the bargaining unit, complained to the Board of unfair labour practices. Two such cases were *Westinghouse*[39] and *Consolidated Bathurst*.[40] In both of them, the Ontario administrative agency found anti-union bias and devised imaginative remedies to promote collective bargaining and to protect trade unionism.

In *Westinghouse*, the employer was required to give the union access to its employees at its new location to afford the union an opportunity to organize them. The laid-off employees from the old plant were given the right of first refusal of jobs at the new locations. The terms and conditions of employment were to be the same as the ones which they had enjoyed at the old plant. The employer was to pay any relocation costs incurred by an employee who took up the offer. It also was required to put up notices admitting its wrongdoing. In *Consolidated Bathurst*, the Board required the employer to pay damages to the employees who lost their employment as a result of the employer's decision. These damages were substantial.

Another decision which was well received by unions was made by the federal labour relations board in the *Eastern Provincial Airways* case. The pilots had gone on strike. The employer had hired replacement pilots, as it was permitted to do. In due course, the pilots' union had to admit that it had lost and that the workers wanted to go back to work. They relied on the Canada Labour Code provision which provides that no employer shall refuse to employ or to continue to employ any person because that person has participated in a legal strike. But Eastern Provincial Airways refused to dismiss its replacement employees. The union complained that this was evidence of the failure to bargain in good faith, as well as of the commission of unfair labour practices. The Board upheld the complaint. It ruled that the employer's refusal to rehire its former employees was prolonging the strike and preventing an agreement to be reached. The duty to bargain in good faith did not end because there had been a strike: the employer had to respect the union. The Board ordered that the parties should resume negotiations and that the pilots be allowed to return to work in order of their seniority.[41]

A similar positive ruling was made in the *Shaw-Almex* case, but the labour relations agency took its time getting there. The Board's assistance was sought repeatedly by the union during tough negotiations. In the early part of the process, however, the Board's findings favoured the employer. A long strike commenced. Eventually, the union said that its members were ready to go back to work on the basis of the last terms which had been offered by the employer some time before. But the employer did not want to sack the replacement employees it had hired, and agreed only to recall the striking workers as scabs left its employ. When the union insisted that, having accepted a legitimate offer, its members were entitled to a full recall, Shaw-Almex took the offer off the table. The Board now intervened. It awarded hefty damages to the striking workers. This was hailed as a victory for the union.[42]

A great number of well-established firms have accepted collective bargaining. Usually, they bargain in good faith. But a great many firms, mostly small, but also including some very large and prestigious ones, such as Radio Shack, K-Mart, Eaton's, Dylex, Canada Trust Co., the Canadian Imperial Bank of Commerce and the Bank of Montreal, do not. Faced by those kind of employers, union rights are not all that well protected. First, the legal costs incurred in organization and in enforcing union rights are crippling. Second, the delays in the enforcement processes may make victories Pyrrhic ones. Third, the imaginative and attractive-sounding remedies devised by the boards may be blunted in time by differently constituted boards. This is typical of all legal decision making: rules and principles are malleable and manipulable. Some further elaboration is in order.

The *Shaw-Almex* saga took an amazing amount of time to play itself out. Negotiations began in January 1983, and the final order of the Board recalling strikers back to work was not made until March 1988. Long delays are characteristic in this kind of toughly fought case, and in adjudicative, legal processes in general. This makes it very hard to turn nice-sounding pronouncements of rights into concrete benefits. We saw this in *Radio Shack*. The exciting, newly crafted remedies did not help the workers in the Barrie plant very much in the end.[43] Indeed, complaints about discriminatory discharges and similar unfair labour practices are taking longer and longer. In 1983, it took the Ontario Board 137 days to deal with such a matter; the delay grew every year thereafter to reach 187 days by 1987.[44] To be sure, the readiness that boards show in these kinds of cases to go to new lengths to protect workers does help to set a new tone and, perhaps, to deter redneck behaviour. But even this possibility is not as promising as it would appear to be; different boards take different approaches.

Our story shows that there are forward steps and backward steps. In large part, this is because words are plastic, and the system thrives on technicality. As soon as one loophole is closed, the very phrase-

Chronology of *Shaw-Almex* Case

January	1983:	expiry of collective agreement
April	1983:	legal strike begins
October	1983:	OLRB complaint filed by union
January	1984:	preliminary evidentiary ruling (1984) O.L.R.B.R. 109
April	1984:	preliminary evidentiary ruling (1984) O.L.R.B.R. 659
October	1984:	ruling on merits, no remedy (1984) O.L.R.B.R. 1502
December	1984:	employer withdraws offer after union rejection of recall clause
January	1985:	OLRB complaint filed by union
May	1985:	hearings again
February	1986:	hearings end
December	1986:	ruling on merits, remedy (1986) O.L.R.B.R. 1800
February	1987:	order amended (1987) O.L.R.B.R. 276
June	1987:	preliminary ruling *re* damage assessment (1987) O.L.R.B.R. 1032
January	1988:	Divisional Court ruling on judicial review (1988) 88 C.L.L.C. 14,007
March	1988:	OLRB orders preliminary recall of strikers as various hearings continue

Source: *The Globe and Mail*, March 8, 1988.

ology used to close it can be exploited to open another. For instance, there is the progressive position taken by some boards in disciplining employers who had made a final decision to close a plant before or during negotiations, and did not tell the union about this decision. Agile employers now realize that all they have to do to escape this obligation is to hide the fact that, when negotiations begin, they are thinking of shrinking the size of the bargaining unit. In Ontario, the labour relations agency has made it a little easier for this kind of "smart" employer to contract out work or to relocate without being found to be acting in bad faith.[45] This puts a premium on cleverness rather than honesty. Similarly, the tactics used in the *Eaton's* case were, in the eyes of any lay observer, blatantly anti-union. Yet, a quintessentially legal form of reasoning — namely, that a plausible argument is a good argument — enabled Eaton's to attack the union while staying within the outer limits of the law.

This litany of difficulties must be kept in perspective. Boards have been successful in establishing a significant substratum of collective bargaining. There is a core of industrial relations activities in which collective bargaining is the norm. It thrives in major economic sectors such as the automobile, electrical equipment, construction and mining industries. The legitimacy of certified trade unions in these areas is not put into jeopardy every time they have to enter into negotiations with their employers. But there is another sphere of industrial relations where things are not so good. Thus, in Ontario, between 1971 and 1981, one in seven newly certified unions was unable to negotiate a collective agreement. This low success rate was only in part due to outrageous and/or illegal behaviour by employers. The more important fact was that employers could fight successfully within the rules. In her study, Anne Forrest found that half the units that did not manage to get even a first agreement were not hampered by counter-petitions and had not laid any charges of unfair labour practices. She saw the built-in weaknesses of small, disparate bargaining units as a problem which was not being overcome by the policies devised by boards to promote trade unionism.[46] Some of the legislatures have stepped in to overcome this problem.

First-Term Contract Arbitration

At the federal level, and in Newfoundland, Quebec, Ontario, Manitoba and British Columbia, governments have passed first-term contract arbitration legislation. This means that, in some circumstances, an agreement will be imposed on the parties.[47] This legislation is diametrically opposed to the precepts of a voluntaristic (that is, a "free") collective bargaining régime. The idea of the legislation is that, if a labour relations board or the minister of labour becomes convinced that because of the intransigence of the parties (read: employer) no collective agreement will be concluded, an arbitration board can impose a first-term contract. The hope is that, once such an agreement exists, the parties will learn to live with each other and develop an ongoing collective bargaining relationship. The hope remains a hope.

When first-term contract legislation was introduced in British Columbia in 1973, a board was to be established only if it was shown that something akin to a failure to bargain in good faith had led to the failure to conclude a first collective agreement. In Quebec, by contrast, there was a willingness to impose a first-term agreement even when the tough requirement of establishing bad-faith bargaining could not be met. It is interesting to note that two other jurisdictions which have passed similar legislation, Manitoba and Ontario, also have not insisted on this requirement which, as we have seen, has given rise to a jurisprudence which is something of a nightmare. Instead, in Manitoba, the legislation — the result of an NDP initiative — allows the Board to impose a first agreement after negotiations have failed to result in agreement after a specified amount of time has elapsed. In Ontario, the requirement is that the labour relations board has to be satisfied that the parties are unlikely to conclude a collective agreement. Nonetheless, it is still doubtful whether this increasing willingness to impose first agreements can overcome the problems caused by fragmented unionization outside the established core of collective bargaining.

When the first-term agreement scheme was introduced in British Columbia, hopes were high that it would succeed. But it has not proved very effective there. The British Columbia Labour Relations Board gathered data for the first three years that the legislation was in effect. It found that twenty-two unions had applied for first-term arbitration during that period. The Board agreed to accept the request to legislate an agreement in eleven of those cases. That is, only 50 percent of those unions (which all were local branches of powerful unions), were held to be entitled to the imposition of an agreement. Of the eleven locals who were assisted in this way, only one succeeded in obtaining a second collective agreement.[48] These poor results should not have been unexpected. If the employer was so anti-union in the first place and the union was so weak, there should have been no reason to believe that the employer would change its attitude the second time around or that the union would have become much more powerful by then.

In light of this, one can better understand the Quebec, Manitoba and Ontario provisions which make the imposition of first-term agreement arbitration more readily available and, in addition, why the statutes of Quebec and Ontario provide that the imposed agreement shall last for up to two years, rather than one, as is the case in British Columbia. In Ontario, the most recent jurisdiction to enact such legislation, the Board has been aggressive in imposing first agreements in order to extend the ambit of collective bargaining.[49] Overall, the record of this kind of legislation has not been good. In Manitoba, the results are better than those in British Columbia, but still far from spectacular. Four out of seven unions which obtained first-term agreements entered into a second collective agreement, but one of them was subsequently decertified.[50]

The advantages given to trade unions by strategies such as first-term contract arbitration and remedies for unfair labour practices or violations of the good-faith bargaining requirement do not go to the heart of the matter. The collective bargaining scheme is best suited to promote organization in large manufacturing and resource-based settings. It was Canada's main Fordist stratagem and, within its terms, it worked. Unionization shot up remarkably as soon as the scheme was implemented. It got another large boost when public sector workers were permitted to organize. But, apart from those two growth periods, the incidence of Canadian unionization has remained relatively static (see Chapter 3). The difficulty always has been to organize the non-primary sectors with their many small firms. By and large, the system has provided a disincentive for unions to go out and organize small workplaces. In contemporary Canada, this presents trade unions with an intractable difficulty.

The fact is that very few new firms that employ large numbers of people are being set up. Most of the large-scale enterprises that can be unionized have been. Many of them are reducing their work-force. The growth in employment is taking place in small firms. The average size of all firms in Canada, excluding governments and their agencies, is nine people; in Ontario, it is only thirteen.[51] More than 90 percent of Ontario's firms employ fewer than twenty people, the average number of employees being 4.4.[52] The difficulties and costs of organizing an ever-increasing number of firms of this kind are obvious. They will not be addressed by artifices such as first-term contract arbitration or citations of anti-union employers for unfair labour practices. What is needed is multi-unit bargaining for small-employment settings. Only if they are grouped together and their workers can combine collectively can the disproportionate power of redneck employers be offset. A labour-favouring government would do well to think about such a scheme. Undoubtedly, a union move-ment that is losing members in the smokestack industries will push for it. Such a strategy would replenish its membership by making it worthwhile for unions to organize small businesses.

Legalism and Labour Relations

The labour relations boards have promoted and created a culture of legalism. This is costly for the unions involved. It enables business, with readily available legal advice, to organize their affairs so as to take advantage of technical arguments and thereby hold the unions in check.

Part and parcel of this emphasis on legalism is that difficult matters can be, and are, dragged out, holding up simpler ones. One of the stated and much-vaunted goals of these facilitating boards — namely, the quick, cheap, expert resolution of problems to promote collectivism and self-determination — is undermined by the obstructive, technical nature of the proceedings.

Moreover, the culture of legalism gives the labour relations boards an air of bureaucratic indifference. This is misleading; these agencies do have an agenda. They always have been mindful of the need to preserve stability in production and to constrain the capacity of trade unions to challenge the political and economic entente underpinning export-led growth and its attendant competitive model. As part of this, they have favoured certain kinds of unionism. At various times, American and business unions were preferred to would-be socialist and nationalist unions. Radical unions remain undesirable. The exercise of the boards' discretionary powers to achieve these kinds of results is rationalized and justified by reference to a very specific conceptual framework: the maintenance of a liberal balance between collectivism and individualism. This has stood employers in good stead. The balancing, requiring as it does the determination of when majoritarian views can override individual ones and when organizational rights must be subjugated to property rights and freedom of speech, inhibits worker militancy. It has persuaded trade unions, who derive their legitimacy from the scheme, that the bureaucratization of their structures and a reliance on expertise, mostly that of lawyers, are necessary to the conduct of efficient organizing drives and successful collective bargaining struggles. This partial depoliticization of trade unions has left the state freer from working-class pressures than it otherwise might have been.

This relative neutering of unions is particularly evident in the way in which they have come to see, and by the extent to which they are allowed to use, the workers' right to withhold their labour in concert. It is to the ambit and scope of the right to strike that we now turn.

The Right to Strike: A Velvet Fist in an Iron Glove

The Strike as Menace

Any strike conjures up a series of threatening images. At one end of this spectrum of images is the picture created by a strike of a group of workers trying to change their own conditions of employment. Even this limited kind of strike is frequently perceived as an act of rebellion by ungrateful, short-sighted people. At the other end of the spectrum is the image conveyed by the possibility of a concerted withdrawal of labour by every worker in the country, with a view to changing the very polity. That this possibility leads to real alarm is not surprising. This perception is given added bite by the fact that Canada is strike prone. The incidence of strikes here is exceeded only by that in France, Italy and Britain. The Macdonald Commission noted that in the period 1966 to 1983, Canada's strikes tended to be longer and more frequent than those in comparable industrialized countries.[1] More immediately important to anxious Canadian observers may be the fact that the strike weapon is used far more often in Canada than it is in the United States. Riddell has shown that in the period 1966–76, strike incidence was from one-half to one-third lower there than it was in Canada.[2] While there has been a diminution in strike activity over the last few years, the basic fact remains that, by any standard, Canada has a high rate of strikes. Even in the eighties, Canadian workers often struck more than their counterparts in the rest of the industrialized world.

Inevitably, this has led to high-pitched demands that workers be made to give up the strike weapon.[3] This clamour for constraint is justified by a series of loosely related arguments. Unions are said to be too powerful and strikes too costly,[4] and they create wage rigidities. Harm is caused to innocent bystanders, it is said, by the thoughtless acts of a few reckless and powerful unions. Strikes are claimed to make Canada's economic and industrial relations system unstable, thereby undermining Canada's competitive position. In addition, the argument is made that the scope of the right to strike and its frequent use make unions too politically powerful, for they are able to hold governments to ransom. For many, then, the strike is a focus of much concern and attention.

The fact is that bargaining Canadian-style cannot take place without according workers the power to strike. Bargaining without it would merely amount to a talking shop. The strike has had to be tolerated and legally sanctioned. Its scope, however, always has been a very limited one. Canada's collective bargaining schemes endorse only the most narrow economic strikes, but not strikes which might have wider political and economic impact. That is, the legal right to strike positions collective worker-power firmly at the safer end of the spectrum. The thrust of the statutory régimes has been to bureaucratize the strike and to sanitize the union movement.

But anxiety remains, because workers and their unions do fight back. It is estimated that in any given year, well over 20 percent of workers involved in strikes in Canada are on unauthorized (and thus illegal) work stoppages.

Table 6.1
Workers Involved in Strikes and Lockouts (%)

	1960–70	1970–80	1980–85
First agreement or recognition	4.5	1.7	2.1
Renegotiation	72.5	68.7	72.0
During term	21.2	29.3	25.4
Other[1]	1.9	0.3	0.4
All Contracts	100.0	100.0	100.0

1. "Other" includes instances where there was no collective agreement in effect prior to the work stoppage and conclusion of a formal agreement was not a basic issue.

Source: Labour Canada, *Strikes and Lockouts in Canada*, and unpublished data adapted from *The Current Industrial Relations Scene in Canada 1989*, *op. cit.*, Collective Bargaining Reference Tables, p. 115.

More importantly, on occasion workers have used the strike explicitly to pursue political change. At those moments in history, the working classes do not look as if they have been tamed. It is for this reason that strikes, both legal and illegal, are a cause of angst for policy-makers; the many non-conforming strikes remind everyone of the potential of this weapon. Many observers, therefore, find it difficult to maintain equanimity even about its legally permitted use. They see the strike as the first step on a dangerous, slippery slope.

We agree with the opponents of the strike weapon on one thing: we believe in its potential as a mobilizing weapon. It is a way for issues broader than the narrow economic self-interest of the people on strike to be put on the political agenda. Its use might play a part in leading to a changed polity, one in which people in the paid and non-paid workforce might be endowed with more political and economic rights, and the powerful with less. But this potential is unlikely to be realized. The efficacy of the legal, institutional and ideological restraints on the right to strike created by Canada's collective bargaining system are not to be underestimated.

The Regulated Strike in Canada

The Changing Uses of the Strike

Prior to the coming of modern collective bargaining, employers were free to deal with anyone they liked.[5] They were under no legal or moral obligation to recognize any union. Workers often had to strike to obtain recognition for their union.[6] Employers, frequently aided by favourable immigration policies, had an ample pool of non-unionized workers to call on should a group of their employees form a union.

Strikes in those days often had several purposes. Ultimately they were concerned with obtaining better wages and conditions of work, but many times they were, first of all, fights about the recognition of the right of a trade union to make demands. Further, in the absence of any formal system, strikes could also be a form of worker protest against employer capriciousness and authoritarianism. They were a way to fight about what today we call rights or grievance disputes.[7] Because all of these collectivist activities were outside the norms of legally sanctioned behaviour, they looked like revolutionary conduct.[8] The perception was that they were, at one and the same time, economic and political acts. The separation of the economic and political spheres was not as neat as it is now. In large part this was true because governments frequently intervened directly to restrain the attempted exercises of collective worker action, on the basis that it was their role to guarantee law and order.

In the absence of any positive legal right to bargain collectively, workers' jobs and livelihood were on the line each time workers were on strike, because an employer was completely free to bring in strikebreakers. Violence was common.[9] Governments would come to the assistance of employers and scabs. Conflicts between employers and governments, on one side, and workers and their unions, on the other, were commonplace. In these settings, there was no hiding the fact that such clashes were political ones, as the government of the day used its coercive legal powers to squash one set of protagonists — workers and their unions — on behalf of their opponents, the employers. Examples abound. The coal miners' strikes in British Columbia and Nova Scotia and the railway strikes in British Columbia between 1900 and 1913 spread like wildfire.[10] They could not be restricted to confrontations between one employer and its employees. State and legal interventions on behalf of employers brought the legitimacy of the status quo into question. The actions of the Wobblies, Winnipeg's 1919 General Strike and the movement towards the One Big Union all were explicit challenges to the existing political order. Governments set themselves to stamp out worker uprisings.[11] While the 1920s and early 1930s were relatively quiescent, the Depression years led to the rekindling of widespread militancy. The early 1940s was a period when unions could, and did, make breakthroughs. Governments had to make the accommodation that led to the establishment of modern collective bargaining. Continued open warfare could not go on.[12] Employers had to recognize and bargain with democratically chosen unions. Organizational drives no longer led to counter-attacks by employers that threatened workers' jobs. To obtain recognition for their unions, workers, for their part, did not have to engage — indeed, were not permitted to engage — in conduct which was bound to bring state intervention down upon them. Workers were given a leg up, but there was a cost. What the new scheme did was to substitute a bloodless, adjudicatively administered process for economic warfare in the effort to obtain recognition.

Most unions viewed the loss of the right to strike in order to obtain recognition to be an acceptable trade-off. The principal reason was that, in the past, unions had lost many of the recognition battles in which they had been forced to engage. As it turned out, the administrative practices which facilitate trade union organization have worked well; trade union membership got a big boost initially and has been maintained at respectable levels since. But the downside is that the heightened awareness and solidarity which attend the waging of a tough recognition battle have become much more difficult to realize. The confrontations on the shop floor which arise when workers have to fight to have the legitimacy of their union accepted have been transformed into protracted technocratic battles in front of labour relations boards. The point is that a strike is not simply a way to win one battle at a time; it is also a powerful educational tool. Woods put it nicely when he pointed out that it is a "constructive social instrument."[13] This cannot be said with equal force of the bureaucratic processes which have replaced the strike for the purposes of recognition. This neutering of the strike as a consciousness-raising instrument is furthered in other ways by Canada's modern collective bargaining régime.

The Ambit of the Legal Strike

Once a collective agreement has been reached, the strike cannot be used by workers who are dissatisfied with their conditions. While it is also true that employers cannot lock out their workers to persuade them to accept less favourable conditions after an agreement has been signed, this is not a corresponding curtailment of power. Employers are primarily interested in remaining in production. Rarely will they want to lock out employees. Rather, they will threaten to close the plant or part of it, or to contract out production work. These activities have been defined by labour relations boards as being distinct from lock-outs and, therefore, permissible during the life of a collective agreement. Workers have no such easy and equally efficient alternatives to the strike.

Workers, however, have been given a remedy to replace the loss of their strike rights during the life of a collective agreement. If they believe that the employer is at fault in administering the agreement, they have been given access to a bureaucratic dispute-resolution mechanism. They must submit their dispute to a grievance process that culminates in arbitration. Therefore, workers involved in a dispute tend to play only an indirect role in its resolution. Moreover, the arbitration mechanism tends to individualize disputes, rather than treat them as problems of the workforce as a whole (see Chapter 7). This does little for the promotion of working class cohesion and empowerment. The switch to an adjudicative-type model to deal with daily workplace conflicts means that unions do not continuously remind their workers of the need to stand shoulder-to-shoulder to resist unacceptable employer demands and orders. Nonetheless, the union movement sees the denial of strike power in this setting as yet another acceptable trade-off, because the costs and risks of threatening to strike about each and every workplace conflict are very high.

It must be remembered as well that the grievance scheme, which excludes strikes as well as lock-outs, gives employers a guarantee of stability for long periods. This stability is threatened only by the fact that the system mandates that workers must be allowed to strike *sometime.*

As a matter of statutory law, the only situation in which workers are allowed to exercise the right to strike is when they are negotiating a first or a new agreement. In most Canadian jurisdictions, workers have to go through a lengthy process of supervised conciliation or mediation. It takes time to appoint a conciliator and/or a mediator, and the conciliation/mediation processes themselves may stretch out over a long period. This may help employers plan for the long term. But in the end, workers may, and indeed do, use the strike to win concessions from their employer. There are some indications that it is taking longer and longer to do so.

Table 6.2
Time Needed to Negotiate a New Contract Covering
500 or More Employees
1975–1988

	Percentage of contracts				Median time (months)
	3 months or less	4–6 months	7–9 months	10 + months	
1975	21.7	51.4	20.2	6.7	5.2
1980	10.2	39.7	23.4	26.7	6.5
1985	11.9	24.6	23.8	39.8	8.2
1986	9.9	28.4	24.1	37.5	8.0
1987	10.4	35.5	16.8	37.3	7.2
1988	10.5	34.4	20.4	34.6	7.3

Source: Labour Canada, *Collective Bargaining Review* (Ottawa, 1989).

When workers finally strike, they must rely on their ability to outlast their employer economically. They are not entitled to call on workers elsewhere to lay down their tools to support them. The strike is to be limited to work done for their own employer and any other firm that is so closely integrated with their employer's enterprise that it is considered to be part of the same business for the purposes of the dispute.[14] The basic rule is clear: in Canada the legal right to strike only exists to negotiate a first or a new agreement with one employer at a time.[15] This rule, with its precisely spelled-out limitations, serves two functions. First, it helps to contain the effect of any strike on the economy; overall stability is the watchword. Second, it militates against workers seeing the problems of all workers as their own; separation and fragmentation are the key.

From this vantage point, it is clear that the strike is a narrowly focused economic weapon, just as it was envisioned to be when statutory collective bargaining was initiated. This limited view of the strike was reaffirmed by the Supreme Court of Canada when it dealt with a trilogy of cases in the 1980s.[16]

The Charter and the Right to Strike

Three important cases arose after the governments of Newfoundland, Alberta and Canada all had passed legislation which forbade unions within their jurisdiction from using the strike power which the ruling collective bargaining legislation had given them. The unions sought to have this restriction set aside. They claimed that, because the *Charter of Rights and Freedoms* gave all citizens a constitutional right to associate freely,[17] their members' right to form a union was inviolate. They then argued that, as the whole purpose of joining a union would be defeated if that union did not have the right to strike, the constitutional guarantee of the freedom to associate must necessarily entail a constitutional guarantee of the right to strike.

A majority of the Supreme Court of Canada refused to accept this reasoning. It noted that the common law had never recognized a right to strike and that the relatively modern collective bargaining statutes did no more than detail a series of limited circumstances in which the concerted withdrawal of labour for economic purposes was to be permitted. That is, there had never been anything which properly could be characterized as a legal right to strike, nor had collective bargaining legislation created one. Inasmuch as freedom to associate was constitutionally protected, the Court held that the purpose of entrenching this guarantee was to enhance the ability of individuals to do what they could legally do as individuals. But as individuals cannot strike by themselves, the constitutionally protected freedom of association did not encompass the right to strike. In short, the highest court in the land was saying that collective action by workers was still to be treated as aberrational by the law, to be tolerated only in those specific circumstances detailed by a statute. To many unionists, the Supreme Court of Canada's decision served as a brutal reminder of how anti–working class the judiciary had always been. The Court's holding was not just a result of institutional bias, however; given the history and politics of labour relations in Canada, it made legal and political sense.[18]

As we have seen, the right to strike always has been seriously limited by collective bargaining legislation. The statutes do not intend the right to strike to be a civil liberty; the focus of the legal strike is to be economic, not political. Indeed, despite their understandable disappointment with the Supreme Court of Canada's decision, in their hearts most unionists must have anticipated the outcome. They knew that the right to strike has never been an embedded right with which no government could interfere arbitrarily. That trade unionists and their political allies understood that there was no deep public commitment to such an unfettered right to strike can be gleaned from a revealing exchange which took place between drafters of the *Charter of Rights and Freedoms*.

Svend Robinson of the NDP had urged that the clause which was to guarantee freedom of association should include the right to bargain collectively. To sell the idea he readily agreed that any guaranteed right to bargain collectively would not signify that the right to strike should be protected constitutionally. That would be going too far.[19] Even so, his fellow drafters rejected his milk-and-water suggestion. This is a clear reflection of the fact that labour's allies understood full well that the idea of the right to strike, as a politically entrenched right on the order of, say, the right to speak, has been — and remains — unacceptable to Canadian decision-makers. Rather, it is conceived of as a right to pursue immediate economic concerns, no more, no less. It is therefore always perfectly justifiable to subordinate it to more universal, more important, interests. These pressing needs are to be identified by the government of the day. This explains why it has been so easy to limit the ambit of the right to strike in respect of time, space and purpose. Provided that the disequilibrium caused by its exercise is likely to be minimal — that is, restricted to localized settings — workers can be allowed to exercise it to settle future conditions of employment. It was, in fact, always meant to be a safety valve which would ensure that workers' resentment of their employers' residual power would not build up over time. As the *Report* of the Woods Task Force on Labour Relations put it:

> 392. There is a basic characteristic of the collective bargaining system that is seemingly contradictory. Paradoxical as it may appear, collective bargaining is designed to resolve conflict through conflict, or at least through the threat of conflict. It is an adversary system in which two basic issues must be resolved: how available revenue is to be divided, and how the clash between management's drive for productivity efficiency and the workers' quest for job, income and psychic security are to be reconciled. Other major differences, including personality conflicts, may appear from time to time but normally they prove subsidiary to these two overriding issues.

> 393. For the most part Canada has deliberately opted for a system in which disputes over these matters may periodically be put to a test of economic strength in the form of a strike or lockout. *Although this system may seem costly, it may well be more healthy and less expensive in resolving labour-management disputes than any other method.* Barring the opportunity to an economic confrontation from time to time, the parties are compelled to contain their differences or submit them to some kind of binding third party intervention. In neither event is there assurance of a result that would settle the matter or clear the air. Resort to economic sanctions will still prove inevitable. An employer might still shut his operation. Employees might engage in absenteeism or slowdowns or industrial sabotage. *The advantage of the present collective bargaining system in allowing the parties to let off steam may, in the long run, be more important than the traditionally accepted role of a potential work stoppage as a means of inducing the parties to resolve their differences. The strike or lockout thus may serve either as a catalyst or as a catharsis, if not both* [emphasis added].[20]

The point is clear. Controlled strikes are seen as functional; they are expected to take place. Industrial relations experts understand this, even if the general public does not. Still, on occasion, professional proponents of the scheme are tempted to deflect the persistent argument that Canada's strike record is unacceptable by noting that stoppages of production are minimal, given the large number of collective bargaining agreements in force. Ninety percent are concluded without resort to a lock-out or a strike.[21] This kind of riposte is sometimes accompanied by the argument that, in any event, more time is lost owing to work accidents and sickness than to industrial disputes.[22] But these kinds of defensive claims do little to appease the perception of unruliness and ungovernability of trade unions and their members, which pervades the public's mind. This impression stems, in large measure, from the fact that a great number of strikes do occur with predictable regularity in ways that are suggestive of dangerous rebellion.

Length of Strikes

Many strikes are very long, and in general strikes have grown longer in the past two decades. In the 1960s, on average, a strike lasted fifteen days; by the eighties, the average was twenty-six days.[23]

The reason for the protracted nature of strikes is rooted in the logic of the system. Because strikes, as a matter of law, are local conflicts, it is safe to let market forces determine their outcomes. Accordingly, there is nothing in the rules governing collective bargaining which provides for the termination of strikes. The consequence of this hands-off approach is that, where one (or both) of the parties is stubborn or, as is more likely, when an employer can stay in production and outlast a union on strike, the strike is often a lengthy one. This increases the number of hours of labour lost owing to strikes. As "hours of labour lost" is the usual way in which strike rates are measured, Canada's proneness to strikes is exaggerated. This adds to the general perception that instability is part and parcel of Canadian labour relations.

Picketing: More Than an Exercise in Free Speech

When a union is on legal strike, Canadian collective bargaining law does not require the employer to stop production. Strikers have to force such a stoppage. One measure commonly used is the setting up of picket lines. These are walking billboards, advising would-be workers and the general public that a legal strike is being conducted and that the strikers are seeking support for it.

Picketing has two features: it supports immediate economic demands and it is also an educational exercise which seeks to broaden support for working class aims and aspirations. In large part, then, it is an exercise in free speech and freedom of association.[24] At the same time, however, picketing often acts as a physical barrier to entry into the struck employer's operations.

As the collective bargaining régime protects the right of the employer to buy, to sell and to maintain production during a strike, the law guarantees unimpeded passage to and from the employer's premises. In addition, of course, since the employer's dominion over its property is unchallenged by collective bargaining law, the striking employees cannot physically stop production by occupying the premises. Thus, in most jurisdictions employers are allowed to hire scab labour to maintain production. This often renders a strike ineffective. For this reason, violence is almost inevitable when police escort non-union people across picket lines to allow them to get in and out of struck premises.[25] Similarly, as workers parade up and down outside plant or office gates, they often will find themselves on private property or on public thoroughfares. The law can be used to move them away in either case.

As a consequence, labour disputes frequently turn ugly. When they do, union activity acquires the character of illegal, violent and wrongful behaviour. The image is one of wilful, lawless mobs which no civil society ought to tolerate.[26] The ease with which this pervasive, harmful characterization has emerged is the result of a conceptual starting point which demands that individualism (as reflected in private property and private contract law), is to be protected against an unnatural collectivism. It is this which permits an employer to enlist the assistance of the police and the courts to help it defeat the otherwise lawful demands made by its employees. Frequently this leads to arrests as police prevent picket lines from obstructing roads, sidewalks and shopping plazas.[27] Employers are further aided by the courts, whose entrenched opposition to collectivism has left them eager to issue orders telling unions how many pickets they should be allowed to have and what their signs are permitted to say. This makes it manifest how contingent union rights are.[28]

Modern collective bargaining history bristles with such incidents. Recent examples include the 1987 Gainers strike in Alberta and the

1988 CUPW strike. Newspapers were filled with headlines about picket-line violence and arrests of strikers. Nightly, television beamed pictures of masses of workers locked in physical combat with the police. This kind of recurring episode undermines the acceptability of strike activity. Much of the violence could be avoided by effective anti-scab legislation which would prevent an employer from hiring non-union labour during a lawful strike. Quebec already has such legislation, and the NDP government in Ontario has proposed some.[29]

Secondary Boycotts

The impression that picketing is out of control and, by implication, that strikes are out of control, is strengthened by the fact that secondary boycotts in which workers must engage are not legally permitted. A struck employer may be able to have its production carried on by an associated firm or have necessary supplies continued by a third party. Striking workers must try to stop these kinds of strike-breaking activities. They will picket the so-called third-party enterprises to this end. If these other firms are so closely intertwined with the struck employer's business that they are really part of it, they will be deemed to be allies of the struck employer. When this is so, the secondary picketing will be legal. But if the third parties are not, as a matter of law, allies, they may not be picketed. As it is very difficult to prove this kind of legal alliance, workers will frequently be held to have used the secondary-boycott weapon wrongfully.[30] Injunctions will be issued which, if breached, may lead to contempt charges, fines and jailings.

This additional limitation on workers is justified by reliance on the principle that an *individual's* right to trade should never be interfered with by a third party.[31] This concept obviously pre-dates modern collective bargaining. Logically, it should have no place in it. Worker collective action has been given a new status and should not be trumped by doctrines invented by the common law courts to counter collectivism. Yet it is on the basis of these doctrines that, in the 1985 *Dolphin Delivery* case, the Supreme Court of Canada specifically upheld the right of a non-allied employer to go to court to ask it to remove pickets from outside its premises. Private property and private contract rights — which underpin the right to trade — were held to be sacrosanct, despite the acknowledgement by the

Supreme Court of Canada that picketing was a form of speech and, hence, notionally protected by the *Charter of Rights and Freedoms*.[32]

Illegal Strikes: Stepping Outside the System

The many restrictions on the right to strike in Canada only serve to emphasize how significant a tool it might be. A paradoxical situation emerges. Something which is mired in legalism and so often maligned is made all the more seductive, especially to people who are at their wits' end. It is likely to be used when it is not permitted to be used.

McDonnell Douglas workers fight back

On occasion, anxiety about health and safety in the workplace leads to illegal strike activity.[33] This happens when employers fail to remedy poor conditions. In this situation, workers often feel they have to resort to direct action. This is what happened at a McDonnell Douglas plant in Toronto in 1989.

The local CAW leadership and the workers had made repeated representations to their employer about the deplorable conditions in the plant. The employer was impervious to these workers' attempts to collaborate with it to ameliorate the problems. The Ministry of Labour's help was sought, but it too failed the workers completely. The workers commissioned an independent consultant's report. It found that there had been hundreds of violations of safety regulations in the plant. This evidence was presented to the employer and the ministry. Nothing happened. In anger, nearly three thousand workers walked out. While workers have the legislative right to refuse unsafe work as individuals, it is doubtful whether they can exercise this right in concert except in some narrow, not very clearly circumscribed circumstances.[34] The walk-out that occurred while a collective agreement was in force was, in all likelihood, an illegal strike. But, in this case, the number of workers involved was so great that coercive sanctions were out of the question. A complicated settlement was worked out.[35]

Alberta nurses defy the law

Another frequent source of illegal actions is the fact that the law does not permit some workers to strike at all. They obtain awards by way of binding arbitration but, when they are dissatisfied with the poor results, they strike despite the legal prohibitions. This is what occurred in Alberta in 1990 when the nurses' union walked out, even though it did not have a statutory right to strike. Hospitals went to court to demand orders requiring the strikers to stop their illegal activity. They got them. When workers refused to go back to work, they and their unions were convicted of both civil and criminal contempt of court. The provincial government passed legislation to order the workers back to work. The workers hung tough. Eventually, they were offered a settlement which they felt they could accept.[36]

In both these examples of illegality, the workers "got away with it." They had claims which had credibility with the general public. At McDonnell Douglas, the intransigent employer, aided and abetted by the government, was endangering the lives of workers who had done their best to stay within the system. In Alberta, nurses, who generally have a good public image and are understood not to want to undermine health care services, were treated by hospitals and the government as pawns in the war they were waging on deficits. Public opinion was unsympathetic to both the employers' and the government's approach. The nurses won support from people right across the nation.

The fact, then, that unions and workers strike illegally can be justified to the public in some isolated cases. But, on the whole, extra-legal activity is easily typed as delinquent behaviour, condemnable and restrainable. Nothing is more proper than to use the law to put it down. And so, with few exceptions, illegality will lead to coercion. Frequently, the right to strike is least available where it is most needed. One example will suffice to make this point.

Often workers are faced with an employer who wants to contract out bargaining unit work during the life of an agreement.[37] Workers cannot respond with their most potent weapon, the strike. This creates a serious imbalance. While this may be viewed favourably by intransigent employers and sectors of the public who have a stake in stability of production, it does create difficulty for policy-makers. They have an interest in maintaining the legitimacy of Canada's collective bargaining system, something which it is very hard to do when arbitrators and courts are allowed to punish workers for doing the only thing that makes sense. Weiler has gone so far as to recommend that this glaring gap in countervailing power be closed. He has proposed that workers should be allowed to strike even during the life of a collective agreement if the employer proposes to contract out bargaining-unit work. He recognizes that there is no logic in giving workers the right to strike in respect of sub-contracting but not when other important issues arise.[38] His argument is one of convenience, not logic. It points to the built-in advantages which employers have retained *vis-à-vis* their workforces, despite the advent of collective bargaining.

The differential in legal bargaining power is so great that workers must resort to illegality. They must strike when the iron is hot. In a boom-and-bust economy, there are few enough opportunities to make real advances. The best moment comes before a boom ends. At that point, workers are often bound by their collective agreement. Illegal strikes simply may make sense. This was particularly true during the 1960s. The illegal strikes of that decade gave collective bargaining an unruly look, which led to coercion and, when that did not work so well, to reform (see Chapter 2).

The pressure to act illegally persists. The narrowness of the right to strike continues to make this a necessary tactic. The reaction of the state to illegality will vary with the economic circumstances of the time. Given the logic of the system, the instruments of both reform and repression are available to it.

The Aura of Public Sector Strikes

Strikes in the public sector always have been a matter of great concern. The idea that government services could be interrupted was a contentious one. In the end, public sector workers got their right to bargain collectively at a time when private sector bargaining was in great upheaval (see Chapter 2). At that time, policy-makers found the militant use of the strike in the private sector disturbing. In this climate, the bestowal of the right to strike on public sector employees was seen as a very special privilege. It was, therefore, even more seriously circumscribed than it was in the private sector, and always more likely to be taken away.

The erosion began very shortly after the right to strike was given. It took from 1965 to 1973 for all governments in Canada to grant collective bargaining rights to their employees. In 1975, the Trudeau government passed comprehensive wage and price restraint legislation. Its success in holding wages down was noted by all. Since then, all governments have used incomes restraint legislation of that kind to constrain their own workers. (For more details, see Chapter 9.) Governments have been able to characterize the use of the right to strike by their employees as an abuse. This has given more credence to the belief that it is proper to curtail everyone's right to strike.

The Potential of the Strike as a Political Weapon

Apparent Limitations
The legal limitations on the right to strike and the low esteem in which the strike is held make it very difficult to entertain the thought that it can be used as a tool for radical political change. There are, in fact, many examples of situations in which it appears that a strike would have been an effective political weapon for workers if used in a less tremulous manner than was in fact the case.

The CLC's Day of Protest
The 1975 Anti-Inflation Board (AIB) legislation was a frontal attack on working Canadians. It was to be amazingly successful. Under the guise of wrestling inflation to the ground for the benefit of all, Canadian workers' attempts at playing catch-up, and perhaps making some real gains, were repressed.

Wages were not the demonstrable cause of inflation. The fact is that prices had begun to increase markedly in Canada before the oil shocks of 1972 had taken effect. Even in 1974, price increases ranged between 38 and 58 percent, whereas wage increases ranged between 8 and 15 percent.[39] Yet the way in which the AIB legislation was implemented amounted to an attack on wages, not on profits. It succeeded. By the end of its operating life, the AIB legislation had enabled employers to make 9.2 percent more profit than they otherwise would have.[40]

The trade union movement, sensing the intent of the legislation, had challenged its constitutionality in the courts. As was to be expected, the Supreme Court upheld Pierre Trudeau's anti-collective bargaining legislation.[41] One important initiative was taken by Canada's trade union movement to oppose this manifestly pro-employer legislation, in addition to its search for a remedy in the undemocratic court system. The CLC organized a one-day nation-wide work stoppage.[42] It claimed that a million people downed tools; opponents claimed that many less did so. The interesting fact is that the CLC felt it was not in a position to label its call to action a general strike.

A general strike to achieve a political objective is, of course, forbidden by collective bargaining law. Further, most unionized workers on whom Canada's labour central was calling were, at that time, working subject to collective agreements. The CLC was urging these workers to breach the prohibition on strike action during the life of a collective agreement and to take the consequences. Indeed, many workers who struck for the day were disciplined, and legal actions were brought against many local unions.[43] In this context, it becomes easy to understand why the CLC called its effort a Day of Protest. Rather than making it a clarion call for a general strike to overthrow anti-worker legislation, it was trying to suggest that it was only asking that people exercise their power to strike in a non-threatening manner, as if it were a symbolic civil-libertarian act of disobedience. It wanted to make it clear that it was not promoting the strike as a political weapon for radical purposes, even though the political actions of a government bent on holding back workers cried out for direct political action.

The 1988 free trade election
During the bitter free trade general election of 1988, the CLC and, indeed, all of the trade union leadership were opposed to Brian Mulroney's conservative agenda. The unionists' protestations were loud and vehement. They backed the Pro-Canada Network, the umbrella group leading the fight against the free trade deal. According to the Network's own figures, it spent close to three-quarters of a million dollars on pamphlets and newspaper advertisements. In the end, this proved futile. The Business Council on National Issues and other major business organizations stole the election by spending millions of dollars in the final days of the campaign.[44] Although organized labour understood the immense problems it was facing, it never reached out for its most powerful weapon: the strike. At no stage was an attempt made to mobilize the workers by calling on them to stop production to achieve a political end.

The GST fight
The Conservatives were not satisfied with having beaten the trade union movement and their allies in the free trade election. They are bent on completing their agenda. In 1990, the federal government proposed a regressive Goods and Services Tax (GST). To the trade union movement this was like a red rag to a bull. The proposal came on top of accelerated privatization, deregulation and attacks on the social wage.

Egged on by the huge popular opposition to the tax, organized labour took a leading part in the resistance. The unionists lobbied fiercely, spoke out publicly, pamphleteered, initiated petitions. In addition, they advised their affiliates to negotiate wage settlements that would offset the anticipated inflationary effects of the GST. Some unionists would have liked to go much further. They came to the CLC convention in 1990 with placards that urged that a general strike be called. They were unsuccessful. The CLC leadership was not about to endorse the use of the strike as an overt political weapon.

The Trade Union Movement's Dilemma

In the fights around the AIB legislation, the free trade election and the GST, governments were not backward in coming forward. Their argument was that necessary economic restructuring required political rearrangements. In the case of the AIB legislation there was to be a suspension of the post-war capital-labour entente. In the free trade election, there was to be a subjugation of national political sovereignty in favour of continental integration. As for the GST, there was a frank acknowledgement that the ideal of levying taxes on a progressive basis was to be abandoned. It might have been expected that such huge political changes would have provoked the trade union movement into an equivalent political response, making use of its economic weaponry. Yet this was not the outcome. There are important structural reasons, as well as (less justifiable) instrumental ones for organized labour's reticence. It is caught in a dilemma.

The trade unions that have emerged as legitimate bargaining agents under the collective bargaining scheme are the ones which have succeeded in persuading the state's labour agencies that they are willing to abide by the system's constraints. These trade unions do not want to endanger the quasi-public status that they have earned. They believe that legal collective bargaining has yielded real benefits for the workers they represent. They understand that their bargaining rights are contingent and fear that, should they be branded as irresponsible bargaining agents, these precious rights may be taken away. In a legally regulated system, the most obvious sign of irresponsibility is a failure to abide by the legal rules. The key here is that all political strikes will fall foul of some rule or another.

To ask workers to take strike action for political purposes often involves asking them to strike during the life of an agreement. This is illegal. To have the state as the target, rather than a particular employer, is also beyond the ambit of collective bargaining norms. To withdraw labour to support the industrial action of workers employed elsewhere is also unlawful. And, of course, to defy a state edict which removes the right to strike is not allowed.

When faced with provocative actions by employers or governments, trade union officials are very sympathetic to their members' desire, and need, to act illegally. But legally they will be forced to contain outbursts from their rank and file; indeed, they must actively seek to restrain them.[45] Failure to do so will lead to penalties that may include fines and, possibly, decertification. Sometimes union officials merely go through the motions so that they can be seen to satisfy the law. At the same time as they are formally saying "desist," they are informally winking and nodding approval. But, over time, the combination of having to accept the limitations of the strike and the need to convince themselves that the system is working has made trade union leaders chary of advocating any far-reaching use of it.

This goes a long way towards explaining the union movement's ambivalence about the use of the strike in vital struggles over issues such as those raised by the AIB legislation, the Canada-U.S. Free Trade Agreement and the GST. The use of the strike has become bureaucratized and depoliticized. This is becoming increasingly important as economic conditions have put unions on the defensive. Employers are demanding concessions. Job security is at risk. In such a climate, even narrow economic strikes are difficult to mount. In fact, there was a sharp reduction in the level of strike action in the 1980s.[46] To arrest those trends, workers need more political control to force a change in Canada's economic orientation. The believable threat of a solidarity-type strike would be a valuable weapon.

Despite the many impediments, the possibility that the strike will be used for militant purposes always exists in a class-divided society. Canada's turbulent labour history provides Canada's élites with many good reasons to be fearful of organized outbreaks. This, in large measure, explains the excessive restrictions on the right to strike in Canada. The culture of resistance always bubbles just underneath the calm sea of industrial relations created by the legal system. Contemporary struggles serve to remind everyone, including Canada's trade union leaders, of this. Blunted though it is, the strike weapon retains its potential as an instrument for social change.[47]

Apparent Possibilities

The very fact that unions have gained a quasi-public status means that they must be given some sort of standing in political decision-making that affects their collective bargaining interests. Decisions about tariffs and excises, trade liberalization, unemployment insurance benefits, training of the workforce, immigration, race relations, social transfers, regional development programs, research and development schemes, environmental planning, taxation laws and the like affect their bargaining power, as well as the public welfare. Unions and unionists are active on all these fronts.

They write briefs and lobby politicians; they participate in electoral politics; they sit on a multitude of tripartite boards along with business and government representatives.[48] Unionists are frequently involved as individuals in single-issue groups formed to deal with struggles around a particular concern; sometimes unions will provide knowledge, and administrative and financial support, for such groups and the floating coalitions to which they give rise. In short, politically linked activities of this kind by unions and unionists are not only legitimate, they are an integral part of trade union life. This fits in with the image trade unionists have of themselves.

By contrast, many Marxists see trade unions primarily as economic, and not revolutionary agents,[49] their role determined by their need to be bargainers for wages in the existing economic system. This characterization was accepted by Marx, Lenin and Trotsky.[50] Yet this glosses over too many historical facts.

Unionists always have played a significant part in enlarging citizen participatory rights. In Belgium and Sweden they used their strike power to get the franchise.[51] Everywhere their struggles have been instrumental in making liberal capitalist societies more democratic. As C.B. Macpherson, among others, has shown, such freedom of speech, assembly and belief as exists today is largely due to workers' efforts to democratize the market mechanism and state apparatus.[52] Whatever the theoretical merit of Marxist views of the limited possibilities of trade unionism, it is clear that trade unions did not always act as if the economic and political spheres were completely discrete. It is thus always possible that they may act as if this artificial division ought to be ignored, especially when they form links with special interest and pressure groups.

There have been many such *ad hoc* coalitions. Take for instance the fight that grew up around the immigrant workers who had to confront a recalcitrant employer at Artistic Woodworkers in Metropolitan Toronto.[53] The strike began as a legal one, but the political support that it attracted led to the kind of picketing and boycotting that the authorities were quickly able to characterize as illegal. Arrests and violence became commonplace. At the same time, the importance of invoking the support of popular groups for unions engaged in struggles for job rights became evident to many people. Similarly, the Fleck strike involved a redneck employer, a parts manufacturer in southwestern Ontario, who was able to call on the police to deal brutally with women engaged in a legal strike. Trade unions and women's groups worked together for a while.[54] More recently, the Gainers strike in Alberta featured many of the same elements. It began as a legal strike: the employer insisted on scabs; violence resulted; workers were arrested; the courts forbade effective picketing while the government supported owner Peter Pocklington with grants. A nation-wide network of support for the strikers among leftist groups and trade unionists was formed.[55]

This kind of occasional coalition building is not the stuff of which mass movements are made. But it does serve to remind everyone, those who fear mass movements as well as those who favour them, of the possibilities of politically linked actions arising from the exercise of collective bargaining. Not every possibility, however, will be realized. While trade unionists are sympathetic to coalition building, and often seek to engage in it, the industrial relations system has made them responsible for the containment of working class politics. So when unions and popular sectors coalesce, the union movement finds itself in an awkward situation. The social agenda and the collective bargaining agenda vie for dominance. Frequently, trade unions are unable to transcend the narrow economic collective bargaining role which the state has bestowed on them. This leaves the popular-sector groups isolated, the trade union movement divided and the state in firm control. The following short accounts of the 1972 Common Front in Quebec and the B.C. Solidarity Movement illustrate this all too well. They also demonstrate the enormous, if rarely achieved, potential of politically linked strikes.

The Common Front, 1972

The emergence of the Common Front was part of a long history of confrontation and militancy that had begun under Quebec's Duplessis régime.[56] Trade union demands in Quebec led to massive confrontations with police, mass arrests and beatings, and a campaign of state terrorism. The 1949 Asbestos strike is the best-known example. The Asbestos strike lasted for over two months, but the workers went back to work with little to show for their efforts. Strikes like these supported the belief that the Duplessis régime was vulnerable, particularly when large-scale mobilization was used to bring together many political activists and groups, including Church officials.[57] Other major labour eruptions which followed served to raise political consciousness further. In 1952, six thousand textile workers fought a violent three-month strike against Dominion Textile at Valleyfield. Landmark strikes broke out at Dupuis Frères in 1954, at Murdochville in 1957, and at the CBC in Montreal in 1959.[58] Political awareness was also heightened by the struggles over language in the workplace in the 1960s and the coalitions that were formed between the trade union movement and the educated sections of the emerging French-speaking middle classes. This political co-operation was part and parcel of a political climate in which nationalism as well as working class activism was on the rise.[59]

By the early 1960s, these alliances helped militants see the possibility of going beyond the confines of the Quiet Revolution. The manifestos of the Common Front in the 1970s later gave voice to these new kinds of aspirations. *"Brisez le système"* and *"maîtres chez nous"* became the rallying cries.[60]

The radicalization of the Quebec trade union leadership was due to the failure of the Quiet Revolution to make good its promises to build a better economic life for Québécois. Despite much talk of reform from the early sixties onward, workers had seen only modest changes. Quebec continued to experience one of the highest rates of unemployment in North America, as well as some of the lowest wage rates in industrialized North America.[61] The political and economic were about to mix.

The three major trade union umbrella organizations formed the Common Front to bargain more effectively with the province. The government, like any employer in the private sector that is used to dealing with a divided labour force, resisted this bargaining tactic. A stand-off resulted. The rhetoric of the Common Front came to adopt overtly class terms as the anti-government economic struggles were supported by the nationalist and populist groups. Organizational structures evolved whose aim it was to politicize the working class movement further. Trade unionists supported the growth of the Comité d'action politique, a rank-and-file organization of union and non-union militants. Some of the flavour of the movement can be gleaned from a 1971 statement by Louis Labèrge, then leader of the QFL: "The system that we live in in Quebec, and more generally in North America, is not made for us ... we live in a violent society and this violence with few exceptions originates from the propertied class and is aimed at the wage earners."[62] The challenge for the Common Front was to maintain the political dynamic of alliance building and not to let traditional economic collective bargaining demands dominate the agenda. The government, of course, had precisely the opposite aim.

From the unions' point of view, the principal claim was a $100-a-week salary for the 210,000 public and quasi–public sector workers they represented.[63] This figure was chosen because both the federal Senate Committee on Poverty, headed by Senator David Croll, as well as the Castonguay Commission on Social Welfare in Quebec, had pointed out that this was the wage needed to allow working Québécois to get out of the poverty trap. At the time, 40 percent of public sector workers in Quebec were making less than $70 a week, and more than half were earning below the family poverty rate of $100 a week. As Marcel Pépin, the leader of one of the trade union organizations, the Confédération des syndicats nationaux (CSN), was to argue, the unusual collective bargaining tactics were adopted to redress the intolerable discrimination perpetuated by supposedly neutral market forces. He was referring to the fact that many public workers were women and that the government was claiming that it should not have to pay them more than the rates which prevailed in the private sector — even though the private sector undervalued women's work.[64] Among other demands, the Common Front wanted equal pay for equal work (not equal pay for work of equal value), a claim which looks very modest by today's standards.

The Quebec government's unwillingness to accede to these demands arose from its belief that such concessions would impinge on labour market rates in the private sector. It launched a massive campaign to break the Common Front. To this end, it reached out for traditional collective bargaining control weaponry.

The government's refusal to negotiate led to a twenty-four-hour work stoppage, followed by a general strike by the Common Front's members. This, of course, was illegal. Back-to-work orders were obtained by the government from the courts. The orders were disobeyed. This resulted in the laying of more than 7,000 charges against supporters of the Common Front. Fines totalling over $6.5 million were levied, and some of the leaders of the strike were jailed for refusing to obey these back-to-work orders. These were draconian penalties when compared to, say, the penalties exacted at that time when corporations broke health and safety or environmental laws. Mr. Justice Deschênes was to justify this later. He made it clear that this kind of strike activity amounted to a form of disobedience that was not to be tolerated, even if it was provoked by the "slowness of the democratic process." He supported state suppression of the trade unionists: "... l'état ne peut se payer le luxe de laisser bafouer la loi ni, par extension logique, les ordonnances des tribunaux."[65]

The strike lasted ten days. It had large popular support. Radio stations were taken over. Roads on the periphery of the province were closed, as well as some ports. Nonetheless, the tough, uncompromising approach of the Bourassa government took its toll. Union leaders sought their members' support for a continuation of the strike. A majority of workers gave that approval but the voter turnout was poor and the leadership of the CSN sharply divided. In the result, the strike was called off. Subsequently, the trade union umbrella groups were to drift apart. Immediately after the termination of the general strike, some sporadic short strikes and demonstrations flared up to protest the imprisonment of the Common Front leaders. These ended when Pépin, Labèrge and Charbonneau were given the right to appeal their convictions and were released from jail.

The Quebec government was able to quell this large syndicalist uprising by characterizing and treating it as a malfunctioning of collective bargaining, rather than as an anti-establishment political movement. It therefore reached out for collective bargaining tools, in particular the coercive aspects of collective bargaining law. Both the type-casting of the uprising and the nature of the weapons to combat it reflect the view which Justice Rand had assigned to the role of trade unions if they wanted to enjoy the privilege of collective bargaining. Justice Deschênes reflected this view when he later pointed out that "... un syndicat répond envers les particulières des dommages directs et immédiats qu'une grève illégale poursuivie avec sa bénédiction peut ... avoir causés."[66] Nothing could be plainer. Collective bargaining power was not to be permitted to bring about changes in the social order. The Quebec trade unions, whose language and organizational efforts had indicated that they were desirous to resist the "economistic" role bestowed upon them by the legal régime, were forced to retreat. The reasons for this were complex but it is clear that, despite the extensive linkages which had been established between the trade union movement and the *groupes populaires*, despite the rich rhetoric of class politics which permeated the struggle, and despite the unifying thrust of nationalist politics, something essential was missing. The Quebec struggle was seriously handicapped by the institutional arrangements which legitimate and condition trade union activities. In particular, these arrangements have had great success in compartmentalizing the economic and the political spheres.[67]

Operation Solidarity in British Columbia

The 1973 reforms introduced by the NDP in British Columbia gave the Woods Task Force recommendations the biggest play they received in Canada. Leading progressive pluralists had been mandated to draft a modern collective bargaining statute. The government conferred the task to implement the new Labour Code on one of these liberal pluralists, Paul Weiler.[68] In the upshot, trade union organization and dispute resolution were to be dealt with by a board which had more sympathy for trade unions' needs and which was given tools to handle matters more expeditiously.

The vexed issue of secondary strikes and boycotts was brought under the aegis of the labour relations board. This was an innovative departure. It was a positive signal to workers that they were no longer to be subjugated as often as before to the antediluvian approaches of the judiciary: collectivism was to be respected. Public servants were given the same rights to bargain and to strike as private sector workers. The intent was to write a new chapter in labour-management regulation. The Labour Relations Board set out with enthusiasm to give life to this progressive structure.[69]

By the 1980s, after the fall of the NDP government, the British Columbia Labour Relations Board was no longer as sympathetic to workers' needs as it had been in earlier days. The progressive legislation, however, was still on the books. It is in this context that the attack by the Bennett government in 1983 was seen as particularly brutal and regressive.[70]

Because of its singular reliance on its resource sector, British Columbia is especially susceptible to downturns.[71] As a consequence, it suffered more from the economic collapse in the early 1980s than any other region in Canada. The growth in unemployment tells the story. In 1981, there were 90,000 unemployed; in 1982, there were

163,000. The jump in the unemployment rate, from 6.7 percent in 1981 to 12 percent in 1982, was matched only in Alberta. By 1984, the unemployment rate had risen to 15.6 percent. Female workers had been the largest-growing segment of the labour force in the 1970s. By the 1980s, the growth in the female unemployment rate matched that among males; women were discouraged from entering the labour force in the same numbers as they had begun to do.[72]

The Social Credit government decided to tackle the economic crisis by adopting policies of restraint.[73] In particular, it sought to undermine the bargaining power of trade unions and the public's recently acquired social welfare and citizenry rights. The government began with an attack on its own employees. It proposed to remove their rights to negotiate about job security, promotion, job reclassification, transfers, work hours and other such work conditions. This was the infamous Bill 2, introduced in July 1983. At the same time, the government presented Bill 3, which would enable government employers to fire employees without cause whenever a contract ended. Wage restraints were imposed; the setting of wage rates was to take account of the employer's ability to pay. This provision was particularly odious to trade unions. As if all this were not enough, it proposed to undermine minimum-protection standards dealing with such matters as pregnancy leave and safety on the job.

The British Columbia Government Employees Union (BCGEU) set out to fight these frontal challenges. It called on unionists in both the private and public sector to support it. It rightly characterized the government's neo-conservative legislation as an attack on all workers. The union struck and, in due course, asked other unions to come out in support. This support was readily offered — indeed, it came from some surprising quarters. Teachers' unions, heretofore not known for their militancy, went on rolling strikes. More importantly, social-movement groups and unaffiliated citizens of all kinds joined in the anti-government movement. And they did so in large numbers.

They were aggrieved because the Bennett government had also proposed legislation to repeal the Human Rights Code and to abolish the Human Rights Commission. The rental review tribunal was to be abrogated; doctors were to be allowed to opt out of the medicare system; the tax base of local school boards was to be reduced and the minister of education's control of these boards was to be bolstered; the minister of education's control over courses and budgets of colleges and other institutions also was to be increased; parliamentary control over Crown corporations was to be diminished, leaving more control with the chief executive officer; "sin taxes" were to be increased; property taxes were to be raised; and tax credits for tenants were to be reduced. The objective conditions for the formation of Operation Solidarity had been created. It was born shortly thereafter.

The province was rocked by a continuous wave of work stoppages and frighteningly large mass demonstrations. The NDP joined in the fray and initiated a filibuster in the legislature to delay the repressive laws. The province was truly in a crisis. Wheeling and dealing began.[74]

Unlike in Quebec, this crisis had been brought about by positive government action rather than by pressures generated from below by a maturing political movement. The British Columbia government's own action precipitated the fast-growing movement. But, despite its name, Operation Solidarity was not a coalition with a single-minded focus.[75]

The union movement primarily wanted to regain and preserve its economic collective bargaining rights. Secondarily, it wanted to protect the social and political entitlements of British Columbians. For their part, the popular-sector organizations were primarily interested in defending their hard-won social benefits packages and anti-discrimination guarantees. Support for trade union rights was part of their agenda, but it was not the central issue for them.

The situation was further complicated by the fact that it was hard to develop a common agenda within the trade union movement itself. Public and private sector trade unions were thrown together. In the past they often had kept each other at arms' length. A good deal of tension existed between American and national unions.[76] On the other side of the fence, the popular-sector groups also had a tradition of fighting their own battles as discrete groups. In the main, they had pursued their narrow goals through electoral politics, allying themselves with trade unionists and other social movements as the situation demanded. In other words, the concept of Operation Solidarity, of a widely based coalition for social and economic change, was a novel one for all involved. People had been brought together by precipitous government action before their experience had prepared them to hold together.

In this context, the Bennett government reflex was to split Operation Solidarity in two. It did so by dealing directly, and principally, with the trade unions.[77] This was a natural thing for it to do, as governments traditionally deal with popular-sector groups only as individual lobby and interest groups, as client groups. Now these groups were coalesced into a hydra-headed, hard-to-define mass. They had no identifiable leadership and their agenda was unspecified, open ended and political. There was no one who could guarantee that any agreement negotiated by the movement's leaders would be honoured by their constituent members (in the absence of a process to ratify it democratically). Given the vague, but notionally radical objectives of the social sector activists, there was no certainty that a compromise which stayed within established political bounds could be arrived at.

To deal directly with the trade unions, however, did not present any conceptual or practical difficulties. The dispute between the government and the British Columbia Federation of Labour could be characterized as dealing with economic rights, rather than with far-reaching political rights. For these purposes, a leadership could be identified which could be said to fully represent the economic bargaining interests of an identifiable constituency and which could be held responsible for implementing any agreement reached on its behalf.

In the end, the B.C. government was successful because the unions were also fearful of the political forces which might be unleashed if Operation Solidarity stayed in full flight. Indeed, they could not be certain that they would be the eventual leaders and thus control the movement as it grew. While the possibilities were intoxicating, the dangers of failure loomed large to a trade union movement allied to a traditional electoral perspective and which looked to the reformist, social democratic NDP to act as its political arm. In this context, the unions accepted the government's distinction between the economic and political spheres. They chose to save their legitimacy as economic bargainers.

In order to push them in this direction, the Bennett government consciously used the supposedly autonomous British Columbia Labour Relations Board as a principal channel of negotiation. The idea was for the Board to convey to the unions how perilous their situation was and that their existing powers were at risk should they continue to contravene the Board's view of what their proper role was. The Board indicated that, as certified unions, they were limited to legislatively sanctioned strike action. If they struck for political purposes, however, the Board would wash its hands of them, leaving them at the mercy of the courts and/or the legislature.[78]

As a result of these many pressures, the trade union establishment followed what, in all likelihood, was its natural inclination. It convinced itself that no viable political alternative was available because there was no political organization which could take charge should the British Columbia government be brought to its knees by a general strike supported by a large mass of the population. It opted for a deal which helped preserve its legal bargaining rights. The protection of social rights was to be left to the NDP, as it had been in the past.

A deal was struck behind the social movements' backs. The government withdrew Bill 2. This helped redress some of the British Columbia Government Employees Union's immediate grievances. But the labour movement got little else. Bill 3 was amended only slightly before it was passed. The wage-restraint law and the provisions which undermined existing labour standards legislation were implemented. The social movements attained virtually none of their goals. The only immediate gain was that doctors were denied the right to extra-bill.

Initially, there was much bitterness among the social groups' leaders. They felt they had been betrayed. This was a natural reaction. In the long term, however, the quick escalation of events in British Columbia showed the enormous potential of politically linked strikes, just as it did in Quebec.[79] For a moment it appeared that the consciousness that the economic and political spheres are one might be internalized, an awareness which, if it is made part of daily struggles, has transformative capacity.

These possibilities still lie ahead in the future. For the time being, trade unions and their members still tend to accept the limits that are imposed on the right to strike. The most important effect of the tight legal confinement of the right to strike is that it makes the inevitable breakouts by workers less dangerous than they might be. Moreover, the trade union movement has paid a heavy price. It has had, or believes it has had, to accept a controlling and disciplinary role over its members. This "management of discontent" function has been given an added dimension by the responsibility imposed on trade unions in the resolution of disputes that arise in the workplace during the life of a collective agreement. We turn to this now.

The Paradox of Grievance Arbitration: Empowerment and Disempowerment

From Arbitrariness to Rationality

For theoreticians who support the collective bargaining system, the grievance arbitration process is a milestone. It is seen as part and parcel of the dynamics of collective bargaining, an inherent component of an enriched industrial democracy. This is so despite the fact that it calls for third-party imposition of settlements to deal with disputes, a seeming paradox in a system which prides itself on its voluntaristic nature.

The way in which it works is that, should a dispute arise during the life of an agreement, if the parties cannot settle it themselves it is to be resolved by means of a negotiation process which must culminate in binding arbitration. Unlike impasses caused by disagreements over future work conditions, conflicts about the interpretation or application of agreed-upon terms and conditions are to be settled by a rational adjudication of the collective agreement's relevant provisions, not by resort to naked power. From the workers' point of view, this is attractive because the need to fight and to take militant action about every workplace dispute is costly and debilitating. To employers, the scheme has the merit of enhancing the stability of production. Does the scheme, then, serve both parties equally well? In the end, this depends on the nature and quality of the outcomes of this form of dispute resolution.

On the face of it, the advent of the grievance arbitration process should be seen as a positive development for workers. In the absence of legalized collective bargaining rights, employers had the economic power to exercise their will unilaterally. Now, capriciously exercised employer power is fettered by the requirement that managerial decisions must be capable of being defended with rational arguments before an impartial arbitration board. Perhaps the most significant curtailment is that an employer can no longer, as a matter of economic and legal fact, determine that a worker should be discharged or punished because she displeases the boss. The supporters of the grievance arbitration régime see this as one of the great advances offered by our model of collective bargaining. Indeed, it is a welcome, necessary step on the road to the enhancement of the dignity of workers. Even so, the question remains as to why this system of third-party intervention does not trouble its proponents conceptually. After all, even if some of the outcomes please them, these results are not the product of freely reached agreements between the parties.

In 1968, the Woods Task Force offered what is still the standard response to this question. Its argument was that collective bargaining is a powerful participatory mechanism. It allows workers — who have control over their unions — to express their wishes from a position of strength. A dispute-resolution mechanism which requires interpretation of work rules obtained in this context complements, rather than detracts from, a voluntaristic scheme. It pays respect to rights won and lost by parties who engaged in bargaining that truly can be characterized as "free collective bargaining," because workers have been granted much-needed countervailing power.[1]

Analytically, this view has merit. But it is posited on two premises: that workers were given equality in bargaining power, and that the ideology of the more primitive master-servant relationship of earlier days has been abandoned. Both these premises are frail. The results bear this out. While the grievance arbitration system has permitted workers to make some gains on some fronts, it also has imposed serious limitations on the scope and quality of the control which workers can exercise over their environment. Indeed, somewhat ironically, the scheme has helped reinforce some aspects of managerial prerogatives. At the same time as the employers' right to fire individuals has been fettered to a great extent, their right to make economic decisions which affect the right of workers to remain employed has not been seriously eroded. Further, while their power to use draconian disciplinary measures as they see fit has been diminished, the scheme has helped employers perfect and refine their ability to manage their workforces on a daily basis. It is in this context that, perhaps somewhat paradoxically, the Woods Task Force acknowledged that grievance arbitration "furnishes the means of legitimizing and making more acceptable the superior-subordinate nexus inherent in the employer/employee relationship."[2] Even more explicit than this were the comments of Feller, a prominent American trade union lawyer and counsel for the AFL-CIO. He wrote that a grievance arbitration process which is limited to the interpretation and administration of the agreement

> confers a substantial advantage upon management which it would not have in its absence. On matters covered by the agreement and within the limits imposed by it either expressly or impliedly, management is free to manage without either immediate or ultimate restraint in areas in which, in the absence of the agreement, it would have both a duty to bargain and the risk of concerted employee reaction in protest against its action. In return for an agreement for what the rules shall be, management gains the freedom to act that it would not otherwise have.[3]

The most intriguing aspect of the grievance arbitration scheme, then, is its two-faced character. It provides some furtherance of industrial democracy by broadening workers' control over their own lives in some respects. At the same time, it is a mechanism which has permitted employers to retain and to refashion some of the fundamental control rights which they always enjoyed. This is particularly useful to employers who have to be able to respond quickly to the many vagaries of an export-led growth economy. They want to be able to increase or shrink their workforce as needed. On this front, grievance arbitration does not hinder them. For workers, then, it is something of a mixed blessing. It certainly is not the great invention that many of its proponents would have us believe. Many institutional and structural constraints have limited the unions' ability to get what the machinery seems to offer on paper.

This chapter is aimed at demonstrating how these constraints work, by examining some aspects of grievance arbitration. The kinds of issues to be resolved through this process are almost infinite in number and kind because the parties may, in theory, bargain about anything they like, in any way they choose. We have had to be selective, then, and have chosen those areas which go most directly to the claims made by those who uphold grievance arbitration as an unquestioned enhancement of industrial democracy in Canada. In particular, we will look at the individual's right to security on the job and the trade unions' ability to limit employers' freedom to decide the size of their workforces.

Discharge and Discipline

Moving Away from the Common Law

As a consequence of the acceptance of modern collective bargaining complemented by grievance arbitration, employers are no longer able to exercise their whim and dismiss an employee for any reason whatsoever. This was not the case under the more primitive legal régime of individual contract of employment. Employers then ran very little risk if they dismissed an employee summarily. The law provided that an employer would be held liable for the wrongful dismissal of an employee only if the employer could not give any justification at all for the termination. Even if the employer failed to meet such a minimal test, the only penalty it would face was the amount of money it would have had to pay in lieu of notice to terminate the contract lawfully. The courts refused to order reinstatement for employees who were wrongfully dismissed.[4] In practice, most workers were entitled to very little notice time, if any. The only judicial remedy on offer, therefore, was the award of very small sums by way of damages. Not surprisingly, workers rarely brought legal actions against an employer who, they felt, had wrongly discharged them. In practical terms, employers could act with impunity. They had little to fear from legal challenges by workers because not only were the available remedies poor, but also because courts made it very easy for employers to justify the exercise of their punitive powers. Almost any scintilla of worker "misbehaviour" gave the employer legal justification for summary dismissal.[5]

The grievance system was envisaged to be, and very quickly proved itself to be, a break from this anti-worker tradition. Early on in modern collective bargaining history, grievance arbitrators came to the conclusion that employers who wanted to rid themselves of a worker had to prove that they had reasonable cause for doing so. Unlike the common law courts, arbitration boards deployed the remedy of reinstatement for workers whom they found to have been dismissed without just cause. But arbitrators arrogated even more power to themselves. They found that there were many situations in which an employer did, in fact, have a right to be displeased with one of its workers, but not to be *that* displeased. The arbitrator, therefore, would determine that the employer had "cause" to discipline the worker, but that the employee's wrongful behaviour had not warranted the ultimate penalty, namely, discharge. The solution they came up with was to order reinstatement with some loss of pay, or some loss of seniority, or with a warning to behave better in the future. They were, in effect, substituting their judgement about the kind of behaviour an employer had to put up with for that of the employer.

Employers thought this initiative to be an attack on their sovereignty. They argued that the arbitrators' power to deal with the discharge of an individual employee could arise only from the words of the collective agreement. The clause which governs this situation is called the "just cause" clause. At the time, it was commonly understood that arbitrators could reinstate workers if employers had acted in breach of the "just cause" clause. The argument of employers was that the substitution of a lesser penalty — as opposed to a full reinstatement or an upholding of the discharge — was an alteration of the collective agreement, rather than an interpretation of it. Their claim, therefore, was that the arbitrators were rewriting the collective agreement made by the parties. In 1969, the Supreme Court of Canada accepted this employer point of view.[6]

This led to something of a legitimation crisis for the grievance arbitration system. If employer power was to be curbed only when it was clear that an employee had not deviated at all from the employer's requirements, or only in the most trivial way, it could hardly be said that the dignity and autonomy of workers had been enhanced much by the new dispute-resolution mechanism. Indeed, the argument that trade unions were losing little by agreeing not to strike during the life of a collective agreement would no longer be persuasive. Collective bargaining adherents and trade unions, therefore, combined to form a lobby to overturn the Supreme Court of Canada decision. They were successful. Both legislative amendments and collective agreement clauses which explicitly gave arbitrators power to vary any discipline imposed by employers ensued.[7] The scheme became capable of offering remedies in respect of discharge and lesser forms of discipline imposed too hastily and too harshly.

It is now easy to see why this aspect of grievance arbitration has come to be seen as a very progressive development. This perception is fuelled, first, by the historic employer opposition to it, second, by the fact that many workers have been able to retain jobs which they otherwise might have lost, and third, by the fact that it constitutes such a clear step up from the ancient common law régime.[8] As a result, trade unions continue to see much merit in the concept of grievance arbitration, even though they may quibble about many of its features. Understandable as this is, however, the outcomes of discharge and discipline cases should not afford unionists the comfort they appear to take from the scheme.

"Just Cause" Clause Applied

The employer's right to monitor, command and control its workforce has not been undermined in a profound way. Indeed, while some power to act unilaterally has been lost, it might be said that overall employer control has been enhanced by the grievance arbitration decisions which have interpreted the "just cause" clauses. Carefully worked-out refinements of the classic individual contract of employment duties imposed by the reactionary judiciary in eighteenth- and nineteenth-century England — the duty to obey, the duty to exercise appropriate skill, and the duty to act in good faith and fidelity — have come to be accepted by arbitration boards as valid bases for the exercise of managerial control over their employees. For instance, the following have been accepted as behaviour that justifies the imposition of discipline on workers:

- failure to notify an employer of absence from work
- absence from work due to incarceration
- abuse of leave of absence
- drinking
- conflict of interest (for example, working for another employer, not necessarily a competitor, in the employee's own time)
- failure to explain criminal charges
- damage to employer's property
- failure to disclose the misconduct of other employees
- failure to get along with other workers
- fighting with other employees or supervisors, or threatening them
- falsification of records
- insolent behaviour or obscene language
- insubordination
- lateness
- leaving work without permission
- off-duty conduct involving criminal behaviour
- unacceptable work performance[9]

This does not mean, of course, that each instance of such behaviour will permit the discharge of offending employees. Arbitrators are to inquire into the nature of the offence, the needs and problems of the offender and the appropriateness of management's reaction to the offence, given the employer's productive needs. This often leads to the imposition of less draconian punishments than dismissal. As a consequence, employees have been educated into accepting that appropriate discipline may be imposed by management. Further, employers have learned that they can calibrate punishment more finely, that they need not discharge an employee whenever she displeases them. Overall, this jurisprudence has had a surprising result: in real terms the employers' ability to control their workers' behaviour has been enhanced.

"Obey Now, Grieve Later"

Arbitrators have demonstrated an unflagging adherence to the idea that managerial prerogative is to be left as unmodified as possible. They start from the premise that, when an employer gives a command, the employee must execute it. The rationale for this was laid down as early as 1944. In his very well known *Ford Motor Company* decision, U.S. arbitrator Shulman wrote:

> An industrial plant is not a debating society. Its object is production. When a controversy arises, production cannot wait for exhaustion of the grievance procedure. While that procedure is being pursued, production must go on and someone must have the authority to direct the manner in which it is to go on until the controversy is settled. That authority is vested in supervision. It must be vested there because the responsibility for production is also vested there: and responsibility must be accompanied by authority. It is fairly vested there because the grievance procedure is capable of adequately recompensing employees for abuse of authority by supervision.[10]

This "obey now, grieve later" rule has become the credo of grievance arbitrators. It has far-reaching implications for workers generally, and most especially for those who have been discharged. While the burden of proving that the summary dismissal or the imposition of any other discipline was justified rests on the employer throughout the grievance process, the employee remains punished until the matter is settled. That is, the initial and heaviest part of the burden of the employer's decision is borne by the employee, regardless of the nature of the offence or the personal characteristics of the employee. While it is true that, eventually, the employer may have to pay the employee for work not done while suspended (and which another employee was paid to do during that time), the employee is much more likely to be adversely affected than the employer — even if, in the end, the employer is held to have been totally wrong.

By way of example, take a typical situation in which an employer dismisses an employee. The employee will have no income from her employment until the matter is settled. This may be a long time indeed, if the dispute goes to arbitration. Until fairly recently, the period between the dispute that led to the dismissal and the arbitration hearing often was as long as eight months in Ontario.[11] This time-lag was so scandalous that a form of expedited arbitration has been established. But it is not always used, and already shows signs of inefficiency.[12] In some jurisdictions, no such expedited arbitration is available. In British Columbia, the time lapse between dispute and date of decision used to be 7.9 months.[13] Again, this may have been ameliorated somewhat by remedial legislation, but, like all administrative reforms designed to free up clogged courts, procedural changes of this kind do not retain their efficacy for very long.

In any event, it is not fanciful to assume that an employee who has been dismissed may have to wait some eight months to receive an arbitration award. A fairly common kind of result is one which reinstates her without any entitlement to back pay because a judgement was made that, while the discharge was too harsh, the employer did have good cause for imposing some discipline. If the worker's earnings are $20,000 per annum, the effective fine imposed by this award is $13,333. There are very few criminal offences for which fines of this order are imposed. Large fines are possible in tax fraud cases, and many crimes do lead to imprisonment, but typically, they are crimes against persons or property, offences that have a different moral stigma than "offences" committed by workers on the job, such as lateness or insolence. More analogous to serious criminal offences would be breaches of industrial health and safety standards by employers which lead to the death of a worker. Yet the fines imposed on employers are typically on the order of $2,000 to $5,000.[14]

Smoothing Out Managerial Rights

Because of these effects, the threat of punishment to workers is immense, even if redress may be obtained eventually. Their understandable fear of discipline is exacerbated because employers do not often lose when challenged before an arbitration board. In discharge cases (and discipline cases constitute more than a third of all cases taken to arbitration), the discharge is upheld 46.5 percent of the time. In 35.7 percent of cases, arbitrators substitute lesser discipline. Whether these are categorized as victories, losses, or something in between depends on who is making the assessment. In only 17.8 percent of discharge cases are dismissed employees reinstated with full back pay. For unions, then — not to speak of workers — the results are disappointing. In fewer than one-fifth of the cases do the unions score complete, unequivocal victories, as opposed to clear wins in nearly half of the cases for employers. It is only when partial successes (reinstatement with or without some back pay, or the like) are added to absolute successes that unions and employees fare roughly as well as employers. But any claim of parity is misleading. Partial wins for unions are also partial wins for employers, making the claim of a fifty-fifty split dubious.[15]

Thus, in the one area in which trade unions think they have made a major breakthrough, the books have to be read in a peculiar way to uphold the claim. And this is not the only negative aspect of the grievance arbitration régime in respect of disciplinary issues.

An important outcome — perhaps the most important — of the arbitration boards' efforts to be more flexible and worker-friendly than their judicial counterparts is that, over time, they have tailored a set of punishments that are considered "right" for particular instances of employee "misbehaviour." Employers have learned to use these with telling effect. The result is a much more sophisticated system of control than the brute exercise of power which existed under a more primitive Taylorist system. It is almost as if Foucault's model of discipline and punishment, with its reliance on criminalization, has been given real life in the workplace. Foucault's thesis is that the goals of the powerful are to be furthered by the punishment of deviants. The lesson that others are to learn is that they are not to challenge the status quo if they want to preserve their security and safety.[16]

It is appropriate to analogize arbitral review of discipline cases with Foucault's analysis of criminal law. The language of arbitral jurisprudence bristles with references to "discipline" and "offence." Discharge is seen as the equivalent of capital punishment.[17] The scheme of lesser penalties, which escalate in severity with the nature and number of offences, has been characterized as being the essence of an elaborate *corrective-discipline* mechanism. Indeed, George Adams, a well-known scholar and arbitrator (now a judge), has characterized the scheme as an educative, penal system. In tracing the development of the discipline criteria by arbitrators, he noted with obvious approval the evolution of a form of corrective discipline that he says is

> tailored to allow the offender to learn from his mistake. It is also sensitive to the fact that an employer usually has to spend money in recruiting employees and, following the recruitment, it is customary for the employer to bear associated training costs whether in the form of formalized training programs or, less visibly, through inadequate productivity and initial employee mistakes. This being so, the employer suffers a capital loss when an employee is dismissed, but emotional and personal considerations very often obscure these economic implications. Corrective discipline is a concept which, by limiting an employer's access to the dismissal remedy, guards against unnecessary capital losses of this kind.[18]

Adams also points out that tailoring of the discipline to the offence will have an appropriate chilling effect on the rest of the workforce, just as the imposition of criminal law penalties on errant citizens serves to educate the rest of us into accepting society's rules. He goes on to note that employers do not have to discharge employees to achieve productive stability and the maintenance of their right to command. Well-applied and appropriately measured lesser discipline will help to "identify those employees who are unlikely to profit from another opportunity," and "ensures that those who abide by the rules will not be disadvantaged. It preserves the morale of the law-abiding citizen ... A final purpose is to achieve *conformity* to workplace norms by permanently removing the offender from this job and replacing him with someone who will *conform*."[19]

By and large, trade unions have learned to live with arbitral approaches that do not question the continued right of employers to discipline and discharge individual employees. Unions fight the cases on the understanding that the long list of causes which arbitrators say might justify management's disciplinary actions is no longer to be contested. Only the facts of the case, the issue as to whether or not the appropriate procedures were followed and as to whether or not the amount of punishment imposed was justified, are usually disputed. The right of the employer to discipline, or the grounds on which it may do so, are rarely contested by unions. In this way, unions send workers a message of what is acceptable industrial behaviour. This is awkward for Canada's trade union movement. Certainly it detracts from the force of the argument that it is in the area of discharge and discipline in particular that the grievance arbitration process has allowed workers and unions to make a major breakthrough, one which has enhanced industrial democracy.[20]

The Employer's Right to Control the Size of Its Workforce

Unions can bargain for job security by obtaining provisions which prohibit lay-offs or the contracting out of bargaining-unit work. But, as is shown in Chapter 3, up to now unions have been relatively unsuccessful on these fronts. In the absence of such specific provisions, grievance arbitrators might have given a narrow reading to management's residual power to order temporary or permanent lay-offs for economic reasons. This would have reduced the employers' right to change the size of their workforces as they see fit. But this has not happened. Arbitrators' decisions, if anything, have increased the control which employers can exercise over the size of the bargaining unit.

This is well demonstrated by the *Air Care* case.[21] The collective agreement contained the following provisions:

Article 2. Purpose of Agreement
2.01 It is the intent and purpose of this Agreement to maintain cordial relations in the Plant, to clearly define hours of work and other working conditions, to provide a method for the orderly adjustment of differences and grievances, and to protect the safety and health of employees.

Article 4. Management Rights
4.01 The Union recognizes the inherent right of the Company to manage the business and agrees that this right shall remain

unimpaired except insofar as the express provisions of this Agreement stipulate otherwise.

Always provided that any dispute as to whether any Rules and Regulations are reasonable, or any dispute involving claims of discrimination against any employee in the application of such Rules and Regulations, shall be subject to the grievance procedure of this Agreement.

Article 7. Arbitration

7.03 The decision of the majority shall be the decision of the Arbitration Board, and if there is no majority, the decision of the Chairman shall be the decision of the Board, but the jurisdiction of the Arbitration Board shall be limited to deciding the matter at issue within the existing provisions of the Agreement and in no event shall the Arbitration Board have the power to add to, subtract from, alter or amend this Agreement in any respect.

Article 10. Shortage of Work

10.01 In all cases of lay-offs, because of shortage of work, employees shall be listed by occupation in order or length of service, the last hired at the bottom of the list. Proceeding upwards from the bottom of the list, the following factors will be considered:

(a) Service.

(b) Knowledge, efficiency and ability to perform the work.

(c) Physical fitness.

Where factors (b) and (c) are relatively equal, factor (a) shall govern.

Article 23. Hours of Work

23.01 A day is a twenty-four (24) hour period beginning with the start of the employee's shift.

23.02 (a) The work week will be forty (40) hours consisting of eight (8) hours per day, Monday to Friday inclusively.

23.09 Nothing in this Agreement shall be read or construed as a guarantee of hours of work per day or week or a guarantee of days of work per week.

When the employer was faced with a downturn in the market, it relied on the management rights and hours of work clauses to justify its reduction of everyone's work week by one working day. The union grieved the issue.

The union did not question the employer's decision-making power to provide less paid work when the employer thought market conditions warranted this. The United Steelworkers of America local's concern was that the employer had used this legitimate power wrongly. It argued that the employer had instituted a lay-off and that, therefore, it was bound by the lay-off and accompanying seniority clauses. In short, it was the union's position that a few workers should bear the brunt of the employer's otherwise justifiable decision to downsize the workforce, rather than have the unavoidable loss of paid work shared equally by all the members of the collective bargaining unit. The contradictory position in which the union is put in this kind of situation is self-evident.

The employer's ultimate control is not at issue in these cases. The reason for this is that, very early on in arbitral decision-making history, it was held by arbitrators that, in the absence of a specific clause to the contrary, employers are deemed to have retained the right to reduce the workload of all workers, to contract out part of the work and/or to lay off some members of the bargaining unit if, in the business judgement of the employer, market conditions call for such downsizing. The landmark decision was that of arbitrator H.W. Arthurs in a case called *Russelsteel*.[22] His rationale was that, where there was no specific language in the collective agreement dealing with these issues, the implication was that the parties had agreed that they should be ruled by the prevailing practices in industry. In his view, the existing climate of industrial relations was such that management should be presumed to have retained the power to manipulate its workforce as it saw fit. The assumption was that the advent of modern collective bargaining had not led to any change in employers' control over the size of bargaining units. This approach, which is still the dominant one, squarely puts the burden on unions to attack this prerogative of management at the bargaining table. Failure to do so leaves them only with the kind of Byzantine arguments that they had to resort to in *Air Care*.

This does not mean that Canada's union movement never wins arbitration decisions in these kinds of cases. For instance, in the *Air*

Care case itself the grievance arbitration board found for the union. This decision eventually was overturned by the Supreme Court of Canada. Usually, arbitral decisions do not go to the Supreme Court. But the fact is that even if the initial union victory obtained at arbitration in *Air Care* had stood up, it would have been something of a Pyrrhic one: the only fettering of the employers' prerogative would have been the application of the seniority clause to the lay-off. Winning on this basis reveals something about the ambivalent position which the logic of collective bargaining, and of the arbitral jurisprudence which reflects it, creates for unions.

Unions frequently claim that the now standard insertion of seniority clauses into agreements is one of the great benefits yielded by collective bargaining. Such clauses inhibit the employers' right to choose capriciously between workers when it comes to such issues as promotion, demotion, overtime, retraining and lay-offs. At the same time, seniority provisions do not affect the right of the employer to lay off. Further, they provide employers with a rational scheme with which to justify the way in which lay-offs, promotions, demotions and other such decisions are to be made. This stops employers from being embarrassed by injudicious decisions made by low-level management. In part, Feller was referring to this when he pointed out the advantages of arbitration generally, and of seniority clauses specifically, for *employers*.[23]

What is clear is that, in the absence of a win at the bargaining table, the unfettered right of the employer to manipulate its workforce, subject only to limitations imposed by the seniority system, makes for difficult choices by the union. After all, it is not obvious that the application of seniority rules reflects the actual needs of employees. The least senior employees may frequently be in the worst position to deal with the costs of a temporary lay-off. Given the need to restrain the otherwise untrammelled power of the employer to deal with its workforce as it wills, it is clear why unions bargain for seniority. But the fact that reliance on such clauses often is the only rational argument they have in subsequent arbitrations puts them in an invidious position and forces them to make decisions which are not necessarily democratic or compassionate.[24]

From business's perspective, the ability of employers to lay off or to contract out work as needed leaves it with great flexibility. Moreover, many of the costs of these lay-offs are picked up by society at large. Unemployment insurance benefits are paid to the laid-off workforce. When workers are laid off temporarily they must make do in this way until they are recalled. This suits employers, particularly in Canada, where they make smaller contributions to unemployment and social benefits packages than do similarly placed employers in other OECD countries. Temporary lay-offs, therefore, are relatively costless to Canadian employers. From the viewpoint of business in Canada, it is cheaper to reduce the payroll than it is to change work practices.[25] A few well-placed unions, such as the Steelworkers and the Autoworkers, have made it somewhat more expensive for employers to lay workers off temporarily by winning longer notice periods and richer supplementary unemployment benefits in their collective agreements; however, as we saw in Chapter 3, this kind of protection is the exception rather than the rule.

At the end of the day, then, unions have not been able to reduce management's power in this critical area of job security. Grievance arbitrators have done little to beef up workers' rights where raw economic power fails. To the contrary, they have legitimated a mindset that makes it increasingly difficult to challenge the employer's prerogative in this crucial sphere of control over job rights.

The Trade Union Dilemma

Grievance arbitration has blunted the ability of employers to engage in arbitrary or discriminatory practices. This is progress. Yet real difficulties remain, and trade unions do not seem to be looking actively for alternatives to the scheme. There are a number of related reasons for this.

Inevitably, because collective agreements are detailed and vary a great deal in emphasis, there is a "wilderness of single instances" to fight. And, for many trade unionists, a fight to correct a wrong is an end in itself. The fact that they do win a number of grievances tends to confirm their occasionally wavering belief in the possibilities of the system. There appears to be very little reflection on the quality of the victories or, equally important, on the effects that arbitration has on relations between unions and their members.

The dynamic of the grievance arbitration system is such that it deepens the tendency to replace the oft-stated aspiration that workers should control their trade unions with its opposite. Collective bargaining Canadian-style generally gives the trade union and its officials a role which drives a wedge between it and its members. Trade union professionals have something of a stake in the maintenance of this gulf, because their prestige and political clout are fortified by their position as needed specialists in a highly technocratic system.

The manner in which collective agreements have come to be interpreted by grievance arbitration boards demands that a great deal of sophistication be brought to the task of fighting grievances. Trade unions have responded to this need. In the early stages of a dispute's resolution the workers and their elected grievance committees are directly involved in the attempts to arrive at a resolution. At this level, lack of technocratic know-how is not a major problem. If no settlement is reached, however, these rank-and-file people are joined and, eventually, replaced by members of the cadre of experts and professionals which trade unions have developed to deal with grievances.

The need to have these professionals available stems from the fact that the grievance arbitration system has not turned out to be the informal, non-legalistic process it was envisaged to be. Often the chair of a board will be a lawyer. Even if this is not so, the arguments to be made by the parties will revolve around the meaning of particular words in a collective agreement. This meaning may have to be found by reference to the prior interpretation given to them in disputes which arise under the same agreement and/or that agreement's antecedents. It may require looking at the interpretation of similar clauses in other agreements entered into by different people. Often it demands giving the words content by reference to the actual practices in the workplace where the dispute arose. Procedural questions are frequently raised: whether the parties are prohibited from raising a point because it has been decided between them on another occasion, or because the conduct of one of the parties has foreclosed the issue (the vexed estoppel question); whether the words of a provision are ambiguous enough on their face to warrant reference to past practice of the parties (the oft-litigated past practice question); and so on. In short, the kinds of arguments which are the meat and potatoes of the adversary system are also daily fare in the grievance arbitration process. Inevitably, lawyers are brought in to fight these legal-type issues. Otherwise, unionists must make themselves legal experts. The role which workers involved in the dispute are permitted to play during the actual arbitration hearing is thereby minimized.

The culture of legalism has other impacts, both material and ideological. Grievance arbitration takes longer and costs more than it ought to do. In 1990, a fully fought-out discharge case in Ontario cost a union somewhere between $3,000 and $4,000.[26] Attempts to simplify the system in Ontario and British Columbia have been only partially successful. The problem of delay and costs remains. Unions have many grievances to bring every year.

It is difficult to get accurate data. In part this is due to the fact that unions keep poor records. For instance, all the International Woodworkers' Association of Canada was able to tell the authors is that the money spent on grievance arbitration as a percentage of budget varied from local to local; Local 78 of the International Association of Machinists and Aerospace Workers could give no information at all; nor could the International Service Employees' Union and the Canadian Automobile Workers, although it stated that it probably was not a major financial burden. The Public Service Alliance of Canada's national office, which deals with one specialized board, advised that $1.6 million (out of a budget of $30 million) was spent on grievances, while the same union's regional unit (Employment and Immigration) was unable to give any idea of the amounts spent on arbitration. In part, the paucity of data is due to the fact that it is hard to calculate the real costs of arbitration, as the time of paid union staff allocated to it is not separated out from time spent on their other functions.

As well, the number of grievances which arise during the life of a collective agreement varies with the style of management and the nature of the enterprise. Further, the proportion of disputes which actually get taken to arbitration differ from place to place. There are a great number of grievances and arbitrations. The *Monthly Bulletin*, a report published by the Ontario Ministry of Labour's Office of Arbitration, indicates that there are some 1,800 arbitral decisions handed down every year, not counting those in the public sector. At an individual union level, the regional office of the Public Service Alliance of Canada (Employment and Immigration) advised the authors that 1,800 grievances a year arose in a unit of 6,000 members.[27] And, in the Post Office, it appears to be management's intention to confront the union over everything and to render it immobile by burdening it with grievance cases. The Canadian Union of Postal Workers spends a staggering amount of money on defending its members' collective agreement rights. In the fiscal year 1989–90, it expended $4,372,191 on arbitrations. In the first four months of 1990–91, it referred 10,434 matters, raising some 13,636 issues, to arbitration. While this is an extreme circumstance, it is clear that in general there is a costly preoccupation with the grievance arbitration process. In addition, the fact that grievance arbitration more often than not is held in hired hotel rooms, away from the workplace, makes the process relatively invisible and inaccessible to the workers.

The legalism that gives the scheme a patina of legitimacy also affects the way unions think about their role and the way in which they treat their members' complaints. In particular, they have come to see the limits of what may be asked for as being properly defined by arbitral jurisprudence. This influences what cases they take up and the extent to which they fight them.

Unions, of course, do take up causes which might seem quixotic to disinterested observers. They may see them as issues of principle. Sometimes the internal politics of the union may dictate that they pursue apparently unattainable results. In addition, and more frequently, they take up questions of policy arising out of the collective agreement, even though nothing the employer has done has given rise to a dispute. They do this in the hope that they will get an interpretation which will help the workers they represent in the future, or that it will provide them with ammunition for the development of future negotiation stances. Although there are quite a number of occasions when unions are motivated by these kinds of concerns, the arbitrations to which they give rise constitute a small part of the grievance arbitration caseload. Most of the grievances arise out of disputes between management and workers over work practices, the interpretation of benefits clauses and, very importantly, disciplinary issues. In deciding whether or not to arbitrate a dispute, costs loom large. While unions will fight cases that are likely to result in losses, they will want to avoid this as much as possible. They prefer to go to arbitration with winnable cases. In determining what is winnable, unions will be guided by their understanding of grievance arbitration law. Consequently, they often will seek the opinion of the lawyers whom they hire.

Lawyers, quite naturally, see the process from their professional perspective, which is inherently conservative. This is true even of lawyers who see themselves as progressive and have chosen to act for trade unions. As a group, they do not have a vision of workers' control and greater participatory rights for workers, nor do they question the fundamental underpinnings of the scheme. This limits the possibility of making radical breakthroughs by means of grievance arbitration, let alone the likelihood of expanding Canadian industrial democracy by the promotion of more direct worker participation in decision making.

The fact that unions choose what ought and what ought not to be arbitrated has, as we noted in respect of discharge cases, an inhibiting effect on the rank-and-file. By their actions — fighting or not fighting a grievance — unions tell their members the extent to which they may resist their employers' demands. This is not just a function of a false consciousness engendered in unthinking trade union officials by the implicit premises of the system. No, the grievance arbitration model is posited on the explicit idea that unions will serve a monitoring function.

A dispute about the meaning of the agreement — even when it is between a foreman and an individual worker — is a dispute between the parties to that agreement, namely, the employer and the union. As a matter of law, it is the union's grievance, not the worker's. This is, of course, the reason why it is for the union to decide whether or not to arbitrate a dispute. This distortion of reality gives rise to unhappy tensions in a variety of circumstances. Two of the most common of these are detailed in the following paragraphs.

Sometimes when a union chooses to support a worker's claim against the employer by grieving the employer's decision, success may adversely affect the rights of other workers. To overcome this problem, arbitrators and courts have decreed that workers who might be affected in this way must be given independent standing at the grievance proceeding. For instance, in one case an employer promoted some employees. The union thought that the employer had ignored the seniority provisions of the agreement and brought a grievance on behalf of the employees who, it claimed, should have been promoted on the basis of their seniority. It was held that the employees whom the employer had promoted in the first place had a right to participate as individual parties in the hearing because they would be adversely affected by the union's success.[28] In short, the system makes it clear that the union cannot represent all of the workers equally when it fights arbitrations.

Similarly, when a trade union determines that a worker's claim ought *not* to be pursued, a possibility arises that a worker with a justifiable grievance will be denied her rights. Legislation has been enacted to overcome this difficulty. It imposes a duty of fair representation on the union. While it does not require that unions pursue every claim that workers wish to make, they must be able to show that they did not act arbitrarily, discriminatorily or in bad faith in any refusal.[29] Even though very few unions have been found to have acted in breach of this legislative duty, it causes unions great concern. This is so because, as we have seen, the logic of the scheme requires them to reject many claims. Furthermore, any inquiry into a breach of fair representation may lead to a public hearing by a labour relations board into the internal affairs of the union, a most delicate and sensitive issue.

At the end of the day, both the actual workings of arbitration and the legislative duty of fair representation serve to delimit the role of the trade unions and the possibilities of grievance arbitration. The union is made responsible to contain its workers' demands. Policy-makers and overseeing administrative agencies have acknowledged this explicitly. Their aim is to ensure that not all irritations and vexations in the workplace will lead to costly grievance arbitrations and unrest. Thus, the Ontario Labour Relations Board noted that giving trade unions the legislative right to determine whether or not to grieve, and to what extent, guarantees that "frivolous and un-meritorious grievance issues can be quickly resolved without the cost and time involved in further steps of the grievance process or at arbitration." This will bolster the union's standing "as the statutory agent and as co-author of the bargaining agreement in representing employees in the enforcement of that agreement." This is necessary, the Board went on to say, because the ability of an "individual employee ... to compel arbitration of his grievance regardless of merit would vastly encumber the settlement machinery required by the Act and hamper the interests of industrial peace." Not only that, but "*it would also destroy the employer's confidence in the union's authority*" (emphasis added).[30]

The union's role as a manager of discontent is in part established by the legal and political requirement that it is to control workers' militancy during the life of an agreement and to promote localized bargaining rather than solidaristic action. It is now also clear that this role is further cemented by the way in which the union is expected to discharge its legal responsibilities in the grievance arbitration scheme. This cannot help but have an influence on what the union sees and promotes as viable bargaining targets. Certainly, the relatively poor clauses protecting against contracting out, lay-offs and harm from technological innovation which unions have sought and managed to obtain — after forty years of experience with "free collective bargaining" — are in some measure reflective of the disempowering effect of the acceptance of arbitral ideology.

In part, unions have come to accept their ambivalent role in the grievance system as a given because it has given them new responsibilities and a new status. And, even though grievance arbitration boards have been jealous of preserving the residual rights of employers, unions can point to substantial gains obtained through the grievance mechanism. The requirement of more even-handed treatment of workers by employers, the right to be given some advance notice of managerial decisions to change work processes and work allocation, and the development of novel, substantive remedies in respect of wrongfully applied discipline do represent real advances. But, as we have seen, they fall short of giving workers the kind of quality of worklife to which a more mature Fordist polity would have permitted them to aspire.

While it probably made sense for Canada's unions to accept serious limitations on the right to strike in order to get legalized collective bargaining rights in the late 1940s, all the benefits of this compromise were reaped very early. No serious qualitative advances have been yielded by the collective bargaining and grievance system since the early seventies.[31] This was to be expected, given that the compromise was based on an understanding that there was to be no challenge to the employers' right to control the running of their enterprises. Both the bargaining and grievance systems are posited on the liberal premise that they are to be mediating mechanisms between disputants who share the ideology of consensus politics. These being the terms of the entente, the fact that it is theoretically possible for the union to bargain about anything and to demand much greater worker control from arbitrators has remained just that: a theoretical possibility.

The continued acceptance of, and support for, a liberal pluralist scheme makes less and less sense for unions. Both the state agencies which administer it and the employers who are party to it are bent on pursuing philosophical and economic goals which are antithetical to liberal pluralism. They want to restore a form of competitive capitalism in which collective labour is, at best, a nuisance and at worst, unacceptable. Yet employers continue to use the language and rhetoric of a shared ideology. Unions must not be fooled by this. They must continue to push grievance arbitration to its limits. But the best they can expect is that their existing rights will not be eroded all that much. They should educate their workers so that they come to understand that the existing mechanism only permits them to fight rearguard battles. To reach anything like an acceptable plateau of industrial citizenship requires structural changes in the capital-labour dispute-settlement machinery. This can only be achieved through direct political intervention. Fragmented collective bargaining and grieving will not do the trick.

Getting the Minimum in Canada: Boosting Private Ordering

The Unprotected Sectors

A single-minded concentration on collective bargaining leads to an incomplete understanding of Canadian labour relations. First, it is not a monolithic mechanism of adjustment; it has many variants and many variegated outcomes. Second, much of the labour market is subject to completely different mechanisms of regulation. Third, the way in which the non-unionized sectors are regulated has an impact on the way in which collective bargaining works.

To begin, then, collective bargaining is the most efficient way for labour to obtain gains. But, as Chapter 2 showed, the gains it yields are not evenly spread. There are many reasons for this. One is that Canada has a vast secondary labour market, much of which is unionized. It features small employers, many of whom operate in an intensely competitive environment. Their workers, unionized or not, may work for rates which may be as much as 40 percent less than those which are earned in the unionized primary sectors.[1] In any event, only 36 percent of Canadian workers belong to unions, and only 50 percent are covered by some form of collective agreement. Fully half the population in the paid workforce, then, does not directly receive any of the protections which unionization may bring. Such flow-ons as do spread to the unorganized sector do so in an uneven and uncertain way. For the most part, people there have to rely on their feeble individual bargaining power and on those support systems that the state has seen fit to provide. The absence of an efficient mechanism to ensure that gains made by labour's "aristocracy" flow through evenly has had a dramatic impact on the unprotected sectors.

The approach of Canadian governments to labour markets makes no serious attempt to protect workers who cannot protect themselves. For the old, young, and women of all ages, this has been a particularly vicious strategy. They are employed in disproportionate numbers in those sectors in which, traditionally, there has been very little unionization, and therefore they have had to rely on minimum standards provided by governments. If anything, this regrettable failure has been exacerbated by the way in which the Canadian economy is being restructured. New entrants to the workforce, predominantly the young and women, are finding employment in the service sectors.[2] Within these disadvantaged groups, there are further differentiations of hardship, as some are even less able to defend themselves than others. Women and part-time workers, two largely overlapping categories, are particularly vulnerable.

The part-time workforce is growing. Since 1981, the number of people who want full-time work but who have been forced to accept part-time work has grown to number three out of every ten people. Part-time workers obviously take home less pay. Moreover, their hourly wage rates are lower than those of equivalent full-time employees. This difference is most pronounced when unionized and non-unionized sectors are compared. The average rate for part-time unionized workers in 1987 was $10.68, as opposed to $5.84 for part-time non-unionized workers.[3]

Women are doubly hit. Not only are many women employed in the mostly non-unionized secondary and emerging tertiary sectors of the economy, but they form the bulk of the part-time work world. In 1985, 72 percent of all part-time employees were women; more than one in four employed women worked part-time, while only 8 percent of males worked part-time. The single fastest growing component of the labour force has been female part-time employment, increasing by 84 percent between 1975 and 1985. In absolute numbers, by 1985, there were 1,263,000 females employed part-time. Compared to the 84 percent growth in part-time employment for women, there was only a 31 percent increase in full-time employment for women.[4]

The poverty of outcomes for those at the bottom end of the labour market suggests that the political economy of Canada puts Canada at one end of the spectrum of welfare state models constructed by Esping-Andersen. He notes that "each model expresses a peculiar synthesis between welfare and efficiency." He characterizes Canada as a country that has adopted a "liberal" model, as have the United States and Australia. The liberal nation's goal, as he puts it, is to nurture the market's autonomy and to offer a minimum of social rights, lest the work incentive be impaired.[5] The plight of the disadvantaged in Canada, and the outcomes and possibilities of collective bargaining, bear out Esping-Andersen's characterization of Canada.

But, just as collective bargaining is not just a coercive-restrictive institution but also one which has autonomous and reformist elements, Canadian governments' interventionist strategies in respect of the social wage are also nuanced. Indeed, it is fair to say that many Canadians would be angered by a classification which makes them sound ungenerous. They do not see themselves as being at the minimalist end of welfare states. Rather, they think of themselves as being closer to the social democratic end of Esping-Andersen's spectrum, one in which there is a focus on equality in terms of social citizenship, regardless of market imperatives. That many Canadians hold something like this view is in large part due to the fact that they tend to compare themselves to their American counterparts. The perception is that if the United States, with its blatant racism, poor minimum wages, lack of adequate health care and an overt anti-union approach, is seen as a liberal welfare state, then surely Canada's institutions reflect adherence to a more progressive model. From this vantage point, Canadian policy-makers and politicians tend to describe our system as one that evinces the compassion and social consciousness that are part and parcel of a mature welfare system. This self-characterization is an illusion.

Canadian governments have remained wedded to the idea that both welfare and efficiency are to be created primarily by private sector actors, relying on the anarchy of the market. This is reflected in the fact that Canadian governments have been slow to intervene with market operations. We have already noted how Keynesian measures were introduced piecemeal and late in Canada and, when they were introduced, it was done in such a manner as to leave the private sector's *modus operandi* as little disturbed as possible. This is not to say that there are any *a priori* reasons why willing governments could not set up universalistic régimes to reduce Canada's entrenched reliance on the private production of welfare. Indeed, when NDP governments are elected provincially, they start off with an agenda to do just that. They are quickly faced with vigorous opposition based on the deeply held ideology of the superiority of free markets. The Rae government in Ontario has come face to face with this reality; it looms large because, in the last decade, neo-conservative governments throughout the land have launched a vigorous ideological assault on Canada's welfare system. The situation is grave because, as we now detail, that welfare system has been an underdeveloped one.

The Minimum Wage

Canada's governments have legislated wages below which people cannot be hired to work. This was necessary because the market, left to its own devices, caused people to work for wages which were below a living wage. The minimum wage rates established in Canada always have been very low. Canadian governments at all levels have embraced the private sector's argument that minimum wage rates which actually lift people out of poverty distort the market and lead to increased unemployment. It has been accepted, however, that the minimum wage rate must be more than the money given to welfare recipients. If the minimum wage rate does not provide sufficient incentive for people to work because they would be nearly as well off by putting themselves on the welfare rolls, the pool of available workers would be reduced, diminishing the employers' capacity to exploit competition amongst workers. Accordingly, Canadian authorities have done no more than is absolutely necessary to overcome this problem, which is referred to as the welfare trap.[6] As welfare rates are low, minimum wage rates have been kept very low. Despite periodic increases, they always have constituted a small fraction of the average industrial wage, and things are getting worse.

In 1974, the average provincial minimum wage was around half the average manufacturing hourly rate; by the mid-eighties the average minimum wage was calculated to be 41 percent of that average hourly rate.[7] Put another way, between 1976 and 1984, minimum wages increased by only 40 percent while the cost of living increased by 100 percent.[8] Gunderson, Muszynski and Keck have found that, starting from a very low base, over the last two decades the drop in the minimum wage in real dollars has been between 20 and 30 percent.[9] The evidence is incontestable: in this sphere, the intervention by Canadian governments has done little to redress serious market imbalances. This has had a significant impact on the lives of many workers and on the union movement's overall bargaining position.

Even in Canada's most prosperous jurisdiction, Ontario, 500,000 employees receive the minimum wage rate or only slightly more.[10] This represents approximately 10 percent of Ontario's workforce. In 1985, in Canada as a whole, over one million people (9 percent of the workforce) worked at or near the minimum wage level.[11] Given that most people who earn below the average industrial wage may be considered low-income Canadians, as defined by the National Council on Poverty, it can be seen that the guarantees provided by the minimum-wage legislation leave many working Canadians pitifully poor.[12] As is to be expected, a majority (67 percent) of those earning minimum wage rates are women. In 1985, all women who earned minimum wage rates in British Columbia lived below the Statistics Canada poverty line.[13] Young people below the age of eighteen are also treated very badly. This is so because, typically, the minimum wage rate to which they are entitled will be lower than that set for adult workers. In addition, they frequently are able to obtain only part-time work. This means that they receive none, or very few, of the benefits attached to a full-time employment contract. Youth constitute a large source of cheap labour.

The result of these state policies is that many of the individuals and families classified as "low income" in Canada are in the paid workforce.[14] The National Council of Welfare, in its 1988 report, showed that most poor families "are headed by persons who work or who are actively searching for a job. In 1986, 55 per cent of low-income families were headed by men or women in the labour force and 26.7 per cent were led by someone who worked 49 weeks or longer." Many of these workers are clearly in the secondary or tertiary labour markets. Not surprisingly, four in ten families headed by women are poor, compared to one in ten by men.

Canada's wage rates reflect the desire of governments to support the cause of employers who have an interest in having workers fight each other for poorly paid jobs. It is an indicator of how feebly Canada has embraced the notion that workers should have the kind of income that could help link mass consumption to mass production. This approach to minimum wages reinforces the argument that it is export-led growth, rather than a modern form of Keynesianism, that has been the primary focus of policy-makers. This also is reflected in the way in which the unemployment insurance scheme, the other side of this labour-market coin, has been administered.

Unemployment Insurance

Canada's economic strategy has made it a mass-unemployment society. The costs of this high rate of unemployment have fallen disproportionately on workers. Federal governments have designed an unemployment benefits scheme that provides for some income maintenance, rather than for total lost-income replacement. The income maintenance benefits have been kept at relatively low levels, which are being lowered even further as the drive towards hyperliberalism intensifies. One of the chief objectives of the scheme always has been to discipline the workforce. This is being reinforced in order to create an even more competitive labour market.

The Persistence of Unemployment in Canada

The table reproduced here makes it clear that levels of unemployment in Canada always have been comparatively high. While in recent years there have been mounting levels of unemployment in France and Germany, this is a new phenomenon for these countries in the post-war period. By contrast, high levels of unemployment always have been tolerated in Canada. Diane Bellemare and Lise Poulin Simon convincingly argue that what this indicates is that full employment policies have been pursued with some seriousness of intent in these Western European nations, whereas the contrary has been true in Canada.[16]

The Focus of Canada's Unemployment Insurance Scheme

Until 1988, people eligible for unemployment insurance benefits were entitled to 60 percent of their earnings, provided this did not

Table 8.1
Unemployment Rates Standardized by the OECD
Selected Years

	1968	1970	1972	1974	1976	1978	1980	1981	1982	1983	1984
W. Germany	1.5	0.8	0.8	1.6	3.7	3.5	3.0	4.4	6.1	7.5	7.3
Austria	2.0	1.4	1.2	1.4	1.8	2.1	1.9	2.5	3.5	4.2	–
Norway	2.1	1.6	1.7	1.5	1.8	1.8	1.7	2.0	2.6	3.1	3.2
Sweden	2.2	1.5	2.7	2.0	1.6	2.2	2.0	2.5	2.5	2.5	3.2
Canada	4.4	5.6	6.2	5.3	7.1	8.3	7.4	7.5	10.9	11.8	11.3

Source: Adapted from Diane Bellemare and Lise Poulin Simon, "Full Employment: A Strategy and an Objective for Economic Policy," in D. Cameron and A. Sharpe, eds., *Policies for Full Employment* (Ottawa: Canadian Council on Social Development, 1989), p. 73.

exceed a set amount. These benefits were payable for up to fifty-two weeks, although extensions might be granted in exceptional circumstances. During the early seventies, a period of social reform and worker militancy, the benefits had been set at 66 percent of a claimant's earnings. The erosion that has taken place since is continuing apace.

Income maintenance at a level of 66 percent of earnings, or even 60 percent, may not sound all that miserly. But, the fact is that the average unemployment insurance benefits paid out left a single individual 16.6 percent below the poverty line, a family of two 30.9 percent below the poverty line and a family of four 59 percent below the poverty line in 1981. These calculations were made on the basis that one person in a family was receiving unemployment insurance benefits.[17] While Muszynski carefully notes that these families might be in receipt of other benefits, he points out that his calculations show that Canada's unemployment insurance "is not meant to be an income security program but rather an income continuity scheme." It is clear that the program envisages that the workers should go back into the paid workforce quickly.[18] Workers who are receiving benefits must show that they are willing to re-enter the workforce if they are to remain entitled to benefits. A heavy-handed supervisory and screening scheme has been developed to this end.

In a hard-hitting article, Reuben Hasson revealed the often arbitrary and cruel nature of the unemployment insurance system.[19] Workers who claim benefits initially can satisfy the Unemployment Insurance Corporation's requirements by showing that they are actively looking for a job of the kind which they have lost. But the administrators of the scheme demand that "after a reasonable interval" the claimants are to lower their job and wage-rate expectations. Amazingly, Professor Hasson found, unemployed people were not necessarily told what a "reasonable interval" was. They had to guess at how the administrators would use their discretion. Nor was it certain that they would be told to what extent they should lower their expectations when that time came. Yet, if they failed to meet what to them may have been unknown criteria, they could be disqualified from receiving benefits altogether.

Hasson also discovered that, in 1981, the Unemployment Insurance Commission had set down policy guidelines for its officers, but that those guidelines were not available to the unemployed claimants. The Commission's internal, but then publicly unknown, rule was that *skilled* employees were entitled to continue to look for the same kind of job as the one they had lost for no more than three weeks unless they had held their previous job for a minimum of thirteen years. In that case, the Commission, unbeknownst to them, might give them thirteen weeks' grace before they had to lower their expectations. It may well be that, in practice, these policies were not applied as coercively as they could have been. After all, administrators are not necessarily evil. But one fact cannot be negated: workers had to be willing to search for jobs at progressively lower pay rates.

Hasson further showed that to remain entitled to benefits, the worker also had to prove to the Commission that she had made a minimum number of job searches per week. This minimum, again not necessarily known to the claimant, varied with the skill, age and ethnicity of the claimant. This requirement meant that claimants had to keep the bureaucracy informed of their job searches. They had to go to a series of personal interviews, conducted by benefit *control* officers. At the time Professor Hasson did his research he found that these officers often were former policemen or debt-collectors.[20]

To back up this blame-the-victim approach, the Commission expends a great deal of energy or money in tracking down fraudulent claimants. Yet the amount of fraud is very slight. The Macdonald Commission put it at less than 5 percent, while other studies peg the rate at an even lower level than that.[21] What is certain is that the number of deviants in respect of unemployment insurance is no greater than it is in any other analogous sphere. But the state expends far more effort in tracking down those who cheat on unemployment insurance than it does on people who defraud the income tax system, even though the losses caused by tax evaders outstrip by far those which flow from violations of the *Unemployment Insurance Act.*[22] Work shyness will not be tolerated. A message is sent to all workers, even those who have the benefit of collective bargaining. This is a weighty bargaining chip for employers.

Not only has the Canadian unemployment insurance scheme supported Canada's employers in these ways, it also has left the private sector more or less free to mould the resulting pool of labour to its short-term needs. While the unemployment insurance scheme, to some extent, has been used as a retraining mechanism, this never has been a major objective of Canadian policy-makers. The scheme has not managed to train people who have lost their jobs in a way that might widen their range of opportunities. Muszynski has traced the history and politics of labour-market policy from the 1960s on. The story he tells shows how early federal attempts were largely thwarted by federal-provincial wrangling and how, later on, efforts to provide more generous schemes failed, primarily because of the confusion of the goals of these programs.

Early efforts had concentrated on teaching people basic skills, including reading and writing, while enrolled in formal educational facilities. There was little by way of on-site training. In the 1970s, well-known programs such as the Local Initiatives Program (LIP) and Opportunities For Youth (OFY) were developed. They proved to be incapable of providing the trainees with the skills needed to keep them fully employed.[23] In 1984, the new Conservative federal government attributed these deficiencies to the thoughtlessness and extravagance of its Liberal predecessors' training schemes. It initiated a program which it called the Canadian Jobs Strategy. But its achievements also turned out to be disappointing.

The government used unemployment insurance funds to support private sector employers who hired unemployed people. The private sector employers were to train these people with a view to improving their long-term employment prospects. Of the 17,000 people who found jobs created in this way, a remarkable 2,900 were placed in employment situations where no transportable skills could be acquired at all. They obtained jobs in doughnut shops, pizza parlours, hamburger and take-out chicken restaurants, submarine sandwich shops, groceries and variety stores. They were employed by retail stores, hotels, motels, video rentals, television and stereo shops, beauty salons, fitness studios, dry-cleaning businesses and drugstores. Service stations, car dealerships, car washes, security companies, taxi firms, bowling alleys, pool halls, arcades, bingo halls and golf courses took some of the others. Still others went to work as janitors. While it is true that the scheme also created jobs which required more skill and which were better paid, a great number of employers, including major national franchisors such as Burger King, Swiss Chalet, Mr. Submarine, Safeway, IGA and Mac's Milk were provided with cheap, subsidized labour. The workers obtained very few skills that would enable them to take advantage of any opportunities which might arise in the high-skill, higher-paying sectors of the economy.[24]

This story reflects the three related policy goals which have underpinned government programs in this sphere for a long time: (1)

not to force employers to bear anything like the real cost of the termination of employment and the retraining of employees; (2) to compensate displaced workers at low levels; and (3) to help private sector employers take advantage of the pressure felt by displaced workers to take any job at all. In sum, rather than committing itself to a policy of full employment with the kind of industrial planning which this necessitates, the Canadian state promotes a relatively unmodified and anarchic market-based system. In recent times, this desire to let employers retain market power *vis-à-vis* labour was given a boost by the reports of top-level government-sponsored commissions.

The prestigious Macdonald Commission Report saw increased liberalized trade as the principal engine of economic growth. The vision it presented was stark. It called for a far-reaching realignment of social, trade and labour-market policies. The idea was to free the state from the moral obligation and the political need to provide jobs for everyone.[25] It recommended a complete restructuring and rationalization of unemployment insurance and social welfare programs. This agenda was the very one which the Business Council on National Issues (BCNI) had urged upon the Macdonald Commission.[26] The BCNI is, of course, the lobby group created by Canada's multinationals, the group which has the greatest interest in promoting trade-led development. The BCNI was very specific. Its focus was on making programs cost-efficient: translated, this meant that benefits and eligibility rules should make the labour force more compliant and adaptable to the needs of business. An attack on the existing unemployment insurance scheme was central to this agenda.

By July 1985, the government had set up the Commission of Inquiry on Unemployment Insurance, the Forget Commission. Its recommendations met with a storm of opposition precisely because they provided a detailed blueprint of how to implement the thrust of the Macdonald Commission Report and the pleas of the BCNI.[27] The effect of these successive reports was to give the impression that Canada's social programs were rich and unnecessarily indulgent. The Conservative government, when re-elected in 1988, was thereby helped to attack the unemployment insurance program frontally. The attack it made was double pronged.

First, there was a declaration that unemployment insurance would be rationalized to make sure that only the most deserving people would get it. To ensure this, eligibility requirements were tightened. In the past, most people qualified if they had worked ten weeks during the year.[28] Under the new policy, the basic eligibility period ranged from fourteen to twenty weeks, a 40–100 percent increase. Consequently, many people who once would have been entitled to benefits no longer were, although some allowance was made for claimants in high-unemployment areas. In addition, in many cases, the length of time for which benefits are payable was also shortened.

The government announced that these measures would save it $1.3 billion in payouts per annum, some of which would be spent on job retraining.[29] Much of the savings was to be given to employers to support training programs. Thus, at the same time that fewer people were to collect stingier unemployment benefits, employers were to be subsidized more directly. Subsidized employer-run training schemes have proved ineffective in the past and are likely to fail again. Wolfe and Yalnizyan have noted that

far from promoting lifetime learning and an activist approach to returning the unemployed to the labour market, the strategy devotes a huge portion of its budget to persuading employers to fill the breech…. Having employers define training needs for the economy … is a recipe for moving the training system closer to meeting short-term, job specific skill requirements, rather than investing in people's long-term learning needs.[30]

Not only are benefits harder to get, but the government is intent on reinforcing the disciplinary effect of its proposals. Whereas, in the past, workers who lost their jobs through quitting voluntarily or misconduct of some kind could be disqualified from receiving unemployment insurance benefits for up to six weeks, this period was now increased to a maximum of twelve weeks. If the standard waiting period of two weeks is added, a claimant may have to wait a full three months before receiving a penny from the fund. The twelve-week period of non-entitlement would also be applied where workers are deemed to have refused to accept other available "appropriate" work. Here it is to be remembered that it is an unaccountable bureaucracy which has been left with the task of determining what a voluntary quit is, what misconduct is, and the extent to which an unemployed person should drop her expectations about what she might look for in a job.[31] As if all this were not bad enough, workers who are being punished in this way may receive benefits that amount to only 50 percent of their previous earnings, rather than the previous standard 60 percent.

The bureaucracy is meant to apply these tough new standards with venom. The minister announced that she expected to save $450 million per annum this way. The message is clear. Employed people had better behave, or else.

A notable aspect of these new measures is that they make the Canadian unemployment insurance scheme resemble that of the United States more closely than before. In particular, the lengthening of the eligibility period, to about fourteen to twenty weeks, brings Canada more into line with the prevailing American norm. Similarly, the entitlement of claimants punished for "wrongful" conduct is the same as that available to *all* people who claim unemployment benefits in the United States, namely, 50 percent of their earnings. This is not a coincidence; it is the first salvo in bringing Canada's levels of social spending in this area into line with the lower ones which prevail in the United States. It is not to be forgotten that during the free trade negotiations the Americans made it clear that no unfair subsidies of any kind would be tolerated and that no Canadian social program was to be exempt from scrutiny, as such programs might constitute unacceptable subsidies. Indeed, there was a specific allegation that Canada's richer unemployment insurance scheme provided an unfair subsidy to seasonal workers in the fishing industry.

The second shoe fell in the budget of 1989. It was announced that Ottawa would no longer contribute directly to the unemployment insurance fund. All contributions were to be made by employers and employees. Up to then, the government had topped up these contributions by up to 25 percent. The stated objective of this change was to save the government an expected $2.3 billion. This saving may be applied to deficit reduction, although some is to be put into retraining programs. The real significance of these policies is that Ottawa is making it clear that it intends to reduce its role as a guarantor of income maintenance programs. This dovetails with Canada's intention to make brute competitiveness the centre of government economic strategy.

The Gender Gap

Cultural, historical and political reasons have led to the undervaluation of work done by women.[32] Employers have come to rely on the female job ghettoes which this has generated. This always has been important to all capitalist economies, but it has become especially so to Canada's. Women constitute the single most important supply of low-wage workers in Canada.

In recent times, the utility of the undervaluation of women's work has been increased as women have entered the paid work force in record numbers. Between 1975 and 1986, the female labour force grew by 56 percent, compared to 12.4 percent for men. Significantly, the gap in earnings between males and females has narrowed very little. In 1985, the average woman employed full-time for a full year earned $18,870; the average comparable male earned $23,640, a gap of almost 30 percent. In the service sectors, the difference between men's and women's wages is close to 50 percent. The average full-time salary of a woman working in a service occupation was $12,844 in 1985 compared to $23,180 for her male counterpart.[33]

It suits employers to have a pool of workers who are organized weakly. This reduces their labour costs. If this source of cheap labour can be characterized as the product of the workings of the market's invisible hand, it can be treated as if it were a natural and inevitable phenomenon. It is this analysis of the development of the gender gap which has left Canadian governments, bent on leaving market forces as much free play as possible, off the hook. They did much less than their counterparts in Europe to attack wage discrimination based on sex. The results bear this out.

Canadian governments did come to act on this front, but despite growing political awareness and associated government action, Abella showed that over the seventy years leading up to 1982, the gender gap remained nearly constant. Her calculations indicated that it was reduced by 2 to 11 percent, depending on one's method of calculation. In 1911, women's earnings were 53 percent of what men earned, and by 1982, according to Abella, the figure had changed to somewhere between 55 and 64 percent.[34] The primary reason for this glacial progress is that the state instruments used to overcome the gender gap have paid undue homage to the logic of the competitive market. In the early days of public interventions, this was reflected in legislation which required equality of treatment only where a woman's work was identical to that done by a man in the same place of employment. As it became clear that this was too rigid, the criterion was changed so that a woman had to show that her work was substantially the same as that of the man to whom she wished to be

Table 8.2
Average Female Earnings as a Percentage of Male Earnings in Selected OECD Countries, 1968 and 1977

	1968	1977
Australia	.70 (1972)	.82
Austria	.67 (1960)	.74
Canada	.54 (1961)	.50 (1971)
Denmark	.74	.85
France	.86 (1972)	.86
Germany	.69	.73
Netherlands	.74	.81
Norway	.75	.30
Sweden	.78	.87
United Kingdom	.60	.72
United States	.66 (1973)	.66

Source: Adapted from Isabelle Bakker, "The Status of Women in the OECD Countries," in *Equality and Employment: Report of the Royal Commission on Equality in Payment* (Abella Commission), Vol. 2 (Ottawa: Ministry of Supply and Services, 1984).

compared. But women still found themselves in situations where their occupations had no apparent appropriate male comparator groups. Effectively, the narrowing of the gender gap could not be achieved, as systemic discrimination remained unrecognized. As Cornish has noted, this permitted "employers ... consciously or unconsciously, [to benefit from] a double standard for wages."[35] In short, the legislatures did not address the basic problem — the ghettoization of women's work.

Sixty percent of Canada's women wage-workers are employed in 20 of the 500 or so available occupations. More telling is that in some sectors women constitute the vast majority of the workforce. They dominate clerical, sales and service positions. Ninety-eight percent of typists are female, 92 percent of nurses are female, 69 percent of people working in food services are female.[36] Clearly, statutes relying on substantially the same kind of work being done by males and females in the same enterprise cannot redress the problems of the mass of low-paid women working in such occupational ghettoes.[37]

The growing strength of the women's movements combined with the massive evidence that poverty in Canada is largely a women's problem has created considerable pressures for a change in approach. What have evolved are a series of schemes promoting pay equity and equal pay for work of equal value. The nature of these régimes is conditioned by pre-existing institutional conceptualizations.

Pay Equity

In an industrial relations system that focuses on atomized productive activities, it seems natural to promote equality in discrete employment settings. Elaborate mechanisms are devised to facilitate the implementation of equality as determined by new, ever more sensitive, criteria which are to be applied to discrete workplaces. Many women will not be able to take advantage of the scheme because of the lack of meaningful male comparator groups. The only thing to do when this becomes obvious is to change the terrain for comparisons from the one-employment setting to a wider one. Ideologically and economically this will meet with strong resistance because it runs contrary to the basic industrial relations model. The kind of struggle that results, based as it is on attempts to modify the constraints of the deeply embedded market ideology, is illustrated by the saga of the Ontario pay equity scheme which came into effect on January 1, 1988, and which has been under constant review ever since.

As earlier equal-pay legislation had posited, the 1988 Ontario statute retains the central idea that, to attain equality, jobs performed primarily by women are be compared with jobs done primarily by men. But there is an important new departure: the scheme no longer relies on individual women or groups of women to bring a complaint of discrimination. The fact that, under the old equal-pay scheme, an individual complaint had to be lodged had proved to be a real inhibition.[38] Under the present scheme as enacted in 1988, there is to be no waiting for a complaint. A pay equity plan has to be developed for all private sector employers in Ontario who employ more than 100 employees. For people in establishments with fewer than 100 but more than 10 employees, different, less favourable, rules are to apply. Where there are fewer than 10 employees, workers are to be left to their own devices.

Where employer plans are to be developed, they are to compare job categories in which at least 60 percent of the workers are female with job categories in which at least 70 percent of the workforce is male. The comparisons are to be made between male and female workers in one employer's establishment, defined as a business entity within a specific geographic region. The selection of comparison groups is to be based on job evaluations in that establishment. The pay equity plan submitted after such an evaluation has to win the approval of the government's Pay Equity Commission, which also has the power to resolve differences between the parties. When the comparisons reveal unacceptable differentials, employers are required to make adjustments. The total amount of the adjustment which an employer is required to make in any one year cannot be less than 1 percent of its previous year's total payroll. People in the lowest job categories may be entitled to receive greater pay increases than other employees.

When this legislation was first presented, it was hoped that, over time, existing differentials in pay between males and females who do comparable work would disappear. But some fundamental problems with the legislation make this goal unreachable.

One of these difficulties is the way in which comparisons are to be made. The Act specifies criteria to be used to do the job evaluations necessary to engage in job comparisons. These criteria are skill, effort, responsibility and working conditions. It is well known that the methodologies which define these criteria for job evaluation are far from neutral.[39] Consequently, they allow the historic undervaluation of women's work to be perpetuated. There are other reasons for concern, as well. The legislation permits the employer to maintain differential wage rates where an acceptable seniority or merit pay scheme justifies them or incentives are needed to address skill shortages. All these exceptions favour males over females, given the occupational history of workers, and given work processes. To a large extent, then, the Act subjugates women's opportunity to attain a greater measure of equality to the perceived needs of employers.

Another facet of the legislation reveals this continued respect for the employer's managerial rights: comparisons are to be made within *one* establishment. The statute leaves it to an employer with several plants and/or offices in one geographical area to characterize them as separate enterprises or to treat them as one integrated operation. The employer's choice changes the groups available for comparison. A bloody-minded employer could use this manipulative power to deny some women the entitlements which the statute purports to bestow. Vital power has been left with employers in a scheme supposedly designed to empower marginalized women.

The Ontario Nursing Association (ONA) has had some success in countering the inherent problems of the employer's right to define its establishment. ONA convinced the Pay Equity Tribunal that nurses working in the public sector in the Haldimand-Norfolk area should be allowed to use male workers in the same municipality as valid comparators for purposes of job evaluation. The nurses argued that male police officers would be an appropriate group. The municipal employer, of course, had argued that it should be permitted to treat its policing and health sectors as different establishments. The tribunal agreed that the municipality could be viewed as one establishment for the purposes of equal pay legislation, but did not conclude that male police workers constituted an appropriate comparator group. That issue was left to further negotiation and/or litigation. The result in the case is something of a bell-wether, but it is hard to know how many other groups can have success on this front, especially as the argument made by ONA is not so readily available to private sector unions. Private sector employers with different, apparently discrete, operations spread over several plants and buildings are not so easily characterized as one establishment.

While it had been the first jurisdiction to intervene on a pay equity basis in the private sector, then, the Ontario government's efforts were compromised by its instinctive protection of the competitive market ideal. If any further evidence is needed for this assertion, it is to be found in the fact that, inasmuch as one of the strengths of the 1988 Ontario legislation is that it is pro-active, for enterprises which employ less than one hundred employees, the scheme is a re-active one. These smaller employers merely have to post a pay equity plan in the workplace. To have a failure to do so redressed, aggrieved workers have to lodge a complaint with the Commission. Just as in the bad old days, in small employment settings a complaint-based system remains in force. Similarly, the frank recognition that the market was yielding outcomes which were unacceptable in a modern liberal society was not sufficient to cause the Ontario government to demand more than tortoise-like gradualism in redressing them. The statute gave some employers as much as six years from the date of its proclamation to *begin* to comply. In addition, employers who do submit pay equity plans recognizing the existence of pay discrimination are not bound to make up the unacceptable difference in one fell swoop. Only 1 percent of their previous year's payroll has to be allotted to this kind of redistribution in any one year.

Thus, while the 1988 Act provides for better and more benefits to women in the private sector than had been available before, true equality was far from assured and any progress it brings is not to be realized at the expense of employers. Here it should be noted that the Act decrees that the requirement of equality will be satisfied when the highest-paid woman makes as much as the lowest-paid man in the comparator group. Equality is to be realized at the lowest level possible. Moreover, it is by no means clear that the 1 percent of payroll to be applied to a successful women's equality claim will be new money rather than money that would otherwise have been available for wage increases. This puts male and female wage earners in potential conflict.

Another deficiency in the scheme is that it seeks to achieve gender equality on a factory-by-factory basis. This has left many people excluded, because a huge number of women work in female-only enterprises. The government's own figures show that 800,000 to 900,000 working women were not to be protected by the legislation as first written.[40]

Despite all these obvious drawbacks, the pay equity régime of 1988 was seen as path-breaking at that time, precisely because it purported to interfere with market operations more directly than any other such scheme.

The many deficiencies of the Act quickly became apparent, however.[41] When the Rae government came to power in late 1990, much was expected from it. It declared that it would amend the legislation in two major ways.[42] First, it set out to deal with the circumstance in which there are no direct comparators for a female job class in a particular employment setting. The proposed amendment to the legislation provides that, as long as there are some male job classes in the employer's establishment, the female job classes without direct comparators will be able to get a proportion of what another female class, which did find a male comparator group, obtained. There are four clear difficulties with this proposed reform. In these job ghettoes, any males found are likely to be poorly paid ones. The benefits obtained will be worthwhile, but they will be small ones, as women get a fraction of the lowest wage paid to poorly paid male comparators. More significantly, the comparisons are still to be in the one enterprise, limiting the possibilities of undermining the systemic discrimination that pervades social and market relations. And, as before, its dilatory application and the cost imposed by the technical nature of the enterprise will impede progress. Further, a lot of women will get nothing, because there are no male job classes at all in the employer's establishment. And it is precisely in these situations that the effect of the undervaluation of women's work is the most pronounced — for example, in daycare employment.

The second major proposed amendment to the 1988 Ontario legislation addresses inequality in the public sector. Women are to be entitled to look for comparators throughout the government services. This will be a boon because it gives the scheme more flexibility and the potential to find more advantageous comparator groups. Yet this very flexibility is likely to give rise to serious problems as female job classes endeavour to find the most beneficial comparator groups and the employer resists. Disputations, confusions and delays are to be expected.

The ideal of pay equity is accepted by all governments as requiring action. Five jurisdictions have pursued this goal in their public sectors, while Ontario is extending it with some vigour into the private sector. At best, however, what has been put on the agenda is the comparison between poorly paid men and worse-paid women in one employment setting. This kind of gender equality régime is not likely to be all that fruitful. Governments ought to be pressured to consider other means of addressing the gender gap, means which cut through the obstructing thickets of employer-by-employer bargaining and the retention of job evaluation schemes that preserve management's prerogative to define the skills, abilities and qualities to be rewarded. One important contribution would be to compress wage scales. Government could do this by increasing the minimum wage. As a disproportionate number of women earn the minimum wage, this would do much to reduce the gender gap. During the election campaign which led to the NDP victory in Ontario, Rae promised to raise the minimum wage to 60 percent of the average industrial wage, in due course.[43] Were the NDP to honour this promise, it would do much to help women.

Retirement Income

Canadian governments have been laggards in the public provision of adequate retirement incomes. The idea that retired people should have a right to live in dignity and reasonable comfort is not a primary government goal. Canada's late acceptance of Keynesian instruments never took it far along this road. Again, the reason is the virtually unquestioned belief that private is better than public.

The Public Domain

It was not until 1965 that Canada instituted its first nation-wide income retirement scheme, the Canada Pension Plan (CPP). Quebec, as an emerging modern state, instituted a mirror-image of this plan over which it was to exercise sole control, the Quebec Pension Plan (QPP). The way these plans work is that employees and employers contribute into a central fund at rates specified by the government. The benefits are available only to those who participated in the paid workforce, and what they get depends on their level of contributions and the amount of time worked. By definition, this excludes home-workers who, of course, are mainly women. In addition, those who will get the least benefits, if they get any benefits at all, are part-time and irregularly employed people. These include the differently abled, native people, those who can work only on a seasonal basis because of where they live, and the least skilled of the workforce. In short, the most disadvantaged workers are the worst protected.

All governments, therefore, have had to supplement this very limited earnings-related retirement scheme. The federal government has done so through two welfare programs. The first is Old Age Security (OAS), which is available to anyone who has resided in Canada for forty years. The other is the Guaranteed Income Supplement (GIS), which is available to all people whose combined retirement income from all sources keeps their earnings below a minimum set by the government.

The Private Sphere

In a system which emphasizes that people should look after themselves, they are entitled to bargain privately for their own post-work security. Only organized workers can attempt to do so in any meaningful way. Something less than 40 percent of all Canadian workers are covered by employer-sponsored plans, slightly less than the total number of workers covered by collective agreements. This number has remained relatively static for twenty or so years. It was not until the end of the 1960s that pension bargaining became a real preoccupation of unions, reaching a crescendo when the AIB legislation, the first major income-restraint legislation of the 1970s, left it as one of the few things about which bargaining could take place.

The outcomes of private pension bargaining have been very uneven and unsatisfactory. In large part, this is due to the logic of collective bargaining. Factory-by-factory bargaining means that a worker's pension rights are based on the number of years she has worked for a particular employer. In a fragmented bargaining scheme it is difficult to develop portable pensions, as each employer (if it agrees to a pension plan at all) provides one specifically tailored to its own and its employees' needs.[44] This means that workers cannot take their accrued rights and have them be part of the base of any other plan that they join during their lifetime. The ability to do that would give them the best possible return on the contributions which they have made to all the private pension plans in which they were participants during their worklives.

As if this were not bad enough, workers do not become entitled to collect monies from the plan until they have participated in the plan for a specific period. This is called the vesting period. The length of this period may be subject to bargaining. Initially, Canadian unions were unable to win very much here. From the workers' perspective, the shorter the vesting period the better. Until the pension is vested, the only entitlement of workers is to have their own contributions, if any, returned to them. Thus, workers might participate in a pension plan for some years without developing any equity in the plan's yield. Legislation had to be passed to address this serious deficiency. A maximum statutory vesting period of ten years was established by most jurisdictions. This still left many workers out of luck. Canada has a competitive, flexible labour market. Many employees do not spend ten years with one employer. Each year sees roughly 40 percent of workers either changing employment, leaving or entering the labour market, or unemployed.[45] In the same vein, the Forget Commission found that the number of people who were unemployed at some time during any given year was 25.4 percent of the labour force.[46]

Recently, therefore, there was renewed pressure on legislatures to reduce the vesting period. Workers have met with some success on this front, getting shorter vesting periods by legislative fiat in some jurisdictions than they could win at the bargaining table. But this much-needed reform has not solved the problem of lack of portability. As long as workers depend on fragmented bargaining, it will be extremely difficult to harmonize the thousands of plans in existence, something which is needed if portability is to work.

Not surprisingly, there is a good deal of support for the proposition that workers be allowed to take their vested pension rights with them when they leave their employment so that they might invest them privately. The idea is to roll them into retirement savings plans.[47] There are two difficulties with this option. First, workers frequently will not be in a position to keep adding to the fund to the same extent that they do under the forced-savings mechanism of the employer-sponsored plan. The likelihood is that they will contribute to a number of funds, individual and collective, over their lifetime. They may not be able to maximize the return on their monies so invested. The second difficulty is that individual retirement savings plans yield good results only because of the tax advantages that they offer. Such tax advantages are worth more to the rich than to the less well off.[48] Very few workers are likely to choose to spend whatever precious disposable income they may have in this way, given the poor tax incentive they have to do so and the difficulty of postponing their enjoyment of this income.

The difficulties associated with the lack of portability of private pension plan schemes, then, are caused by the fragmented nature of collective bargaining. Adherence to a model of private planning is pushing policy-makers towards a solution which requires even further fragmentation. A better solution would be a comprehensive social retirement plan. The logic of collective bargaining, however, is a barrier to its being put on the agenda.

Another serious concern is the failure to index benefits. Contributions are to be invested to yield agreed-upon benefits to retirees.[49] Long time horizons are involved; the potential price fluctuations are many and unpredictable. From the retirees' point of view, contributions to the plans should be costed on the basis that the benefits returned will keep up with the cost of living. The risks of doing this are considered too great by private pension plan administrators. Finlayson claims that, in 1984, "93.7 percent of all private sector pension plans in Canada had no automatic form of inflation protection whatsoever."[50] Even for those few workers who become entitled to a full pension but who are unlucky enough to live for a few years after retirement, this means a quick descent into poverty. For instance, Finlayson reports that a pension worth $1,000 a month in 1980 "saw its real value decline to $634 by 1985."[51]

The dramatic erosion of privately bargained-for retirement income benefits has put pressure on governments to force employer-sponsored pension plans to adopt indexation. The Friedland Commission, created by the Ontario government, recommended that pensions be partially indexed.[52] Workers responded that the indexation would still allow their pensions to be eroded severely, while employers and underwriters claimed that even this partial indexation would cause pensions to become too expensive.[53] A statutorily guaranteed right to partially indexed pensions remains a contentious issue; at this time full indexation seems out of reach.

In the private sector, well-placed unions are seeking to enrich their pension rights along the lines of the Friedland proposals. Thus, the Canadian Automobile Workers union has achieved something of a breakthrough in recent pension settlements. For current workers who serve thirty years (and who, therefore, might become entitled to a full pension well before reaching the age of sixty-five) the average monthly pension is to be increased sharply, with generous — though not full — indexation. Workers will be entitled to CPP and OAS as well. Thus, employees who become entitled to full pension rights might expect a retirement income of up to 85 to 90 percent of their pre-retirement income.

Most employer-sponsored pension plans, however, are not that rich, nor do they offer this much protection against inflation. The CLC has reported that more than one-half of retirees covered by employer-sponsored pension plans received less than 30 percent of their pre-retirement income, while more than 35 percent of retirees received less than 20 percent of their pre-retirement income.[54] If one of the objectives of this kind of forced savings scheme is to help avoid poverty for employees who have retired, it is not being achieved. And if this is true for the best-positioned workers — that is, those who have collective bargaining power — it is even more true for those who have no private pension plan to rely on in the first place. They must depend on CPP/QPP to the extent that they have participated in the paid workforce and on Old Age Security and Guaranteed Income Supplement benefits if they qualify for them. In 1986, of 2.6 million people potentially eligible for GIS, half were poor enough to receive GIS benefits: 290,000 people received the maximum, while another million received partial GIS benefits.[55]

Beneficiaries of the Retirement Income Schemes

The wonder of it all is why this dreadful mix of public and private pensions continues. In part, the reasons are ideological. The Canadian state has maintained its commitment to let private arrangements flourish, believing that welfare of all kinds is best generated in this way. The fact that employer and employee contributions are made to fund private plans to keep this private ordering dream alive means that there are less monies available to fund public social security schemes. Not only is the establishment of an adequate comprehensive public plan inhibited by this lack of reserves, but the most disadvantaged Canadians who must rely on the existing public régimes as their principal source of retirement income are hardest hit by the plans' resulting miserliness. For their part, unions have been forced to look after their own members in the absence of a centralized retirement income scheme. They have bargained privately for pensions. Thousands of such agreements exist, creating rights and expectations. Suggestions for a change-over to a totally different system are technically daunting, and frightening to participating workers, as it may require giving up existing benefits. Unions know that improvements are needed, but they are limited to doing what appears to be the only pragmatic thing. They urge governments to enrich the CPP/OAS régimes and to improve the private pension plans in which they participate by passing laws mandating better portability and indexation provisions. If they meet with success, their efforts will reinforce the existing private pension schemes' legitimacy. While this perpetuation of the private/public mix serves workers and their families poorly, it does produce a number of winners who have a stake in the maintenance of the régime. These profiteers are investors and financial institutions.

The contributions made by workers and/or on behalf of workers are deferred wages.[56] In the aggregate, the contributions constitute a huge amount of money. These vast pools of capital grow ever larger as they are invested and re-invested and benefit from inflation, a benefit which is not passed on to the workers. From time to time, this permits employers to lessen the contributions they have to make under the plan.[57]

At the end of 1984, $168.4 billion was held in reserve to meet future pension entitlements. The largest portion of such reserves was to be found in the care of trust companies and associated investment counselling firms that administer these plans. Their holdings amounted to $94.4 billion, much of it invested in marketable securities and bonds. As a single source of investment capital, the pension funds rated second only in size to the combined reserves of the chartered banks.[58] In effect, the state's commitment to promote privately negotiated pensions permits workers' money to be used to support a competitive economic model that causes so many workers to be impoverished in old age. The workers' money, invested by the private sector for its own needs, is not used to promote full employment and a better quality of life for all Canadians.[59] This needs to be re-thought if workers are going to influence the state of the economy and their own part in it.

Occupational Health and Safety

The economic costs of the carnage that goes on in workplaces are staggering. (See Chapter 3.) The direct and indirect costs of traumatic injuries alone amount to close to $7 billion a year.[60] The amount would be even greater if the social welfare and health-care costs incurred because of occupation-related diseases were included. Nearly all of these enormous bills are paid by tax-paying workers. Employers contribute the least and suffer no occupational injuries or diseases. The victimization of workers seems almost malicious. At the very least, it is an anachronism in a society which publicly maintains that good health and physical well-being are fundamental rights.

Setting Standards

Canada's dismal occupational health and safety record is a tinderbox. It has the potential to lead to the kind of conflict between employers and employees that might destabilize the carefully cultivated perception of the consensual nature of labour relations. Governments throughout Canada have gone to great lengths to convey the impression that workplace disputes generally are technocratic ones and, in the main, are fights about shares of the co-operatively produced pie, rather than struggles about power and control in a class-divided society. This is particularly true in respect of the regulation concerned with occupational diseases. Generally, the floors established are those which would have been yielded by an unfettered market.[61] This was the finding of a major study. Tuohy indicated that, with one exception, no standard had been selected for exposure to toxic substances which would have imposed a new cost on major industrialists in Ontario. The standards set were no more rigorous than those already being met by the majority of large employers in each of the industries where the newly legislated standards were to be applied.[62]

Enforcement of Standards

Governments are very lax about the enforcement of their own standards. They rarely appoint an adequate number of inspectors. Ontario, which has the largest government occupational health and safety agency in the nation, employs no more inspectors than it does gamekeepers to look after the province's wildlife.[63] Further, there is almost no effort to punish employers for flagrant contraventions of what are, after all, minimum requirements. Thus, at the federal level there were only two prosecutions in 1983; Ontario, after initiating a get-tough policy in 1986–87, launched some 400-odd prosecutions arising out of nearly 37,000 violations.[64] The emphasis of government is not on punishment but rather on getting employers to comply voluntarily with existing standards. The results of this strategy continue to be horrible. Awareness of the ongoing toll, usually deepened by a particularly dramatic accident, leads to vociferous worker demands for action, sometimes accompanied by illegal militancy. Governments then may be forced to announce that they will increase their use of criminal sanctions. Usually, there is a flurry of activity, but, in the end, such promises are not kept. The basic reason is not that governments lie. Rather, it is that it is central to their thinking that private settlement is vastly preferable to resolution by state intervention.

Consultation Rather than Enforcement

A key component of these statutory health and safety régimes is the establishment of joint employer-employee committees. They are to ensure that standards are complied with and to make recommendations about the creation of a safe workplace. But the emphasis is on "recommendation." Even if the workers on a committee can persuade the employer's representatives to ask the employer to upgrade conditions, the employer is not bound to accept the recommendations. Its prerogative to run its workplace as it likes is not to be undermined that easily.[65] Workers then have to go to the state for help. Because of governments' general emphasis on voluntary settlement, their departments respond reluctantly. A spectacular example of this was provided by the tension created when some inspectors in Ontario supported labour's position before a commission of inquiry. The argument they made was that there were conscious efforts to impede investigations and prosecutions. The commission, of course, rejected the claims and recommended more of the same — that is, more consultation, more emphasis on internal responsibility.[66]

The Workers' Right to Refuse

What is notably absent from the scheme is a strong right for workers to stop production when they feel endangered. They have been given the right to refuse unsafe work, but it is a severely curtailed right. Most importantly, they can only refuse work on an individual basis. This de-emphasizes collective needs and the legitimate use of collective power in this sphere. Further, the very large number of workers who do not have the support of an existing union have to be very courageous indeed to exercise the right of refusal. Unsurprisingly, they rarely do so. Tucker has shown that 90 percent of work refusals take place in the unionized sectors.[67]

When a worker does exercise the right to refuse, there often is no pay for the down-time that results. This acts as a brake on the right to refuse. Not only do workers face a loss of wages but fellow employees who may be stood down because of a work refusal may resent their militant brother or sister. In the end, the right to refuse to work in unsafe conditions is rarely used. As a weapon it is a very blunted one.

When the NDP was in opposition in Ontario, it criticized the government for relying on this consultative approach. It argued that workers should be empowered. Curiously, when it was elected, it enacted, without change, Bill 208, a bill drafted by the predecessor Peterson Liberal government. If anything, Bill 208 reinforces internal responsibility mechanisms. It provides for more joint health and safety committees in more industries than were covered previously. The only added power that workers have been given is that certified worker representatives may halt production where they believe health and safety conditions warrant. But they cannot do so without the agreement of a managerial representative, or, should they fail to get it, a government order. The utility of this mechanism is highly questionable, as the NDP was fond of saying when in opposition.

In addition, Bill 208 provides for a bipartite overseeing agency. Capital and labour are to control training and education of personnel officers and workers to administer health and safety regulations. This agency is intended to generate proposals for research and regulation. At the time when this bipartism was established, it was seen as something of a victory for labour. Labour had believed that, when the business-favouring former government was directly responsible for policy determination and implementation, it gave too much weight to the employers' agenda. Paradoxically, the Ontario labour movement has agreed to bipartism at the very moment when a friendly government is in power.

There is a good deal of anecdotal evidence to show that Bill 208 was the product of a series of compromises engineered by the Ontario Federation of Labour (OFL) and CAW leaderships. Spontaneous militancy had forced government and employers to sit down with labour to find a new stabilizing system while the NDP was in opposition.[68] At the time, the bipartite system looked good, and it may have been difficult for the new NDP government to renege on the settlement, even though its flaws were many. In the upshot, however, Ontario's workers are left with a system which, at the top, reinforces the consultation between employers and unions and increases government passivity. At the bottom, however, little has been done by way of direct worker empowerment. Workers' lives still depend on deals done at the top in a market setting.

Must Welfare Be Inefficient?

Esping-Andersen puts Canada at the extreme liberal end of his spectrum of advanced industrialized nations. He believes that Canada has foregone welfare to promote efficiency. The data assembled in this chapter, as well as the earlier analysis of collective bargaining and its outcomes, support this characterization. But the fact that there has been a good deal of intervention with the market on many fronts, despite fierce resistance from private sector employers, has given the impression to many people that Canada leans to the welfare end, rather than to the efficiency end, of the spectrum. It is regrettable that this erroneous view has been maintained.

In the last several years, Conservative governments at the federal level have used this misperception as a basis for renewed attacks on Canada's minimal welfare state system. Ottawa has been willing to attack even the principle of universality, which was so well entrenched that even Prime Minister Mulroney had called it a "sacred trust." In 1985, the year after it was first elected, the federal Conservative government tried to de-index public pension benefits. It was forced to back down in the face of an unprecedented co-ordinated counter-attack by senior citizens. Immediately after its re-election in 1988 it announced its intention to institute a series of "clawbacks" of family benefits and old age pensions. It had taken its cue from the BCNI, which repeatedly had urged governments to replace wasteful universality with cost-efficient selective programs. The not-so-hidden agenda is that, when universality disappears, there will be less support from the electorally powerful middle classes for such social spending. At the same time as universality is being challenged, the federal government has been busy attacking the whole social welfare benefits package.

While the increasing number of older voters have made it politically necessary to enrich the publicly provided benefits for the aged (CPP/QPP, OAS, GIS, GAINS), making that segment of the population the only one which has improved its position, other welfare programs have been cut. In addition to unemployment insurance, these include family allowances and transfers to the provinces for health and secondary education. The overall effect is that, while in constant 1989 dollars the amount of social spending has remained roughly the same, all sectors of the population but the old lost ground.[69]

The impact has been exacerbated by the fact that working Canadians affected by these cuts have lost an increasing share of their income to income taxation. Between 1984 and 1989, in constant 1989 dollars, the tax burden on a working family of four with two income earners who earned less than $24,000 (this would classify them as working poor) *increased* by 44 percent; the burden on a similar family with earnings of $49,000 *increased* by 10 percent; while a very rich family, with a combined income of $122,000, enjoyed a *decrease* of 6 percent.[70] The greater revenues obtained from working taxpayers were not reflected in increased social spending levels, even though these levels were low by European standards.[71]

The focus of the federal government is easy to discern. It wants to diminish its supporting role for labour, such as it is, and to enhance the ability of business to compete internationally. As a result of Ottawa's tax policies, the corporate sector's contribution to collected revenues was a mere 18 percent. Individuals contribute four times as much. Yet, as late as the 1960s, individuals were only contributing about one-half of all income tax collected. Clearly, there has been a long-term movement in support of business's interests and a decline in the state's willingness to support the social wage, from the early seventies on. Both the support for business and the withdrawal of the state from its commitment to social welfare programs are increasing in intensity.

Nonetheless, the prospects for improvement are not as bleak as they seem from this account. After all, all Canadian policy-makers and politicians continue to pay lip service to Canada's social commitment to welfare for all citizens. Moreover, a model is just a model. While Canada's welfare programs are efficiency-oriented, and hence minimalist in nature, the same forms and policy instruments could be used to provide more and better-quality welfare. In a way, this has become more plausible as the attacks on the existing schemes increase in vehemence. This is so because the justification for these assaults is that they will improve competitive efficiency. Basic to this argument is the idea that welfare programs and positive government interventions are a drag on corporate Canada's competitive position. The logic is that, if competition improves, economic abundance will be created, welfare will be spread and there will be no need for government intervention and welfare creation. Each one of these claims is based on contentious theoretical premises. For instance, even if more economic abundance is created by deregulation and privatization, there is nothing in a market-driven economy which guarantees its equitable diffusion. But the niceties of theoretical debate are beside the point. There already is a mass of evidence which causes this set of justifications for attacks on liberal welfarism to have less and less resonance.

For instance, while it is difficult to show how many jobs have been lost as a result of the Canada-U.S. Free Trade Agreement, it is clear that many have been lost. By contrast, there is no evidence at all that, on balance, Canadians have profited from it. Canadians have been asked to make sacrifices on the basis of short-term pain for long-term gain. But the pain is deep and is suffered now; the gains are not in sight.

In this context, there is a good case to be made that politicians should intervene to create welfare first and worry about competitive efficiency less. The pressure to adopt this approach always exists in a liberal democracy. In contemporary Canada, trade-union-minded governments may be able to exploit the immediate, concrete need for more social welfare. As they set up better programs they can, by highlighting the disappointing results of the unmoderated drive for efficiency, push us towards the welfare end of the Esping-Andersen spectrum. There are straws in the wind which indicate that this is a plausible scenario.

One of these is a forward-looking report made to the Liberal government which preceded the Rae government in Ontario. The Thompson Task Force was the result of pressure exerted by the NDP on a minority Liberal government. Its recommendations constituted an integrated set of proposals for welfare reform. When the Peterson government received the Thompson Report, it implemented only a small piece of it. The NDP has promised to put the whole thing into effect, enriching welfare benefits throughout the province on a rational basis. If this is done, the stigma of welfare and the disciplinary effects of welfare administration could be sharply reduced. As education and retraining of the displaced workforce are part and parcel of the recommendations, implementation of the report should in no way detract from the goal to maintain and to promote economic efficiency. But resistance to implementation will be fierce. The economy is in recession and the government must deal with increasing deficits, making funding of enriched welfare programs very difficult. Yet the payoff could be handsome.

Implementation would be a clear indication that Ottawa's approach to the balance between competitive efficiency and social welfare is not the only one available. It could act as a spur to similar policies in other jurisdictions, particularly British Columbia and Saskatchewan where the NDP has come into power. At the federal level, the NDP would be strengthened in its opposition to the liberalization of trade, privatization and deregulation. This could shift the focus of the national political economy debate. The idea that there is no choice for Canada but to engage in global competition by bringing itself under the American umbrella could be challenged more seriously than it has been. The potential is there.

The Canadian State as Employer: Fortifying the Private Sector

The Dimensions of Public Sector Industrial Relations

The state is one of the largest employers in Canada. It employs workers at the municipal, provincial and federal levels. As well, it provides public services through state enterprises such as Saskatchewan Potash, Canada Post, Ontario Hydro, and the like. In 1975, two million people worked directly for public sector employers.[1] By 1988, more than 2.5 million Canadians were employed in the state sector.[2] The size of the discrete state enterprises and the numbers they employ also have been impressive. In the early 1980s, Canada's 40 Crown corporations and their 130 subsidiaries accounted for $40 billion in assets and employed more than 200,000 additional public sector workers.[3] The Macdonald Commission Report said that, in 1980, government employment accounted for one-quarter of the total wages paid in the economy. Even this figure is a conservative estimate. It does not include the total wages paid in the post-secondary education sectors, nor the cost of doctors' fees in the public health sphere.[4]

The level and density of unionization in the public sector is higher than it is in any other part of the economy. Close to 80 percent of the public sector workforce is unionized. The Canadian Union of Public Employees, the National Union of Provincial Government Employees and the Public Service Alliance of Canada are three of the largest unions in the land. Today, more than one in five of the unionized workforce belong to these major unions.[5]

Many factors have led to this rapid growth of unionization. Among the most important was the militancy of Post Office workers who, in the early sixties, refused to accept the fact that the law denied them the right to strike. Their defiance of the law forced the government to take a second look at the need for introducing wide-ranging reforms to public sector unionization. Another key development was the emergence of public sector unionism in Quebec in the 1960s.[6] As part of the mood of reform sweeping the province at the height of the Quiet Revolution, the Quebec government was forced to legitimate public sector bargaining and grant its employees new status and new bargaining rights. This, in turn, put pressure on the federal government, and then on other provincial governments, to give their employees similar rights.[7] The ensuing growth of public sector unionization was dramatic. It went from 37 percent of the workforce in 1967 to close to 68 percent by 1974.[8] It was a major feature of the socio-political movements which swept Canada from the mid-sixties to the early seventies, a period which was pivotal to the development of the modern industrial relations system.

The bestowal of legal collective bargaining rights on public sector workers did much to make the industrial relations system look progressive. Governments were seen to endorse the goal of unionization and the legitimacy of worker demands. The industrial relations machinery adopted for the regulation of public employees' bargaining was a variation on the already established private sector collective bargaining model which, uniformly, had been regarded as a step-up for private sector unions. The extension of this kind of bargaining to the public sectors was seen as an equally liberal development. In practical terms, it was to improve public sector workers' position at the negotiating table; politically, it was thought to perfect the ideal of industrial citizenship for all. As it has turned out, these views were too sanguine. At all times there was an underlying difficulty that prevented governments from granting their employees the same range of collective bargaining powers that is found in the private sector. The problem was that the economic logic of the competitive market model, which lies at the heart of private sector bargaining, has little direct impact in the public sphere.

Governments are held, and hold themselves, responsible for the welfare of the whole of society. It is this sense of accountability which imposes very real and immediate restraints on public sector bargaining rights and practices. Governments reserve the right to decide the initial scope of collective bargaining rights and the degree to which they should be further fettered in order to serve what they deem to be the public good. As a result, public sector bargaining, despite its antecedents, always has been a distorted version of private sector bargaining. It has been subject to constant modification. Different governments responding to changing political and regional needs have created a patchwork system of industrial relations in the public sectors. Rights and practices vary enormously from jurisdiction to jurisdiction; the right to strike faces many restrictions; and many public sector workers have no collective bargaining rights whatsoever.

Variations in Public Sector Collective Bargaining Rights

In British Columbia, New Brunswick, Newfoundland, Quebec and Saskatchewan, government workers have strike rights fully comparable to those of their private sector counterparts. This is not true in Alberta, Manitoba, Nova Scotia, Ontario and Prince Edward Island, where some public sector workers, as identified by the government,[9] are not legally entitled to strike at all.[10] For instance, Ontario and Alberta have denied strike rights to all Crown employees, hospital workers and police workers, as well as firefighters.[11] Workers in the federal public service face different kinds of restrictions. The matters about which they may bargain are limited expressly and severely. They are given an option as to whether they want to exercise the right to strike as the way to settle labour disputes about such matters. If they do not, any impasse which arises will be settled by third-party arbitration. This is the situation in which federal government workers who are members of the Public Service Alliance of Canada, often portrayed as a militant force which can hold the government to ransom, find themselves. These workers' union rights are regulated by the federal *Public Service Staff Relations Act.* As a matter of law, they are not permitted to bargain about the assignment of duties, classifications, promotions, demotions, transfers, lay-offs, pensions or any other matter spoken to by federal legislation; therefore, they cannot enforce their claims about these matters with a legal strike.[12] For other public sector workers, there are yet other, and different, kinds of restrictions.

Crown corporations and state enterprises such as Ontario Hydro, Saskatchewan Potash and the Canadian National Railways, as well as hospitals and schools, are run at arm's length from the government. The concern is that whimsical decision making by elected politicians would endanger long-range planning in respect of conservation and use of energy and resources, and the stability of certain sensitive key markets. Further, the delivery of some services is of such importance to the people who need them that they should be given as much say in the delivery as possible. As a consequence, independent government entities are set up. Crown corporations or controlling boards of trustees, whose members either are appointed by the state and are given security of tenure or are directly elected by citizens, are established.

In principle, governments are expected to take no interest in any bargaining which is to take place between these separate entities and their unionized employees. To all the world, a circumstance has been created in which independent corporations and boards bargain with their employees' unions much the way General Motors does with the CAW. Hidden from view is the fact that bargaining is not really conditioned by a competitive market position. Rather, it is subject to the financial will of governments not sitting at the bargaining table. Frequently, this enables governments to control outcomes of supposedly discrete economic bargaining while not being held politically accountable for the policies which form the substratum of the dispute. Workers who have been given full strike rights are handicapped by not being able to confront their real opponent directly. Moreover, as seen, some of the workers in these very same groups are denied the right to strike altogether because they are claimed to be essential workers.

A case in point are police and firefighters. They have to bargain with their local boards without the benefit of the use of the strike. As seen, hospital workers in Ontario and Alberta are in a similar situation. They have been deprived of their main bargaining leverage. In addition, some of the workers who have to bargain with supposedly independent, publicly accountable boards, have been given very restricted strike rights. Typically, this is the case for schoolteachers.

Not only do many public sector workers face major restrictions on their collective bargaining rights, but new fetters are imposed from time to time. It is relatively easy for governments to justify them by invoking the logic of the private sector model.

In Canada's private model of collective bargaining, workers can only use their collective power to make demands that their own private sector employer can grant directly. This is because collective bargaining is restricted to a one-on-one situation in which employers and their employees square off against each other. Trade unions are not allowed to go beyond the workplace-by-workplace scheme to attempt to use the leverage that concentrated withdrawal of workers' services across the board gives them to attain political goals. If these rules are violated, the state will feel justified in using its coercive powers: the right to strike is not meant to be a political weapon. (See Chapter 6.)

When this logic is applied to the public sectors, it cannot help but have a sharp and immediate impact. Collective *economic* demands there, by definition, have a direct *political* effect on budgets, taxation, government spending and debt reduction. The state, therefore, has a ready-made pretext to intervene and to restrain its own employees should it decide that, for reasons of state, its workers' economic collective bargaining demands can be categorized as "excessive," "unreasonable" or "unjustified," — that is, political in nature.

The Government Uses Its Tools

Not surprisingly, Canadian governments have used this justificatory framework with increasing frequency to reduce public sector workers' rights since the late 1970s. They have done this for a variety of purposes, across a broad front.

Post Office Workers

When Post Office workers were first given statutory collective bargaining rights, they were granted them under the federal *Public Service Staff Relations Act (PSSRA)*. It gives unions the right to bargain about a limited number of issues but, within that framework, they may choose to use the strike to back their demands. The inside Post Office workers always did prefer the strike route, and chose it over arbitration.

In 1978, after more than a year of negotiations, the Canadian Union of Postal Workers (CUPW) exercised its legal right to strike. In due course, back-to-work legislation was passed. Its enactment made headline news throughout the country. Workers felt compelled to go back to work, lest they be punished. The reason was that the back-to-work legislation contained a clause which continued the old collective agreement until a new one was negotiated or imposed by an arbitrator. Concerted refusal to go back to work would be an offence, as strikes are prohibited during the life of a collective agreement. The legislation spelled out the penalties which might be imposed on individuals, union officials and the union should there be a violation of the back-to-work provisions. A separate clause required union officials to tell their members that what had been a statutorily authorized call for a legal strike under the *PSSRA* was now rescinded. This was the sticking point.

Jean-Claude Parrot, the leader of CUPW, refused to make such a statement. This was an understandable position. His union had chosen the strike route rather than the compulsory arbitration one and had bargained in good faith, just as the statute mandated and required. It had exercised its legal right to strike. It was an untenable position for a principled union leader to have to say that a wrong had been committed in this.[13] Curiously, the statutory clause which required this public act of humility by CUPW's leaders did not provide for a penalty should there be a violation of it. As a consequence, its enforcement was left to be implemented by resort to a little-used *Criminal Code* provision.

Section 115 of the *Criminal Code* [now s.126] states that it is a criminal offence to breach any statutory provision of the land which does not set its own penalty. A conviction under s.115 could lead to imprisonment for up to two years, a most serious penalty. Parrot was convicted under this section and sent to jail for three months. His offence was one of exercising his right *not* to speak against his beliefs and values. It was his commitment to his trade union and his cause that motivated him. It was precisely that commitment which goaded the state to exercise its repressive power in this ugly way. It wanted to de-legitimate the idea that any trade union had the right to set its economic and political will against that of the state. This is not idle speculation; it can be proved by looking at the way the government used s.115 of the *Criminal Code* in an analogous case decided at about the same time.

Section 115 was invoked by the state against an RCMP officer who had burned down a barn in Quebec which, supposedly, had been used by the Agence Presse Libre, a group viewed with disfavour by the government. The RCMP officer could have been charged with burglary and arson, two very serious criminal offences with stiff penalties attached to them. Instead, he was charged with a breach of a trivial statutory requirement for which, understandably, there was no penalty. This meant that the government could seek to penalize him under s.115 of the *Criminal Code*. It did so, and he was convicted. But the court found that he did not deserve to suffer any penalty. He was discharged because the motivation behind his wrongdoing was said to be laudable. He had pursued, zealously and misguidedly, what he believed to be hidden government-supported policies. Parrot, by contrast, had had the temerity to pursue a public policy vociferously supported by the state — namely, free collective bargaining; but he had done so at a time when the government had decided, arbitrarily, to suspend the rights it had claimed to have given so whole-heartedly to workers.[14]

CUPW has continued to be met with frontal assaults upon its apparent legal rights. In 1987, another legal strike was met with back-to-work legislation. This time the return-to-work statute contained a provision which decreed that any union officer who did not abide by its requirements would be forbidden from being employed by, or from holding any official position within, the trade union for five years. The workers went back and the union entered into negotiations to deal with the problem. The lesson the federal government wants to teach is clear: it is not going to let full economic bargaining take its natural course, even if it means that it has to negate its own proclamations about the fundamental value of free trade unionism and the freedom of individuals to make choices and to act upon their principles.

In addition to these draconian measures by the government, CUPW has had to cope with the serious limitations on what could be bargained for under the *PSSRA*. It supported a change of status for the Post Office from a directly government-run service to a Crown corporation. In part, the union's hope was that the creation of a Crown corporation would establish a sufficient chasm between its collective bargaining and the political process to enable it to use its economic weaponry to better effect. But the advent of the Canada Post Corporation as the employer, and the associated right of CUPW to use the much fuller collective bargaining powers given to private sector workers by a *Canadian Labour Code*, have not resulted in the realization of this hope. Post Office workers continue to be a target of government hostility.

The singling out of CUPW as public enemy number one has had a lot to do with the fact that it has been a thorn in the side of Liberal and Tory governments alike, for quite a long while. It prides itself on being a union with a social vision. It has championed the legitimacy of the use of economic power to achieve wider social goals. In 1981, it struck the government in order to obtain paid maternity leave. Given the prominence of the union and the fact that the employer was the government, this was seen as a demand for a radical breakthrough in the making of collective agreements. The leadership of CUPW managed to identify itself with the aspirations of women throughout Canada during this successful struggle. As a result of this and other such stances, it is fair to say that CUPW's approach to collective bargaining has been somewhat atypical. It has been natural, therefore, for governments to see CUPW's militancy as a series of challenges to their political authority. Successive governments have characterized this union as a disruptive force, heedless of the public's needs and convenience for which they, the government of the day, have sole responsibility. Governments have justified their many interventions in Post Office bargaining on this basis. The Mulroney government continues to use this fierce ideological battle to its advantage.

Canada Post has become a *cause célèbre* in the struggles that surround privatization. While it is part of big business's agenda to encourage this kind of privatization, there is much public scepticism about its wisdom. In this context, Ottawa uses every opportunity it has to show that worker demands in market-insulated situations are one of the prime causes of inefficiency and costliness. Each CUPW demand is painted as outrageous and as further evidence of the need for market discipline. The federal government has been aided in furthering this image by the way the supposedly autonomous Crown corporation has conducted its industrial relations. The Canada Post Corporation makes life very difficult for CUPW. Daily work practices give rise to endless disputes as supervisors insist on strict obedience to rigid work rules and practices. Just to get an idea of the scope of this campaign of harassment, at any one time there are in excess of 40,000 grievances outstanding. (See Chapter 7.) In addition, the Corporation tends to drag out the bargaining processes and when, finally, CUPW seeks to exercise its right to strike, the government can hardly wait to add its weight to the dispute. When it does so, its focus is to discredit the public sector collective bargaining process.

In 1988, CUPW struck Canada Post once again. It had obeyed all the legal requirements which have to be satisfied to exercise the right to strike. A few days after the commencement of the strike, the government imposed savage back-to-work legislation. As usual, it justified the intervention on the basis that the public was being seriously inconvenienced. An additional reason given was that serious violence was occurring on the picket lines. Both of these arguments were distortions.

Canada Post was telling the public that it was keeping the flow of mail at a satisfactory level, despite the strike, when Ottawa enacted its back-to-work legislation. As to the incidents on the picket line, they were far less serious than those which had occurred a few weeks earlier when the Letter Carriers' Union of Canada was on legal strike against the same employer. There had been no back-to-work legislation in the Letter Carriers' case. Of course, that union had never been as economically and politically militant as CUPW.

The ongoing saga of Post Office labour relations demonstrates that the interposition of a Crown corporation as "employer," which notionally gives workers fully fledged strike rights, still leaves unions more subject to the will of the government of the day than workers in the private sectors are subject to the will of their employers. Moreover, it also shows the great willingness, indeed eagerness, of governments to exercise their power to interfere with a supposedly autonomous industrial relations scheme to achieve their broader political ends.

Designating Some Workers to Be More Vital than Others

To facilitate government's control, some workers in a bargaining unit may be designated "essential workers." This signifies that, should collective bargaining lead to an impasse, all but the designated workers may go on strike. The effectiveness of any ensuing strike will be determined by the number of workers designated as essential employees. If the government can maintain a high level of services during the strike, the striking workers will have no bargaining leverage.

This tactic has gained favour in recent times with Canadian governments as they have sought to undermine the collective bargaining process in their sectors. For instance, in Newfoundland, where public sector employees had been granted the right to strike, the government designated more than one-half of its employees as essential workers.[15] This made public sector strikes there ineffective. Newfoundland has now backed off from this extreme use of designations. It was found to flaunt international labour standards. Ottawa, however, continues to use the tactic with increasing vigour.

Under the federal *Public Service Staff Relations Act*, the politically sensitive task of determining whether a group of workers shall be designated as essential workers belongs to the Public Service Staff

Relations Board (PSSRB), the administrative agency overseeing the operation of the statute. This makes a good deal of political as well as administrative sense. To allow a relatively autonomous agency the responsibility for designations gives the practice of designation an appearance of fairness. The government has to appear before the board as if it were any other party, a *de jure* equal of the union. For a while, the scheme worked well enough and gave workers some protection. In 1982, the Supreme Court of Canada's decision in the *Air Traffic Controllers* case changed all this.[16]

The Canadian Air Traffic Controllers union had announced that it wanted to support fellow unionists in the United States who were members of the Professional Air Traffic Controllers Association (PATCO). PATCO's members had been dismissed by the Reagan administration when they struck for better wages and working conditions. To assist them, their Canadian counterparts threatened not to land flights which had been serviced by PATCO replacements. The Treasury Board, the employer of Canada's air traffic controllers, sought to have all the union's members designated as essential workers. The union responded to this claim by making the incontrovertible point that the employer's ability to obtain such a wholesale designation would render their right to strike meaningless. Moreover, the union argued, this employer tactic ran counter to the requirement that the Public Service Staff Relations Board needed to be convinced by an applicant-employer that the withdrawal of services by employees would affect air safety and security. Only the number of workers who were needed for these purposes should be designated as essential employees. The Public Service Staff Relations Board accepted this argument. The Treasury Board appealed right through to the Supreme Court of Canada. There it was held that the government employer had the unilateral right to determine what level of services had to be maintained by it.

The 1982 *Air Traffic Controllers* decision has had a profound effect, especially in the federal sector. The number of employees sought to be designated as essential by the Treasury Board has increased dramatically since then. Prior to that date, as a consequence of having to apply to the PSSRB for permission to designate, the numbers of workers it suggested should be designated as essential were far more modest than they are now. The Treasury Board had proposed, on average, that 46 percent of each unit's members be so designated and, in some units, less than one-third. By 1984, the

Treasury Board was proposing that 76 percent of its workers be deemed essential and that no bargaining unit have less than one-third of its members designated as essential workers.[17] The Mulroney government has thus been able to diminish actual bargaining rights without having to renounce its publicly proclaimed commitment to freedom of association, with an attendant right to strike, for its own employees. This is quite a coup for a neo-conservative government which has a real interest in the dilution of public sector workers' power.

Purposeful Ad-Hocery

Sometimes governments will claim that a legal exercise of the right to strike is too effective, even if some workers have been designated as essential employees. They then will suspend the right to strike, arguing that innocent people are being hurt and that it is the government's ultimate responsibility to maintain public welfare. In short, the government takes away the collective power of its workers precisely because its exercise is effective. Its justification is that it, and it alone, is to determine how best to protect the public interest. The mechanism used is back-to-work legislation, tailored to deal with the particular strike. In these circumstances, the government does not say that it is abandoning its commitment to its workers' legal right to strike, but rather that it is temporarily suspending it. The argument is that it is merely passing *ad hoc* legislation, necessitated by a temporary difficulty.

More often than not, workers are forced to go back to work on terms they had the legal right to reject. A collective agreement is imposed by an independent arbitration board. If the arbitration board has been given no criteria for imposing an award, it must fashion its own. Sometimes, the back-to-work legislation may provide guidelines as to how the arbitration board is to carry out its task. In the abstract, it is difficult to say whether these processes will lead to better or worse results for workers than untrammelled collective bargaining would have yielded. After all, governments, unlike private sector employers, are not subject to the same kinds of economic pressures. Indeed, very often governments make money during a strike, as wages do not have to be paid, facilities are not opened, monies are not paid out, and so on. Economic strikes are not necessarily effective against government employers. What does make governments come to terms with workers is the political embarrassment of being seen not to pay their own employees well enough and/or being seen as unwilling to give good-quality services. But even if compulsory arbitration imposed by *ad hoc* legislation does not in itself lead to unacceptable results for unions, this weapon of restraint has important effects: First, workers are not given the option to find out whether or not their strike would have yielded good results. Second, this kind of government intervention robs them of one of the most important incidents of industrial citizenship, namely, the right to stand up for themselves.

This option is being removed increasingly often as governments become ever more intent on cutting wage costs and worker power, regardless of the political costs. Between 1950 and 1954, on average, the federal and provincial governments used back-to-work legislation 0.2 times per year; this rose to 0.4 times per year during the period 1955–59, and to 0.6 times per year in the years 1960–64. The equivalent figures for the periods 1975–79, 1980–84, and 1985–87 were 5.0, 4.4 and 7.0 respectively.[18] Governments obviously are finding it easier to claim that the public interest is threatened by strikes and, equally clearly, they see real political value in doing so.

Blanket Restraints

Ad-hoc back-to-work legislation characterizes an otherwise lawful strike as being too harmful. Increasingly, governments are saying that there should be a blanket prohibition on strikes for the foreseeable future. The justification for these kinds of decrees is that the economy simply cannot tolerate the threat of strikes. Production must be stable and the lid must be kept on wage costs.

The ball was set rolling by Trudeau's Anti-Inflation Board (AIB) legislation in 1975. Its stated aim was to attack the unacceptable inflationary effect of collective bargaining wage settlements in the private sectors. As noted in Chapter 2, the success of this strategy in dampening wage gains was enormous. Governments learned that it was possible to exercise effective income restraint. Of course, it is politically difficult to use AIB-type legislation on a regular basis. Canada's public policy has been supposedly steadfast in its commitment to free collective bargaining, especially in the private sector, where a market-dominated régime makes sense. But this logic has not precluded augmented use of income-restraint legislation in the public sectors.

Since 1975, the year in which the AIB legislation was introduced, a flood of federal and provincial legislation has temporarily suspended the right to strike of all public sector workers.[19] Objectively, this could not be justified on the basis that public sector wage gains were too rich. Rather, the idea was to signal the need for private employers to hold the line, as will be shown below.[20]

Public Sector Bargaining Rights and the Right-Wing Agenda

There are plans afoot to adapt the economy to the demands of global competitiveness. To this end, it is the state's aim to make unions less resistant, less confrontational than they are perceived to be at present. Government is intent on creating a highly flexible, willing and competitive labour force. It is in this context that the intensification of attacks on public sector unions has to be understood. Erosion of public sector workers' standing is crucial to obtaining public support for the conservative economic agenda.

Governments have become increasingly confident that their tough wage-restraint legislation does not meet with much disapproval from the public at large. There are instances, of course, when the public has supported public sector worker demands. Examples already given include the case of British Columbia's Operation Solidarity and the Alberta nurses' illegal strike. But governments have been relatively successful in their efforts to convince the public that they are entitled to set limits on the participatory rights of their own workers. Their right to strike has been characterized as an exercise in selfishness, and their demands are successfully portrayed as being out of line with their productivity. The proliferation in Canada of neo-conservative governments has turned up the volume of these arguments. These governments have been keen to discredit the delivery of social and public services. Implicit is the thought that, if these employees were in the private sector, they would soon be brought to heel. As a consequence, what seems on the surface to be a series of *ad hoc* responses to many unrelated industrial disputes is starting to amount to a reversal of the public commitment to the maintenance of public sector bargaining rights.

While it is hard to know to what extent governments have actually saved money by these tactics, it is certainly clear that they have sent an unmistakable message to the private sector. Not only is it permitted to be tough with trade unions but, in fact, it is laudable to undermine them. That this is the intent is illustrated by evidence provided by the *Public Service Alliance* case.[21]

When the federal government passed its "6 and 5" legislation in 1982, it suspended its employees' right to strike. The Public Service Alliance of Canada complained that its constitutionally guaranteed freedom of association had been violated, and challenged the legislation in the courts. The government argued successfully that the *Charter*'s guarantee of freedom of association did not include the right to strike. It also had contended that, even if there was a constitutionally protected right to strike, the government was entitled to take it away, at least for a while. Such a restriction would amount to a reasonable limitation on this constitutional right in a free and democratic society. To buttress this argument, the government's lawyers argued that the federal government was charged with the responsibility of reducing inflationary pressures arising from a wage push. Accordingly, it was proper for it to seek to contain wage gains sought by its own workers.

The problem with the argument was, as the government frankly admitted, that there was not enough evidence to show that public sector workers were in the vanguard of a national wage push. This did not matter, said the lawyers, because what the government was setting out to do was to restrain its own workers in order to demonstrate to private sector employers that there was an urgent need to resist wage demands made upon them by their unions.[22]

The government's motive is not always articulated so explicitly. More typically, governments wink and nod at private sector employers, egging them on to adopt union-restraining strategies. A form of duplicity is at work. As employers, governments continue to suggest to the public that they believe in freedom of association for their workers and that, in a liberal democratic welfare state, an employer should not have the unilateral right or power to determine its employees' conditions of work. But, at the same time, the private sector is being told that these are not such important principles; after all, the governments themselves do not adhere to them. To many employers this may indicate that governments may be losing their eagerness to enforce the rules that promote trade unionism. Some of the more draconian measures taken by governments against their public sector unions certainly have had this effect.[23]

In 1982, the Parti Québécois (PQ) ordered its public sector workers, who had been on strike, to resume work on conditions which were to be set by decree.[24] There was not even to be an arbitration process during which the workers would get an opportunity to present their view as to what conditions ought to obtain. Normally, when governments take away the right to strike, they acknowledge the need to make up for this loss by providing an alternative dispute-resolution scheme to mediate employer power. The failure to do this in this case, in the very province in which public sector unionism made its initial breakthrough, cannot but have an impact on the industrial relations climate in both the public and private sector. Similarly, in British Columbia, following Operation Solidarity, the government eventually passed legislation which made strikes and lock-outs subject to supervision by the minister if he or she believed that an essential service whose withdrawal could harm the health and well-being of the provincial economy was affected. This too was an unambiguous message that, for that government, free collective bargaining was no longer a valued priority.

The signals conveyed by Canadian governments are amplified by non-analytical media coverage of public sector strikes. The press tends to concentrate on picket-line unrest and sentimental stories about individuals who are adversely affected by interruptions to public services. This reinforces the general perception that, when workers are protected from job insecurity and when they have been given the right to exercise collective power, the results are rigidities, inefficiencies and unnecessary costs. The production of goods and the delivery of services becomes costly and unpredictable. The implication is that a more effective form of market discipline is needed. This will make workers compete harder for new employment opportunities and for the better-paying jobs. Not only the federal but also several provincial governments have done their utmost when they could to push labour markets in this direction. Bourassa in Quebec, Bennett and Vander Zalm in British Columbia, Devine in Saskatchewan and Getty in Alberta — each has embraced a return to market fundamentalism.

Part of the logic of these neo-conservative governments is to let the private sector provide as many services as possible. Since it is clear that, in Canada, the service sectors show the greatest potential for growth, the tendency is to have governments get out of the delivery of public services and to turn them into traded services supplied by individual firms. For instance, there is increasing pressure on the publicly funded health sectors to contract out intensive care work for the aged and chronically ill, as well as aspects of hospital management.[25] In addition, governments have instituted other practices which follow the lead of private sector behaviour. A great number of government clerical workers are now hired on a contractual basis rather than as permanent employees. This yields conservative-minded governments savings since they do not have to pay the social benefits package that their unionized employees receive. These kinds of changes often are not obvious to the public. There are occasions, however, when governments are more brazen about their intent to transfer business to the private sector. Then they are likely to be met by opposition from the workers affected. Indeed, these workers may be supported by a public that fears that the level of services to which it has grown accustomed will be reduced. A British Columbia experience provides a telling case in point.

The Bennett government had decided to sell some of its road-building and road-maintenance equipment. Workers were alarmed by the potential job losses and the worsening of working conditions for those who were to be employed by the new contractors. To counter their resistance, the government proposed that workers could bid to become the new owners of the services to be put on the auction block. This was unacceptable to the unionized workforce, which did not have the means to be a credible bidder. The British Columbia Government Employees Union (BCGEU), the relevant union, went to court and won a decision which upheld the right of a worker to remain a government employee if his or her job was privatized as a result of the contracting out of government services.[26] The government reacted by announcing that workers should have to show that they were turned down for a job by the new employers before they would be offered back their government job (or severance pay in lieu thereof). Workers could not accept this arrangement, which meant that they might be forced to accept low-wage employment by the new operators. The union conducted a successful strike on the issue. In September 1988, it won a settlement which entitled the workers to turn down a job offer by the new private sector employers and yet retain a position as government employees. In this case, the privatization effort failed.[27]

The B.C. government's crude behaviour, while more transparent than most, is symptomatic of a general movement to discredit public sector bargaining rights, something which has been occurring at an accelerated rate over the last ten to fifteen years. Governments have been able to make good use of the argument that their employees, because they pursue their own narrow self-interest, are a barrier to modernization. This tactic has been more than useful to them. Public employee-bashing not only goes some way towards cutting down the payroll during a time of rising deficits, it also reduces the standing of the delivery of social service programs to the public by public means. Contracting out and privatization are made progressively easier and the notion that competition is good and, inferentially, that monopolistic labour practices are bad, is advanced.

This recasting of public policy involves the dilution of the little Keynesianism that Canada has experienced. Its logic also demands the imposition of ever-increasing discipline on labour markets. To achieve this, the federal government, in particular, has held the line on social expenditures. Grattan Gray has calculated that "federal social expenditures [have] declined from 8.1 per cent of Gross Domestic Product in 1984/85 to a projected 7.1 per cent of GDP in 1990/91. The 17.5 per cent real increase in GDP from 1984 to 1991 far surpasses the 2.0 per cent rise in social spending over the same period."[28] While the Mulroney government has not succeeded in slashing as much as it wants, there is little question that it has gone a long way towards its ultimate goal. Its rhetoric, especially in respect of unemployment insurance, bristles with the notion that a serious moral hazard is presented by the many people who seek to rely on public handouts. This is why UIC qualifications have been made much tougher and the benefits lower.[29] The idea being peddled is that paternalism is a thing of yesteryear and that, if only people were willing to adapt themselves to a competitive market, the general welfare level of all would increase. The atmosphere thus created is a very encouraging one for non-unionized employers. It is demoralizing for workers in general and for public sector employees in particular.

From Defence to Offence?

The institutions that signalled progress for public sector unions during the 1960 reform period are still in place, formally. But these institutions were based on concepts more apposite to the market model, and therefore always had a problematic life in the public sector. Governments have been able to exploit the inherent contradictions. They have done so with ever more telling effect as they make radical changes in their economic planning. Public sector workers have become pawns in a larger game. But the very fact that there is a supposed commitment to full collective bargaining rights means that unions may be able to resist this trend. To do so, however, they will have to show the electorate that the delivery of services by governments can be of high quality and that it is a public good which must be protected. If this case can be made more successfully than it has been to date, it can be demonstrated that public sector workers' rights should be guaranteed and respected. This case needs to be part of a larger strategy which Canada's progressive forces must develop.

Technology: Promise or Threat?

Possibilities and Vistas

Technology is a term that describes how productive work is undertaken. In its broadest sense, it encompasses the machinery, materials and substances, special processes, and managerial strategies in use, as well as the deployment of the workforces. In market economies, technology is used to maximize return on investment. The idea is to produce a compromise between quality and quantity of product, on the one hand, and the cost of producing it to make the firm as competitive as it can be, on the other. In this sense, there is nothing fundamentally new about the modern technologies: they are used to achieve the same efficiency-inspired goals that the older technologies served. But the contemporary interest in technology arises from the belief that new scientific capacities will make a revolutionary difference in lowering the cost of production and restoring profit levels.[1]

The potential is there to permit quantum leaps in productivity and to achieve the wholesale realignment of work processes. In manufacturing, the new technologies make possible advances in design, in drafting, in the lay-out of manufacturing products, in engineering analysis and design, in the establishment of systems for storing and transmitting instructions, in resource planning and ordering, in the utilization of recording capacity (both to initiate work orders and to control inventory on the basis of sales orders), and in the development of machine tool re-programming and robotics.[2] In addition, they have the capacity to improve inspection systems and to provide statistical quality control. They can enhance flexibility in manufacturing by facilitating small- to medium-scale batch production, the re-tooling of machines and the introduction of multi-product production on the same production line. Similar advantages can be obtained in telecommunications by way of electronic mail, fibre optics, and facsimile transmissions. Office automation has become possible, and innovations such as improved electronic funds transfers and automatic teller machines are likely to lead to dramatic changes in the production and delivery of services. A major impetus for the wholesale deployment of these new computer-based technologies, then, is the fact that they are capable of yielding great benefits in those very sectors where the Fordist assembly-line production methods have outlived their usefulness.

Fordism was a unique blend of efficiency, waste and rigidity. As a system of production, it allowed for only one kind of product on any one assembly line at a time. This limited the ability of firms to produce a wide range of products or to respond to sophisticated and highly unpredictable changes in consumer demands; it relied on stable, predictable markets, long production runs and a relatively unskilled workforce. On the factory floor, its principal drawback was the fragmentation of the work process.[3] It led to high levels of worker alienation and absenteeism which, in turn, led to worker resistance. This made it difficult to increase output. These aspects of the Fordist model have forced management to look for new social and technical forms of organization in order to renew sources of productivity within the firm.[4]

The new scientific machinery is, therefore, very attractive. There is now an opportunity to produce more for less by marrying mass-production techniques with flexible production systems; to produce better-quality goods more cheaply by introducing rigorous zero-defect production standards and to be more competitive by innovating constantly in response to changing markets. The buzzwords used to describe the new modes of production are "lean" and "innovative." It is part of this vision to have people work harder and smarter in work teams in a new factory setting.

The idea of this electronic factory is that there will be multi-skilled workers who work in cohesive units and who are capable of moving efficiently between different modules of the operation. Under the old system — despite the best efforts of Taylorism — manufacturing, design and information co-ordination were discrete activities, with only rudimentary forms of inter-sphere integration.[5] The new technologies not only allow, but their efficient deployment requires, consolidation of all these constitutive elements of production to connect what would otherwise be disparate spheres of production.

To make this work, employees will need to be given a greater amount of discretion. In the words of technology expert Shoshana Zuboff, "anyone with the wit to access the data can discern patterns

Table 10.1
Flexible Automation Performance in Japan

	"Hard" Automation	"Flexible" Automation	Effect
Toshiba Tungaloy (cutting tool plant)			
No. of machine tools	50	6	88% decline in use of machines
Operating rate as a percentage of downtime	20%	70%	350% increase in operating rate
Floor space (sq. metres)	1480	350	76% decline
Work time as a percentage of output (days)	18.6	4.2	77% decline
Niigata Engineering (section of diesel engine plant)			
No. of machine tools	31	5	84% decline
Work time as a percentage of output (days)	16	4	75% decline

Flexible Automation Performance in Ontario

	1979 Machines	1983 Machine System
Price of equipment	c. $2MM	c. $2MM
Labour requirement	9/shift	1/shift
Machining time/unit	300 min.	71 min.
Downtime	required on third shift	none

Source: Daiwa Securities, Research Report on Flexible Manufacturing Systems, 1982, cited in *The Technology Challenge: Ontario Faces the Future* (Ministry of Industry and Trade, 1984), p. 81; Limur Ltd., Ariss, Ontario, 1983, cited in *The Technology Challenge*, p. 87.

Table 10.2
Fordist and Post-Fordist Practices Compared

Labour Skills	Fordist	Post-Fordist
Training amount	limited	continuous training
Training frequency	one-time	continual
Responsibility	narrow execution of tasks	self-activating, multi-skilled
Accuracy	few special skills, low technical-process competence	continual improvement, increased production precision
Expertise	manual, by rote	self-starting, problem-solving
Interaction	individual work station	teamwork, small station or group assembly

Source: Adapted from Ontario Task Force on Employment and New Technology, Appendix 3 (Toronto, Ontario), 1985, tables 4 and 5.

and dynamics, anticipate problems and opportunities, and make connections.... The informated business invites the whole work force to think strategically."[6] This will empower workers.

The prospects that this idealized version conjure up are pleasing to business. Profitability should be enhanced, efficiency increased and global competitiveness improved. By the same token, workers understand that increased productivity should mean a larger economic pie to bargain for and a potential increase in their standard of living. Moreover, more involvement in production decisions should enrich workers' lives. In theory, all parties should favour the wholesale introduction of these new production methods. The question is whether this will be the way it will work out in practice. The issue is not a straightforward one.

To get a handle on it, we are going to look at the adaptation of technology in Canada in three sectors. The format in which policymakers and researchers utilize technology in Canada is structured in this way; we are adopting it for our own purposes.

Figure 10.1
The Pre-Electronic Organization of Factory Production

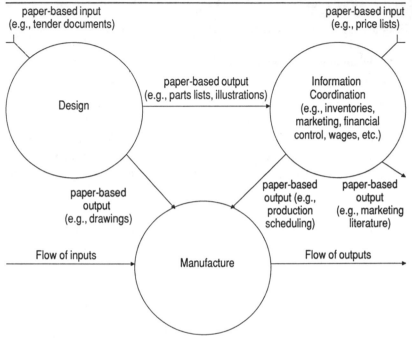

Electronic Organization of Production: Intersphere Co-ordination of Design, Information and Manufacturing

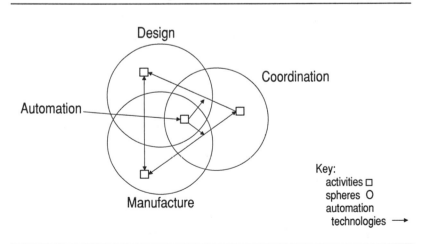

Source: Raphael Kaplinsky, *op. cit.*, pp. 24–27.

The first sector is that of leading-edge users. Many government commissions and think-tanks, typified by the Premier's Council of Ontario, start off with the presumption that Canada has no choice but to try to establish a prominent presence in the new global economy. To obtain such a foothold, it is argued, it will be necessary to acquire niches based on Canada's strengths in resources, manufacturing and communication industries. The new technologies are to be used to this end. The hope is that a handful of multinational firms will emerge, enabling Canada to participate fruitfully in the wide-open global economy. If the ideal deployment of technology is likely to take place anywhere, it will happen in these leading-edge enterprises. It is anticipated that the impetus given by the development of new processes by these home-grown multinationals will accelerate the diffusion of technology throughout the Canadian economy. This, it is said, should strengthen the competitive position of both small- and medium-sized firms. The plan reads well, but the results thus far raise many questions about the wisdom of this strategy.

The use made of new technologies in small- and medium-sized firms is the second issue to be examined. One would expect these businesses to find it more difficult to make profitable use of the new technologies. Indeed, Canada remains a laggard in the adaptation of technologies in this sector.

The third sector to be examined is constituted by the service industries. Our finding here is that new technologies are put to great use in this segment of the economy. But, regrettably, not in the way technology enthusiasts envisage.

Leading-Edge Users of Technology in Canada

The most technology-intensive goods-producing sectors in Canada are transportation equipment, electrical products, non-electrical machinery and fabricated metal products.[7] The firms involved include car manufacturers, aerospace corporations (such as Boeing, Pratt and Whitney, McDonnell Douglas, Spar) and communications enterprises — particularly one giant, Northern Telecom. The technologies these firms have introduced range right across the spectrum of available machinery. They include computer-aided design and engineering, numerical control machines, pick-and-place robots, laser-based fabrication, more complex robots, automated material-handling systems, sensor and testing equipment, as well as communications and control networks, both on and off the factory floor. The introduction

of these machines has had a positive effect on the competitive position and productivity of the firms which employ them. For instance,
at Northern Telecom, the profits per employee increased from
$2,293.00 in 1976 to $9,359.00 in 1986.[8] While this looks hopeful,
it does not tell the whole story.

First, the level of sophistication shown by the leading-edge users
of technology is an underdeveloped one. These firms use the new
devices and work processes mainly to enhance the efficiency of
existing product lines. In this aspect they are successful users of
technology and, importantly, they are a match for their American
competitors. But they lag badly when it comes to the creation of new
technologies that speed up the development of new product lines and,
therefore, the creation of specialized niches for their businesses. In
part, as we shall see, this is due to the short-sightedness of Canadian
governments.[9] More directly, it is a result of Canadian business's lack
of interest in investing to promote and take advantage of innovative
thinking. As a percentage of the GDP, the amount of money spent
on research and development by individual Canadian firms is lower
than that of their counterparts in France, the Netherlands, the United
Kingdom, the United States, Sweden and Japan. Indeed, their research and development expenditure is only one-third that of Japanese and Swedish industrial leaders.[10]

Thus it is that even in the most technology-oriented sectors
(telecommunications and electrical equipment production), Canadian
firms, on average, adopt the technology to compete on new product
lines some five to nine years after their foreign competitors do.[11] This
makes it improbable that even these relatively efficient users of new
production technologies can become the cutting-edge firms which
Canadian policy-makers would like to see emerge.

A second factor that casts doubts on the possibility of our lead-
ing-sector actors becoming the engine of a new kind of economy is
that they employ very few people themselves. And in some, employment actually has declined. It is not true, of course, that the increased
output per worker which new technological applications bring necessarily leads to job losses. After all, firms may expand in new
directions. In some circumstances, however, job displacement is not
only a possible but a likely outcome of new processes and technologies. The experience at Northern Telecom is telling. In 1982, at its
London plant, 1,725 workers produced one million telephone units.
In 1987, only 909 workers produced 1.8 million units. The workforce

Table 10.3
Percentage of Firms Using Selected Technologies

Technology	Percentage of firms using the technology
CAD or CAE	18.2
CAD/CAM	10.5
CAD for procurement	7.7
Stand-alone NC/CNC machines	19.2
FMC or FMS	10.8
Laser fabrication	3.4
Robots	8.0
Automated materials handling	7.3
Computer-based inspection/testing	18.1
Local area or intercompany networks	23.1
Programmable controllers	25.4
Computerized factory control	16.3

Source: Adapted from D.G. McFetridge, "The Distinguishing Characteristics of Users of New Manufacturing Technologies," Report prepared for Ontario Ministry of Industry, Trade and Technology, November 1988, Table I, p. 14. Establishments surveyed accounted for 51.2 percent of the value of 1986 manufacturing shipments.

had been cut in half, while the output had doubled. Again, at the same plant, the new automated plastic moulding presses now require only one operator for every two machines, whereas the old presses required one operator per machine. The potential is clear: in some situations, the new technologies will lead to lessened employment.[12]

In addition, there is no solid evidence that the firms that produce high technology in Canada contribute very much to indirect employment growth by improving the competitiveness and profitability of firms in other sectors.[13] This is so because Canada imports, rather than develops, most of the technology it deploys. The failure to generate much new employment within the leading sectors and the incapacity to create backward and forward links does not bode well for a strategy built around a reliance on the development of leading-edge firms; it is difficult to see how the kind of leading-edge firms we do develop will give a spur to the establishment of better and more competitive small firms to service them, which, in turn, will lead to more employment and welfare.

Technology Laggards: Small and Medium-Sized Firms

Much of Canada's industrial and manufacturing economy is composed of small firms employing less than 100 employees. This is where most of the industrial and manufacturing workers are employed. Many of these firms are suppliers to leading firms in their industries. Their position is fiercely competitive. For many of them, the new technologies represent as much of a problem as a solution.

Nonetheless, new computer-based innovations are being employed by some of these firms. But those that use the new devices on a large scale and in sophisticated ways constitute only a very small percentage of all high-technology users. Data derived from responses to a survey of 4,600 respondents conducted by Statistics Canada in 1987 show this clearly.

These results are particularly telling because 50 percent of the surveyed firms were large firms and 50 percent medium-sized ones. It is reasonable to assume that medium-sized and small firms will make below-average use of the new production machines and techniques. The figures show just how spotty the use of available technologies is. Canadian small and medium-sized firms adopt only bits and pieces of the latest production techniques and they do even this hesitantly. In short, a large number of Canadian workers are exposed only to the most limited deployment of new technologies. Likewise, it is rare that whole sectors, or even a majority of small firms in any given sector, come anywhere near to approaching their European, let alone their Japanese, counterparts in the use of sophisticated systems of technology.

The reasons for this are two-fold. First, acquiring leading-edge technology is beyond the reach of many small firms. They cannot afford the high cost of the new computer-driven technology and do not have the managerial expertise necessary to deploy it efficiently. Second, Canada's business culture sees its authority threatened by flexible work practices and tends to resist the intelligent use of such new production systems. What is remarkable is that Canadian governments have done little to surmount these obstacles, either through funding research or by means of positive intervention.

Government: All Talk and No Action

That Canadian governments lag badly in their support for the private sector has become conventional wisdom. There has been a massive outpouring of important policy documents and government statements in Canada over the last twenty years to this effect. A partial list includes reports by the Science Council of Canada, Ontario's Premier's Council, the Royal Commission on Canada's Economic Future, the Canadian Manufacturers' Association and the Economic Council of Canada.[14] These agencies and commissions have urged the private sector to modernize, and point to the fact that many of the new production techniques will have to be imported unless government funds are available to bring Canada up to the standard of industrial competitors. That funding has not been forthcoming. A 1989 Canadian Manufacturers' Association study found Canada second-last among eight leading industrial countries in the provision of government-funded research and development as a percentage of GDP.[15] The results reflect this.

The Economic Council of Canada found that, in 1984, Canada ranked ninth out of ten countries in the number of robots used per 10,000 workers in manufacturing — well behind Japan and Sweden. The Evans research corporation places Canada three to four years behind the United States in the rate of adoption of robot technology — and the United States ranks well below Japan and Sweden. The situation with respect to numerically controlled machine tools is disturbing. As a proportion of all machine tools in use, Canada, with a deployment of 4.4 percent in 1983, ranked well behind Japan (38.1 percent), the United States (12.9 percent), and the United Kingdom (8.1 percent). There were two areas where Canadian firms' adoption of technologies fared relatively well. The rate of adoption of automated inspection and quality control equipment and of automated materials handling equipment had nearly caught up with Japan by 1985.[16]

Although the adverse impacts of the government's failure to commit itself financially to R&D are felt across the economic spectrum, it is particularly small and medium-sized firms that are caught between a rock and a hard place. They need to compete with the many alternative suppliers of component parts. Foreign competitors often have the advantage of lower cost structures and greater government and industry commitment to the new technologies. But, in Canada, where this support is not readily available, small and medium-sized firms are able to afford only bits and pieces of the available machinery. The costs of innovation are too high and, from their viewpoint, there is no guarantee that their competitive position will be sufficiently enhanced to make it worthwhile. The importance of the cost-risk factors to Canadian businesses is reflected in the findings of two business researchers. Their inquiry was aimed at finding out what factors their employer-respondents took into account when considering the purchase and introduction of new technology. In order of descending importance they were as follows:

- total costs involved (63 percent)
- uncertainty regarding benefits (54 percent)
- expertise required (45 percent)
- perceived payback (45 percent)
- technical requirements (38 percent)
- employee attitudes (35 percent)
- union or employee group relations (32 percent)[17]

All of this means that, in the absence of effective government subvention, employers caught in the dilemma of high costs and uncertain returns are tempted to perfect their old methods to turn a profit. The natural tendency is to find ways to push wages down rather than to invest in value-adding practices.[18] This tendency conforms with prevailing Canadian managerial thinking and practice.

Business Culture: New-Tech Talk and Old-Tech Thinking

The need to restructure work organization and deploy new technologies is part of contemporary conventional wisdom. Many managers are aware that this means that they should reconsider the role and significance of the production worker. Phrases such as "we believe that people who are actually producing in plants know what's going on with it"; "you work at a job eight hours a day, who knows more about the job than that person?"; "number one, start talking with the operator"; " 'line' operators have the best practical knowledge ... the primary function ... of management is to focus on the needs of the production operator" are often heard.[19]

These statements of respect for employee know-how contain two thoughts. First, an understanding that workers should be more directly involved in designing work processes; second, an acknowledgement that they are to be offered more control and responsibility.

This dovetails with the views of technology experts such as Adler.[20] He argues, with a great deal of vigour, that the new technologies will not be put to their best use unless a new business culture evolves, one which allows for a more egalitarian relationship between managers and workers. His contention is that it is essential to develop an atmosphere which leads to spontaneous co-operation. This is to be made possible by the acceptance of values which are truly shared by employers and employees. Industrial democracy, in its widest sense, is to become the *sine qua non* of the modernized workplace. Only in this context can a strategy be developed which will permit the efficient integration of the new technologies.[21] In Canada, however, not only are firms ill-placed to create truly integrated automated production units but, despite their well-intentioned pronouncements about the need for flexibility and co-operation, Canadian managers spend relatively little money on educating their workers (or themselves) in the use of the new technologies.

The Economic Council of Canada has found that Canadian workers get only 2 hours of in-plant training compared with 100 to 200 hours for their Japanese equivalents. Further, out of 1,000 Canadian establishments surveyed, less than 5 percent provided occupational training for their workers. The Council concluded, with obvious chagrin, that most firms did little more than "adopt[ing] existing skills to new equipment."[22] The required workplace reorganization simply is not taking place. But it is not workers who are at the core of the problem. Despite all the talk acknowledging the need for new workplace relations, managers continue to see workers as adjuncts to the machines, rather than the other way around. Why is this so? Some useful data that cast light on the nature and origin of the contradictions created by the availability of technology and the need to deploy it imaginatively, and on existing managerial practices, have been furnished by the CAW Technology Project.

It found that the most important development on the shop-floor is that team work has been organized so that people can be asked to do several tasks, instead of the one repetitive task to which they had been restricted previously. These new demands on workers may not involve the learning of any significant new skills. Often, it is more a case of multi-tasking than of multi-skilling. At the other end of the spectrum, the teamwork concept has been used to integrate previously discrete spheres of production. When this has happened, the level of new skills required might be quite high. One of the other observations of the CAW study was that, as job categories become unnecessary and unproductive, persons who were in low-level managerial positions often become part of the new work teams. In the same vein, there has been a tendency for engineers to replace technicians, as the specialized skills of engineers are needed less and less. The other side of the coin is that, as the old classifications systems break down, workers are being given responsibility that used to belong to supervising personnel under the pre-existing scheme of organization. Inspection, too, has changed in character. In some cases, it can be done by machines. This reduces the need for inspectors. Fewer people, with a greater understanding of technology, can do better and more quality testing of the product line.

The CAW study is balanced in its appraisal of these kinds of workplace innovations. It recognizes that some real advances have been made but that much depends on management's attitude towards the deployment of the new technologies. In this context, the CAW study expresses strong disappointment with the kind of training that is on offer in the industries it organizes, although it carefully notes that the educational efforts vary in sophistication from plant to plant and from firm to firm. Workers told the CAW that frequently there was no efficient — or, indeed, any — formal training programs for them at all. They have had to learn their new tasks as they go along. As a result, they often feel stressed and express discontent with their worklife. This is hardly evidence that the new technologies are fostering a more humanized workplace. The new responsibilities which many workers have been given have not made them feel better. The CAW identified a partial explanation for this malaise. Some managers show a marked preference for training young, more educated workers rather than for retraining their older existing workforce. The CAW also discovered that some managers, despite proclamations to the contrary, tend to make decisions on their own about the introduction of new technology. When this happens, the workers feel that they are being confronted with a *fait accompli*. It is made clear to them that their managers believe, as they always have, that training is meant to ensure that workers are made to adapt to machines, rather than the other way around.

Nonetheless, the CAW found that workers remain hopeful. After all, some workers have become multi-skilled and many have been entrusted with more responsibilities. On the whole, workers are quite supportive of the introduction of the new technologies and processes.

They tend to accept the argument that these new work practices are essential to their job security and the maintenance of their living standard. Further, they believe that the quality of their worklife will be improved greatly by the innovations. This dovetails with the findings of Munro and Noori, cited earlier. Those scholars reported that even in the non-leading sectors, employee attitude is not a serious obstacle when firms decide whether or not to introduce new production methods.[23] This is reflective of the fact that, on the whole, workers are positive, even optimistic, about the new technologies, and not the luddites they are often portrayed to be. This being so, we can now face more directly the question as to why, despite the lip-service paid to the desirability of new, flexible work methods and technologies by business, Canadian management is so slow and heavy-handed in the introduction and adaptation of the new technologies. In part, the explanation is to be found in the structure and culture of labour relations in Canada.

This study has emphasized that the collective bargaining system has left the prerogative of management largely unfettered. Rigid, hierarchical top-down management techniques continue to dominate Canadian production. The power to bargain collectively allows Canadian workers to off-set this only marginally. They protect themselves from the arbitrary power of supervisors by negotiating for seniority ladders and discrete job classifications. This restrains the employers' capacity to exercise whimsical preferences and to instigate unilateral alterations of the work process. Something of a paradox has emerged: as workers are limited to alienating, precisely detailed functions, discretion and disciplinary power are vested in line supervisors; the top-down concept of management is reinforced. A consequence is that low- and middle-level managers have much to lose should workers come to have more of a say and become multi-skilled, the preconditions for effective modernization.[24] These lower-level managerial cadres are all too likely, especially in smaller firms, to resist the adoption of more flexible work practices. This means that when new schemes are introduced, they often tend to be reflections of the older modes of managerial thinking. The emphasis remains control over workers, rather than workers' control. This pill is sweetened sometimes by giving it a coating of "flexibility," but its content all too often remains bitter, because "flexibility" often signifies flexible workers rather than flexible processes.

Workplace Flexibility: Myth or Reality?

Workers are being asked to vary their hours of work to accord with the productive needs of their employer. In addition, very often, even in the less technologically sophisticated spheres, workers are organized into semi-autonomous work groups. These re-arrangements have many forms. They include concepts such as socio-technical systems (STS), employee involvement (EI), quality of worklife (QWL), and flexi-time arrangements. While these innovations are not, in and of themselves, harmful to workers' interests, they are more market-oriented than focused on industrial democracy. This is already well documented. The Economic Council of Canada found that, while only 30 percent of respondents in a survey of enterprises it conducted had joint management-labour committees, what was even more telling was that "most (of these committees) do not have a major role to play with respect to technological change."[25] This indicates that most of the innovations are introduced in a top-down way, reflecting the existing business culture. Furthermore, the same Economic Council of Canada study shows that "schemes to redesign jobs through enlargement, rotation, and enrichment were practised by fewer than one-quarter of [the] survey respondents."[26] That is, not only are they top-down when they are introduced, but innovations of this kind are not all that common.[27]

There are other consequences of the dominant business culture's response to the need for workplace restructuring. When innovative technologies are introduced, firms take it to be an opportunity to get rid of expensive unionized work. Firms often characterize this as the natural corollary of the development of the flexibility mandated by the new competitive pressures. But, while there can never be enough flexibility of this kind for employers, there may be too much for workers.

For instance, at Northern Telecom, one of the leading users of technology, the lead time of orders has become much shorter and the ability of the firm to respond to variable market conditions much greater. This is referred to as "numeric flexibility." What it is, in fact, is an increase in the employer's ability to change its level of employment in response to changing market conditions. Lay-offs and recalls have become more frequent. As one worker told the CAW research unit: "The way Northern is looking at it, they are going to have a full-time staff and a part-time staff. 'We'll lay them off when the work is slow but we will get ninety-five percent of them back so who cares.' That is Northern's attitude." As the CAW summed it up: "Northern has taken to recalling people on a temporary basis rather than laying them off on a temporary basis."[28]

The shift from full-time to part-time labour is also furthered by the ability of firms to contract out work. This is much easier in Canada than it is in many of the more advanced European countries because, until now, Canadian labour has not been very successful in constraining employers' prerogative to contract out work. (See chapters 3 and 6.)

One of the things which permits Canada's business class to use technology in this narrow, worker-unfriendly manner, is that labour has never had any serious input into workplace decision making. Fragmented bargaining, focused on periodic wage increases and some job protection, has left management relatively unchallenged in its control over the enterprise. As was noted in Chapter 3, only 54.6 percent of major collective agreements contain any technology-protection clauses, and most of these are feeble and ineffective. Further, half the population has no collective bargaining protection at all and, despite the intransigent approach of Canadian business, governments are unwilling to intercede meaningfully on labour's behalf.[29]

Many business and government representatives make the argument that the increased incidence of contracting out will not necessarily result in a net loss of jobs if the contracted-out work is to be done in Canada. This may or may not be the case. Just as the new technologies make it possible to have high-quality products manufactured just-in-time in Canada, they make it feasible to have them produced in the same way in low-wage regions of other nations.

The potential to go offshore already is being exploited by many manufacturing sectors in Canada. This is particularly so for Canadian auto parts producers and other industries integrated into the United States economy. Canada always has suffered from being at the bottom end of the market; it specializes in manufacturing component parts for American multinationals, rather than putting out finished goods. A lot of small branch-plant firms vie fiercely with each other to supply parts to these large multinationals. Since, increasingly, the Americans can get component parts manufacturing done more cheaply in areas such as the Mexican-Texas border, and in other such places, they are all the more likely to move out of Canada and/or to get their parts from elsewhere. The trend is clear. The recent Canada-United States Free Trade Agreement has made it more possible for American multinationals to close their Canadian branch-plant operations and to move them to less costly areas without losing their hold on the Canadian market. This North American rationalization poses additional new dangers for a workforce already facing major structural change. Many jobs are being shed.[30]

Employers understand the bargaining potential of their ability to contract out work. They may use it as a disciplinary tool when workers resist the introduction of new technologies. The threat is often put to the workers explicitly. Indeed, Holmes has suggested that the introduction of new technologies in this way is one of the most significant features of the labour relations scene.[31]

Canadian managers and policy-makers make it clear that employees should be flexible as the world-wide availability of production techniques challenges Canadian competitiveness and, therefore, job security and welfare. This gives a resonance to their demands for concessions from the labour force. Workers with some seniority may be pressured to agree to a reduced workforce to guarantee their own job security or they may be cajoled into accepting a two-tier employment system. They may agree that future employees will be hired at lower wage rates and/or that the employer be allowed to hire temporary workers as it needs them. None of this is calculated to improve trade union strength; nor are other aspects of the way in which new work methods are being deployed in Canada.

There is a drive towards tying workers' welfare more directly to the employer's profitability. A whole host of new pay systems are being developed which are best characterized as incentives to improve productivity. They are to replace, at least in part, annual across-the-board increases. The Economic Council of Canada has noted that some of the major innovations in organizational structure include employment stock ownership plans, gains-sharing and bonuses, as well as pay-for-knowledge.[32] This may work out well when times are good. But any downturn in the economy will cost workers dearly. Bonuses are not usually built into base wage rates. They are one-time cash pay-outs which do not become an integral part of an employee's pay structure.

If, as a result of these kinds of schemes, workers feel that they must assume more responsibility for the profitability of the enterprise than the traditionally more openly adversarial relationship has required, they will be at a sharp disadvantage when militant opposition to the employer's demands would be in their interest. In accepting a consensual model, they will have been hooked into the argument that employer-employee relations are essentially symbiotic, rather than inherently conflictual. Once it becomes accepted that the workforce has both a need and a duty to help the employer to be as competitive as possible, by such means as contracting-out of work or by discontinuing less profitable lines, it becomes difficult to resist these trends even if they are likely to hurt both future and fellow workers.

Another aspect of tying workers' income directly to output is that, when workers are grouped together in discrete work teams, there will be an incentive for workers to police each other. This, too, is not conducive to the creation of a sense of solidarity, something which will be needed should things turn sour. In a similar vein, the continual pressure for all kinds of process innovations that have workers acting as semi-autonomous cells, each with a production quota, lessens the need for the union to act as a mediating agent in the regulation of daily work practices. This erosion of the union's claims on the loyalty and support of its membership is dangerous.

It should be clear by now why labour has cause to be suspicious of Canadian employers who ask their employees to adapt themselves to the new circumstances without any thought for the consequences. But, trade union leaders are very conscious of the fact that it is bad politics to take a luddite position and to oppose all change on the factory floor or in offices. Indeed, it not only makes for bad politics; it is a fundamental error to believe that the new technology cannot be used to enrich workers' lives. Labour leaders know that there is nothing crudely deterministic about the introduction of new technologies and more flexible work practices. The outcomes can be good, neutral or bad. It all depends on the way in which they are introduced and deployed.

To this end, the United Steelworkers and the Energy and Chemical Workers Union, for instance, have begun to develop their own ideas for Quality of Work Life programs. Their notion is that the new work practices may well bring real benefits to workers, provided that the issue of technological change becomes a central focus of collective bargaining. What is to be avoided is the unilateral introduction of new processes by employers. The Steelworkers' position has been made clear by Docquier:

People who are seriously interested in job satisfaction will have to first tell me that they are in favour of strong unions, that they want all obstacles to union organization removed from the laws and that they want governments to make sure that employers keep their hands off the right of workers to organize.[33]

In a similar vein, Guillet has noted that

... if the government's concern about Quality of Working Life is to be understood as a sincere policy direction, the introduction of sectoral or regional certification procedures for workers who want union representation is a step toward proving government's commitment to QWL and industrial democracy. Anti-scabbing and first-contract legislation would strike a further blow for industrial democracy.[34]

In the same way, the CAW has indicated that it sees nothing inherently wrong with restructuring work practices. What matters to it, however, is the context of the changes: "What we *are* saying no to is concessions and to structures that undermine union solidarity."[35]

In short, labour has indicated its willingness to co-operate with innovative practices provided that they form part of a package to enhance employment and income security during a time of renewal. This requires a commitment by employers and governments to greater economic and social democracy all around. The crucial factor for labour on technology issues is whether or not labour has a real seat at the decision-making table when innovations are devised and productivity is being defined.[36] In Canada, this has not been the case, so far, in the heavily unionized goods-producing side of the economy. Is there hope elsewhere?

Technology in the Service Sectors: Success of a Kind

A 1987 OECD study has suggested that 80 percent of technological advances in the near future will be innovations which support the development of banking, insurance, telecommunications, retail trade, and the like.[37] The Economic Council of Canada has found that the Canadian experience mirrors this tendency. Most of the new technologies have been deployed in the service sectors, with only 24 percent of the existing micro-computer technology being used to advance productive processes directly in factories. It is, then, the impact of the new technologies in the service sectors' setting, rather than their potential to create an idealized electronic factory, which gives a realistic indication of their effect on work practices in Canada and of the opportunities they offer for increased welfare and job creation.

In a most useful series of studies, the Ontario Task Force on Employment and New Technology[38] gathered information on employment and technological change. Part of its research agenda was to gather information of a historical nature. As well, the task force commissioned surveys designed to obtain data to help forecast the occupational and employment implications of technological change for the decade 1985–95. There is a remarkable sameness to the sectoral reports written as a result of these surveys. Each of them showed that the new information technologies would lead to the possibility of rendering more, as well as more varied, services to the public and to increase the extent of automation of office work. The observable results are much as anticipated by the task force.

The work revolution in banking is striking. Banks are handling a higher volume of transactions at greater speed. Typical of the new services are daily interest calculations, payroll services, the cross-referencing of different accounts of one customer, daily cash management systems for business, and so forth. Multi-branch banking already has been developed. There is an increasing use of automated teller machines. These machines can handle about four times as many transactions per month as human tellers because they can be located in places where workers cannot be, and they can be kept open during hours when workers are not readily available. Banks are starting to offer clients single-stop access for all their banking business, including computerized scrutiny of loan qualifications and approvals. Electronic fund transfers are increasingly used for inter-branch, inter-bank, corporate, commercial and retail transactions. Home banking has become possible.

In the offices of the banks themselves, main-frame and micro-computers and interval data-based management systems have long been in use. Electronic filing is being implemented and integrated work stations adopted. Electronic mail and fax systems as well as video-conferences are already much used.[39]

The task force reported similar innovations in the insurance industry. Indeed, computers already are used to aid the processing of orders. Customized telecommunications systems, as well as voice synthesis and recognition applications, have been extensively developed. Automatic branch systems and electronic mail, including fax systems and video-conferences already are everyday things. The uses of office automation technologies in insurance are much the same as those to be found in banking.[40]

In retail, electronic cash registers that allow single handling of food items have been widely adopted. Optical scanning systems are becoming almost universal. At the same time as they speed up check-outs, they monitor inventories and the performance of the cashiers, and indicate whether more or fewer people are needed at the check-out counters. While in the retail industry office automation is not widely deployed, there are developments which will change this, such as automated credit card verification and TV shopping. Similar modernization has been evolving in telecommunications and other service sectors.

The task force asked what these changes and innovations will mean for employment opportunities in the service sectors. Many banks projected that there would be an insufficient supply of workers in certain occupational categories, especially of managerial and financial officers, systems analysts, computer programmers and statistical clerks. However, at least half of the banking employers expected to be saddled with a surplus of clerical supervisors, typists, book-keepers and accounting clerks, finance clerks, general office clerks, cashiers and tellers. This is highly significant.

In 1981, only 25 percent of all bank workers were managerial administrators, 5 percent or less were experts in the natural sciences, engineers or mathematicians and fewer than 5 percent were involved in sales. An amazing 68 percent of all bank workers were clerical workers. It is clear, then, that the expected gains in employment as a result of the new innovations will not compensate for the number of jobs lost in the clerical classifications.[41]

In insurance, the picture is similar, but not quite as stark. By 1981, the managerial forces represented over 10 percent of the employees, the scientific experts more than 6 percent and sales people around 30 percent, while clerical workers represented only 30 percent of the insurance workforce.[42] The survey showed that managerial and administrative occupations were expected to increase by 1.3 percent by 1995. By contrast, there would be a 4 percent increase in the natural sciences, engineering and mathematics occupations. It projected an increase of about 1 percent in the sales forces, but a 5 percent drop in the clerical occupations. On the basis of this industry's predictions, a sharp downturn in employment is not to be expected; nor is a significant employment spurt in the offing.

In the retail industry, a similar increase in managerial and science-based personnel was anticipated by the study. Whatever the actual numbers of such additional employees, they were expected to amount to a large percentage increase because, in 1981, these occupational categories constituted only about 1 percent of the retail industry's workforce. Sales and clerical workers each made up 30 to 45 percent of the labour force in the retail industry.[43] The employers' responses to the survey showed that they expected increases in management and science-based occupations, a stable sales force and, again, a decline in clerical occupations, particularly in the general office categories. The retail industry employers, as a group, expected employment growth to be well below the rate experienced in the decade 1972–81. Moreover, they indicated that they expected the proportion of part-time employees to increase from 50 percent to 60 percent.

In sum, the task force concluded that the service sectors would not continue to provide the boom in employment growth that they did from the early 1970s onwards. It saw the technological advances which had helped the service sectors flourish and to employ an increasing percentage of the labour force as likely to lead to some displacement of the very jobs which the initial wave of technological innovation created. This is particularly troublesome for women. Between 1971 and 1981, clerical, service and sales occupations accounted for almost two-thirds of female employment growth; clerical occupations alone accounted for 40 percent of the new jobs taken by women.[44] These are the very occupations in which the survey expected that there would be no job growth or, in some sectors, that there would be job losses.

These expected results have come true. Cohen's analysis of recent studies caused her to conclude that the growth in employment for women in clerical and sales occupations in the 1970s was over 40 percent of the women entering the workforce. By 1989, this number had dropped to just under 15 percent. More women (one-third) were entering the managerial cadres than before (8 percent), but the number of managerial employees remains small.[45]

The idea that the new technologies in these sectors will create a never-ending explosion of job opportunities, then, is not being borne out. This may mean that, contrary to the hopes of many policy-makers and technological enthusiasts, the large-scale job displacement from the primary and smokestack industries will not be offset by a corresponding growth in employment in the secondary and tertiary sectors. In 1983, Leontief warned of the limits of the service sectors' ability to take up the slack. His fears seem to have been well founded.[46] Moreover, the potential of the new work processes in the service sector is not only disappointing in respect of job opportunities; it is also true that the work environment of many people will be anything but enriched.

The largest increase in job satisfaction will accrue to people who are highly skilled and whose ability to deal with new technology will be central to the service sectors' efficiency. Managers, scientists and computer experts will be given a good deal of discretion and increased job satisfaction as they design and operate information-based technology. They will be well placed to know and understand the processes they administer. But these people were never the most alienated persons in the workforce and, in absolute terms, they will never be very numerous. For vast number of workers in these sectors the story is a different one. Once again, experience contradicts the conventional wisdom.

The standard suggestion is that the introduction of the new information technologies in the service sector means that all workers will learn many new skills to deal with the increasingly complex and interrelated work processes. Inherent in this idea is the notion that individual workers will gain control over their working lives. The implied promise is that these new skills will reunite conception and execution. This linkage had been destroyed, systematically, by the assembly-line mode of organization, both in the factory and in the office. However, it appears that it is not about to be reforged.

The skills to operate the new machines have to be learned. As we have seen, Canadian employers have been loath to put much effort into training. In the service sectors, as well as elsewhere, there is a tendency not to train older workers — more often than not female — but to replace them with younger and more educated people who require less training and can more easily learn the particulars of the job as they go along.[47]

Once the skills have been acquired, many workers will be doing highly repetitive, non-discretionary work. Such work will require a great deal of concentration and attention but little, or no, initiative, in the sense of planning or designing the work to be done. Much of the work consists of reading and manipulating electronic symbols. The symbols of the computer language create a barrier between the workers and the work they once performed more directly. Zuboff has referred to this as "the abstraction of work routines." She argues that this leads to greater stress and alienation.[48]

Andrew Clement has demonstrated that the new technologies have the capacity to monitor the activity of telephone operators working on a visual display terminal. As the keyboard is struck, the stroke is recorded and the operator's performance is monitored. The average work time per call and the amount of time the operator spends away from the machine is registered. Airline reservation agents are watched in a similar way with regard to the number of calls they make and how long each one takes. Clement notes that at one airline, workers are subjected to individual counselling if they do not meet the expected standards. If they are found to deviate from specified performance and production standards, they will be disciplined. In a similar vein, he found that data entry clerks at a large insurance firm are expected to maintain an average of 11,500 keystrokes per hour. Their wages depend on the rate of keystrokes they maintain. Retail check-out clerks can be surveyed equally easily by monitoring the number of items they ring in. At some workplaces, those who exceed a reasonable rate (about 20 to 23 per minute) are rewarded with gold stars on a computer printout that is posted publicly; those who fall below expectations have their names circled in red.[49] The unfolding story in the service sectors acts as a cold shower, dampening the warm glow spread by technology enthusiasts.

Employers who persist in their use of microcomputer-based mechanisms in this primitive manner meet with little resistance because the rate of unionization is very low in the service sector. In 1985, only 5 percent of insurance brokers had to deal with trade unions. By 1990, only a handful of banking employees had been organized.[50] Only in the retail industry is union representation a numerical factor of any significance: in the mid-1980s, 48 percent of the employees were members of a trade union,[51] but a large number of them were part-time workers, lessening the impact of unionization on the relevant employers. The Ontario Task Force on Employment and New Technology reported that employers expected union representation to grow in only one service industry, the telegraph and cable systems sector. There is no anticipated growth in unionization in the banking and trust sectors, amongst the insurance brokers, insurance companies, computer services and management business consultants, nor does the retail industry expect any notable change.[52]

The Post-Fordist World of Work

The new era of labour relations has sometimes been referred to as post-Fordist. The idea is that the new technologies, driven by fierce competition, should make assembly-line production, with its primitive notions of scientific management, a thing of the past. This has been realized to some extent in a few firms in some special industries, notably telecommunications, automobile manufacturing and aerospace. Leading-technology firms in the automobile industry are forcing their fiercely competing suppliers to harmonize their processes with those established in the dominant firms. Even so, post-Fordism is not yet established; while new work methods are widely employed, they have not created a new paradigm as much as they have reinvigorated many aspects of the old one.

In the vast majority of firms, particularly in the service sectors where 70 percent of Canada's workers are employed, the new technological possibilities are leading to a return to a more pristine Taylorism. Despite all the rhetoric to the contrary, many — perhaps most — employers have not given up on the maintenance of the hierarchical workplace, with themselves at the top of the management chart. As the Economic Council of Canada put it: "On balance ... it appears that many firms ... are operating according to traditional principles of work design and decision-making.... Far too many Canadian firms pay only lip-service to the 'people' side of the enterprise."[53]

It is apparent, then, that Canada is not yet that close to the flexible, automated factory which can provide sufficient welfare and agreeable work conditions for all, a vision that is not that new. In 1946 there was a lead article in *Fortune* magazine by two prescient Canadians who saw the potential of transforming assembly-line production methods in much the same way as enthusiastic technology analysts do today. They argued that the full integration of workers with electronically controlled machinery would be both profitable and humane. They contended that work-upskilling and increased control could lead to nothing but improvement. They noted that the performance of workers during the war showed that they could be trusted and that there was no reason not to deploy machines in a way that would subject them to the workers rather than the other way around:

> Here for the first time we have a productive system so poten-
> tially efficient that the two-or-three-day week is feasible....
> This system must ... balance out at a higher level of living than
> ever before.... Our present industrial system tends to regiment
> the worker and destroy his skills and initiative, without a com-
> pensating measure of economic security. Regimentation of ma-
> chines can't hurt the machines, and can emancipate the worker
> forever from degrading and or monotonous toil.[54]

This dream is far from being realized anywhere in the world. In Canada, it appears to be more remote and unattainable than in most industrialized countries. Much needs to be done to ensure that the inevitable deployment of the new work methods and devices gener-ates greater economic welfare, security and job satisfaction. Difficult though it may be, these are attainable goals.

Entrepreneurs, pushed by competitive pressures, will argue ever more strenuously for government-sponsored research, and for sup-port for private research and development, and skills development. This is already happening. A brief written for the blue-ribbon mem-bers of the Canadian Manufacturers' Association[55] calls for a major government offensive along these lines. Employers recognize the need for some kind of industrial strategy, one which gives them financial and technical support and then *carte blanche* to deal with their assets and workers as they see fit. Workers can turn to their own advantage the logic of capital's drive to restructure by using new technologies. Workers should argue and fight for a strategy that promotes the effective deployment of the new machinery so as to advance the dignity and aims of working people. Technology yes, technological determinism no.

Tooling Up for Change

Reprise: The Problem

The globalization of markets seems to have the force of unbounded nature driving it. Capital, goods, services and labour are to move according to the logic of competition, in much the way as the earth's plates are propelled by forces beyond anyone's control. But economic arrangements are the creation of, and subject to, human agency. History has proven that people have always fought off efforts by the few and the powerful to treat them as disposable, inorganic objects.

At what seems to be the zenith of capital's latest offensive, there are signs of discontent. The growing inequality that the new modes of production are engendering heightens disabling sexism and racism among workers, and also increases alienation and sows the seeds of rebellion. To maintain control, governments are intensifying their commitment to support employers in their drive to weaken workers' resistance. Increasingly they turn to discipline and punishment strategies.[1]

All the effort that goes into moulding the workforce suggests that there is a great deal of resistance as employers, aided by governments, exercise their new market strength in a remarkably unified way. One of the peculiarities of the present circumstance is that while, on the face of it, individual businesses and governments seem to be following their own star, on fundamental issues there seems to be a unity of purpose. There appears to be a co-ordinated push to develop a new kind of political economy, one which will no longer have to pay any respect to labour's needs.

The logic of liberalized trade, the stress on competitive efficiency and the demand that workers engage in direct competition against their brothers and sisters, no matter where they are, must be denied. These policies are a prescription for turning Canada into the kind of liberal economy of which Adam Smith used to — and Canada's Business Council on National Issues does — dream. This is why a co-ordinated, coherent response is needed. The battle will be a tough one. What stands in the way is not only the vehemently argued ideology of hyper-liberalism that inheres in the logic of collective bargaining, but also on-the-ground conditions. These barriers must be tackled in an integrated way.

This is one of the reasons why this book has been written as it has. We have tried to lay bare the economic and institutional frameworks of Canadian state-capital-labour relations that have conditioned labour relations in the post-war period. This may have given the study a somewhat bloodless appearance. But the approach was chosen so that people will know better what it is they must do to defend themselves and change the system. That system has created fragments and divisions which are all too easily exploited by capital and the state as restructuring takes place.

The industrial relations system separates a single union's locals from each other. The law does not permit them to coalesce their bargaining efforts; the right to do so is contingent on employer acquiescence. Factory-by-factory bargaining separates trade union from trade union. Each has an interest in maintaining itself and growing, for the stated purpose of serving its members better. A great deal of energy is sapped by inter-union rivalry and overlap. Trade union organization is fragmented along provincial lines. The system tends to drive a wedge between trade unions and their members, because technocracy and legal culture play such a dominant role in the collective bargaining process. Because trade unions bargain about economic matters at the local level and cannot use collective power for political ends, an unnatural division is created between the economic and political spheres. The ability and willingness of unions to help the unorganized achieve better conditions is undermined. The state feels little pressure to enrich the social net but, when it does, it does so on the basis of interfering as little as possible with private-market decision making. It has been encouraged to take this approach by another fundamental assumption of Canada's Fordist collective bargaining model: the scheme was always seen as having been designed to provide the male industrial breadwinner with a family wage. Male-dominated unions shared this understanding and its corollary that there was no need for the state to support the male unionized worker directly. Minimum-standards legislation was to regulate working conditions for dependent, rather than independent, workers — that is, for women, not men. The model does not, and cannot, easily, accommodate the needs of the burgeoning number of women entering the workforce.

Workers and their organizations must seek to overcome these socially and institutionally constructed fissures. One way to do this is to create bargaining and work relationships which will force co-alescence on both employers and employees. Conceptually, what this requires is to link the need for institutional change to a plan for political action. This involves two sets of connected strategies. One is to find ways to empower workers by building stronger collective bargaining institutions so that they transcend employer and corre-sponding trade union organization. The other is to develop a different kind of politics, one which has as its starting point that all of Canada's workers have an interest in state intervention premised on the need to shape markets, rather than having invisibly structured markets dictate to governments.

The instability created by the policies of hyper-liberalism will inevitably lead to an attempt to stabilize capital-labour relationships. Agency is important in this context. There is no *a priori* reason to believe that conscious workers and their allies should not or cannot play a dominant role in shaping a new regulatory accord.

For this to happen, however, workers' most effective organiza-tions, trade unions, must not only overcome the imposed fragmenta-tion from which they suffer, but they must also define themselves differently than they do now. This is a tall order.

Structurally, Canadian Fordism has led to defensive trade unions. Primarily, their role has been to address narrow economic distributio-nal issues and, politically, they have been little more than vocal lobby groups.[2] They must see themselves as agents for radical redistribu-tion, rather than as hard bargainers who seek to maintain or increase the share of the productive pie for their own members. If they push to reduce inequalities in this way, they will have a stake in redefining social welfare. It will no longer be useful to treat social welfare as a means of partial income replacement for those people who have lost their job or cannot get access to one. Retention of this scheme would continue to punish victims of the economic system and it would perpetuate inequality; that is, it would be opposed to the consciously adopted political stance.

If this kind of thinking becomes part of a grassroots movement encouraged by trade unions determined to become actors rather than reactors, it will necessarily lead to demands that government change its role because it will be clear that investment, planning and training decisions are seen as too important to be left to private sector actors with short-sighted self-serving goals.

Of course, unions must first fend off the ongoing attacks and rebuild in a way that permits them to reach out to the non-union sectors and, from this new base, influence governments. Without attempting to provide a blueprint, we want to look at some of the things that could be done to further this agenda. First, we deal with ways to strengthen and broaden trade unionism from within the existing institutions. We then offer some ideas on how to confront the conventional wisdom that hyper-liberal policies are unavoidable. We show that it is plausible to argue that a considerably enriched social wage of a conceptually different kind can be implanted without threatening productivity. Finally, we look at one mechanism which could be used to tilt state policy so as to favour this kind of agenda.

Using the Precepts of the System to Change It

The Extension and Deepening of Collective Bargaining

Making it easier to organize
Unions ought to look for legislation that reverses what is, in reality, an opt-in system of union representation. The safeguards for individualism and private property have permitted employers to withhold crucial information from organizers about employees, such as their numbers, addresses, pay rates, seniority, qualifications, job classification and duties, nature of employment (casual, part-time, full-time and so on). More damaging still is the fact that organizers do not have full and unimpeded access to the employer's premises where people are most easily contacted. Employers are only mildly hampered if they want to warn (read: intimidate) their workers about the dangers of unionization. Further, because they retain their basic right to modify the work processes and to discipline employees, clever and/or intransigent employers can create fear in the minds of workers who might be interested in joining a trade union. Consequently, organization is carried on in secret, as if a trade union were still an illegal society, not one acknowledged to be a legitimate component of a liberal democracy.

But, precisely because Canada purports to be a liberal democracy, there are no logical difficulties to the demand for more access to information and to the employer's premises, and no shortage of practical means for achieving it. For instance, employers could be required to put the necessary access to information on a central registry controlled by the Ministry of Labour. In this way, unionization could begin without having to alert the employer. This would remove a good deal of the employees' anxiety and end the need for the cloak-and-dagger tactics in which trade unions now have to engage.[3]

To complement these protective measures, any discipline imposed during an organizational campaign should be treated presumptively as an unfair labour practice and the discipline set aside until the employer proved beyond a shadow of a doubt that it had not been motivated by anti-unionism. This requires only a mild strengthening of existing provisions; the sanctions could be increased by making the remedy for violation of these new rules automatic certification of the union. As a consequence of these or like measures, the issue of anti-union petitions would lose some of its centrality. The petitions that cause most of the heat and fury are those initiated by employers. If employers are coerced into a more neutral stance, it will be more likely that any such petitions will reflect the wishes of those workers who genuinely do not want a union, or, at least, not the union making the application for certification.

It is perfectly realistic to argue for these reforms within the present scheme. Steps along some of these lines (and there are many possible variants) have been taken by some jurisdictions already. The Ontario government's 1992 proposals for labour law reform contain some weak provisions of this kind. They are completely compatible with the existing institution of collective bargaining. In particular, even the strongest versions continue to treat dissent with respect, while diminishing the potential for employer intervention. The reforms will fulfil the immediate need of helping organization in a practical way, and have a political impact beyond that, as well. Workers will be treated more like industrial citizens who have a right to vote for their own government without having to worry about outside interference. A union would be treated more like a representative political body than as an agent serving the narrow economic interests of individuals.

Redesigning the bargaining unit
As discussed, when it suited employers in automobile manufacturing, meat packing, construction and the Post Office, the basic unit-by-unit bargaining approach has been modified in practice, as was done in

law by the Michelin Bill to appease one dominant enterprise in Nova Scotia. The bargaining unit also has been redesigned when it suited both the parties and the state agencies, as in the case of supermarkets and banks. As a liberal, pluralistic entente is supposed to entertain symmetrical demands no matter who makes them, this kind of bargaining unit adaptation should be demanded on behalf of labour as it confronts changing forms of business organization.

To begin with, unions need to have the means to organize and strike in shopping malls.[4] The spatial reorganization of retail, office and entertainment businesses has permitted landlords, exercising the legacy of feudal property rights, to make it extremely difficult for unions to leaflet and to picket targeted employers in such a shopping mall. It is time for labour law to acknowledge the conventional wisdom that shopping malls are public spaces. The right to approach workers and to conduct a legal strike should take priority over ancient and inappropriate property law conceptualizations.

More directly, unions should be able to win the right to treat various branches of a firm in a defined geographical area as one entity. This already happens to some extent. It should be made the norm, at labour's behest. More difficult to obtain, but still a realistic demand, would be to treat all the franchisees of a given business, in a given area, as one employer. The fact that they are separate employers as a matter of contract and corporate law should be seen to be the fiction it is. There is a good deal of useful jurisprudence and business organization literature which can be used to support this strategy.[5] A more ambitious extension of the collective bargaining scheme would force truly distinct employers, for example, the owners of private nursing homes in one defined area, to be treated as one employer. This does happen occasionally; it should be made standard practice.

Again, these reforms are functionally compatible with the model. They will not necessarily yield marked increases in wages and benefits, but they will send a signal that the right to be represented by a union is the right of everyone, including those who have been left out thus far. In particular, they should help the organization of small employment settings. This is important. For instance, in 1990, half the new bargaining units in Ontario contained fewer than twenty employees. Under the old Fordist model it made no sense for unions to organize these kinds of places, as the cost was high and the bargaining leverage which could be obtained minimal. Consolidated bargaining begins to address these problems.

Improving bargaining leverage

The extension of representation rights will not have much more than symbolic significance unless it gives workers clout. Bargaining rights without adequate weapons merely add up to talking rights. The only thing that gives a trade union power is the right to strike. The existing law needs to be changed.

Anti-scab protection

If employers are not directly involved in a lawful strike, the law upholds their right as wealth owners to buy and sell commodities, including labour power. The same legal principle supports the right of a struck employer to maintain its productive activities if it can. It is permitted to hire workers to help it do so.

Unions must demand far-reaching anti-scab laws which will enable them to engage in effective secondary boycotts and which will protect workers who refuse to cross lawful picket lines. This kind of legislation has been enacted in Quebec and a very weak form of it exists in Manitoba.[6] The demand can be put on the legislative bargaining table. It can be supported by the fact that it would reduce the violence associated with picket-line struggles and by the argument that strikes and lock-outs would be more likely to be avoided and, if they occur, would be of shorter duration. Again, the reform could be justified using the very premises of the scheme itself.

Mid-term strikes

Trade unions must be given the right to strike when the bargaining unit's size or composition is likely to be seriously affected during the life of a collective agreement. This happens when the employer contracts out work or unilaterally introduces new technologies and work processes.

As the drive to restructure by parcelling out work and introducing new work processes intensifies, Canada's unique peace obligation during the life of a collective agreement has become even more of an anachronism than it already was. The denial of the right to strike when the bargaining unit's size and composition are affected by an employer's unilateral decision makes a mockery of the grant of representational rights to workers.[7] The force of this argument has been recognized, as seen by the enactment of some minor statutory modifications in some jurisdictions. This is not good enough. The argument for a mid-term right to strike can be posited on the assumptions of the system: they purport to respect the bargaining rights of the parties for the duration of the negotiated relationship. The grant of the mid-term strike right would force an employer to negotiate with the union when it wanted to change the size and shape of the bargaining unit.

The only other sensible alternative would be to make it illegal for an employer to contract out work or to introduce far-reaching work process changes during the life of a collective agreement, unless certain requirements are met. For instance, the legislation could provide that workers who are to do contracted-out work should be paid at the same rate as the relevant bargaining-unit members were. Or, if new technologies are introduced, the trade union should be given economic and technical research assistance at the employer's expense to enable it to judge whether the proposed changes are acceptable to it. The right to introduce new technologies would remain with the employer, but it would be forced to consult and discuss with the union in a serious way. Workers would be more likely to co-operate with necessary technological innovation if they could participate in its implementation and in the devising of adequate training and severance schemes.

In short, the claim of trade unions would be based on the argument that the voluntarism on which collective bargaining is supposedly based must be given full sway; failing that, the state should be asked to provide better protection to the disadvantaged bargaining partner.

Justice and dignity
The argument for the extension of union representation is not just about giving workers the possibility of better economic protection. It also is meant to denote an upgrading of the status and dignity they should be accorded.

Grievance arbitration jurisprudence has modified the employer's right to discipline, but has not abrogated it. Indeed, in many ways it has perfected it. For workers, the problem is that discipline is imposed first and a hearing is held later. Even though workers may be fully restituted eventually, they live in fear of the costs they will have to bear until they are fully vindicated (which is rare). There is nothing in the logic of the law, as opposed to the logic of capital, which mandates this imbalance.

Some unions already have used this line of reasoning to win limited status quo ante clauses, significantly referred to as "justice and dignity" clauses. These are very hard to win at the bargaining table. Unions must demand legislation that decrees that this kind of clause be a mandatory provision of every collective agreement. This will mean that when an employer decides to punish an employee, it must continue to pay that employee until the grievance is finally determined. It will make employers think harder about using their coercive powers and will give them a much greater interest in expediting arbitration and in making it less costly. At the other end, workers will not be so fearful and will be enabled to speak up for their rights more often than they do now.

Bargaining with a Difference

Reliance on the logic of the system to obtain reforms needed to broaden the base and scope of bargaining is dangerous. It could legitimate some of the more coercive aspects of collective bargaining, while leaving the source of employer power relatively untouched. Thus, the claims for this kind of reform must be linked to a more holistic approach. The idea should be to create linkages between terrains of struggle which have been kept separate by the logic of the institutional arrangements imposed on labour. This will require some imagination, but it will not require taking unwarranted risks. The possibilities are many.

Linkages on the shop floor

Right now, trade unions bargain about health and safety issues and about the impact of new technology as separate issues. These struggles should be linked more often than they are.

It is the modern cry of employers that new technologies and more flexible work organization will lead to better productivity and, therefore, more welfare, security and contentment for workers. Workers will be multi-skilled and will be given more control over the work processes. Employers thus make it sound as if achieving workers' welfare and autonomy is one of their principal goals. What is true is that, given the new technologies and the flexible, more educated, workforce that the employer intends to deploy to achieve zero-error production, workers will be empowered to stop the processes when the machinery goes awry. This has already occurred at some Northern Telecom plants.

Workers should use the employers' own justifications to argue that, if employees are so prized and the employer truly intends to make them more satisfied workers, they should be allowed to stop the processes whenever their reliable judgement tells them that conditions present an occupational health and safety danger. For workers to learn to make demands in this way would constitute a breakthrough. Right now, they do not believe that they have a right to exercise that kind of autonomy. If they can cross that threshold, it may give workers a fresh vision of what non-hierarchical work could be like. Part of the learning process is to deepen what is already their instinctive understanding, namely that, in Canada, the untrammelled prerogative of management is the source of their discontent and growing alienation.

The difficulties and potential of the feminization of labour

As unions in the private sector are losing members rapidly, especially in the mass-assembly industries, the family wage is eroding while its cultural and social meaning still is propagated. The ensuing crisis of distribution has caused more and more women to vie for paid jobs. These women need to earn a wage that will sustain them and their dependents. The market, however, continues to undervalue women's work, leaving many of them exploited. Strategies must be devised not only to do economic justice, but to ensure that women come to be treated as sovereign equals in our society.

Changing social relations require new forms of organization. The typical Canadian trade union, structured as it is on "malestream" notions of hierarchical bureaucracy, is antagonistic to the vision of many women. The essence of the Fordist collective bargaining scheme is its characterization of the worker as a one-dimensional person, the epitome of "rational economic man." Not only has this disadvantaged many men who have participated in collective bargaining, but it is a particularly inapt starting point for women workers. As it is, society as it is constructed expects them to be not only typical self-optimalizing wage-workers, but also mothers and housewives. The model of rational economic man does not fit the lived experience of progressive feminists. Moreover, they see this deeply economistic approach as a reactionary and oppressive one. They do not intend to replicate it in the new gender-neutral world they want to create.

This is a problem because, for the immediate future, it will be these old malestream-model unions that will have to spearhead many of the drives to organize women. They must, therefore, become sensitized to women's needs and aspirations. Self-education is important; affirmative action to give more prominence to women within their trade unions is a prerequisite. This is easier said than done, but the process is underway. A few women have risen to positions of influence in a handful of unions. The pace needs to be accelerated. More than this, however, the emphasis must be on feminizing unions, rather than on unions seeking to grow in the same old way by recruiting women members. What is involved is a change in both composition and character.

An opportunity is provided by the contemporary pay equity struggles. Many unions understand that reliance on the existing legislative pay equity schemes, supplemented by collective bargaining, is not adequate. Progressive women's groups, and unions such as the Municipal Workers of British Columbia, CUPE, the Ontario Provincial Service Employees Union and the CNTU in Quebec, have advocated a variety of schemes different in kind to the existing legislative schemes.[8] All of these proposals are aimed at overcoming the problems of existing bargaining fragmentation and of the stereotyping and evaluation systems promoted and controlled by employers. These proposals have surfaced because it is understood that the pay equity schemes on offer will not necessarily lead to a living wage for women, even though some equalization may result. None of the alternative strategies devised thus far is much better than any other. What is important is that all reject the premise that the private market should hold sway. As unions support women in these fights, they will become more conscious of the limitations of employer-by-employer bargaining and of the need to transcend it. In particular, it will be easier for them to see that the best way to make an immediate impact in pay equity is to fight for a sharp increase in the minimum wage for all workers.

Two positive developments, then, are underway. Women are organizing and are being organized. This yields positive economic results. The data show that unionized women have the best chance of catching up with male counterparts. On the political front, as workers' organizations become less economistic and their daily struggles to transcend market practices educate them, alternative visions are more likely to be turned into reality.

Public sector workers as bridge-builders
The state has been leading the way in finding ways to help capital to satisfy its aims in the new economic order. To do so it has sought to cut state expenditures to the detriment of the non-propertied. In addition, it has attacked its own employees with a vengeance. This puts its own employees in the forefront of the struggle. Both for their own protection and for the good of all workers, it seems logical to urge public sector workers to identify their interests with those of the state's clientèles. This is particularly necessary because business is setting the tone of contemporary public discourse.

Corporate Canada has succeeded in characterizing government deficits as the evil to end all evils. Government borrowing is portrayed as *the* cause of impaired economic welfare, while corporate debt is seen as a productive instrument which creates well-being for all. Public sector workers are in an ideal position to provide credible evidence for the argument that public expenditure on human needs, such as education, health care, housing, skills development and the environment, are investments which yield positive returns for the entire society and are not a crippling mortgage on the future. They must demand their right to speak on these issues and exercise that right vigorously. This is one labour need that could be furthered by the *Charter of Rights and Freedoms.*

A major benefit that can be obtained by having public sector employees engage in political action on behalf of the general public they serve is that they will reap direct economic advantages from such conduct. The logic is straightforward: the expansion of the state's services enhances public servants' job security. In addition, it will help build bridges to all workers.

By way of example, when teachers bargain with their employers they should make it clear that their struggle is for better education for all, as well as for better pay for themselves. Indeed, they ought to oppose all proposals for cutbacks, even if their own wages or security are not directly threatened. Further, they should ask public sector workers everywhere to support their drive to enrich the lives of all Canadians. Similar approaches ought to be adopted by public sector workers who deliver unemployment insurance benefits, publicly funded pension plans or daycare programs. Public sector workers always have understood the need to act in this way, but their efforts have not been very effective. Their limited bargaining rights, the legal constraints on their civil rights, and the gulf between private and public sector unions all have proved to be serious obstacles. Their efforts on this front have to be intensified if they are to succeed in reversing the state's neo-conservative agenda.

If public sector workers can be seen to defend all workers' rights, it will be easier for industrial unions, environmentalists, women's organizations and welfare-rights activists to see the interests they share with each other and with government employees. This will aid in the development of the understanding that inequalities and insecurities can best be countered by the establishment of national industrial strategies, rather than through private bargaining in an *ad hoc,* fragmented way.

The Need for a Different Political-Economic Entente

Institutional reform and the building of alliances are the necessary first steps to establish a different vision of political economy. As people fight for these reforms they must be convinced that this is not a hollow exercise but a realistic way in which to confront the determinism driving the contemporary public policy agenda. Conservative policy-makers champion the idea that competitive trading will create sufficient welfare for domestic populations everywhere. Labour-friendly advisors must discredit this dominant view. They have to show that this kind of planned anarchy cannot sustain a high level of evenly shared welfare. Further, it should be demonstrated that it guarantees little by way of improvement in social and political life. One way to do this is to make it clear to workers and their allies that there is no empirical evidence that shows that unrestricted global trading would make any one country better off.

The argument for complete freedom in the exchange of capital, goods, services and labour is a theoretically elegant one. It assumes that the private actors in each nation state will maximize their resources and capacities to meet global demand. The optimum division of production will ensue, generating the greatest amount of wealth possible. But this argument tells us nothing about the distributional effects or the impact of this growth model; most importantly, it does not look at the participants' starting points. It may be a very bad model for most countries, given the uneven distribution of military, political and economic power. This should make any serious person pause before embracing the wide-open trade model, particularly as such calculations as have been made show that the benefits of unrestricted trade are relatively minimal and that the adverse effects of protection are vastly overstated by hyper-liberalism's ideologues.

Paul Krugman is a leading light in the school known as the "New International Economics." This is a group of staunch proponents of liberalized global trade. Krugman has acknowledged that the increased wealth that is likely to result is not sufficient reason to support a world without trade restrictions. He admits that the free trade model's attraction is largely ideological. He writes that

> [a]mong advanced countries, ... protectionism at current levels is not a first-class issue. Without a doubt the major industrial nations suffer more, in economic terms, from unglamorous problems like avoidable traffic congestion and unnecessary waste in defense contracting than they do from protectionism. To take the most extreme example, the cost to taxpayers of the savings and loan bailout alone will be at least five times as large as the annual cost to U.S. consumers of all U.S. import restrictions.[9]

He goes on to demonstrate that, if the United States, Japan and the European Community, as trading blocs, imposed a tariff of 100 percent on all imported goods, the world economy would be deprived of only 2.5 percent of its income. If tariff rates were "only" 50 percent, the diminished income would be 0.75 percent.

This calculation is sufficient to reveal some of the exaggerations that buttress the trade-at-all-costs argument. It does not address, however, the more serious question as to what happens to a country which does not open its borders if everyone else is doing so. But the fact is that not everyone is doing it; the commitment to liberalized trade is often more rhetorical than real. Business interests stand to gain an immediate advantage from the competition on wages which a declaration of a free trade war seems to mandate. They play on the overblown rhetoric of unthinking politicians and captive academics. Still, this does not prevent them from seeking government handouts and assistance, or from seeking favourable trade concessions for the sectors in which they principally operate. The larger issue is not whether to trade, but how unfettered trade should be, whose interests ought to be paramount and what the real costs of adjustments are. To allow policy-makers to use the promotion of decentralized, uncoordinated competition as a starting point for all discussion only permits leading business firms and their supplier firms to sweat their work-forces to maintain price advantage.

This kind of argument to discredit the dominant view must be supported by an argument that an alternative set of strategies can be pursued. Indeed, a large number of proposals are available. In each of the many models they offer, more control over footloose capital is the essential ingredient.[10]

Canada's existing growth model mandates that the particulars of a progressive industrial strategy have to be part of a macro-economic policy tailored to overcome Canada's structural weaknesses and, in particular, the openness of its economy and its governments' dependence on foreign corporate actors.

If a vision of this kind is kept in mind by trade unions and their allies who are simultaneously engaging in the kinds of strategies proposed earlier, pressure may be put on governments to act differently than they do now. But during these struggles, business will have a great deal of countervailing power. It would be all too easy for progressive forces to consider their efforts futile. Here the need to fight for a different kind of social welfare becomes central.

Social Security

Canada spends over 30 percent of its GDP on social welfare. There is a good deal of inefficiency and meanness in the system. There are huge numbers of different schemes: unemployment insurance benefits, family assistance, child credits, workers' compensation, old age pensions, disability pensions, housing subsidies, welfare assistance, and so on. The bureaucratic costs of administering so many, often overlapping, schemes are immense. Moreover, the amount and extent of support is based on fortuity rather than rationality. Vastly different amounts will go to a person injured at work as opposed to one hurt in her bathroom, even though the extent of the injury, and the subsequent income-replacement needs, are the same. This arbitrariness not only sets people apart from one another, it also subjects them to ugly discipline. To qualify for a benefit under a particular scheme, the claimant must prove eligibility. This means not only showing, say, that she is a single mother, or was attached to the workforce long enough to quality for UIC benefits or that a heart-attack was due to poor work conditions, but also that she is willing and able to comply with the conditions imposed for the receipt of the benefits.

This social security scheme is a reflection of two connected ideas. First, it is the result of the reluctant and piecemeal way Keynesian policies were introduced in Canada (see Chapter 2). This goes some way towards explaining its uneven effects. Second, and relatedly, the relatively poor benefits of Canada's social security net are a consequence of the uni-dimensional understanding of a social security scheme. Canadian policy-makers perceive social security solely in terms of income replacement, at a minimal level, for the victims of a relatively uncontrolled market-based economy. A rethought social welfare system would also have to provide for those who, through no fault of their own, cannot participate fully in waged work. Its aim, however, would be to provide a level of social welfare that does not leave a pool of people which, by the blaming-the-victim nature of the scheme, exercises a downward pressure on wages and working conditions.[11] This would help safeguard workers in employment and put pressure on employers to train and invest in people and new technologies.

To create such an enriched scheme will require governments to raise taxes. This means that there is a built-in logical limit. But a lot can be accomplished before that limit is reached.

A great deal of money can be captured by closing tax loopholes, doing away with pointless tax breaks and making corporations pay money they owe.[12] There is a limit, of course, as to how much money can be obtained by taxing the corporate sector. At some point, the incidence of taxation will cause investment to dry up. But there is a long way to go before this point will be reached in Canada, indeed in many countries. This does not stop corporations from using this argument to whip-saw nation states. They point to the need for countries to harmonize their tax rates to create a level playing-field for investors. To follow this advice will lead to a race to the bottom. What needs to be done is to counter the argument that high taxation rates result in inefficient economies. There is good empirical data to mount an effective campaign of this kind. Indeed, there are strong indications that "there is a positive relationship between increases in taxes and productivity growth."[13] Maybe a high-tax régime forces firms to be efficient producers by investing in plant and equipment and the training of the workforce. Certainly, Germany and Japan, the leaders of the industrial world, pay high taxes and have an unequalled economic performance.

Figure 11.1
Taxes and Productivity Growth

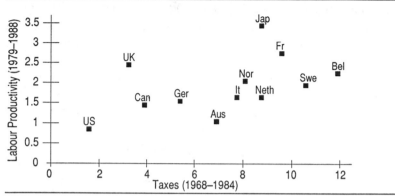

Sources: Taxes: OECD *Revenue Statistics 1965-1989*, Paris: 1990, Table 3.
Productivity growth: OECD, *Economic Outlook*, no. 47., Paris, 1990, Table 43.

When set against Canada's low taxation rate, Canada's lagging productivity indicates that a low-taxation régime has not encouraged Canadian firms to invest. This suggests that higher corporate taxes are in order. Further, a high-productivity/high-wage economy, which is a premise of an alternative economic vision in which competition on wages is not the dominant fact, should yield increased government revenues. They will help pay for a better social security régime. Again, there is a limit on this source of revenue because, at some point, increases in the tax burden erode the gains made by productive workers and will cause them to oppose a generous welfare scheme which supports less-productive people. While the cost of such a scheme will become a problem at some point, there is no question that, in a different kind of growth model, Canada's social security benefits package can be improved considerably without impairing the country's economic efficiency.

A second argument that will have to be confronted is that a generous welfare net will discourage people from working very hard. This argument is a favourite of conservatives. Their belief is that only the fear of unemployment and impoverishment will cause people to work at alienating jobs. This allows a counter-argument to be made that it is preferable to entice people to work by creating better work relationships than to coerce them into productive work. And, as already noted, a different kind of social welfare scheme puts pressure

Figure 11.2
Equality and Productivity Growth

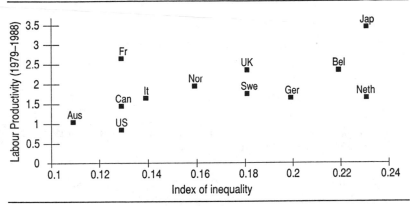

Source: Neil Brooks, "The Changing Structure of the Canadian Tax System: Accommodating the Rich." Forthcoming, *Osgoode Hall L.J.*, p. 35.

on employers and governments to develop a high-wage, high-skills economy. Furthermore, an improved social wage will diminish inequality. This has positive possibilities because it has been demonstrated that the greater the degree of income equality in a country, the greater its productivity is. For instance, Esping-Andersen characterizes Australia, Canada and the United States as efficiency-driven, rather than welfare-oriented nations. These countries exhibit some of the greatest inequalities in income distribution among OECD countries, and they remain firmly fixed at the lowest end of the productivity scale. By contrast, Japan, Belgium and the Netherlands are among the most productive countries in the OECD bloc; they exhibit a great deal of income equality. The only country that does not fit this analysis is France. It is on the highly productive end, although it maintains a great deal of inequality.[14]

These data are strongly suggestive that income maintenance policies that reduce differences between people are associated with improved efficiency.

But logic alone will not be sufficient to overcome business intransigence. Governments must feel that a change in industrial strategy by them will be politically expedient as well as wise. Only then will it make sense for governments to devise policies to integrate production, provide better training for workers and focus research and development so as to enhance Canada's export possibilities and diminish its import needs. To tilt the state in this way, it will be necessary to find a counterweight to business's most potent weapon: its ability to invest and disinvest at will.

Countering Capital Mobility — a Little

The vast pool of funds collected in retirement schemes belongs to workers. The premiums are paid by them either directly or indirectly out of foregone wages. If they were all pooled into one fund and if workers could control it democratically, it would constitute a powerful bargaining chip to diminish the threat of a capital strike. It would be less difficult to influence governments to adopt a very different kind of industrial strategy.

There are a number of technical and political obstacles to this plan. First and foremost, the monies are collected in discrete retirement plans. It will be difficult to satisfy workers who are potential retirees that the integrity of their own tailor-made retirement scheme will be maintained if it is subsumed into a large plan. Second, there are jurisdictional problems; each province has different pension rules. Third, there is a large number of professional investment houses and financial institutions which have an interest in maintaining the status quo. Fourth, it is not clear that the union movement would be prepared to take on the responsibility of controlling investment funds outside of the comforting restrictions of existing pension plan law. This point relates to the very real difficulty of making the exercise of control over such a unified pool of capital truly democratically accountable. These formidable difficulties militate against trying to transform all the separate pension plan funds into one large one.

A more modest approach might be easier to implement and still give workers some necessary muscle. It is more feasible for workers to seek to exercise control over their own pension fund monies. This gives them, as a collective, the possibility of influencing their particular employer's investment and managerial decision making. Co-ordination of these kinds of initiatives across an industry could support a government's efforts to restructure it. There are other ways in which collectivized funds can be used as a counterweight to capital. For instance, forced savings out of wages, commonly referred to as wage funds, are one fairly well known variant; a few wage-earner funds — equity holdings derived from collective profit sharing — also exist; a government might create a collective fund by taxing profits or by imposing duties on productive activities or, more naturally, by taking control of a number of public sector funds, such as hospital, teachers' and hydro workers' funds, which now function as discrete private plans.[15]

This is not the place to determine the best mechanism to democratize capital. What is important to note is that it can be done, to some extent. We argue that it must be done. The formation of collective capital has been on the agenda of social democratic governments and unions in Europe for a long time. They have seen it as a means to achieve a broad range of objectives, including the use of its funds to

- promote more productive investment
- redistribute wealth
- improve workers' rights and democracy in the workplace
- promote research and training.[16]

These goals are part and parcel of giving the state and its policies a more egalitarian and democratic tilt. While there is always the danger that it will lead to a kind of workers' capitalism, the strategy to democratize collective funds is an essential part of the politics to create an alternative growth model.

A Final Word

Canadians need to develop a co-ordinated and practical plan which emphasizes that the generation of welfare by public means is better than reliance on private initiatives, and that equality and the sharing of burdens in all spheres, public and private, are important values. Social and political empowerment is our aim. If the strategies we have proposed, or similar ones, are pursued with a shared vision of the need for a truly transformed society, they may form the basis of a politics of democratic socialism. While this may sound more tame than a ringing call for industrial militancy by way of strikes, it has more political credibility; that kind of industrial militancy can be confined, rather easily, to struggles about local issues and wage gains.

It bears repeating that, in Canada, where the institutional context has laundered the strike and narrowed collective bargaining, old-style industrial conflict lacks a political dimension. It seems somewhat unreal to expect strike activity to be the launching pad for any significant kind of political change. Proponents of this route have to believe in spontaneous combustion. It could happen, and let us hope that it does, but waiting for it is not a strategy.

Our proposals are aimed at overcoming the sense of powerlessness which results from a system of fragmented collective bargaining, a highly legalized order of industrial relations and a labour movement which has been kept outside the main centres of political power, where business holds sway. Their purpose is to ensure that people do not struggle mightily to retain the very régime that is proving detrimental to them. This is why it is so important for unions not only to refashion themselves, but to see themselves differently, as agents for redistribution and promoters of an alternative growth model in which democratic accountability, rather than the logic of private profit, has pre-eminence. The actual details of the legal, political and economic activism we have proposed are not as important, therefore, as their thrust. In today's Canada, capital-labour conflict is being fought on ground highly favourable to the owners of wealth and their corporations. We must set ourselves to find a practical way to change the terrain of struggle and thereby to put the transformation to a different society back on the agenda.

NOTES

Introduction

1. Some non-unionized people will be fortunate enough to benefit from collective bargaining even if they are not members of the union who signed the contract. At best their role is a passive one.
2. See Michael Mandel, *The Legalization of Politics* (Toronto: Thompson and Wall, 1990).
3. A central theme of this book is that the law which governs industrial relations both reflects and helps to embed a certain ideology and a set of social relations. To make this argument, frequent references are made to the state of the law. This necessitates a caveat. Even in a traditional legal text, it is difficult to give an all-encompassing, up-to-date account of the law in Canada. Each jurisdiction generates its own legislation and its own judicial and administrative agencies' decisions. It is hard to account for all the variations. In this book we do not attempt this task. What we have set out to do is to give an overview of the principal thrust of labour law and industrial relations, so that a generalized analysis can be offered.

   As we work in Ontario, it has been convenient to use a somewhat disproportionate number of Ontario sources and cases. We are aware of different practices in other parts of the country, and we try to take note of those which, in our view, make an analytical difference. We trust, therefore, that our representation of the way in which industrial relations at large function in Canada is not flawed by our bird's-eye-view approach.

Chapter 1

1. The literature on the global economic revolution is voluminous. It includes Robert Cox, *Production, Power and World Order* (New York: Columbia University Press, 1987); Kenichi Ohmac, *Triad Power: The Coming Shape of Global Competition* (New York: Free Press, 1986); Robert Boyer, *La théorie de la régulation: Une analyse critique* (Paris: La Découverte, 1986); Michel Beaud, *L'économie mondiale dans les anneés 80* (Paris: La Découverte, 1990); Richard Barnet and Ronald Muller, *Global Reach* (New York: Simon and Schuster, 1974); Susan Strange, *States and Markets* (New York: Basil Blackwell, 1988); A. Madison, *The World Economy in the 20th Century* (Paris: OECD, 1989); Daniel Drache and Meric Gertler, eds., *The New Era of Global Competition, State Policy and Market Power* (Montreal: McGill-Queen's U.P., 1991).

2. Orville Freeman and W. Persen, "Multinational Corporations: Hope for the Poorest Corporations," *The Futurist* 14:6 (1980): 3, estimate that transnationals "turn out about one-third of the world's gross product." For a more detailed analysis, see Frederick F. Clairmonte and John H. Cavanagh, "Transnational corporations and services: the final frontier," *Trade and Development; An UNCTAD Review* 5 (1984).

3. Here we refer to the facilitation of capital accumulation and the rationalization and co-ordination of production through the increasingly flexible device of incorporation.

4. J. Grunwald and Kenneth Flamm, *The Global Factory: Foreign Assembly in International Trade* (Washington, D.C.: Brookings Institution, 1985); Michael Dertouzos, Richard Lester and Robert Solow, *Made in America* (Cambridge, Mass.: MIT Press, 1989).

5. This included heater hoses from Austria, speedometers from Switzerland, valve lifters from the United States; see M. Anderson, "Shakeout in Detroit: New Technology, New Problems," *Technology Review* 85 (Aug./Sept. 1980).

6. Forty-eight percent of Canada's manufacturing sector is foreign-controlled and some 80 percent of that foreign control is exercised by U.S. corporations. Under the impetus of North American rationalization many of the Canadian plants might be phased out, since the Canadian market can be served from the United States or from offshore production in the newly industrializing countries. See A. Rotstein, *Rebuilding from Within; Remedies for Canada's Ailing Economy* (Toronto: Lorimer, 1984), chapters 2 and 3; Jack Baranson, "What happens to the Branch Plants?" in Duncan Cameron, ed., *The Free Trade Papers* (Toronto: Lorimer, 1985).

7. Thomas Hout, "How Global Companies Win Out," *Harvard Business Review* 60:5 (1982): 98.

8. See the study prepared for the Science Council of Canada, G.A. Jewett, *Metal Markets: An Analysis of Future World Consumption*, 1986; see also, Dr. Stuart Smith, "Future Consumption of Minerals," Science Council of Canada, September 1986; and Winston G. Chambers and P. Lafleur, *Market Share and Market Access: The Canadian Mineral Industry in a Changing World Economy* (Ottawa: Department of Energy, Mines and Resources, December 1982).

9. *The Toronto Star*, May 27, 1986; for other specific examples see Patricia Lush, "Going, going, gone," *Report on Business Magazine*, January 1987, p. 36.

10. Canadian Autoworkers Union, "Can Canada Compete?" in D. Drache and D. Cameron, eds., *The "Other" Macdonald Report* (Toronto: Lorimer, 1986).

11. For a detailed account, see B. Bluestone and B. Harrison, *The De-industrialization of America* (New York: Basic Books, 1982). In addition, *The Wall Street Journal*, Oct. 7, 1986, notes that southern states have increased their share of direct foreign investment at the expense of the Great Lakes and mid-Atlantic regions. Between 1974 and 1983, offshore investors in the United States beat a path to the sun-belt and the deep South. Not surprisingly, Georgia, Texas and Arizona, states with restrictive labour legislation, have had the greatest success in attracting foreign money.

12. Rae Murphy and Scott Sinclair, "Mission to Mexico," *This Magazine* 24:1 (June 1990); see also *The Multinational Monitor* 6:16 (Nov. 15, 1985). Canadian employers are also reaching out for Mexico's favourable conditions.

13. J. Grunwald and Kenneth Flamm, *The Global Factory*, p. 12.

14. Murphy and Sinclair, *op. cit.*, indicate that, while General Motors is closing nine plants in the United States and Canada, it will be opening twelve in Mexico.

15. Wendy McKeen, "Export Processing Zones: A Threat to Women, Unions and All Canadian Workers," Women's Bureau, Canadian Labour Congress (undated).

16. Arthur J. Cordell, *The Multinational Firm, Foreign Direct Investment and Canadian Science Policy*, Science Council of Canada, Special Study, No. 22 (Ottawa, 1971); J. Niosi, *Canadian Multinationals* (Toronto: Between the Lines, 1985); B. Bellon and J. Niosi, *The Decline of the American Economy* (Montreal: Black Rose, 1988).

17. "Free Trade One Year Later," Special Issue, *Financial Post*, Jan. 2, 1990. Many of the firms involved are branch plant operations as, in an integrated North American market, there often is little reason to continue full-fledged operations in Canada. The list reads like a Who's Who of Canadian business. It includes Bendix Safety, Gerber, Fiberglas, Galtco, Consumer's Glass, Burlington Carpet, Sklar-Peppar, Outboard Marine, Toro, Bovie, Kimberly-Clark, Campbell Soup, Gillete, Schlegel, Leviton, Coleman, United Maple, ITW, Kesley-Hayes, Ivaco, and Sysco.

18. *The Globe and Mail*, June 9, 1990. By 1991, employment in Ontario had declined by 250,000 jobs, most of which were in manufacturing; see *The Globe and Mail*, March 19, 1991. For other appraisals, see Daniel Drache, "New Work Processes, Unregulated Capitalism and the Future of Labour," in G. Szell, Paul Blyton, and Chris Cornforth, *The State, Trade Unions and Self-Management* (New York: Walter de Gruyter, 1989); and L. Muszynski, *The De-Industrialization of Metropolitan Toronto: A Study of Plant Closures, Layoffs and Unemployment* Vols. I and II (Toronto: Social Planning Council of Metropolitan Toronto, 1985).

19. In Robert Reich's influential study, "Beyond Free Trade," *Foreign Affairs* 61:4 (Spring 1983), the author shows that wage competition is not the only possible response to the world's new economic conditions. It is, of course, the most inimical to labour in high-wage countries such as Canada because there is always some less-fortunate country which can produce the same goods with cheaper labour. For a full discussion of these issues, see his *The Work of Nations* (New York: Knopf, 1991).

20. *The Toronto Star*, Nov. 16, 1986.

21. For a general account of the impact of new work technology on productivity, see H. Shaiken, *Work Transformed: Automation and Labor in the Computer Age* (Lexington, Mass.: D.C. Heath, 1984), and H. Menzies, *Fast Forward Out of Control* (Toronto: Macmillan, 1989). For a more detailed analysis, see Chapter 10 below.

22. For a detailed examination of job creation, the wage rates and impact on women's employment, consult *The Final Report* of the Ontario Task Force on Employment and New Technology (Toronto, 1985); Julie White, *Women and Part-time Work* (Ottawa: Canadian Advisory Council on the Status of Women, 1980); and J. Fudge and P. McDermott, eds., *Just Wages: A Feminist Assessment of Pay Equity* (Toronto: University of Toronto Press, 1991).

23. Studies documenting the growth of part-time employment include Arthur Donner, *Working Times: The Report of the Ontario Task Force on Hours of Work and Overtime* (Toronto: Ontario Ministry of Labour, 1987); *Ontario Study of the Service Sector* (Toronto: Ministry of Treasury and Economics, December 1986).

24. J. Myles, G. Picot, and T. Wannell, "Wages and Jobs in the 1980s: Changing Youth Wages and the Declining Middle," *Statistics Canada Analytical Studies*, Branch Research Paper Series No.17, Oct. 1988.

25. These figures overstate the extent of unionization. They exclude the agricultural workforce from the calculation. When these workers are included, the percentage of unionized people as a percentage of the total paid workforce, in 1987, was 29.7 percent; Labour Canada, *Directory of Labour Organization 1987* (Ottawa: Labour Canada, 1987).
26. Richard B. Freeman, "Canada in the World Labour Market to the Year 2000," (Ottawa: Economic Council of Canada, 1988; typescript). The figures are adapted from Table 2, p. 6.
27. Mary Lou Coates, et al., *The Current Industrial Relations Scene in Canada, 1990* (Kingston: Industrial Relations Centre, Queen's University, 1990), Table 5, p. 48.

Chapter 2

1. For a general account of Canadian labour history, see Craig Heron, *The Canadian Labour Movement: A Short History* (Toronto: Lorimer, 1989); Harold Logan, *State Intervention and Assistance in Collective Bargaining: The Canadian Experience, 1943-54* (Toronto: University of Toronto Press, 1956).
2. The U.S. literature on the introduction of the *Wagner Act* (the colloquial name for the *National Labour Relations Act* 29 U.S.C. para. 141) and its subsequent role and interpretation has led to some interestingly different analyses. See, for instance, S. Bowles, David Gordon, and T. Weisskopf, *Beyond the Wasteland* (New York: Anchor Books, 1984); M. Piore and C. Sabel, *The Second Industrial Divide* (New York: Basic Books, 1984); Karl Klare, "Judicial Deradicalization of the Wagner Act" (1988), 62 *Minnesota L. R.* 265.
3. There is some controversy as to whether the union was to be *the* bargaining agent from the inception of the scheme in Canada. Warrian argues that, initially, only named representatives were to act as agents for workers, rather than certified unions; see P. Warrian, "Labour is not a Commodity: A Study of the Rights of Labour in the Emergent Postwar Economy in Canada 1944-1948," Ph.D. thesis, Department of History, University of Waterloo, 1986. He attaches a good deal of importance to this finding. For a different interpretation of this early history, see J. Fudge, "Voluntarism and Compulsion: The Canadian Federal Government's Intervention in Collective Bargaining from 1930 to 1946," D. Phil. Thesis, University of Oxford, 1988.
4. Many proponents of the scheme saw grievance arbitration as furthering the industrial democracy provided by collective bargaining. For sharply differing general assessments of the nature of Canada's system of collective bargaining as it evolved, compare H.J. Glasbeek's "Law, Real and Ideological Constraints on the Working Class," in Gibson and Baldwin, eds., *Law in a Cynical Society?* (Calgary: Carswell, 1985), p. 282 and his "Voluntarism, Liberalism and Grievance Arbitration: Holy Grail, Romance and Real Life," in G. England, ed., *Essays in Labour Relations Law* (Don Mills, Ont.: CCH Canadian Ltd., 1986) with B. Laskin, "Collective Bargaining and Individual Rights" (1963), 6 *Can. Bar J.* 278, and with H.W. Arthurs, "Developing Industrial Citizenship: A Challenge for Canada's Second Century" (1967), 45 *Can. Bar Rev.* 786.
5. Daniel Drache, "Industrial Relations as a System of Regulation: Canada and the Economic Crisis" in Hans Diefenbacher and Hans G. Nutzinger, eds., *Gewerkschaften und Arbeitsbeziehungen im Internationalen Vergleich*, FEST, Band II (Heidelberg, 1984).
6. Rand, J., *Ford Motor Company Award 1946*, 1946 Labour Gazette, pp. 123–24.

7. For a comprehensive statement of the work of this school, see R. Boyer ed., *La fléxibilité du travail en Europe* (Paris: La Découverte, 1986). Also B. Coriat, *L'atelier et le chronomètre* 2nd ed., (Paris: C. Bourgeois, 1982).
8. See Michel Aglietta and A. Brender, *Les métamorphoses de la société salariale* (Paris: Calmann-Lévy, 1984), and G. Esping-Andersen, *The Three Worlds of Welfare Capitalism* (London: Polity Press, 1990).
9. Alain Lipietz, "The Globalization of the General Crisis of Fordism," in J. Holmes and C. Leys, eds., *Frontyard, Backyard: The Americas in the Global Crisis* (Toronto: Between the Lines, 1987).
10. For a somewhat fuller account and references to the literature, see H.J. Glasbeek, "Labour Relations Policy and Law as a Mechanism of Adjustment" (1987), 25 *Osgoode Hall L. J.* 179.
11. See the influential OECD study, *Economies in Transition* (Paris: OECD, 1989). It argues that, to make economies more flexible, countries have to strengthen their market mechanism, the very antithesis of the premise of the post-war Fordist mechanisms described by the *régulation* scholars.
12. Richard Belous, "Flexibility and American Labour Markets," ILO, Labour Market Analysis and Employment Planning, World Employment Programme Research (Geneva, June 1987), has made the following calculation:
Annual Rate of Growth of Real Compensation[*]

	1979-82	1982-84
United States	-0.1	0.5
West Germany	1.1	1.0
France	1.8	1.0
United Kingdom	0.3	2.1
Italy	1.3	0.5

[*]Real Compensation includes wages and fringe benefits adjusted for compensation. Compensation per employed person was divided by a nation's gross domestic product price deflator. Estimates are based on OECD data.
Source: Richard Belous, *op. cit.*, p. 22.
13. There will be very real difficulties standing in the way of defining, let alone enforcing acceptable binding standards in respect of minimum wages, the right to strike and the inhibition of discriminatory practices. For a short, but insightful listing of these problems, see Roy Adams, "A Social Charter for European Labour?" *Labour Relations News* (May 1990). The point, however, is that the agenda for the creation of a liberalized trading block includes a Social Charter. No thought was given to this possibility in the U.S.-Canada free trade dealings. Belatedly, a social covenant has been proposed in Canada, although it comes as a sop to NDP participants in the constitutional wheeling and dealing. From the start it has been clear that the social covenant is to have symbolic value only. At no stage was it seen as necessary to give in to labour.
14. Despite the rhetoric of open markets, the U.S. market was heavily protected in the post-war era. This, combined with America's corporations' great competitive strength, meant that imports remained a low or declining share of the U.S. gross domestic product until the late 1960s when U.S. manufacturers began to face import competition from the Europeans and the Japanese. Between 1948 and 1965 imports constituted an average of only 5 percent of the U.S. market's supplies, while U.S. merchandise exports accounted for 32 percent of the imports of the major capitalist economies. See Samuel Bowles, David Gordon, and Thomas Weisskopf, *Beyond the Wasteland: A Democratic Alternative to Economic Decline*, esp. Chapter 4, and M. Piore and C. Sabel, *The Second Industrial Divide*, Chapter 7.

15. These were amendments to the *National Labor Relations Act* (Wagner Act), 29 USC, para. 141. They were a response to an increase in strikes, the perception that they were violent and that too many unions restricted membership and engaged in internecine fights over jurisdiction. In the result, violence and intimidation were outlawed specifically and strikes to force employers to deal with one union rather than another or not to employ certain people were forbidden. Most significantly, secondary boycotts were outlawed and the right to sue in court in respect of collective agreements was inserted. Union activities were restricted and the scheme became more legalistic.

16. Piore and Sabel, *op. cit.*, Chapter 7.

17. *Ibid.*

18. See Audrey Freeman and William Fulmer, "Last Rites for Pattern Bargaining," *Harvard Business Review* (March-April 1982): 30–31. Indeed, by 1973, the ability of workers to insist on this kind of agreement had been considerably weakened. Thus, in the Steel Industry Agreement mentioned in the text, the union had to give up the right to strike for ten years in order to obtain the kind of basic productivity agreement which had been granted without such concessions during the period when a more generous compromise was possible because of America's dominant position in the world economy.

19. M. Piore, "Fissure and Discontinuity in U.S. Labour-Management Relations," MIT occasional paper, 1984, p. 4.

20. Samuel Bowles, *et al.*, *Beyond the Wasteland*, Chapter 4.

21. Piore, *op. cit.*, p. 7. This underlying weakness was institutionalized by the Taft-Hartley amendments, referred to above, which had imposed prohibitions on secondary strike activity. In addition, the congressional attacks on unions by allegations of corrupt practices, and purges initiated in the name of anti-communism in the 1950s, had made it clear that the status of trade unions depended on their acceptance of the political status quo in the United States.

22. For the pioneering works which established that the Canadian political economy is founded on resources and staples export-led growth, see Harold Innis, *Essays in Canadian Economic History*, ed. Mary Q. Innis (Toronto: University of Toronto Press, 1956); Mel Watkins, "A Staple Theory of Economic Growth," in W.T. Easterbook and M.H. Watkins, eds., *Approaches to Canadian Economic History* (Toronto: McClelland and Stewart, 1967); D. Drache, "Harold Innis and Canadian Capitalist Development," *Canadian Journal of Political and Social Theory* 6 (Winter-Spring 1982); for a contemporary overview of recent contributions to export-led growth, see Gordon Laxer, ed., *Perspectives on Canadian Economic Development: Class, Staples, Gender and Elites* (Toronto: Oxford U.P., 1991).

23. For a discussion of Canada's attempt to adapt Fordist principles to Canadian public policy, see Robert Campbell, *The Full-Employment Objective in Canada, 1945–85*, A study prepared for the Economic Council of Canada (Ottawa: Minister of Supply and Services, 1991); G. Boismenu and D. Drache, eds., *Politique et régulation: Modèle de développement et trajectoire canadienne* (Montreal/Paris: Méridien/L'Harmattan, 1990); and Jane Jenson, "'Different' but not 'Exceptional': Canada's Permeable Fordism," *Canadian Review of Sociology and Anthropology* 26:1 (1989).

24. As quoted by Donald V. Smiley, *Constitutional Adaptation and Canadian Federalism since 1945*, Documents of the Royal Commission on Bilingualism and Biculturalism (Ottawa: Information Canada, 1970).

25. See David Wolfe, "The Rise and Demise of the Keynesian Era in Canada," in *Readings in Canadian Social History*, Vol. 5 of M. Cross and G. Kealey, eds., *Modern Canada 1930–1980s* (Toronto: McClelland and Stewart, 1984); and

David Wolfe, "Economic Growth and Foreign Investment," *Journal of Canadian Studies* 13 (Spring 1978); Robert Campbell, *Grand Illusions: The Politics of the Keynesian Experience in Canada 1945–1975* (Toronto: Broadview Press, 1987).

26. For a detailed examination of the roots of this kind of state intervention see Hugh Aitken, "Defensive Expansionism," in W.T. Easterbrooke and M.H. Watkins, eds., *Approaches to Canadian Economic History* (Toronto: McClelland and Stewart, 1967); and Glen Williams, *Not For Export: Toward a Political Economy of Canada's Arrested Development* (Toronto: McClelland and Stewart, 1983).

27. In addition to Innis, *op. cit.*, see Hugh Aitken, *American Capital and Canadian Resources* (Cambridge, Mass.: Harvard University Press, 1961); R.T. Naylor, *The History of Canadian Business*, Vol. 1 (Toronto: Lorimer, 1975); Kari Levitt, *Silent Surrender; The Multinational Corporation in Canada* (Toronto: Macmillan, 1970).

28. See J. Laxer, *Rethinking the Economy* (Toronto: New Canada Publications, 1984).

29. Wallace Clement, "Uneven Development: A Mature Branch-Plant Society," in Wallace Clement, ed., *Class, Power and Property: Essays on Canadian Society* (Toronto: Carleton University Press, 1983).

30. R.S. Letourneau, *Inflation, The Canadian Experience* (Ottawa: Conference Board of Canada, 1980).

31. Leon Muszynski, "The Politics of Labour Market Policy," in Bruce Doern, ed., *The Politics of Economic Policy*, Collected Research Studies, Royal Commission on the Economic Union and Development Prospects for Canada, Vol. 40 (Toronto: University of Toronto Press, 1986).

32. A useful summary of Canada's slow march towards social Keynesianism is offered by Leslie Pal, "Revision and Retreat: Canadian Unemployment Insurance 1971–1981," in J.S. Ismael, ed., *Canadian Social Welfare Policy, Federal and Provincial Dimensions* (Montreal: McGill-Queen's U. P., 1985).

33. For an overview of Canadian social welfare developments, see Denis Guest, *The Emergence of Social Security in Canada* (Vancouver: University of British Columbia Press, 1980); for an account of more recent developments, see David P. Ross, *The Working Poor: Wage Earners and the Failure of Income Security Policies* (Toronto: Lorimer, 1981), Chapter 3.

34. Social Planning Council of Metropolitan Toronto, "The Rise and Fall of the Welfare State," in D. Drache and D. Cameron, eds., *The Other Macdonald Report*, p. 51.

35. For findings of a similar kind, see Ontario, Social Assistance Review Committee, *Transitions, Report of the Social Assistance Review Committee* (Thomson Report) (Toronto: Queen's Printer, Ontario, 1988).

36. Julia O'Conner, "Welfare Expenditure and Policy Orientation in Canada in Comparative Perspective," *Canadian Review of Sociology and Anthropology* 26.1 (1989), p. 143.

37. *Ibid.*, citing M. Rugge, *The State and Working Women* (Princeton: Princeton University Press, 1984), p. 13.

38. Jenson, *op. cit.*, points to the "profound structuring effects of a resource-based economy in which natural wealth [is] distributed by geographic lottery." She argues that unless specifically tailored measures are taken, "uneven development [is] bound to follow" (p. 80).

39. It is common for proponents of collective bargaining to argue that this is not a failure of the institution because it was never its purpose; see *infra*.

40. S. Ostry and M.A. Zaidi, *Labour Economics in Canada*, 2nd ed. (Toronto: Macmillan, 1979), pp. 215–17.
41. U. Zohar, *Canadian Manufacturing: A Study in Productivity and Technological Change* (Toronto: Lorimer, 1982).
42. *Bank of Canada Review*, Table H2, April 1988.
43. Final Report, Task Force on Labour Relations (Woods Task Force) (Ottawa: Privy Council, 1968), Table 8.
44. See Arthur Donner, *The Facts* 10:3 (Fall 1988): 17.
45. *Final Report*, Task Force on Labour Relations. Its role was to make recommendations for reform, without abandoning the system. To this day, its final report and the great number of studies it commissioned comprise the richest source of information on labour relations and state policy available. The other major inquiry was that of A.W.R. Carrothers and E.E. Palmer, *Report of a Study on the Labour Injunction in Ontario* (Toronto: Ontario Department of Labour, 1966).
46. See Carrothers and the Woods Task Force, *op. cit*. They, and other thoughtful proponents of collective bargaining, understood full well that the pent-up demands of workers had to be recognized somehow and that the existing constraints of collective bargaining should not be seen as an insurmountable barrier to workers' inevitable aspirations to maintain their living standards. If collective bargaining were seen as too much of an impediment to these natural pressures it could not survive as a successful mediating mechanism. They recommended, therefore, that trade unions should be allowed to encourage workers to exercise their legitimate strike power when a "catch-up" period was manifest. Accepting the legitimacy and necessity of unions' support for localized interruptions to production was to help the strike serve as a catalyst and catharsis, while at the same time help unions retain the respect they needed to discipline the workforce when instability truly threatened the system. J. Crispo and H. Arthurs, "Industrial Unrest in Canada: A Diagnosis of Recent Experience," *Relations Industrielles* 23 (1968), put this crisply, at p. 282: "[I]f union leaders are to do what is responsible in the long run, they may have to do what seems irresponsible in the short turn, or the membership will depose them."
47. Claude Morin, *Quebec vs. Ottawa: The Struggle for Self Government 1960–72* (Toronto: University of Toronto Press, 1976).
48. M. Thompson and E. Swimmer, eds., *Conflict or Compromise: Public Sector Industrial Relations in Canada* (Montreal: IRPP, 1984); H.W. Arthurs, *Collective Bargaining by Public Employees in Canada: The Five Models* (Ann Arbor: Institute of Labor and Industrial Relations, 1971); and S. Goldenberg and J. Finkelman, *Collective Bargaining in the Public Service: The Federal Experience in Canada* (Montreal: IRPP, 1983).
49. The Woods Task Force, *op. cit.*, recognized that collective bargaining and protective legislation were complementary parts of a tacit agreement that "government had to take cognizance of the hardships created by unemployment, underemployment, sweated labour, low wages, long hours, brutal supervision and unsafe and unhealthy working conditions" (para. 35). Note that at the same time the conclusion of the *Final Report* was that collective bargaining was not a national incomes policy. Therefore, redistribution of national income or abolition of existing inequalities could not be attributed to, or expected from, it. The contradictory nature of the theoretical underpinning of the system is apparent.

Chapter 3

1. Pradeep Kumar, "Estimates of Unionism and Collective Bargaining Coverage in Canada," *Relations Industrielles* 43 (1988): 757.
2. Kumar, *ibid.*; Roy J. Adams, "The Extent of Collective Bargaining in Canada," *Relations Industrielles* 39:4 (1984).
3. Richard Freeman, "Canada in the World Labour Market to the Year 2000," prepared for the Economic Council of Canada, November 1988, Table 2; see Chapter 1 for additional details.
4. Joseph B. Rose and Gary N. Chaison, "New Measures of Union Organizing Effectiveness," *Industrial Relations* 29:3 (1990).
5. The data are derived from the agreements concluded in bargaining units of more than 500 employees. It will be remembered from the account in Chapter 1 that these are gigantic locals by Canadian standards. The latest data available at the time of writing were those found in *Provisions in Major Collective Agreements in Canada Covering 500 and More Employees* (Bureau of Labour Information, Labour Canada, April 18, 1990). The data found in this Labour Canada tabulation are the ones referred to in the ensuing text, unless otherwise noted.
6. For the best articulation that a new industrial citizenship has been created, see H.W. Arthurs, "Developing Industrial Citizenship: A Challenge for Canada's Second Century," *Canadian Bar Review* 45 (1967): 786.
7. Labour Canada's report, which details the provisions of collective agreements of bargaining units of 500 or more employees, also provides similar information about units of 200 or more employees covered by federal labour law.
8. D.A. Auld, L.N. Christofieds, R. Swidnisky and D.A. Wilton, *The Determinants of Negotiated Wage Settlements in Canada 1966–1975* (Ottawa: Anti-Inflation Board, 1979), have argued that, as a general economic principle, COLA provisions never can provide more than 75 percent of the cost-of-living increases.
9. Woods and Kumar, *The Current Industrial Relations Scene in Canada* (Kingston, Ont.: Industrial Relations Centre, Queen's University, 1987), p. 484.
10. In 1991, the CAW claimed that it had won a more generous COLA in its settlement with the Big Three auto makers than it had in the past.
11. The extent of this protection will be evaluated in Chapter 7. It suffices to note that it is largely improvement on this front which has helped liberal pluralists justify their claim that a more democratic, a more humane, workplace has been promoted by the collective bargaining system.
12. For a survey of these provisions throughout Canada, see H. Arthurs, D. Carter, J. Fudge, and H.J. Glasbeek, *Labour Law and Industrial Relations in Canada*, 3rd ed. (Toronto: Butterworths, 1988), pp. 136–37.
13. Francois Sellier and Jean-Jacques Silvestre, "Unions in the Economic Crisis in France," p. 221, and Paolo Garonna and Elena Pisani, "Italian Unions in Transition: The Crisis of Political Unionism," in R. Edwards, P. Garonna and F. Todling, *Unions in Crisis and Beyond: Perspectives From Six Countries* (Dover, Mass.: Auburn House, 1986). In addition, the OECD countries have imposed a set of guidelines which require that when a branch of a multinational decides to close down, its parent must justify it to the nation state concerned. As the multinational usually wants to maintain good relations with the governments of countries in which it wishes to continue to do business, this gives nation states a measure of control over this kind of contracting out. It has been used with telling effect in Europe. Canada is a signatory to these guidelines, but they have not been given any sway here at all; see R.

Blanpain, *The OECD Guidelines for Multinational Enterprises and Labour Relations, 1976–1979: Experience and Review* (Deventer, Netherlands; Boston: Kluwer; Hingham, Mass., 1979).

14. S.235, *Canada Labour Code* R.S.C. 1985, c.L-2; s.40a *The Employment Standards Act*, R.S.O. 1980, c.137.

15. Proof that the eligibility requirements have been met has to be provided by the terminated employees. Employers, particularly failing employers, may rely on this to avoid payments, or at least to delay them. One instance in Ontario indicated that two years' delay was not uncommon. The hardship for workers is obvious; see "Cleaners win severance pay after 2 years," *The Globe and Mail*, March 15, 1990.

16. The characterization of these benefits as meagre is a comparative assessment; European safeguards are much better. This is not to say that European workers are satisfied with their protections. For two different views of the statutory rights in Europe, see OECD, *High Unemployment: A Challenge For Income Support Policies* (Paris: OECD, 1984). Many of the contributors to this volume argue that, despite the fact that protection is stronger than it used to be and richer than that found in North America, benefit levels are still too low and do little for the long-term unemployed. For the contrary position, see OECD, *Economies in Transition: Structural Adjustment in OECD Countries* (Paris, 1989).

17. John Holmes, "The Organization and Locational Structure of Production Sub-Contracting," in A.J. Scott and M. Storper, eds., *Production, Work Territory* (London: Allen and Unwin, 1986).

18. The landmark case in which this was laid down is *Re Russelsteel Ltd.* v. *United Steelworkers* (1966), 17 LAC 253 (H.W. Arthurs).

19. Holmes, *op. cit.*; see also Robert Boyer, "The Eighties: The Search for Alternatives To Fordism," (Paris: CEPREMAP, 1987).

20. The Premier's Council of Ontario has been one of the most vociferous proponents of economic restructuring and of the need for labour to adapt; see its *Competing in the New Global Economy*, Vol. 1 (Toronto, 1988); see also Economic Council of Canada, *Innovation and Jobs in Canada* (Ottawa: Economic Council of Canada, 1987).

21. H.D. Woods and Pradeep Kumar, *Trends in Collective Bargaining 1986 and 1987* (Kingston: Centre for Industrial Relations, Queen's University, 1988).

22. Where collective agreements contain provisions which are to govern the introduction of new technologies, the unions have rarely won more than what is available by dint of statutorily provided protection; see Patricia McDermott, "Technological Change and the Canada Labour Code," prepared for the Science Council of Canada, January 1984.

23. A. Craig, *The System of Industrial Relations in Canada* (Scarborough, Ont.: Prentice-Hall, 1983), p. 262.

24. D. Brown and D. Beatty, *Canadian Labour Arbitration*, 3rd ed. (Aurora, Ont.: Canada Law Book Co., 1989), para. 6:2210.

25. *Cryovac Division, Grace Chemicals Ltd.* (1972), 24th A.C. 127 (Weiler).

26. Waldie, Brennan and Associates, *Labour Standards: An Interjurisdictional Comparison*, A Study Prepared for the Government of Ontario (Toronto: Ministry of Labour, July 31, 1990).

27. *Canadian Labour Law Reporter*, Vol. 1 (Don Mills, Ont.: CCH Canadian Limited), para. 1500. Any social democratic party which wins government would be well advised to move to enrich these benefits in the same way that they should change hours of work legislation. Unions should support them by bar-

gaining for better provisions. The CAW has made a good beginning in its 1990 negotiations with the automobile companies.
28. See *Post Office Agreement*, 1981.
29. The two jurisdictions are British Columbia and New Brunswick. Most jurisdictions require twelve months' service.
30. The Northwest Territories provides for twenty weeks.
31. See H.W. Arthurs, D.D. Carter, J. Fudge, and H.J. Glasbeek, *Labour Law and Industrial Relations in Canada*, 3rd ed. (Toronto: Butterworths, 1988), paras. 285–86.
32. For a comparative description of parental benefits, see ILO, *Maternity Benefits in the Eighties*, an ILO Global Survey (1964–84) (Geneva, 1985).
33. The CAW has succeeded in making employers pay for daycare provision in Windsor.
34. Statistics Canada, *Pension Plans in Canada 1988* (Ottawa: Supply and Services, 1990), Appendix II.
35. For a comparative description of European retirement income schemes which provide considerably better benefits for workers and their families, see Government of Ontario, *Report of the Task Force on Inflation Protection for Employment Pension Plans* (Friedland Report) (Toronto, 1986), Chapter 3.
36. There are many varieties of works councils and boards of directors structures in Europe. Their efficacy is a matter of some controversy. See Paolo Garonna and Elena Pisani, "Italian Unions in Transition: The Crisis of Political Unionism," in R. Edwards *et al.*, *op. cit.*, pp. 130–137.
37. The story of the struggle at Radio Shack will be told in greater detail in Chapter 5.
38. OECD, *Women and Employment: Policies for Equal Opportunities* (Paris, 1980).
39. Isabella Bakker, "The Status of Women in OECD countries," *Equality in Employment*, A Royal Commission Report, Research Studies (Ottawa: Minister of Supply and Services, 1985), p. 504.
40. As reported in *The Globe and Mail*, December 24, 1988.
41. Women's groups and unions realize this and are busily trying to pursue alternative bargaining and legislative strategies. Thus far, progress is poor; see Debra J. Lewis, *Just Give Us the Money*. The election of the NDP in Ontario in the fall of 1990 opened up the way for more intervention. As we shall detail in Chapter 8, the NDP's efforts thus far have been disappointing.
42. Royal Commission on the Economic Union and the Development Prospects for Canada, *Final Report*, Vol. II (Ottawa, 1985), Chapter 17.
43. H.J. Glasbeek, "A Role for Criminal Sanctions in Occupational Health and Safety," in *New Developments in Employment Law*, Meredith Memorial Lectures 1988 (Cowansville, Que.: Les Editions Yvon Blais, 1989), p. 125.
44. Paul Weiler, *Reconcilable Differences: New Directions in Canadian Labour Law* (Toronto: Carswell, 1980); H.W. Arthurs, "'The Dullest Bill': Reflections on the Labour Code of British Columbia" (1974), 9 *Univ. B.C. L. Rev.* 280.
45. See the *Industrial Relations Act*, R.S.B.C. 1979 c.212, as amended; Part 8.1; for more details, see the discussion in Chapter 5.
46. Section 109.1, *Labour Code*, R.S.Q. 1977 c. C-27.
47. S.45, *The Trade Union Act* R.S.S. 1978, c.T-17.
48. S.39-40, *Labour Relations Act* R.S.O. 1980, c.228.
49. E.g., *Fuller and Knowles Co. Ltd; Strathcone Mechanical Inc. and P.P.T. Mechanical Services Inc.* unreported (Alta. L.R.B.), File no's L.R. 174-S-12, L.R. 174-S-11, L.R. 174-P-23, 31 Oct.'84. See also E.G. Fisher and S. Kush-

ner, "Alberta's Construction Labour Relations During the Recent Down-Turn," *Relations Industrielles* 41:4 (1986).

50. These and previous stirrings of this kind have been thoroughly studied by Barbara Heather MacAllister, "Labour and the State: The Canadian Labour Congress, Consultative Forums, and Incomes Policies 1960–1978," unpublished Ph.D. thesis, University of Toronto, 1982, and David I. Langille, "From Consultation to Corporation? The Consultative Process between Canadian Business, Labour and Government, 1977–1981," unpublished M.A. thesis, Carleton University, 1982; also A. Giles, "The Canadian Labour Congress and Tripartism," *Industrial Relations* 37:1 (1982).

51. Leo Panitch, "Corporatism in Canada," *Studies in Political Economy* 1 (1979): 84.

52. Clare H. Pentland, *A Study of the Changing Social, Economic and Political Background of the Canadian System of Industrial Relations*, Task Force on Labour Relations (Ottawa: Privy Council Office, 1968), p. 339. See also Frank Scott, *Essays on Law and the Constitution* (Toronto: University of Toronto Press, 1980).

53. The malfunctioning of Canada's labour markets was a principal finding of the Woods Task Force, although it did not exploit this insight to the degree it might have. See Task Force on Labour Relations, *Final Report* (Ottawa: Privy Council, 1968); and Henry Pold and Fred Wong, "The Price of Labour," *Perspectives on Labour Income* 3 (Autumn 1990).

54. Clare H. Pentland, *A Study of the Changing Social, Economic and Political Background of the Canadian System of Industrial Relations*, *loc. cit.*; also, Daniel Drache, "Industrial Relations as a System of Regulation: Canada and the Economic Crisis," in Hans Diefenbacher and Hans Nutzinger, eds., Gewerkschaften und Arbeitsbeziehungen im Internationalen Vergleich, FEST, Band II (Heidelberg, 1984), pp. 211–216; see also Jane Jenson, *op. cit.*

55. Bill 40, An Act to Amend certain Acts concerning Collective Bargaining and Employment, July 1992. It is to be noted that although these proposals are even less than a rather modest Ontario Federation of Labour had demanded, the government has had to deal with a marvellously organized and vituperative opposition from business, giving substance to the argument next made in the text. The proposals fail to do much for the prospects of unorganized women and workers in small employment settings.

Chapter 4

1. "Labour relations board" is used here to refer to Canada's collective bargaining administrative agencies. Sometimes they are called something different; for example, in New Brunswick the agency is known as the Industrial Relations Board. Nothing hinges on this. In Quebec, however, the structure is legally different. There is a Labour Court which is to hear and decide appeals from investigating commissioners and has the power to impose penal sanctions. The work referred to as labour relations board work in this chapter basically is done by labour commissioners in Quebec, a separate branch of the administrative agency.

2. In part, this claim is made by juxtaposing labour relations boards' dispute resolution with that which takes place in civil courts. Thus, Gerald E. Phillips, *Labour Relations and the Collective Bargaining Cycle*, 2nd ed. (Toronto: Butterworths, 1981), argues at p. 102: "In contrast to traditional courts of law, labour relations boards substitute relevant expertise for rigid precedents, compromise for the adversary system and 'flexible solutions' for predetermined

remedies. Thus the proponents of the 'tribunal' concept claim that in matters involving employee-employer relationships, such boards theoretically have more potential than traditional courts of law for operating in an optimal manner." For a fuller account of the way in which these boards are to function, see A.W.R. Carrothers, E.E. Palmer, and W.B. Rayner, *Collective Bargaining Law in Canada*, 2nd ed. (Toronto and Vancouver: Butterworths, 1986) pp. 79–80, chs. 8 and 9; H.W. Arthurs, D.D. Carter, J. Fudge, and H.J. Glasbeek, *Labour Law and Industrial Relations in Canada*, 3rd ed. (Toronto: Kluwer/Butterworths, 1988).

3. Beatrice and Sydney Webb, *Industrial Democracy* (London: Longmans, Green and Co., 1926), pp. 807–850.

4. Unless the organizers have called in a union with an existing constitution, they need technical knowledge which they must hire. It is hard for lay people to know that the following steps must be taken: "1. A constitution should be drafted setting out, among other things, the purpose of the organization (which must include the regulation of labour relations) and the procedure for electing officers and calling meetings. 2. The constitution should be placed before a meeting of employees for their approval either as originally drafted or as amended at the meeting. 3. The constitution should be ratified by a vote of the members.... 4. Officers should be elected pursuant to the constitution." See *Federation of Teachers in Hebrew Schools and Associated Hebrew Schools of Toronto*, [1978] O.L.R.B. Rep. 797; *Canadian Union of Bank Employees and Canadian Trustco Mortgage Co.*, [1976] C.L.R.B.R. 725.

5. The boards' eagerness to devise a policy which would encourage unionization, while still paying lip service to the rights of individuals, was anathema to the judiciary. The Supreme Court of Canada, the bastion of rugged individualism, thought the policy a sham; see *Metropolitan Life* (1970), 11D.L.R. (3d) 336 (S.C.C.). Legislative action restored the boards' approach. For a history of these developments, see *Windsor Raceway Holdings*, [1979] 2 C.L.R.B.R. 89, a case which reveals that many technical difficulties continue to plague boards in respect of this issue.

6. For instance, s.13 *Labour Relations Act*, R.S.O. 1980, c.228 provides: "The Board shall not certify a trade union if it discriminates against any person on any ground of discrimination prohibited by the *Human Rights Code, 1981* or the *Canadian Charter of Rights and Freedoms.*"

7. This was a favourite tactic in the 1920s. The boards have been fairly successful in eliminating this threat to real collective bargaining. In the last few years, however, the political and economic climate, first in the United States, and now in Canada, has encouraged many employers to avoid unionization by these means again; see, e.g., *Faultless Doerner Manufacturing Co.*, [1980] O.L.R.B. Rep. 214 where an employer, on advice of a "consultant," provided draft by-laws to employees, discussed them with their employees and encouraged them to adopt them in order to form an association, all of this to avoid organization by an "outside" union. The board thwarted this particular effort. But the fact that some employers get caught does not mean that the practice is not used successfully by many others.

8. See *The Joseph Brant Memorial Hospital Staff Association and Burlington Nelson Hospital* (1963), 63 C.L.L.C. 16,269 (Ont.). The date of the case indicates that this technical requirement is easily met these days but, as the text below argues, the conceptual implications have great practical importance.

9. S.24 a, *Trade Unions Act*, S.N.S. 1972, c.19, as amended.

10. For an academic's articulation of the angst created in the ranks of liberal supporters of collective bargaining Canadian-style by the Michelin Bill, see B.

Langille, "The Michelin Amendment in Context" (1981), 6 *Dalhousie L.J.* 523.

11. Trade unionists who want this picture to be real reacted angrily to the Michelin Bill. Then-CLC President Dennis McDermott emerged from a meeting to say it would be fought nationally and internationally because it made "a deplorable sham of democracy"; see CCH, *Canadian Industrial Relations and Personnel Developments Newsletter*, Feb. 6, 1980. The Nova Scotia Federation of Labour resolved that all labour representatives serving on provincial government boards and agencies should resign their posts and that representatives of labour should not consult with members of the then government; CCH, *Canadian Industrial Relations and Personnel Development*, March 12, 1980. These responses indicate the extent to which the legitimacy of the scheme is contingent on the extent of labour relations boards' autonomy.

12. See, generally, Paul Weiler, *Reconcilable Differences* (Toronto: Carswell, 1980); H.W. Arthurs, "'The Dullest Bill': Reflections on the Labour Code of British Columbia" (1974) 9 *Univ. B.C.L. Rev.* 244.

13. For an analysis of these cases, see J. Baigent, "Protecting the Right to Organize," in J.J. Weiler and P.A. Gall, eds., *The Labour Code of British Columbia in the 1980's* (Calgary: Carswell, 1984), p. 45. This kind of turnabout has not been restricted to British Columbia. After a political turn to the right in Saskatchewan, the Labour Relations Board there changed its ground rules for certification in the construction industry. This made it increasingly difficult for trade unions to maintain their strength and position; see Robert Sass, "The Tory Assault on Labour in Saskatchewan" (1987), 7 *Access to Justice* 133.

14. *Canada Post Corporation and Canadian Union of Postal Workers, and various unions*, Can. L.R.B. Board files 530-1218, 530-1481, Decision No. 675, 10 Feb. 1988, p. 35, unreported decision.

15. Canada Post did not hesitate to add fuel to the fire. LCUC used the International Brotherhood of Electrical Workers (IBEW) as a Trojan horse. The IBEW launched a raid against CUPW. Canada Post, in the interest of "democracy," gave IBEW organizers access to its premises, something it never afforded its own unions.

16. For a discussion of efforts to organize the banks, see Graham Lowe, "Causes of Unionization in Canadian Banks," *Relations Industrielles* 36:4 (1981); E.J. Shelton Lennon, "Bank Workers Unionization," *Osgoode Hall L. J.* (1980) 18; Elizabeth Beckett, "Unions and Bank Workers: Will the Twain Ever Meet?" (Ottawa: Women's Bureau, Labour Canada, 1984).

17. *Bank of Nova Scotia, Kitimat* (1959), 59 C.L.L.C. 18,152 (C.L.R.B.).

18. The workers' account of the bank organizing drive is described by the Bank Book Collective, *An Account to Settle* (Vancouver: Press Gang Publishers, 1980).

19. *Canadian Imperial Bank of Commerce* (1977), 77 C.L.L.C. 16,089 (C.L.R.B.).

20. See E.J. Shelton Lennon, *op. cit.*; see also P. Weiler, *op. cit.*, pp. 15–20.

21. *Union of Bank Employees, Local 2104 (CLC)* v. *Canadian Imperial Bank of Commerce* (1985), 85 C.L.L.C. 16,021 (Can.L.R.B.). Of course, if the employer had permitted the employees to use the internal mail system for diverse purposes before the organizational drive had begun, a prohibition at that point would smack of crass anti-unionism rather than a proper exercise of an employer's property rights. In that case, the employer's conduct might be invalidated, see *C.U.P.E.* v. *University of Toronto*, Labour Law News, Vol. 14, No. 5, 4 March 1988 (O.L.R.B.).

22. E.g., *Union of Bank Employees (Ontario) Local 2104 CLC* v. *Bank of Montreal Devonshire Mall Branch, Windsor* (1983), 83 C.L.L.C. 16,015; *Union of*

Bank Employees, Local 2104, CLC v. *C.I.B.C.* (1980), 80 C.L.L.C. 16,002; *Union of Bank Employees, Local 2104* v. *C.I.B.C.* (1985), 85 C.L.L.C. 16,021; *Union of Bank Employees, Local 2104* v. *C.I.B.C.* (1986), 86 C.L.L.C. 16,023. The recidivism speaks volumes about the banks' anti-union- ism and the ineffectiveness of the sanctions imposed by the administrative agencies.

23. Rosemary Warskett, "Bank Worker Unionization and the Law," SPE 25 (Spring 1988).

24. *Syndicat des employés des Banques Nationales de Rimouski and National Bank of Canada* (1986), 86 C.L.C.C. 16,032 (C.L.R.B.). It is not yet clear whether this approach will win out. In one case, the Ontario Labour Relations Board, dealing with a trust company which fell under its jurisdiction, accepted the cluster approach; see *Union Bank of Employees, Local 2104 C.L.C.* v. *National Trust* (1989), 86 C.L.L.C. 16,026 (O.L.R.B.), only to go back to a branch-by-branch approach when the same parties came before it in 1987; see 87 C.L.L.C. 16,026 (O.L.R.B.).

25. *The Globe and Mail*, March 18, 1986.

26. Gad Horowitz, *Canadian Labour and Politics* (Toronto: University of Toronto Press, 1968).

27. For details of the CSU story, see L.W. Kaplan, *Everything that Floats: Pat Sullivan, Hal Banks and the Seamen's Unions of Canada* (Toronto: University of Toronto Press, 1987); for the Mine Mill saga, see John Lang, "A History of Organized Labour in Sudbury, Ontario," unpublished M.A. Thesis, Guelph University, Ontario, 1967.

28. The boards held that, as communism and free collective bargaining were in- compatible, the communist-led CSU was not a legitimate trade union for pur- poses of Canadian law. See, *Branch Lines Limited and Canadian Seamen's Union* (1950), 52 C.L.L.C. 16, 622; for a similar judicial view, see *Smith and Rhuland* v. *R.*, [1953] 3 D.L.R. 690 (S.C.C.) in which, by the slimmest of ma- jorities, the Supreme Court of Canada held that merely to have communist leaders did not disentitle a union to its bargaining rights, but that it could do so if there was evidence that having such leaders would lead to an erosion of the legitimate purposes of a trade union. Given a context in which judicial no- tice was being taken by our highest courts of the fact that communism was anathema in a society to which free trade unionism was essential, boards had lots of ammunition. Any finding by them that the presence of communists or communist sympathizers was undermining a trade union was likely to be up- held.

29. During the Mine Mill saga, the Ontario Labour Relations Board at one stage changed the definition of an appropriate bargaining unit in much the same way as the Nova Scotia legislature did in the case of Michelin. When Mine Mill had signed up a majority of employees at one of the two plants in Elliot Lake, the Board accepted an argument made by the Steelworkers that the ap- propriate bargaining unit ought to consist of three plants in the geographic area, rather than one, as the norms and practices had previously decreed; see Lang, *op. cit.*

30. For a discussion of the CCF and its acceptance of the Cold War ideology, see Horowitz, *op. cit.*

31. See *Canadian Association of Industrial, Mechanical and Allied Workers, Lo- cals 23-27* v. *Cominco* (1981), 82 C.L.L.C. 16,146 and the subsequent case be- tween the same parties, (1981), 82 C.L.L.C. 16,163.

32. The story of CAIMAW is not unique in recent times. When national unions sought a footing in the Toronto construction industry, American unions, often

assisted by employers, asked the Ontario Labour Relations Board to abandon
its existing practices so as to deny the newcomers their place in the sun. Delays and costs hindered the challengers. The Board never did accede to all the
demands made by the established American unions, but the national unionists
were convinced that the eventual failure of their organizational drive had
much to do with the belief system which motivated the Board.

33. Because the boards are interested in stability, they want secure unions. When
a challenge to a certified trade union has failed, the applicant is barred from
applying again for at least six months.

34. Sam Gindin, "Breaking Away: The Formation of the Canadian Auto Workers," SPE 29 (Summer, 1989); Charlotte Yates, "CAW Militancy in the
1980s," SPE 31 (Spring 1990); John Holmes and A. Rusonik, "The break-up
of an international labour union: uneven development in the North American
auto industry and the schism in the UAW," *Environment and Planning A* 23
(1991).

Chapter 5

1. R.D. McDowell, "Law and Practice before the Ontario Labour Relations
Board" (1977-78), *Advocates Quarterly*, 198. Designating bargaining units
and dealing with applications for certification by unions to acquire agency for
them is the meat and potatoes of labour boards' work. For instance, Ontario's
Labour Relations Board has a yearly caseload of circa 3,500 applications and
complaints, about 1,000 of which are applications for certification and 800 are
complaints about unfair labour practices, many of which arise during organizational drives; *Annual Report 1988-89*, Ontario Labour Relations Board.

2. For a general outline of standard units, see J. Sack and M. Mitchell, *Ontario
Labour Relations Board Law and Practices* (Toronto: Butterworths, 1985);
Claude H. Foisy, Daniel E. Lavery, and Luc Martineau, *Canada Labour Relations Board Policies and Procedures* (Toronto and Vancouver: Butterworths,
1986); L. McGrady, *A Guide to Organizing Unions*, (Toronto: Butterworths,
1989).

3. John R. Kilcoyne, "Developments in Deployment Law: The 1987-88 Term"
(1989), 11 *Supreme Court L. R.*, 241, 245; G. Adams, *Canadian Labour Law*
(Toronto: Carswell, 1985), p. 312; H.W. Arthurs, D.D. Carter, J. Fudge, and
H.J. Glasbeek, *Labour Law and Industrial Relations in Canada*, 3rd. ed. (To-
ronto: Butterworths, 1989), pp. 209 *et seq.*; see also *Usarco Ltd.* [1967],
O.L.R.B. Rep. 526.

4. *Insurance Corp. of B.C.*, [1974], 1 Can. L.R.B.R. 403, 407 (P. Weiler).

5. *The Board of Education for the City of Toronto*, [1970] O.L.R.B. Rep. 430,
435–36 (O. Shime).

6. The Canada Labour Relations Board was citing its British Columbia counterpart; see *British Columbia Ferry Corporation*, [1977] 1 Can. L.R.B. 526.

7. See Leo McGrady, *op. cit.*, paras. 12.01 to 12.10.

8. In the 1960s, the automobile industry with its complex system of fragmented
part-supplies, was particularly vulnerable to wildcat strikes. Parts
manufacturers' employees were usually members of the UAW. This helped to
persuade the Big Three automobile companies to propose sector-wide bargaining. See John Holmes, "The Globalization of Production and the Future of
Canada's Mature Industries: The Case of the Automotive Industry," in Daniel
Drache and Meric Gertler, eds., *The New Era of Global Competition* (Montreal: McGill-Queen's U.P., 1991).

9. For an account of the power of the craft unions and their ability to extract wage and other concessions from the construction trades, see Stuart Jamieson, *Industrial Relations in Canada*, 2nd ed. (Toronto: Macmillan, 1973), pp. 132–33.

10. For a more general discussion of the push towards inflation-control mechanisms, see P. Weiler, *Reconcilable Differences: New Directions in Canadian Labour Law* (Toronto: Carswell, 1980). He properly does not cite the construction industry as the only impetus but it was the wage advances in this industry which attracted most attention during the contemporary debates.

11. See C. Goldenberg and J. Crispo, eds., *Construction Labour Relations* (1968). This study was followed by similar ones: Report of the Commission of Enquiry into Industrial Relations in the Nova Scotia Construction Industry, H.D. Woods, Commissioner (Halifax: Department of Labour, 1970); Report on Accreditation and the Construction Industry (Fredericton: New Brunswick Department of Labour, 1972), Joseph B. Rose; Special Commission of Inquiry into British Columbia Construction (Victoria: Queen's Printer, 1976), James Kinnard, Commissioner; Rapport de la Commission d'enquête sur l'exercice de la liberté syndicale dans l'industrie de la construction (Quebec: Editeur Officiel du Québec, 1975), Robert Cliché; Report of the Industrial Inquiry Commission into Bargaining Patterns in the Construction Industry in Ontario (Toronto: Ministry of Labour, 1976), D.E. Franks, Commissioner.

12. See Richard H. Brown, "The Reform of Bargaining Structure in the Canadian construction Industry" (1979), 3 *Industrial Relations L. J.* 538, for a description of the statutory frameworks.

13. J.B. Rose and K. Wetzel, "Outcomes of Bargaining Structures in the Ontario and Saskatchewan Construction Industries," *Relations Industrielles* 41:2 (1986): 256. Of course, legislatures can change the power balance in different ways. In Alberta, legislation was passed in 1983 which took away the discretion of the labour relations board to give collective bargaining rights to a union when an employer created a non-union spin-off corporation to bid on business against itself. This gave employers in the construction industry the go-ahead to establish a virtually union-free employment climate. The earlier help offered to employers by the Alberta Board when it read the unions' successor rights rather narrowly apparently had not been favourable enough; see E.G. Fisher and S. Kushner, "Alberta's Construction Labour Relations during the Recent Downturn," *Relations Industrielles* 41:4 (1986): 778.

14. *Burns Meat Ltd* (1984), [1984] O.L.R.B. Rep. 1049.

15. Anne Forrest, "The Rise and Fall of National Bargaining in the Canadian Meat-Packing Industry," *Relations Industrielles* 44:2 (1989): 393.

16. Adams, *op. cit.*, p. 322; see also Arthurs, *et al.*, *op. cit.*

17. For a discussion of the literature and for his own analysis, see J. Rose, "Legislative Support For Multi-Employer Bargaining: The Canadian Experience," *Industrial Labour Relations Review* 40:3 (1986).

18. H.J. Glasbeek, "TIP: Another Weapon in the Class War Waged Against Workers," *Canadian Taxation* 3 (1981): 94; Kilcoyne, *op. cit.*

19. *The Corporation of the District of Burnaby*, [1974], C.L.R.B.R. 1,3; see also *Porcupine Mines Ltd*, [1975] 2 C.L.R.B.R. 234 (O.L.R.B), *Cominco Ltd* (1980), 80 C.L.L.C. 16,045 (C.L.R.B.).

20. E.g., *Pre-Con Murray Limited*, [1965] O.L.R.B. Mthly. Rep. 328.

21. For an extended discussion, see *Cominco Ltd.*, *op. cit.*

22. *United Steelworkers of America* v. *The Adams Mine, Cliffs of Canada Ltd.* (1983), 83 C.L.L.C. 16,011 (O.L.R.B.).

23. *Oil Chemical and Atomic Workers International Union* v. *Syncrude Canada Ltd and Gulf Oil Canada Ltd*, 78 C.L.L.C. 16,168 (Board of Industrial Relations).

24. *United Cement, Lime and Gypsum Workers International Union, AFL-CIO CLC* v. *G.T.E. Sylvania Canada Ltd, Electrical Components and Systems Division*, 79 C.L.L.C. 16,193 (O.L.R.B.).

25. *Bell and Howell*, [1968] O.L.R.B. Rep. 695.

26. It is a sign of the times, however, that employers increasingly are challenging boards which rule in favour of union successor rights. They have had a good measure of success in the courts; see J.M. Evans, "Jurisdictional Review in the Supreme Court: Realism, Romance and Recidivism" (1991), 48 *Administrative Law Review*, 225.

27. For a definitive analysis of the principles used by administrative agencies when dealing with good-faith bargaining, see *De Vilbiss (Canada)* [1976] O.L.R.B. Rep. 49 (Haladner).

28. A. Cox, "The Duty to Bargain in Good Faith" (1958), 71 *Harvard L. Rev.* 1401,1409. Despite its antiquity and foreignness, this passage is frequently cited by contemporary Canadian labour relations boards.

29. This well-known tactic, also known as Boulwarism, is considered unacceptable by all American and Canadian labour relations boards. It was conceived by a Mr. Boulware of General Electric in the United States.

30. This was the approach taken by the employers in the first *Radio Shack* and the *Eaton's* cases, both of which are discussed at some length below.

31. A good example is provided by the facts of *De Vilbiss (Canada), op. cit.*

32. *Radio Shack* (1980), 80 C.L.L.C. 16,003

33. *United Steelworkers of America, Local 9011* v. *Radio Shack Division of Tandy Electronics Limited* (1985), 86 C.L.L.C. 16,006 (O.L.R.B.).

34. In 1980, the Board had been faced with another viciously anti-union employer. It had noted how hard it was to distinguish between hard bargaining and surface bargaining, but then, this other case being very close in time to the first *Radio Shack* decision, it held that here there had been bad-faith bargaining; see *Fotomat Canada Ltd.*, [1980] O.L.R.B. Rep. 1397.

35. *Westroc Industries Ltd.*, [1981] 2 C.L.R.B.R. 315 (O.L.R.B.)

36. The significance of this kind of reading of labour law can be grasped from the tactic used by Nation Air in its dispute with its employees in early 1992. Anticipating a bargaining impasse, the employer trained replacement workers and then locked out its unionized employees. A different holding in *Westroc* may have prevented the employer from using this tactic which vastly expanded its bargaining leverage.

37. *Paccar of Canada Ltd.* v. *Canadian Association of Industrial, Mechanical and Allied Workers, Local 14* (1989), 89 C.L.L.C. 14,050 (S.C.C.).

38. *Construction Labour Relations A.A.* v. *Alberta Labour Relations Board* (1984), 33 Alta. L.R. (2d) 143, aff'd (1985), 37 Alta. L.R. (2d) 1 (Alta. C.A.), leave to appeal to S.C.C. denied; *Clark Roofing (1964) Ltd., Westeel-Rose Ltd. and Flynn & Associates Ltd.* (1985), 9 C.L.R.B.R. 96 (Sask. L.R.B.).

39. *Westinghouse Canada Limited*, [1980] O.L.R.B. Rep. 577.

40. *Consolidated Bathurst Packaging Ltd* (1983), 83 C.L.L.C. 16,066 (O.L.R.B.). For the decision on remedies, see (1984), 84 C.L.L.C. 16,027.

41. *Eastern Provincial Airways Ltd.* (1984), 84 C.L.L.C. 16,012 (C.L.R.B.).

42. *Shaw-Almex Industries Ltd.* (1988), 88 C.L.L.C. 14,007 (Ont. S.C.).

43. In the first *Radio Shack* case, the union was certified in March 1979. The negotiations broke down and a judicial decision ordering the employer to conclude a settlement was rendered in February 1980, a full year later. In the

second case, the final decision upholding the employer's bargaining tactics was delivered two years after negotiations had begun. The financial, social and emotional costs to workers are manifest.

44. Peter G. Bruce, "The Processing of Unfair Labour Practice Cases in the United States and Ontario," *Relations Industrielles* 45:3 (1990).

45. *Kennedy Lodge Nursing Home* (1981), 81 C.L.L.C. 16,078 (O.L.R.B.). (The purpose of the employer here was similar to that of Westinghouse, but the Board found that no real decision had been taken to close at the time of bargaining.)

46. Anne Forest, "Bargaining Units and Bargaining Power," *Relations Industrielles* 41:4 (1986).

47. The relevant legislation is described in Arthurs, Carter, Fudge, and Glasbeek, *op. cit.*, par. 539–540.

48. These data are culled from a memorandum written by J. Johnson, Research Officer, British Columbia Labour Relations Board, 26 August, 1978 (available on request). For a more general discussion see P. Weiler, *Reconcilable Differences, op. cit.* For a discussion of the federal provision, see S. Muthuchidambaram, "Settlement of First Collective Agreement; An Examination of the Canada Labour Code Amendment" *Relations Industrielles* 35:3 (1980): 387.

49. Its willingness is displayed in the language found in *Nepean Roof Truss Ltd*, [1986] O.L.R.B. Rep. 1005.

50. J.M.P. Korphsho, "First Contract Experience in Manitoba," Paper presented to the Canadian Industrial Relations Association, 1986. In Ontario, the trade union movement's disappointment with results has caused it to pressure the NDP government into making proposals for further legislative reform. These may become part of the law by the end of 1992.

51. Government of Ontario, Ministry of Industry, Trade and Technology, *The State of Small Business 1989: Annual Report on Small Business in Ontario* (Toronto: Government of Ontario, Small Business Branch, 1989), p. xiv. As a percentage of total employment, the firms employing fewer than 20 employees increased from 24 to 37 percent between 1967 and 1982; see Jean-Michel Cousineau and Elmustopha Najem, "L'effet du développement de la petite entreprise sur l'évolution du syndicalisme au Canada," *Relations Industrielles* 45:3 (1990).

52. For detailed examination of this aspect of industrial restructuring, see *Job Turnover in Canada's Manufacturing Sector* (Ottawa: Statistics Canada, 1989); *Structural Change and the Adjustment Process: Perspectives of Firm Growth and Worker Turnover* (Ottawa: Economic Council, 1990).

Chapter 6

1. Robert Lacroix, "Strike Activity in Canada," in W. Craig Riddell, ed., *Canadian Labour Relations*, Vol. 16, Royal Commission on Economic Union and the Development Prospects for Canada (Toronto: University of Toronto Press), p. 189.

2. Craig Riddell, "Canadian Labour Relations: An Overview," in *ibid.*, p. 35. Riddell's figures allow for the fact that many public sector workers are allowed to strike in Canada, whereas this is the exception in the United States.

3. The Canadian Manufacturers' Association has recently proposed that, once again, Ottawa should impose wage controls on Canada's labour movement should labour not "restrain" itself at the bargaining table. *The Globe and Mail*, February 25, 1991, p. B1.

4. Paradoxically, the same nay-sayers may argue that workers are often misled by their leaders who take them out on strike because losses, suffered while on strike, are rarely made up. This last point is hard to reconcile with the claims made by these same people that the possession of the right to strike has made workers too powerful. This controversy has spawned a thriving academic industry of spade-diggers who try to determine whether or not workers win anything by striking. For a discussion of the strike studies, see Robert Lacroix, "Strike Activity in Canada," in Craig Riddell, *op. cit.*

5. For the early period, see Clare Pentland, *Labour and Capital in Canada, 1650–1860* (Toronto: Lorimer, 1981); Paul Craven, *"An Impartial Umpire": Industrial Relations and the Canadian State, 1900–1911* (Toronto: University of Toronto Press, 1970); Daniel Drache, "The Formation and Fragmentation of the Canadian Working Class," SPE 16 (November 1984).

6. H.D. Woods, "Canadian Collective Bargaining and Dispute Settlement Policy: An Appraisal," *Canadian Journal of Economics and Political Science* 21:4 (November 1955).

7. *Ibid.*

8. There is a large body of literature on political unionism in Canada. For a sampling, see Martin Robin, *Radical Politics and Canadian Labour, 1880–1930* (Kingston, Ont.: Industrial Relations Centre, Queen's University, 1968); and Gregory Kealey and Bryan Palmer, *Dreaming of What Might Be: The Knights of Labour in Ontario, 1880–1900* (Cambridge: Cambridge University Press, 1982).

9. Desmond Morton, "Aid to the Civil Power: The Canadian Militia in Support of the Social Order, 1867–1914," in Michiel Horn and Ronald Saborin, eds., *Studies in Canadian Social History* (Toronto: McClelland and Stewart, 1974); and Stuart Jamieson, "Some Reflections on Violence and Law in Industrial Relations," in D.J. Bercuson and L.A. Knafla, eds., *Law and Society in Canada in Historical Perspective* (Calgary: University of Calgary Press, 1979).

10. Larry Peterson, "The One Big Union in International Perspective: Revolutionary Industrial Unionism, 1900–1925," *Labour/Le Travailleur* 7 (Spring 1981); Norman Penner, *Winnipeg 1919: The Strikers' Own History of the Winnipeg General Strike* (Toronto: Lorimer, 1973); and Charles Lipton, *The Trade Union Movement in Canada, 1827–1959*, 3rd ed. (Toronto: NC Press, 1973).

11. S. Jamieson, *op. cit.*; and D. Morton, *op. cit.*

12. S. Jamieson, *Industrial Relations in Canada*, 2nd ed. (Toronto: Macmillan, 1973).

13. Woods, *ibid.*

14. This is referred to as the ally doctrine. It is complicated by legal conceptualizations underlying corporate law. In brief, each corporation is a separate legal entity. No matter how integrated their activities, the law will treat them as discrete persons, unless there is a compelling need to "pierce the corporate veil." For labour-dispute purposes, to find that an "ally" situation exists all that is technically necessary is a determination that there is a measure of integration — but the legal overhang of corporate law which requires respect for the separateness of corporate envelopes often makes such findings more difficult than they ought to be. As usual, technocracy comes to play a dominant role in determining power relations. This disadvantages unions.

15. As seen in Chapter 5, there have been some agreed-upon modifications from time to time, allowing industry-wide bargaining. This does not change the basic structure.

16. *Reference re Public Service Employee Relations Act (Alta.)*, [1987] 1 S.C.R. 313; *Public Service Alliance of Canada (P.S.A.C.)* v. *R. in Right of Canada,*

[1987] 1 S.C.R. 424; *Retail, Wholesale and Department Store Union (R.W.D.S.U.) Locals 544,496, 635 and 955* v. *Government of Saskatchewan*, [1987] 1 S.C.R. 460.

17. Section 2 of the *Charter of Rights and Freedoms* provides that "Everyone has the following fundamental freedoms:...(d) freedom of association."

18. H.J. Glasbeek and M. Mandel, "The Legalization of Politics in Advanced Capitalism: The Canadian Charter of Rights and Freedoms," *Socialist Studies* 2 (1984); see also, M. Mandel, *The Charter of Rights and the Legalization of Politics in Canada* (Toronto: Wall and Thompson, 1989), especially Chapter 5; Judy Fudge, "Labour, The New Constitution and Old-Style Liberalism," in *Labour Law Under the Charter* (Kingston: Queen's Law Journal and Industrial Relations Centre, Queen's University, 1988).

19. *Minutes of Proceedings and Evidence of the Special Committee of the Senate and the House of Commons on the Constitution*, Issue No. 43:69 (Ottawa: Queen's Printer).

20. *Final Report, Canadian Industrial Relations*, The Report of the Task Force on Labour Relations (Ottawa: Privy Council Office, 1968).

21. A.W.Craig, *The System of Industrial Relations in Canada*, 3rd ed. (Toronto: Prentice-Hall, 1989), p. 286.

22. These kinds of defensive claims rely on the treatment of the strike as a dysfunctional phenomenon. This is not a very clever way for liberal proponents of the scheme to characterize the strike, seeing that they argue that the use of the strike is essential to the effective functioning of collective bargaining.

23. Riddell, *op. cit.*, and Lacroix, *op. cit.*

24. This was acknowledged by the Supreme Court of Canada in *Harrison* v. *Carswell* (1975), 62 D.L.R. (3d) 68 and affirmed by it in *R.W.D.S.U., Local 560* v. *Dolphin Delivery*, [1986] 2 S.C.R. 573.

25. See S. Jamieson, *Times of Trouble: Labour Unrest and Industrial Conflict in Canada, 1900–1966*, Study No. 22, Task Force on Labour Relations (Ottawa: Privy Council Office, 1968); also, S. Jamieson, *Industrial Conflict in Canada 1966–75*, Economic Council of Canada, Discussion Paper No. 142, December 1979.

26. It is well established that this is the focus of the media's coverage of strikes. Several studies show that the concentration on confrontation and violence is the meat and potatoes of labour relations coverage; see, for example, Marc Zwelling, *The Strikebreakers*, Report of the Strikebreaking Committee of the Ontario Federation of Labour and the Labour Council of Metropolitan Toronto (Toronto: New Press, 1972).

27. For a pre-*Charter* decision by the Supreme Court of Canada in which a shopping plaza owner's property right was held to outweigh the rights of workers to exercise their right of free speech by picketing, see *Harrison* v. *Carswell*, *loc. cit.* More recently, the property rights of a shopping plaza's owners were subjected to the rights of unions to picket, provided that the property owner's business was not adversely affected. But the decision was not a complete reversal; it hinged on the fact that the targeted employer was a major shareholder in the corporation which owned the shopping plaza; see *T. Eaton Company Ltd., The Cadillac-Fairview Corp. Ltd. and T.E.C. Leasehold Ltd. and R.W.D.S.U.* (1985), 10 C.L.R.B.R. (N.S.)(O.L.R.B.). The picketers' rights clearly remain seriously circumscribed and contingent.

28. See E.E. Palmer, "The Short Unhappy Life of the 'Aristocratic' Doctrine" (1960), 13 *Univ. of Toronto L. J.*, 166. For a contemporary analysis of union-busting and the ensuing violence, see Alain Noel and Keith Gardner, "The

Gainers Strike: Capitalist Offensive, Militancy and the Politics of Industrial Relations in Canada," unpublished paper, March 1988.

29. Employers do not like this kind of protection for workers. The Ontario government is facing a fierce struggle on this issue.

30. The practical difficulty is well illustrated by the fact that learned legal scholars cannot agree on the ambit of permissible secondary boycott activity; compare D. Beatty, "Secondary Boycotts: A Functional Analysis" (1974), 52 *Can. Bar Rev.* 388 with J. Manwaring, "Legitimacy in Labour Relations: The Courts, The B.C. Labour Board and Secondary Picketing" (1982), 20 *Osgoode Hall L.J.* 274.

31. In 1963, Ontario's Court of Appeal was crass enough to say that the right of an individual to trade freely was a right exercised for the benefit of the whole of the community, whereas the right to engage in secondary picketing was only exercised for the benefits of a particular class and, therefore, must give way to the right to trade freely; per Aylesworth, J.A. in *Hershey's of Woodstock* v. *Goldstein* (1963), 38 D.L.R. (2d) 449. The decision was met with a storm of protest by progressive collective bargaining proponents, who called it typical of a backward judiciary. Nonetheless, some of these very critics acknowledged the necessity to curb secondary picketing, given the many competing interests, including free trade for property owners, as well as worker needs; see H.W. Arthurs, "Labour Law — Secondary Picketing — Per Se Illegality — Public Policy" (1963), 41 *Can. Bar Rev.* 580.

32. *Op. cit.*

33. For a discussion of health and safety issues, see H.J. Glasbeek, "A Role for Criminal Sanctions in Occupational Health and Safety," in *New Developments in Employment Law*, 1988 Meredith Memorial Lectures (Cowansville, Que.: Les Editions Yvon Blais, 1988), p. 124.

34. See *Re Pharand and Inco Metals*, [1980] 3 Can. L.R.B.R. 194 (Ont.) and the discussion in Katherine E. Swinton, "Enforcement of Occupational Health and Safety Legislation: The Role of the Internal Responsibility System," in Kenneth P. Swan and Katherine E. Swinton, eds., *Studies in Labour Law* (Toronto: Butterworths, 1983), p. 141, 166.

35. Stephen Nathan, "Direct Action at the McDonnell Douglas: The Right to Refuse Unsafe Work," *Our Times* 7:1 (February 1988): 26. See also discussion in Chapter 7.

36. The trade union was assessed fines of $400,000 for criminal contempt; 62 nurses and many local branches of the union were fined $350 (individuals), up to $1,000 (locals) for civil contempt; over 2,000 nurses were disciplined by their employers for striking illegally and 150 were terminated; see *Our Times* 7:1 (April 1988): 8–9; see also *United Nurses of Alberta* v. *A.G. Alberta* (1992), 92 C.L.L.C. 14.023.

37. In Chapter 3 we saw that very few collective agreements contain restrictions on this employer right. Further, parcelling bargaining-unit work out to non-union labour during the life of a collective agreement is not — as a matter of law — a lock-out, even though its effect on the union may be the same.

38. Paul Weiler, *Reconcilable Differences: New Directions in Canadian Labour Law* (Toronto: Carswell, 1980).

39. T. Gigantes, *"Structural Change and Capital Accumulation, in the Latter Part of the Twentieth Century: An Essay in Economic History,"* unpublished manuscript (Statistics Canada, July 1989).

40. The Conference Board of Canada, *Inflation and Incomes Policy in Canada* (Ottawa, May 1979). This report also indicated that wage levels were 7.7 percent lower than they otherwise would have been. See also Canadian Depart-

ment of Finance, *Discussion Paper on Anti-Inflation Policy Options* (Ottawa, 1981).

41. *Anti-inflation Reference*, [1976] 2 S.C.R. 373. The legal reasoning used by the Court to justify this anti–working class decision was so threadbare that even conventional suppporters of the legal system were seriously perturbed; see P. Hogg, "Proof of Facts in Constitutional Cases" (1976), 26 Univ. of Toronto L. J. 386.

42. Leo Panitch, "Wage and Price Controls," in D. Drache, ed., *Debates and Controversies from This Magazine* (Toronto: McClelland and Stewart, 1979).

43. See *Domglass Ltd.*, [1976] 2 Can. L.R.B.R. (Ont.), upheld *Domglass Ltd.* (1978), 190 R. (2d) 253 (Ont. Div. Ct.); *Robb Engineering and United Steelworkers of America, Local 4122* (1978), 86 D.L.R. (3d) 307 (N.S.). In British Columbia, where the legislative definition of a strike is different, labour boards did not treat political strikes as illegal under the statute; *British Columbia Hydro and Power Authority*, (1976) 2 Can. L.R.B.R. 410. But this has left the unions subject to judicial sanctions, potentially a worse fate.

44. Nick Fillmore, "The Big Oink: How Business Won the Free Trade Battle," *This Magazine* 22:8 (March–April 1989).

45. This was stated very clearly and very early on by Bora Laskin, one of the leading proponents of statutory collective bargaining as a progressive scheme; see *Re Polymer Corporation and Oil, Chemical and Atomic Workers, Local 16-14* (1958), 10 L.A.C. 31,51, aff'd by the Supreme Court of Canada [1962] S.C.R. 338. This has never been questioned, and reflects the approach laid down by Rand, J. in 1946; see Chapter 1.

46. In 1979, time lost as a percentage of total working time was 0.3 percent; by 1985 it was less than 0.1 percent; it "peaked" at 0.2 percent and dropped back to less than 0.1 percent in 1989; see Labour Canada, Bureau of Labour Information, Ottawa, 1990.

47. For a pessimistic but, nonetheless, penetrating view of this potential, see André Gorz, *Farewell to the Working Class* (London: Pluto Press, 1980).

48. There are no precise figures on the number of boards, commissions and government agencies where Canada's unions are present, but the figure probably runs into the hundreds.

49. For a discussion of these and other issues, see Colin Crouch, *Trade Unions: The Logic of Collective Action* (London: Fontana Books, 1982).

50. Richard Hyman, *Marxism and the Sociology of Trade Unionism* (London: Pluto Press, 1971).

51. Eric Hobsbawm, *Worlds of Labour, Further Studies in the History of Labour* (New York: Pantheon Books, 1984), Chapter 17.

52. C.B.Macpherson, *The Rise and Fall of Economic Justice* (Toronto: Oxford U. P., 1985).

53. Daniel Drache and John Lang, "Immigrants and Small Factories: The Lessons of Artistic," *This Magazine* 8:1 (January 1974).

54. Ellen Tolmie, "Fleck: Profile of a Strike," *This Magazine* 12:4 (October 1978); Constance Backhouse, "The Fleck Strike: A Case Study in the Need for First Contract Arbitration" (1980), 18 *Osgoode Hall L.J.* 495.

55. Noel and Gardner, *op. cit.*

56. Jean-Marc Piotte, D. Ethier, and J. Reynolds, *Les travailleurs contre l' état bourgeois* (Montreal: L'Aurore, 1975).

57. P.E. Trudeau, *The Asbestos Strike*, trans. James Boake (Toronto: Lorimer, 1974).

58. Carla Lipsig-Mummé, "The Web of Dependence: Quebec Unions in Politics before 1976," in Alain-G. Gagnon ed., *Quebec: State and Society* (Toronto:

Metheun, 1984); Alain-G. Gagnon and Mary Beth Montcalm, *Quebec: Beyond the Quiet Revolution* (Toronto: Nelson, 1990), especially Chapter 4.

59. See Hubert Guindon, "The Social Evolution of Quebec Reconsidered," *Canadian Journal of Economics and Political Science* 26:4 (1960), and "Social Unrest, Social Class and Quebec's Bureaucratic Revolution," *Queen's Quarterly* 71:2 (1964).

60. Daniel Drache, ed., *Only the Beginning: The Manifestos of the Common Front* (Toronto: New Press, 1972); see the Introduction.

61. Quebec's economic difficulties are discussed by William Coleman, *The Independence Movement in Quebec, 1945–1989* (Toronto: University of Toronto Press, 1984), and Michael D. Behiels, *Prelude to Quebec's Quiet Revolution: Liberalism versus Neo-Nationalism* (Montreal: McGill-Queen's U. P., 1985).

62. Quoted in Daniel Drache, *op. cit.*, p. xxii.

63. Robert Chodos and Nick Auf Der Maur, *Quebec: A Chronicle 1968–1972*, A Last Post Special (Toronto: James Lewis and Samuel, 1972); see also Gagnon and Montcalm, *op. cit.*, Chapter 4.

64. See Chodos and Auf Der Maur, *op. cit.*, p. 114.

65. Cited in *Le Devoir*, November 30, 1982, p. 13.

66. *Op. cit.*

67. Carla Lipsig-Mummé, "Quebec Labour, Politics, and the Economic Crisis of the 1980's: The Roots of Defensive Accommodation," unpublished paper, argues that, in the end, the strike was a form of anarcho-syndicalism. She argues that the unions' disdain for electoral politics caused them not to co-opt the machinery and institutional position of the Parti Québécois. They lost an opportunity to unify the nationalist sentiments with working class aspirations.

68. On a related front, the Barrett government brought in another progressive academic, T.G. Ison, to head the workers' compensation board, which also was responsible for the regulation of occupational health and safety.

69. Paul Weiler, *op. cit.*

70. A useful compendenium on the background, events and strategy of Operation Solidarity is Warren Magnusson, William Carroll, Charles Doyle, Monika Langer, and R.B.J. Walker, *The New Reality: The Politics of Restraint in British Columbia* (Vancouver: New Star, 1984).

71. Paul Phillips, *Regional Disparities*, 2nd ed. (Toronto: Lorimer, 1982).

72. Stan Persky and Lanny Beckman, "Downsizing the Unemployment Problem," in Warren Magnusson, *et al.*, *The New Reality*, pp. 193–96.

73. See Magnusson, *et al.*, *op. cit.*, Appendix A, The "Restraint Package."

74. Bryan Palmer, "A Funny Thing Happened on the Way to Kelowna," *Canadian Dimension* 18:1 (1984); "The Rise and Fall of British Columbia's Solidarity," in Bryan Palmer, ed., *The Character of Class Struggle: Essays in Canadian Working Class History, 1850–1985* (Toronto: McClelland and Stewart, 1986).

75. For the deep-seated differences about the nature of politics and strategies of Operation Solidarity, see the exchange between Cliff Andstein (the secretary-treasurer of the B.C. Federation of Labour) and Bryan Palmer in "Solidarity — An Exchange," *New Direction* 3:3 (Jan.–Feb. 1988).

76. The Confederation of Canadian Unions (CCU), for instance, was excluded from Operation Solidarity. This is not surprising given the bitterness and rivalry between CAIMAW (one of the CCU's major affiliates) and the United Steelworkers of America.

77. William Carroll, "The Solidarity Coalition," in Magnusson, *et al.*, *op. cit.*

78. See the run of decisions in to the fall of 1983: *Douglas College*, BCLRB No. 353/83, *University of British Columbia*, BCLRB No. 358/83, *University of*

Victoria, BCLRB No. 359/83, *School District No. 81 (Fort Nelson)* BCLRB No. 406/83 and the discussion of *Domglass op. cit.*

79. And there are some who argue that, in the aftermath of the split, a restructuring of the alliance between the popular-sector groups and the union movement emerged; see Peter Cameron, "Is there life after the (almost) general strike?" *New Directions* 1:3 (Nov.–Dec. 1985): 8–12.

Chapter 7

1. This is the reasoning which permitted the Task Force to argue that full collective bargaining was a prerequisite to setting the terms and conditions of work, but that third-party adjudication was sufficient to deal with disputes arising out of such established terms and conditions; see the Report of the Task Force on Labour Relations (the Woods Task Force), *Canadian Industrial Relations* (Ottawa: Privy Council Office, 1968), paras. 395-99:

   "[C]ompulsory arbitration of... rights disputes has been substituted for open economic warfare during the term of a collective agreement.... If grievance disputes are by law to be arbitrated, why not interest disputes? In grievance disputes, the issue is the interpretation and application of already established rights. In interest disputes, the rights themselves are at stake. It is one thing to submit two parties to arbitration on the terms of an agreement which they have negotiated and signed; it is another to impose a settlement in the absence of their mutual consent."

   For a modern iteration of this conventional, liberal pluralist view, see P. Weiler, *Reconcilable Differences* (Toronto: Carswell, 1980).

2. *Op. cit.*, para. 291. The Task Force further noted, at para. 299, that union inroads into management prerogatives were relatively limited.

3. D. Feller, "A General Theory of the Collective Bargaining Agreement" (1973), 61 *Yale L.J.* 663, 704.

4. This approach was seen as a progressive one. If workers could be reinstated when an employer breached a contract, the prevailing reciprocity of contract doctrines were thought to require that employees could be forced to work for employers if employees broke their contract, that is, slavery would be built into a free contract scheme. What this noble sentiment ignored was that workers, desperate for a job, were never free as to whether or not they were to work for some employer, even if some very lucky ones might have a number of employers who were willing to buy their labour power.

5. When workers did go to court, they would lose, more often than not. But Engels showed that, should they pursue their case to the appellate levels — and this was very rare — they had a good deal of success; Engels, *The Condition of the Working Class in England* (Panther ed., 1969).

6. *Port Arthur Shipbuilding Co.* v. *Arthurs*, [1969] S.C.R. 85.

7. For an instructive résumé of the fierce lobbying led by well-known arbitrators and leading academics, see *Labour Relations Law* (Kingston: Industrial Relations Centre, Queen's University, 1974), p. 333. For a prototype legislative provision which gives arbitrators this remedial power, see s. 44(9) *Labour Relations Act*, R.S.O. 1980, c.228. The proposition that arbitrators should have this power is now so widely accepted that the Supreme Court of Canada has indicated that, if confronted by the issue again, it will read it into collective agreements even where the legislation is silent on the issue; for this change of

mind by the highest court in the land, see *Heustis* v. *The New Brunswick Electric Power Commission*, [1979] 2 S.C.R. 768.

8. It must be noted here that the common law today is much less inflexible than it used to be. In the late 1970s, the downturn in economic conditions meant that unorganized middle-level managerial personnel were fired in large numbers. They had to go to common law courts for remedies. The judiciary proved itself to be more receptive to them than it had been to menial workers in the past. Sympathy was evinced for managers faced with bullying behaviour by employers, and damage awards were enriched. The legal practice dealing with workforce dismissal now has become respectable and provides a thriving living for a small number of lawyers. How-to manuals have proliferated; see, e.g., David Harris, *Wrongful Dismissal* (Toronto: Richard de Boo, 1978); Brian A. Grossman, *The Executive Firing Line: Wrongful Dismissal and the Law* (Toronto: Carswell/Methuen, 1982). Conferences to brief lawyers in this field are held regularly; see *The Lawyer's Weekly*, July 27, 1990.

9. D. Brown and D. Beatty, *Canadian Labour Arbitration Law* (Toronto: Canada Law Book Co., 1977), paras 7: 3110, 3422, 3120, 3560, 3330, 3426, 3410, 3312, 3580, 3430, 3322–4, 3660, 3140, 3130, 3422–41, 3500. The list is not exhaustive. For a discussion of these employee duties at common law, see Arthurs, Carter, Fudge, and Glasbeek, *Labour Law and Industrial Relations in Canada,* 3rd ed. (Toronto: Kluwer/Butterworths, 1988), paras. 267–81. For a short account as to how and why the common law courts came to impose these duties, see H.J. Glasbeek, "The Contract of Employment at Common Law," in J. Anderson and M. Gunderson, eds., *Union-Management Relations in Canada* (Don Mills, Ont.: Addison-Wesley Publishers, 1982), Chapter 3. For an analysis of the interrelationship of these common law duties and arbitral decision making, see H.J. Glasbeek, "The Utility of Model Building — Collins' Capitalist Discipline and Corporatist Law" (1984), 13 *Industrial Law Journal* 133; and "Voluntarism, Liberalism and Grievance Arbitration: Holy Grail, Romance and Real Life," in G. England, ed., *Essays in Labour Relations* (Don Mills, Ont.: CCH Canadian Limited, 1986).

10. *Ford Motor Co.,* (1944) 3 L.A. 779 (Shulman).

11. As recorded by the Kelly Report, which was the result of an inquiry set up to examine the delays; see *Report of the Industrial Inquiry Commissioner Concerning Grievance Arbitration under the Labour Relations Act 1976–78* (Ministry of Labour). The expedited arbitration which was the outgrowth of this report is to be found in s.45 *Labour Relations Act,* R.S.O. 1980, c.228. It was enacted in 1980. At that time, the assessment of eight-month delays was, if anything, an underestimation. In an unpublished study of 144 grievances which arose at Stelco and which went to an arbitration hearing, the average time which elapsed between the dispute and the decision was 350 days; see Patricia McDermott, "Grievance Arbitration at Local 1005 of the U.S.W. Stelco's Hilton Works, Hamilton, Ontario," (available on request). Our own interviews(1990) indicate that delays remain a significant problem in all jurisdictions. The International Woodworkers Association and the Public Service Alliance of Canada (Employment and Immigration) advised us that an average discharge case takes one-and-a-half years to complete, while the Canadian Automobile Workers indicated that disputes generally took between nine months and a year to settle and that it had noted that there was a tendency for the lag to increase.

12. Ontario's expedited arbitration process mandates that an arbitrator be appointed within three weeks. While there are no hard data available, there is a good deal of anecdotal evidence to the effect that the scheme does not work

that expeditiously. Often one of the parties raises a jurisdictional or other procedural issue on the first hearing day. An adjournment may result. To get a new date that suits all parties may result in the same kind of delay as plagues non-expedited arbitrations. Second, even if a hearing is held promptly, the handing down of the award sometimes takes a long time. Most importantly, reliance on expedited arbitration means that the parties have no control over who will be appointed to arbitrate the expedited matter. Given their belief that most people who want to act as arbitrators are conservative and ignorant of the real world of industrial relations, many unions are wary of the expedited arbitration process and avoid it whenever they can.

13. See John Stanton, *Labour Arbitrations: Boon or Bane for Unions?* (Vancouver: Butterworths, 1983), p. 35. The author studied 2,830 cases, of which 1,434 reported on the time taken. Public sector cases took an average of 9.8 months, private sector ones 7.3 months.

14. See *Workplace Pollution*, Working Paper 53, Law Reform Commission of Canada, 1986. See *R. v. Ontario Gypsum Co. Ltd* (1982)(Unrep'd) C.C.H. Empt. Safety and Health Guide, para. 95,051, where the corporation was fined $1,500 and the main supervisor $500. There are signs of change. Lower courts began to increase fines but appellate courts turned them back. The ensuing outrage led to an upholding of a "tough" fine ($12,000 for a death caused by a violation of a statute) in *R. v. Cotton Felts Ltd.* (1982) 2 C.C.C. (3d) 287 (C.A. Ont.). This has led to an inflation in fines, e.g., $10,000 for a fatality in *R. v. Inco Limited* (No. 2)(Unrep'd), C.C.H. Empt. Safety & Health Guide, para. 95,010. The "heavy" fines are imposed on the corporation, the supervisors being treated leniently, but there is a continuing increase in fines in unadjusted dollar terms. As a proportion of income, however, they remain way below the burdens imposed on disciplined employees.

15. George Adams, *Grievance Arbitration of Discharge Cases* (Kingston: Queen's University Industrial Relations Centre, Research and Current Issues Series No. 38, 1978), pp. 42–43 and studies cited; see also Stanton, *op. cit.* There are claims that unions win about 50 percent of all arbitrations: see the survey complied from the Ontario Ministry of Labour, Office of Arbitration Monthly Bulletin by the Ontario Federation of Labour, assisted by the United Steelworkers of America (District 6), 1988. But these studies refer to all arbitrations fought. Many of the disputes giving rise to arbitration are ones relating to procedural points — for example, the right of an arbitrator to assume jurisdiction over a particular issue. That unions may win a disproportionate number of less important cases, cases which often have little to do with challenges to employer control, does not make the grievance arbitration régime more attractive from a worker's point of view.

16. See Michel Foucault, *Discipline and Punish: The Birth of the Prison*, trans. A. Sheridan (New York: Pantheon, 1977). Of course, Foucault did not identify criminal law as the sole coercive instrument. He described the development of a carceral archipelago through a widening network of state and semi-private agencies, as well as through the influence of ecclesiastical rules and the nuclear family ethos.

17. See S. Kadish, "The Criminal Law and Industrial Discipline as Sanctioning Systems: Some Comparative Observations" and the comments on this paper by Ross, both found in "Proceedings of the 17th Annual Meeting, National Academy of Arbitrators, 1964" *Labour Arbitration — Perspectives and Problems* (Washington: The Bureau of National Affairs, 1964).

18. George Adams, *op. cit.*, pp. 27–28.

19. *Ibid.* (emphasis added).

20. Note here that the grievance arbitration mechanism in respect of discharge is seen as a relatively toothless tiger by many employers. Anti-union employers frequently offer it to their employees in respect of discharge to dissuade them from unionizing; see "The antiunion grievance ploy," *Business Week*, February 12, 1979, p. 117. They feel safe in doing so because non-unionized employees frequently have no way to ensure that ensuing arbitral decisions will be enforced. Even with this caveat, it is implicit in these tactical manoeuvres that one of the greatest attractions that unions offer potential members is the grievance process. The federal government, Quebec and Nova Scotia have instituted grievance arbitration for non-unionized employees in respect of dismissals. It is seen as the kind of reform which a modern society ought to implement to alleviate undue hardship and which can be afforded without affecting the productive processes seriously; see G. England, "Recent Developments in Wrongful Dismissal Laws and Some Pointers for Reform" (1978), 16 *Alberta L. Rev.* 471; K. Swinton, "Contract Law and the Employment Relationship: The Proper Forum for Reform," in B. Reiter and K. Swan, eds., *Studies in Contract Law* (Toronto: Butterworths, 1983), p. 357.

21. *Air Care Ltd* v. *United Steelworkers of America* (1974), 49 D.L.R. (3d) 467 (S.C.C.).

22. *Re Russelsteel Ltd and United Steelworkers* (1966), 17 L.A.C. 253 (Arthurs).

23. *Op. cit.* text at n. 3. This point is reinforced by taking note of some common employer strategies. For years now, many large enterprises that are not unionized have set up seniority systems for bureaucratic, organizational reasons. See P. Selznick, *Law, Society and Industrial Justice* (New York: Basic Books, 1969), who noted that, in two separate studies, 80 and 85 percent respectively of non-unionized firms used seniority lists to deal with promotions, lay-offs and rehirings. Of course, this does not give workers the same kinds of rights as do seniority ladders in a unionized setting. After all, there is no compulsory binding arbitration system to enforce them.

24. Difficulties also arise when unions bargain for seniority. For instance, long-time employees may prefer plant-wide seniority clauses, whereas others may have an interest in small, departmental or craft-based seniority ladders. While these issues may be settled democratically, because members can participate in drafting the demands, the problems and the tensions they may create are manifest.

25. D. Drache, "The Way Forward for Ontario," in D. Drache, ed., *Getting on Track: Social Democratic Strategies in a Global Economy* (Montreal: McGill-Queen's U.P., 1991).

26. These figures come from discussions with union-based labour lawyers in Ontario. In 1990, arbitrators charged somewhere between $1,000 and $2,000 per hearing. If the union hires a lawyer, this will cost it around $1,000 per case. Then, there are the hotels, meals, travel expenses, the fees or absorbed costs of providing employee representatives and, in many cases, wage replacements. In addition, there are the costs of administration and preparation. Stanton, *op. cit.*, estimated that, in British Columbia, in 1983, the cost to the union of a discharge which went to arbitration was $3,500 (pp. 37–38).

27. None of the other respondents listed in the preceding text were able to tell us how many grievances they dealt with each year.

28. *Re Bradley and Ottawa Professional Firefighters Association*, [1967] 2 O.R. 311 (C.A.). See also *Re Hoogendoorn and Greening Metal Products and Screening Equipment Co.* (1968), 65 D.L.R. (2d) 641 (S.C.C.). The need to give a hearing to people likely to be affected by a decision has complicated the process a good deal. Arbitrators have reacted by developing a series of

practices which relieve the procedural difficulties, but the means devised have meant that the requirement to give third parties standing is often only given token respect; see S. Taçon, "The Effect of Judicial Review Grievance Arbitration" (1976), 14 *Osgoode Hall L.J.* 661, 680–702.

29. For a discussion of these provisions, see Arthurs, Carter, Fudge, and Glasbeek, *op. cit.*, paras. 358–69.

30. The quotations are from the Ontario Labour Relations Board's benchmark decision in *Ford Motor Company of Canada, Ltd.*, [1973] O.L.R.B. Rep. 510, paras. 42,43. The legislation and the administrative agencies' interpretation of it concretize what was always one of the main objectives of the post-war *Wagner Act* model: making trade unions "responsible." See the early writings of theorists and policy-makers such as A. Cox, "Rights under a Collective Agreement" (1956), 69 *Harvard L. Rev.* 601; see also the approach taken by Rand, J., set out in Chapter 2.

31. The date is chosen rather arbitrarily but we think somewhat generously. It was in the early 1970s that collective bargaining was extended to the public sector and that grievance abitrators' and labour relation boards' remedial powers were perfected.

Chapter 8

1. Chan F. Aw, *A Dual Labour Market Analysis: A Study of Canadian Manufacturing Industries*, Labour Canada, Economic Analysis Branch (Ottawa: Minister of Supply and Services, 1981).

2. They include industries such as "trade, transportation, communication, utilities, insurance, real estate, business, community and personal service" in which "total employment grew by 61 percent between 1960 and 1985." See Colin Lindsay and Craig McKee, "Annual Review of Labour Force Trends," *Social Trends* (Autumn 1986): 2–7. By 1985, the service industries' share of jobs was 66 percent of available employment; by 1987, it had risen to 70.8 percent; see David Gower, "Annual Update on Labour Force Trends," *Canadian Social Trends* (Summer 1988): 17–20. Generally, see *Quarterly Labour Market and Productivity Review* (Winter 1988), Table II-2.

3. Shirley Neill, "Unionization in Canada," *Canadian Social Trends* (Spring 1988): 12–15.

4. Mary Anne Burke, "The Growth of Part-Time Work," *Canadian Social Trends* (Autumn 1986): 9–14.

5. G. Esping-Andersen, "Labour Movements and the Welfare State: Alternatives in the 1990s," in D. Drache, ed., *Getting on Track: Social Democratic Strategies for a Global Economy* (Montreal: McGill-Queen's U.P., 1991).

6. An Ontario task force has made some positive recommendations to overcome this problem. The extent of its implementation is uncertain at this time, but a program called STEP has commenced to address the issue; see Ontario Ministry of Community and Social Services, Social Assistance Review Committee, *Transitions* (Toronto, 1988).

7. *Work and Income in the 1990s*, Working Paper No. 8, Phase 1: Income Security Reform, Canadian Council of Social Development (Ottawa, 1987; see also Sharpe, Voyer, and Cameron, "Unemployment: Its Nature, Costs and Causes," in D. Cameron and A. Sharpe, eds., *Policies of Full Employment* (CCSD, 1988), p. 4.

8. "Towards a New Deal for Part-time Workers," brief presented to the Federal Commission of Inquiry into Part-Time Work by the Canadian Union of Public Employees, Oct. 1, 1982. (Figures updated to 1984.)

9. M. Gunderson, L. Muszynski, and J. Keck, *Women and Labour Market Poverty* (Ottawa: CACSW, 1990), p. 158.
10. Interview with Brian Evans, policy advisor, Ministry of Labour, Ontario, August 17, 1988. Mr. Evans explained that there were no firm data available anywhere in Canada.
11. E.B. Akeyanpong, "Working for a minimum wage," *Perspectives on Labour and Income* 1:3 (1989). This figure did not include homeworkers.
12. Gunderson, Muszynski, and Keck, *op. cit.*, note that in 1985, minimum wage incomes fell to about 84 percent of the poverty line for single persons without dependents and to 65 percent of the poverty line for single persons with one child. The latter are mostly women.
13. See *Women, Poverty and Public Policy*, Women for Economic Survival and the Community Council of Greater Victoria, November 1985. See generally S. Baxter, *No Way To Live: Poor Women Speak Out* (New Star Books: Vancouver, 1988).
14. Statistics Canada defines "low income" as the income of an individual or family in which 58.5 percent of the income goes for food, clothing or shelter. The average is 38.5 percent. The National Council for Welfare understandably uses "poor and "low-income family" as synonyms.
15. National Council of Welfare, *Poverty Profile 1988*, A Report by the National Council on Welfare (Ottawa: Minister of Supply and Services, 1988), p. 55.
16. Diane Bellemare and Lise Poulin Simon, "Full Employment: A Strategy and an Objective For Economic Policy," in Duncan Cameron and Andrew Sharpe, eds., *Policies for Full Employment* (Ottawa: Canadian Council on Social Development, 1989).
17. Leon Muszynski, *Social InfoPact* 1:5 (December 1982), Social Planning Council of Metropolitan Toronto. The figures used were based on 1981 data. The unemployment benefits scheme has not altered substantially in real terms since then.
18. For a detailed examination of the changes in government labour market policy, see Leon Muszynski, "The Politics of Labour Market Policy," in G. Bruce Doern, ed., *The Politics of Economic Policy* (Toronto: University of Toronto Press, 1986).
19. See R.A. Hasson, "Social Security Abuse," *Canadian Taxation* 3 (1981): 121.
20. *Ibid.*
21. *Final Report*, The Royal Commission on the Economic Union and Development Prospects for Canada (Toronto: University of Toronto Press, 1986); see also Hasson, *op. cit.*, who cites a number of studies in England and Canada which produced similar conclusions.
22. R.A. Hasson, "Tax Evasion and Social Security Abuse: Some Tentative Observations," *Canadian Taxation* (1980): 98.
23. Economic Council of Canada, *People and Jobs A Study of the Canadian Labour Market* (Ottawa: Information Canada, 1976).
24. *The Globe and Mail*, July 4, 1988, p. A1.
25. For a review of the Macdonald Commission Report, see "The 'Right' Stuff: A Critique of the Macdonald Commission Report," Michael Henderson, ed., *Atkinson Review of Canadian Studies* 3:1 (Spring 1986). For an analysis of the largely ignored popular sector submissions to the Commission, see Daniel Drache and Duncan Cameron, eds., *The Other Macdonald Report* (Toronto: Lorimer, 1985).
26. Business Council on National Issues, *National Priorities*, A Submission to the Royal Commission on the Economic Union and Development Prospects for Canada, December 12, 1983.

27. *Report of the Commission of Inquiry on Unemployment Insurance* (Claude Forget, chairman) (Ottawa: Minister of Supply and Services, November 1986). For a short discussion of the notoriety of this commission's work, see Drache and Glasbeek, "The New Fordism: Capital's Offensive, Labour's Opportunity" (1989), 27 *Osgoode Hall L.J.* 517. The furor helped create an atmosphere in which the unemployed were easily characterized as unworthy people, as malingerers.

28. The period could be shorter in some specified high-unemployment regions.

29. See the report of the minister's announcement of the new policy, *Success in the Works, A Policy Paper: A Labour Force Development Strategy* (Ottawa: Minister of Employment and Immigration, April 11, 1989); *The Toronto Star*, April 12, 1989.

30. David Wolfe and Armine Yalnizyan, "Training the Jobless," *The Globe and Mail*, May 18, 1989, p. A7; for a full exposition of these writers' views, see *Target on Training: Meeting Workers' Needs in a Changing Economy* (Toronto: Social Planning Council of Metropolitan Toronto, 1989).

31. See Reuben Hasson, "Discipline and Punishment in the Law of Unemployment Insurance — A Critical View of Disqualifications and Disentitlement" (1987), 25 *Osgoode Hall L.J.* 615.

32. The interrelation of patriarchy and class are a well-known subject of theoretical debate. For a useful synthesis, see Joy Parr, *The Gender of Breadwinners: Women, Men and Change in Two Industrial Towns, 1889–1950* (Toronto: University of Toronto Press, 1990), Introduction. For our purpose, it suffices to note that even conventional wisdom accepts the fact that the undervaluation of work is systemic. As Muszynski and Gunderson note: "most researchers now agree that a substantial part of the wage gap between men and women is due to discrimination. Women are paid substantially less than men, even when hours of employment, education, and experience are taken into account." *Women, Poverty and the Labour Market A Study of the Working Poor in Canada*, Canadian Advisory Council on the Status of Women, Ottawa, February 1989.

33. Equal Pay Coalition, Bringing Pay Equity to Those Presently Excluded from Ontario's *Pay Equity Act* (Toronto, December 13, 1988).

34. *Equality and Employment*, p. 233.

35. Mary Cornish, "Equal Pay: Collective Bargaining and the Law, Minister of Labour, Government of Canada, 1986, p.4.

36. Judy Fudge, "Labour Law's Little Sister: Employment Standards Legislation" (Ottawa: Centre for Policy Alternatives, 1991).

37. This discriminatory effect is aggravated by the fact that some very well paid occupations — such as those of university teachers, engineers, architects, and the like — are, in effect, male ghettoes.

38. Seldom unionized and unable to obtain relevant statistical data, women could not complain effectively. For instance, between 1972 and 1979, women in Ontario recovered $1,200,000 as a result of successful pay discrimination claims. This averaged out to the equivalent of $0.79 for each woman worker in Ontario. Given the acknowledged fact of a 35 percent wage differential (of which at least 15 to 20 percent is due to unacceptable discrimination in the market), the scale of the failure of the complaint system is self-evident.

39. Patricia C. McDermott, "Pay Equity in Ontario: A Critical Legal Analysis" (1990), *Osgoode Hall L. Rev.* 381; Pat and Hugh Armstrong, "Lessons from Pay Equity," SPE 32 (Summer 1990): 29.

40. *Report to the Minister Of Labour by the Ontario Pay Equity Commission*, February 1989.

41. See Judy Fudge and Patricia McDermott, *Just Wages: A Feminist Assessment of Pay Equity* (Toronto: University of Toronto Press, 1991).
42. Its suggested additions to the 1988 law are contained in a legislative proposal, Bill 168, An Act to amend the Pay Equity Act, which may become law in late 1992.
43. Doubling the minimum wage is one of the principal demands of the Equal Pay Coalition, which calls for an "integrated, broad-front approach" to end wage inequality for women. See its brief, *Bringing Pay Equity to Those Presently Excluded from Ontario's Pay Equity Act* (Toronto, December 13, 1988). Union and women's groups are aware of the shortcomings of these existing pay equity and equal pay for work of equal value schemes. They have been proposing a variety of alternatives. Many of the proposals, however, still involve job evaluation as a central element. For a listing of the more important proposals, see Debra J. Lewis, *Just Give Us the Money: A Discussion of Wage Discrimination and Pay Equity* (Vancouver: Women's Research Centre, 1988), pp. 113–28.
44. There are multi-employer-sponsored pension plans, but they are relatively rare.
45. For the findings of the Economic Council of Canada, *People and Jobs: A Study of the Canadian Labour Market* (Ottawa: Queen's Printer, 1976) see Chapter 2. In 1976, the Régie des rentes du Québec found that, of the employees involved in employer-sponsored pension plans, a mere 3.1 percent satisfied the existing vesting requirements at any one time. While this does not mean that none of these employees would ever work long enough to get pension benefits, these figures show that the majority of people would not get a full return on their lifetime contributions. *Les Régimes de Retraite en Québec*, no. 3 (Quebec, 1976) pp. XXIX–XXXVII.
46. *Summary Report of the Commission of Inquiry on Unemployment Insurance* (Ottawa: Minister of Supply and Services, November 1986), p. 10.
47. Employer-sponsored plans are retirement régimes. This is so because employers can deduct the contributions they make to a plan only if it is a retirement plan. This means that, once a worker has earned a right to a pension, she cannot collect the money until she has reached the retirement age specified in the plan. Workers will have money sitting there which is theirs but they cannot touch. This works particular hardship when the business is shut down before a worker reaches retirement age.
48. National Council of Welfare, *The Hidden Welfare System* (National Council of Welfare, 1976) (Neil Brooks).
49. Benefits are defined at the time of the pension plan or they are agreed to be a share of the yield available as a result of the investment.
50. Ann Finlayson, *Whose Money Is It Anyway? The Showdowon on Pensions* (Markham, Ont.: Viking, 1988).
51. *Ibid.*, p. 120.
52. Government of Ontario, *Report of the Task Force on Inflation Protection for Employment Pension Plans* (Toronto: The Task Force Report, 1988). (Chairman: Martin Friedland).
53. Friedland recommended that pensions be indexed at one percentage point less than 75 percent of the consumer price index. For instance, if the CPI rose by 10 percent, private pension entitlements would be increased by 6.5 percent. Even this partial indexation was not meant to be applied to its fullest extent to people who have retired already or to people who are to retire in the next twenty years.

54. CLC's Submission to the Royal Commission on the Status of Pensions in Ontario, cited in Glasbeek, "A Proposal For a Non-Earnings Related Retirement Income Scheme," *Canadian Taxation* 2:4 (Winter 1980): 190.
55. Hubert Frenken, "Retirement Income Programs in Canada," *Canadian Social Trends* (Winter 1986): 23.
56. For the argument as to why they are deferred wages, see the elaboration in Glasbeek, *op. cit.*
57. Indeed, some employers claim entitlement to these occasional surpluses on the basis that they have to make up any shortfalls, should they occur, and that therefore they are entitled to surpluses when they occur. That is, employers treat these surpluses as their money. Their legal right to do so is contentious; see *Re Reevie and Montreal Trust Co., of Canada* (1986), S.O.R.(2d) 595, aff'd.(1986),56O.R.(2d)192 (S.C.C.): Re *Collins and Pension Commission of Ontario* (1986),56O.O.R.(2d)274 (Ont.Div.Ct.). Ontario's NDP government has promised to prohibit employers from expropriating the surplus funds in these ways. This, and some better indexation of benefits, are probably pension-law reforms this government will introduce. There is no indication as yet that it will do something more radical by, say, giving workers control over private pension funds, a much-needed step.
58. Hubert Frenken, *op. cit.*
59. In part, the possibility for doing so has been exploited by the Quebec Federation of Labour in a very limited manner. The QPP was originally used to advance the economic interest of Quebec. The potential is enormous.
60. See Rohan and Brody, "Frequency and Costs of Work Accidents in North America, 1971–80," *Labour & Society*, 9:2 (April–June, 1985).
61. There are two kinds of standards. The first deals with the physical nature of the workplace, such as the requirement to put devices on machines. They are the result of a century of interventions necessitated by body counts arising out of the repetition of identical accidents. The second kind relates to the substances and materials used in production. Action on this is of more recent vintage. The process is initiated when governments are made aware that there is a link between exposure and an alarming incidence of disease. Much of the supposedly neutral scientific information comes from experts employed by industry. These scientists serve vested interests and their research is biased, even if it is not consciously so. The need to submit regulations to industry and unions guarantees slowness in the setting of standards. In the first ten years of the modern Ontario occupational health and safety omnibus scheme (*Occupational Health and Safety Act*, R.S.O. R90, c. O.1), only eleven standards were set by a government that acknowledged that, at the bare minimum, there were 2,500 toxic substances in use, with hundreds being added every year. The government was forced into accepting, without research of its own, 600 standards set by the American Conference on Industrial Hygienists, an industry-based organization. See Glasbeek, "A Role for Criminal Sanctions in Occupational Health and Safety," in *New Develpments in Employment Law*, 1988, Meredith Memorial Lectures (Cowansville, Que.: Les Editions Yvon Blais, 1989), p. 125.
62. C. Tuohy, "Decision Trees and Political Thickets: An Approach to Analyzing Regulatory Decision-Making in the Occupational Health Arena," Law and Economics Workshop, Faculty of Law, University of Toronto, 1984.
63. In Ontario in 1987, there were 295 inspectors to look after more than 3.5 million workers dispersed over 178,194 establishments. See Ministry of Labour, *Annual Report 1986–87*.
64. Glasbeek, *op. cit.*, p. 26.

65. For an excellent discussion of the lack of power of joint health and safety committees, see Eric Tucker, "The Persistence of Market Regulation of Occupational Health and Safety: The Stillbirth of Voluntarism," in G. England, ed., *Essays in Labour Law* (Don Mills, Ont.: CCH, 1986). He shows that not only are these committees relatively ineffective but that they are most useful where there are strong unions. In short, they are the least help where they are the most needed.

66. *Report on the Administration of the Occupational Health and Safety Act*, Ministry of Labour, Ontario, January 1987 (McKenzie-Laskin).

67. *op. cit.*

68. See Chapter 6 for the discussion of the health and safety uprising at Macdonnell Douglas, which had been preceded by similar difficulties at de Havilland. This had forced the government to propose a new "refuse to work" law which was slightly stronger than the eventual provisions in Bill 208. At the same time, the union leadership, wanting to gain control over local leaders, bought into a bipartite model. Opposition to this amongst rank and file occupational health and safety activists was beaten back by arguments that the new right to refuse work and bipartite control over worker education were giant steps forward. Once labour leaders had won the internal fight to go for bipartism, they felt that they had to get it at almost any price, and subsequently made concessions to government and employers on the issue of direct worker empowerment; see Nick di Carlo, "The Right to Refuse — Bill 208," *Our Times* (May 1989): 9–11.

69. National Council of Welfare, *Social Spending and the New Budget* (Ottawa, 1989).

70. *Ibid.*, Table 3.

71. Canada had one of the poorest records on social spending amongst advanced industrial nations. Canada ranked thirteenth out of eighteen in social spending as a percentage of GDP.

Chapter 9

1. Richard Bird, *The Growth of Public Employment in Canada*, IRPP (Toronto: Butterworths, 1979), p. 50.

2. It is difficult to determine the exact number of public sector workers. Experts disagree on definitions and, therefore, who should be included. However, *Taxation Statistics* 1988, Revenue Canada (1986 taxation year) gives the following figures for public sector employment: institutions, 984,030; teachers and professors, 243,670; federal government employees, 312,180; provincial government employees, 389,530; municipal government employees, 628,310 (Table 3, pp. 130–31). This estimate does not include sectors of the economy which depend directly on government contracts and services. Using this measure, it appears that close to a third of the labour force is directly and indirectly dependent on the state for its employment.

3. Jean Kirk Laux and Maureen Appel Molot, *State Capitalism and Public Enterprise in Canada* (Ithaca: Cornell University Press, 1988), p. 63.

4. *Royal Commission on the Economic Union and Development Prospects for Canada*, Vol. II, p. 36.

5. *The Financial Post*, August 20, 1988, p. 7.

6. Kenneth McRoberts, *Quebec: Social Change and Political Crisis*, 3rd ed. (Toronto: McClelland and Stewart, 1988).

7. See H.W. Arthurs, *Collective Bargaining by Public Employees in Canada: Five Models* (Ann Arbor, Institute of Labor and Industrial Relations, 1971); *The Re-*

port of the Task Force on Labour Relations (Ottawa: Privy Council, 1968); J. Finkelman and S. Goldenberg, *Collective Bargaining in the Public Service; The Federal Experience in Canada* (Institute for Research in Public Policy, 1983). Finkelman and Goldenberg note that in Saskatchewan in 1944, "a socialist government" had included government employees in the coverage of the *Trade Union Act*. No other jurisdiction did the same until the Lesage government did so in Quebec in 1965. Then followed the federal government in 1967, New Brunswick in 1968, British Columbia in 1973. By 1975, all governments had given some bargaining rights to their employees.

8. N. Meltz, "Labour Movements in Canada and the U.S.: Are They Really That Different," Centre for Industrial Relations, University of Toronto, July 1983. See Table I.

9. Governments have the legislative authority to determined whether workers are to be regulated by special collective bargaining legislation. For instance, nurses in Manitoba have been given the full right to strike, whereas nurses in Ontario have not been given any right to strike at all.

10. For an overall view, see J. Sack and T. Lee, "The Role of the State in Canadian Labour Relations" *Relations Industrielles* 44:1 (1989): 195.

11. *Crown Employees Collective Bargaining Act* R.S.O. 1980, c.108; *The Hospital Labour Disputes Arbitration Act*, R.S.O. 1980, c.205; *The Fire Department Act*, R.S.O. 1980, c.164; *The Police Act*, R.S.O. 198 , c.381. Firefighters and police workers are precluded from striking everywhere. For the Alberta prohibitions on the right to strike, see s.4, *Labour Relations Code* S.A. 1988, c.L-12.

12. S. 7, 57, 87(3), *Public Service Staff Relations Act*, R.S.C. 1985, c. P-35, as amended.

13. H. Glasbeek and M. Mandel, "The Crime and Punishment of Jean-Claude Parrot," *Canadian Forum* (August 1979).

14. *Ibid.*

15. An Act to Amend the Public Service (Collective Bargaining) Act, 1973, amended to June 28, 1985.

16. *Canadian Air Traffic Control Association* v. *The Queen*, [1982], S.C.R. 696.

17. Leo Panitch and Donald Schwartz, *The Assault on Trade Union Freedoms* (Toronto: Garamond Press, 1988).

18. *Ibid.*, p. 31.

19. *Ibid.*, Appendix.

20. David Wilton, "Public Sector Wage Compensation," in Craig W. Riddell, *op. cit.*, Vol. 16, p. 264. He clarifies the dynamics of the relationship between private and public wage settlements; see pp. 262–75, where he reviews the findings of economists who have studied the structure of wage settlements.

21. *Public Service Alliance of Canada* v. *R.* [1987], S.C.R. 424.

22. See factum of the Respondents (federal government) in *Public Service Alliance* v. *R. op. cit.*

23. This may explain, partly, why the Ontario government's mild proposals for labour law reform have attracted so much co-ordinated opposition. They are bucking a trend.

24. *An Act Respecting Remuneration in the Public Sector* 1982, c.35.

25. The federal Progressive Conservative government has worsened the situation as it is bent upon reducing transfers to the provinces. It has been calculated that at the present rate of diminished contributions, by the year 2009–10, "not one cent of federal cash for health or education would go to any province or territory." See National Council of Welfare, *Funding Health and Higher Edu-*

cation: Danger Looming (Ottawa: Minister of Supply and Services, Spring 1991), p. 21.
26. *B.C.G.E.U.* v. *British Columbia (Industrial Relations Council)* [1988] B.C.J. No. 2009 (B.C.C.A.).
27. *The Globe and Mail*, Sept. 1, 1988, p. B8.
28. Grattan Gray, "Social Policy by Stealth," *Policy Options* (March 1990): 20.
29. *The Globe and Mail*, Oct. 23, 1990; and Chapter 8.

Chapter 10

1. James P. Womack, Daniel T. Jones, and Daniel Roos, *The Machine That Changed the World* (New York: Rawson, 1990).
2. Raphael Kaplinsky, *Automation, Technology and Society* (London: Longman, 1984).
3. Charles Sabel, *Work and Politics* (Cambridge: Cambridge U.P.), p. 194.
4. Robert Boyer, "Labour Flexibility: Many Forms, Uncertain Effects," *Labour and Society* 12:1 (1987).
5. Raphael Kaplinsky, *op. cit.*
6. *Harvard Business Review* (March–April 1990): 22.
7. Ministry of Industry Trade and Technology (MITT), *A Comparison of Canadian and U.S. Technology Adoption Rates* (Toronto: Technology Policy Branch, November 1989).
8. CAW Technology Project, *Changing Technology and Work: Northern Telecom* (Toronto, October 1989).
9. MITT, *op. cit.*, p. 9.
10. CMA, *The Aggressive Economy: Daring to Compete*, June 1989, p. 3-2.
11. D. Demelto, K. McMullen, and R. Willis, "Preliminary Report: Innovation and Technological Change in Five Canadian Industries," Economic Council of Canada, Discussion Paper 176 (Ottawa), p. 18.
12. CAW study, *op. cit.*, p. 8. What seems clear is that it is unlikely that the introduction of new technology leads to employment growth. Between 1981 and 1986, employment in U.S. manufacturing declined by 10 percent. Michael L. Dertouzos, Richard K. Lester, and Robert M. Solow, *Made in America: Regaining the Productive Edge* (Boston: MIT Press, 1989) noted that this decline in jobs accounted for about 36 percent of the recorded growth in labour productivity; p. 31.
13. M. Gertler, "Investing in the Future: Canada's High Tech Crisis," in D. Drache and M. Gertler, eds., *The New Era of Global Competition* (Montreal: McGill–Queen's U.P., 1991).
14. For a review of these and other reports, see A. Blais, "The Debate on Canadian Industrial Policy," in A. Blais, ed., *Industrial Policy*, Vol. 44 of Background Studies for the Macdonald Royal Commission (Toronto: University of Toronto Press, 1986).
15. CMA, *op. cit.*, p. 3-3.
16. Evans Research Corporation, "The Canadian CAD/CAM Market," ERC paper no. 65 (Toronto, 1985), cited in Economic Council of Canada, *Innovation and Jobs in Canada* (Ottawa: Minister of Supply and Services, 1987), p. 78
17. H. Munro and H. Noori, "Reflecting Corporate Strategy in the Decision to Automate: The Case of Canadian Manufacturing Companies," *Business Quarterly* (March 1986): 115–20, as summarized in D.G. McFetridge, *op. cit.*, p. 10. This article also summarizes an earlier study, covering the period 1980–85, in which similar findings were made. See the Economic Council of Canada study conducted by G. Betcherman and K. McMullen, *Working with*

Technology: A Survey of the Automation Process in Canada (Ottawa: Economic Council of Canada, 1986).
18. Ernst and Young, *Canada's High Technology Industries in the 1990s* (Toronto: 1990), p. 11.
19. CAW brief, *op. cit.*, p. 37.
20. Paul S. Adler: "Managing Flexible Automation," *California Management Review*, 30:3 (Spring 1988): 44–45.
21. *Ibid.*
22. Economic Council of Canada, *Making Technology Work* (Ottawa: Minister of Supply and Services, 1987), pp. 15–16.
23. Other researchers, too, have found that labour is not an obstacle to the introduction of new technologies; see Jackie Mansell, *Workplace Innovation in Canada: Reflections on the Past ... Prospects for the Future,* Economic Council of Canada (Ottawa: Minister of Supply and Services, 1987).
24. It was seen above that the sophisticated use of technology has meant that lower-level managers are often included in new work teams.
25. Economic Council of Canada, *op. cit.*, p. 19.
26. *Ibid.*, p. 20.
27. There are exceptions. One we found was at Budd Manufacturing, a large multi-national car parts firm. An employee involvement (EI) program was set up with the endorsement of the union; a steering committee, with equal management and union representation, with two full-time facilitators was established to oversee those groups of workers who were to be engaged in special production organizations. As a result of this joint effort, a collective agreement was reached which provides that no job losses are to result directly from the employment-involvement practices. But this gave no protection to lay-offs attributable to other factors. Since we discovered this progressive-looking EI scheme at Budd, there have been extensive lay-offs at this enterprise.
28. CAW Technology Project, *op. cit.*, p. 41.
29. In its recent study, the Economic Council of Canada has lamented labour's failure to make a dent in employers' prerogative by bargaining for better provisions relating to technological change. It implicitly rebuked labour relations boards and arbitrators for failing to be more innovative with respect to the existing collective agreement clauses and statutory provisions. It found that they were employer-oriented in their interpretations. *Op. cit.*, p. 23.
30. For a pre–free trade assessment of likely job losses, see Jack Baranson, *An Assessment of the Behaviour of U.S. Industrial Subsidiaries in Canada* (Government of Ontario, Ministry of Industry, Trade and Technology, 1985). These fears have proved to be all too well founded; see *The Financial Post*, Special Issue: "Free Trade, One Year Later," Jan. 2, 1990.
31. John Holmes, "The Organization and Locational Structure of Production Subcontracting," in Allen Scott and Michael Storper, eds., *Production, Work Territory* (Boston: Allan Unwin, 1986).
32. Economic Council of Canada, *op. cit.*, p. 18, Fig. 16.
33. Jackie Mansell, *Workplace Innovation in Canada*, quoting Gerald Docquier, p. 27.
34. *Ibid.*
35. CAW Statement on The Reorganization of Work (Toronto, November 1989).
36. Kumar's survey of QWL shows that unions believe that "for QWL and Quality Circles to be meaningful and successful, the management should take concrete steps towards (a) greater information sharing with the union on organizational plans and operations; ... (c) limitation on management rights; ... (e) formal union involvement in participatory forums." See his article, "Re-

cent Labour-Management Relations Approaches in Canada: Will They Endure?" Queen's Papers in Industrial Relations 1987–9 (Kingston: Industrial Relations Centre, Queen's University, 1987).

37. OECD, *Information Technology and Economic Prospects* (Paris: OECD, 1987).
38. The Ontario Task Force on Employment and New Technology, *Final Report* (Toronto, 1985).
39. See the Ontario Task Force on Employment and New Technology, *Employment and New Technology in the Chartered Bank and Trust Industry*, Appendix 13 (Toronto: Government of Ontario, 1985). Indeed, the use of new technologies to streamline office work everywhere, including the relatively backward industrial sectors, is a fact of life; see Ministry of Skills Development, *Adjusting to Change: An Overview of Labour Market Issues in Ontario*, Labour Market Research Group, June 1988, Table 16, p. 44. The study shows that much of the office automation is not very sophisticated. Only 8.9 percent of the establishments had set up office networks, while, for 34 percent, new technology meant the use of word-processing machines.
40. *Employment and New Technology in the Telecommunications Industry*, Appendix 16.
41. *Ibid.*, Appendix 13, p. 24.
42. *Ibid.*, Appendix 14, p. 21.
43. *Ibid.*, Appendix 17, p. 14.
44. Ontario Task Force on Employment and New Technology, *Final Report*, pp. 60, 69, and 72.
45. Marcy Cohen, "The Feminization of the Labour Market: Prospects for the 1990s," in Daniel Drache, ed., *Getting on Track; Social Democratic Strategies for Ontario* (Montreal: McGill–Queen's U.P., 1991), p. 106; see Table 7.1. She sums up as follows:

> In general, these studies have identified three trends in the reorganization of office employment with computerization: an integration of managerial/professional jobs with senior-level clerical functions; the elimination of many traditional clerical occupations; and the expansion of more routinized computer-related clerical jobs, such as data entry operators. The consequence of these changes has been to create a smaller, more polarized clerical work force with two distinct labour markets for clerical workers and few routes for mobility from routine to senior-level jobs. Increasingly, senior-level clerical jobs are being transformed into para-professional positions that require some college-based training in data processing, business practices, and general problem-solving.

46. Wassily Leontief, "Technological Advance, Economic Growth, and the Distribution of Income," *Population and Development Review* 9:3 (1983). A recent Ontario government study was not quite as bleak, although its tone also was sombre; Ministry of Skills Development, *op. cit.*, pp. 49–50.
47. Heather Menzies, *Computers on the Job* (Toronto: Lorimer, 1982).
48. S. Zuboff, "Problems of Symbolic Toil: How People Fare with Computer-Mediated Work," *Dissent* (Winter 1982): pp. 51–61.
49. Andrew Clement, "Electronic Management, The New Technology of Work Place Surveillance," paper presented to the Canadian Information Processing Society, Calgary, May 1984.
50. For banks, see Chapter 4; in finance, insurance and real estate, the heart of the fast-growing service sector economy, in 1987 only 3 percent, or 20,000, of

the paid workers were organized. *The Current Industrial Relations Scene in Canada 1990* (Kingston, Ont.: Industrial Relations Centre, Queen's University, 1990) p. 51.

51.Ontario Task Force on Employment and New Technology, *op. cit.*, Appendix 12, p. 77.

52.*Ibid.*

53.Economic Council of Canada, *Making Technology Work: Innovation and Jobs in Canada, A Statement* (Ottawa, 1987), p. 20. For an excellent account of how these same technologies could be used to give workers more autonomy and an enriched worklife, see David Noble, *The Forces of Production: A Social History of Industrial Automation* (New York: Oxford U.P., 1986).

54.E.W. Leaver and J.J. Brown, "Machines without Men," *Fortune* magazine (1946): 204.

55.CMA, *The Aggressive Economy: Daring to Compete.*

Chapter 11

1. Despite the well-established Bill of Rights in the United States and the more recent *Charter of Rights and Freedoms* in Canada, there are now more people incarcerated and under direct state surveillance than ever before in these two countries. Those least connected to the workforce are the prime object of this repression. This makes it easier for employers to discipline their workforces. See Douglas Hay, "Time, Inequality and Law's Violence," a paper presented at Mellon Lecture Series, Amherst College, Mass., April 11, 1991; Michael Mandel, "Rights, Freedoms and Market Power: Canada's Charter of Rights and the New Era of Global Competition," in D. Drache and M. Gertler, eds., *The New Era of Global Competition* (Montreal: McGill–Queen's U.P., 1991).

2. Naturally, individual trade unionists see themselves in a different light, but the structures restrict their role and the possibilities for more innovative kinds of strategies; see Chapter 6.

3. It would also obviate the need to legislate curbs on the employer's speech rights during campaigns, something which would be very hard to justify under the *Charter of Rights and Freedoms.*

4. Again, the Ontario NDP's 1992 labour law reform proposals contain some modest provisions to promote this aim.

5. Employment standards tribunals have held that people who manage franchises, ostensibly as independent entrepreneurs, are employees of the franchisors for the purposes of minimum wage, maximum hours and vacation entitlement legislation; *Re Becker Milk Co. Ltd* (1973), L.A.C. (2d) 337 (Carter).

6. And as it is proposed to be by the 1992 Ontario labour law reform proposals. More than any other aspect of that reform package, this has attracted the ire of business, underlining how difficult it is politically to maintain the logical argument made in the text which follows.

7. As seen in Chapter 3, a few jurisdictions give unions a limited right to be notified and to bargain in respect of mid-term technological-change proposals. Aside from this, Canadian labour arbitration jurisprudence has accorded the power to act unilaterally on these fronts to employers during the life of the collective agreements, unless the union has won a specific clause to the contrary during bargaining. The right to strike over such issues has to be recognized. Without this kind of security, the benefits of certification often are illusory.

8. For details, see Debra J. Lewis, *Just Give Us the Money: A Discussion of Wage Discrimination and Pay Equity* (Vancouver: Women's Research Centre, 1988), pp. 113–28.

9. Paul Krugman, *The Age of Diminished Expectations: U.S. Economic Policy in the 1990s* (Cambridge: MIT Press, 1990), p. 104.

10. For an overview of the debate on economic restructuring and market power which includes the creation of industrial clusters and the integration of finance, trade and industry on shifting bases, see Michael Storper and Richard Walker, *The Capitalist Imperative: Territory, Technology and Industrial Growth* (Oxford U.P.; Basil Blackwell, 1989); D. Drache, ed., *Getting on Track: Social Democratic Strategies in a Global Economy* (Montreal: McGill–Queen's U.P., 1991); as to the potential of small businesses within an industrial strategy which favours government intervention, clustering and making use of other forms of integration, see D. Moberg, "Markets in the casino economy," *Dissent* (Fall 1990): 501–9.

11. Guy Standing, "Fragmented Flexibility: Labour and the Social Dividend Solution," in D. Drache, ed., *Getting on Track*.

12. Linda McQuaig and Neil Brooks, "Taxing Our Intelligence," *This Magazine* (November 1987). A recent Statistics Canada study has argued (to Statistics Canada's formally expressed horror) that much of the national deficit is attributable not to social welfare expenditures but to revenues lost by tax concessions and the lower rate of corporate taxation. See H. Minto and P. Cross, "The Growth of the Federal Debt," *Canadian Economic Observer* (June 1991), cat. 11-010.

13. Neil Brooks, "The Changing Structure of the Canadian Tax System: Accommodating the Rich," unpublished paper, presented at Toward the 21st Century: Canadian/Australian Legal Perspectives, Centre for Public Law and Public Policy and Faculty Law, Monash University, Osgoode Hall Law School, York University, June 1991, p. 35.

14. Neil Brooks, *op. cit.*

15. For a detailed examination of the advantages and disadvantages of these schemes, see John Mathews, *Age of Democracy: The Politics of Post-Fordism* (Melbourne: Oxford U.P., 1989), pp. 90 *et seq.* The Caisse de dépôt et placement is the result of a Quebec government decision to amalgamate the public sector plans. The Caisse, as it is known, is the largest pension fund in Canada and in Quebec. It has been used to promote local entrepreneurship. Such a fund could be used more directly to help workers realize their needs.

16. Gosta Karlsson, *Trade Unions and Collective Capital Formation*, European Survey, European Trade Union Institute, Brussels, 1984.

SELECTED BIBLIOGRAPHY

Primary Sources

Canada. *Report of the Industrial Inquiry Commissioner Concerning Grievance Arbitration under the Labour Relations Act 1976–78.* Ministry of Labour. Judge Kelly, chair.

———. Department of Finance. *Paper on Anti-Inflation Policy Options.* Ottawa: May 1979.

———. *Report of the Commission on Equality in Employment.* Ottawa: Minister of Supply and Services, 1984. Rosalie Abella, chair.

———. Royal Commission on the Economic Union and the Development Prospects for Canada. *Final Report.* Ottawa: Minister of Supply and Services, 1985. Donald Macdonald, chair.

———. *Report of the Commission of Inquiry on Unemployment Insurance.* Ottawa: Minister of Supply and Services, November 1986. Claude Forget, chair.

Canadian Council of Social Development. *Work and Income in the 1990s.* Working Paper no. 8, Phase 1: "Income Security Reform:" Ottawa: 1987.

Carrothers, A.W.R., and E.E. Palmer. *Report of a Study on the Labour Injunction in Ontario.* Toronto: Ontario Department of Labour, 1966.

Coates, Mary Lou, et al. *The Current Industrial Relations Scene in Canada, 1990.* Kingston: Industrial Relations Centre, Queen's University, 1990.

Economic Council of Canada. *People and Jobs: A Study of the Canadian Labour Market.* Ottawa: Queen's Printer, 1976.

———. *Making Technology Work: Innovation and Jobs in Canada, A Statement.* Ottawa: Minister of Supply and Services, 1987.

———. *Good Jobs, Bad Jobs: Employment in the Service Economy.* Ottawa: Minister of Supply and Services, 1990.

———. *Structural Change and the Adjustment Process: Perspective on Firm Growth and Worker Turnover.* Ottawa: Queen's Printer, 1990.

ILO. *Maternity Benefits in the Eighties.* An ILO Global Survey 1964–84, Geneva: ILO, 1985.

Labour Canada. *Provisions in Major Collective Agreements in Canada Covering 500 and More Employees.* Bureau of Labour Information, April 18, 1990.

Law Reform Commission of Canada. *Workplace Pollution,* Working Paper 53, (1986).

National Council of Welfare. *Funding Health and Higher Education: Danger Looming.* Ottawa: Ministry of Supply and Services, Spring 1991.

————. *The Hidden Welfare System.* Ottawa: Minister of Supply, and Services, 1976.

————. *Poverty Profile 1988.* A Report by the National Council on Welfare. Ottawa: Minister of Supply and Services, 1988.

————. *Social Spending and the New Budget.* Ottawa, 1989.

OECD. *Women and Employment: Policies For Equal Opportunities.* Paris: OECD, 1980.

————. *Information Technology and Economic Prospects.* Paris: OECD, 1987.

————. *Economies in Transition: Structural Adjustment in OECD Countries.* Paris: OECD, 1989.

Ontario. Task Force on Employment and New Technology. *The Final Report.* Toronto: 1985.

————*Report of the Task Force on Inflation Protection for Employment Pension Plans.* Toronto: 1986. Martin Friedland, chair.

————. *Working Times: The Report of the Ontario Task Force on Hours of Work and Overtime.* Toronto: Ontario Ministry of Labour, 1987. Arthur Donner, chair.

————. *Report on the Administration of the Occupational Health and Safety Act.* Ministry of Labour, Ontario: January 1987. G.G. McKenzie and John Laskin, co-chairs.

————. *Competing in the New Global Economy.* Vol. I and II. Toronto: The Premier's Council of Ontario, 1987/89.

————. Ministry of Community and Social Services. *Transitions, Report of the Social Assistance Review Committee.* Toronto: Queen's Printer, Ontario, 1988. George Thomson, chair.

————. Ministry of Skills Development. *Adjusting to Change: An Overview of Labour Market Issues in Ontario.* Labour Market Research Group, June 1988.

————. *Report to the Minister of Labour by the Ontario Pay Equity Commission.* February 1989.

————. Ministry of Industry, Trade and Technology (MITT). *A Comparison of Canadian and U.S. Technology Adoption Rates.* Technology Policy Branch. Toronto: November 1989.

————. Ministry of Industry, Trade and Technology, *The State of Small Business 1989: Annual Report on Small Business in Ontario.* Toronto: Government of Ontario, Small Business Branch, 1989.

Statistics Canada. *Job Turnover in Canada's Manufacturing Sector.* Ottawa: Minister of Supply and Services, 1989.

————. *Pension Plans in Canada.* Ottawa: Minister of Supply and Services, 1990.

Task Force on Labour Relations. *Final Report.* Ottawa: Privy Council, 1968. H.D. Woods, chair.

Secondary Sources: Books and Reports

Abella, Irving. *Nationalism, Communism and Canadian Labour: The CIU, the CP, and the CCL 1935-50.* Toronto: University of Toronto Press, 1973.

Adams, George. *Grievance Arbitration of Discharge Cases.* Kingston: Queen's University, Industrial Relations Centre, Research and Current Issues Series No. 38, 1978.

Aglietta, Michel, and A. Brender. *Les métamorphoses de la société salariale.* Paris: Calmann-Levy, 1984.

Aitken, Hugh. *American Capital and Canadian Resources.* Cambridge, Mass.: Harvard University Press, 1961.

Armstrong, P., and H. Armstrong. *Double Ghetto: Canadians and Their Segregated Work.* Rev. ed. Toronto: McClelland and Stewart, 1984.

Arthurs, H.W. *Collective Bargaining by Public Employees in Canada: The Five Models.* Ann Arbor: Institute of Labor and Industrial Relations, 1971.

Arthurs, H.W., D.D. Carter, J. Fudge, and H.J. Glasbeek *Labour Law and Industrial Relations in Canada.* 3rd ed. Toronto: Butterworths, 1989.

Auld, D.A., L.N. Christofieds, R. Swidnisky, and D.A. Wilton *The Determinants of Negotiated Wage Settlements in Canada 1966-1975.* Ottawa: Anti-Inflation Board, 1979.

Aw, Chan F. *A Dual Labour Market Analysis: A Study of Canadian Manufacturing Industries.* Labour Canada, Economic Analysis Branch. Ottawa: Minister of Supply and Services, 1981.

Bakker, Isabella. "The Status of Women in OECD Countries." *Equality and Employment.* Vol. 11. Royal Commission Report, Research Studies. Ottawa: Minister of Supply and Services, 1985.

Bank Book Collective. *An Account to Settle.* Vancouver: Press Gang Publishers, 1980.

Baranson, Jack. "An Assessment of the Behaviour of U.S. Industrial Subsidiaries in Canada (Ontario)." Government of Ontario, 1985.

Barber, Clarence and John McCallum. *Controlling Inflation Learning from Experiences in Canada, Europe and Japan.* Toronto: Canadian Institutie for Economic Policy and James Lorimer, 1982.

Barnet, Richard, and Ronald Muller. *Global Reach.* New York: Simon and Schuster, 1974.

Baxter, S. *No Way To Live: Poor Women Speak Out.* New Star Books: Vancouver, 1988.

Beckett, Elizabeth. "Unions and Bank Workers: Will the Twain Ever Meet?" Women's Bureau, Labour Canada, Ottawa: Labour Canada, 1984.

Bellemare, Diane, and Lise Poulin Simon. *Le défi du plein emploi.* Montreal: Éditions Saint-Martin, 1986.

Bellon, B., and J. Niosi. *The Decline of the American Economy.* Montreal: Black Rose, 1988.

Belous, Richard. "Flexibility and American Labour Markets." ILO, Labour Market Analysis and Employment Planning, World Employment Programme Research. Geneva, June 1987.

Betcherman, G., and K. McMullen. *Working with Technology: A Survey of the Automation Process in Canada.* Ottawa: Economic Council of Canada, 1986.

Bird, Richard. *The Growth of Public Employment in Canada.* IRPP. Toronto: Butterworths, 1979.

Blanpain, R. *The OECD Guidelines for Multinational Enterprises and Labour Relations, 1976–1979: Experience and Review.* Deventer, Netherlands; Boston: Mass.; 1979.

Bluestone, B., and B. Harrison. *The De-industrialization of America.* New York: Basic Books, 1982.

Boismenu, G., and D. Drache, eds. *Politique et régulation: Modèle de développement et trajectoire canadienne.* Montreal/Paris: Méridien/L'Harmattan, 1990.

Bowles, S., D. Gordon, and T. Weisskopf. *Beyond the Wasteland.* New York: Anchor Books, 1984.

Boyer, Robert. *La théorie de la régulation: Une analyse critique.* Paris: La Découverte, 1986.

————. ed. *La flexibilité du travail en Europe.* Paris: La Découverte, 1986.

————. "The Eighties: The Search for Alternatives to Fordism." Paris: CEPREMAP, 1987.

Braverman, H. *Labour and Monopoly Capital: The Degradation of Work in the Twentieth Century.* New York: Monthly Review Press, 1974.

Brown, D., and D. Beatty. *Canadian Labour Arbitration.* 3rd ed. Aurora, Ont.: Canada Law Book Co., 1989.

Burawoy, M. *Manufacturing Consent: Changes in the Labour Process Under Monopoly Capitalism.* Chicago: University of Chicago Press, 1979.

Cameron, Duncan, and Andrew Sharpe, eds. *Policies of Full Employment.* Ottawa: CCSD, 1988.

Cameron, Duncan, ed. *The Free Trade Papers.* Toronto: Lorimer, 1985.

Campbell, Robert M. *The Full Employment Objective in Canada, 1945–85.* A Study prepared for the Economic Council of Canada. Ottawa: Minister of Supply and Services, 1991.

————. *Grand Illusions: The Politics of the Keynesian Experience in Canada 1945–1975* Toronto: Broadview Press, 1987.

CAW Technology Project. *Changing Technology and Work: Northern Telecom.* Toronto, 1989.

Chodos, Robert, and Nick Auf Der Maur. *Quebec: A Chronicle 1968–1972.* A Last Post Special. Toronto: James Lewis and Samuel, 1972.

Canadian Manufacturers' Association. *The Aggressive Economy: Daring to Compete.* Toronto: June 1989.

Clement, Andrew. "Electronic Management, The New Technology of Work Place Surveillance." Paper presented to the Canadian Information Processing Society, Calgary, May 1984.

Cohen, Marcy. "The Feminization of the Labour Market." In D. Drache, ed., *Getting on Track: Social Democratic Strategies for Ontario.* Montreal: McGill-Queen's U.P., 1992.

Coleman, William. *The Independence Movement in Quebec, 1945–1989.* Toronto: University of Toronto Press, 1984.

Conference Board of Canada. *Inflation and Incomes Policy in Canada.* Ottawa, May 1979.

Cordell, Arthur J. *The Multinational Firm, Foreign Direct Investment and Canadian Science Policy.* Science Council of Canada, Special Study, no. 22 Ottawa, 1971.

Coriat, B. *L'atelier et le chronomètre.* 2nd ed. Paris: C. Bourgois, 1982.

Cornish, Mary "Equal Pay: Collective Bargaining and the Law," Ottawa: Minister of Supply and Services, 1986.

Cox, Robert. *Production, Power and World Order.* New York: Columbia University Press, 1987.

Craig, A. *The System of Industrial Relations in Canada.* 3rd ed. Scarborough, Ont.: Prentice-Hall, 1990.

Dertouzos, Michael L., Richard K. Lester, and Robert M. Solow. *Made in America: Regaining the Productive Edge.* Boston: MIT Press, 1989.

Drache, Daniel. "Industrial Relations as a System of Regulation: Canada and the Economic Crisis." In Hans Diefenbacker and Hans G. Nutzinger, eds. *Gewerkschaften und Arbeitsbeziehungen im Internationalen Vergleich*, FEST, Band II, Heidelberg, 1984.

————. "New Work Processes, Unregulated Capitalism and the Future of Labour." In G. Szell, Paul Blyton, and Chris Cornforth. *The State, Trade Unions and Self-Management*. New York: de Gruyter, Walter, 1989.

————. "The Way Forward for Ontario." In D. Drache, ed. *Getting on Track: Social Democratic Strategies in Ontario*. Montreal; McGill-Queen's U.P., 1991.

————. ed. *Getting on Track: Social Democratic Strategies in Ontario*. Montreal: McGill-Queen's U.P., 1991.

————. ed. *Only the Beginning: The Manifestos of the Common Front*. Toronto: New Press, 1972.

Drache, Daniel, and Meric Gertler, eds. *The New Era of Global Competition, State Policy and Market Power*. Montreal: McGill-Queen's U.P., 1991.

Easterbrooke, W.T., and M.H. Watkins, eds. *Approaches to Canadian Economic History*. Toronto: McClelland and Stewart, 1967.

Edwards, R. *Contested Terrain: The Transformation of the Workplace in the Twentieth Century*. New York: Basic Books, 1979.

Edwards, R., P. Garonna, and F. Todling. *Unions in Crisis and Beyond: Perspectives From Six Countries*. Dover, Mass.: Auburn House, 1986.

Engels, F. *The Condition of the Working Class in England*. Panther, 1969.

Ernst and Young. *Canada's High Technology Industries in the 1990s*. Toronto: 1990.

Esping-Andersen, G. *The Three Worlds of Welfare Capitalism*. London: Polity Press, 1990.

Finkelman, J. and S. Goldenberg. *Collective Bargaining in the Public Service; The Federal Experience in Canada*. Montreal: Institute for Research in Public Policy, 1983.

Finlayson, Ann. *Whose Money Is It Anyway? The Showdown on Pensions*. Viking, 1988.

Foisy, Claude H., Daniel E. Lavery, and Luc Martineau. *Canada Labour Relations Board Policies and Procedures*. Toronto and Vancouver: Butterworths, 1986.

Foucault, Michel. *Discipline and Punish: The Birth of the Prison*. Trans. A. Sheridan. New York: Pantheon, 1977.

Freeman, Richard B. "Canada in the World Labour Market To the Year 2000." *Economic Council of Canada*. Ottawa: Minister of Supply and Services, 1988.

Fudge, Judy. "Labour, The New Constitution and Old-Style Liberalism." In *Labour Law Under the Charter*. Kingston: Queen's Law Journal and Industrial Relations Centre, Queen's University, 1988.

————. "Voluntarism and Compulsion: The Canadian Federal Government's Intervention in Collective Bargaining from 1930 to 1946." D. Phil. thesis, University of Oxford, 1988.

————. "Labour Law's Little Sister: Employment Standards Legislation." Ottawa: Centre for Policy Alternatives, 1991.

Fudge, J., and Patricia McDermott eds. *Just Wages: A Feminist Assessment of Pay Equity*. Toronto: University of Toronto Press, 1991.

Gigantes, T. "Structural Change and Capital Accumulation in the Latter Part of the Twentieth Century: An Essay in Economic History." Unpublished manuscript. Statistics Canada, July 1989.

Glasbeek, H.J. "The Contract of Employment at Common Law." In J. Anderson and M. Gunderson, eds. *Union-Management Relations in Canada*. Don Mills, Ont.: Addison Wesley, 1982.

———. "Law, Real and Ideological Constraints on the Working Class." In Gibson and Baldwin, eds. *Law in a Cynical Society?* Calgary: Carswell, 1985.

———. "Voluntarism, Liberalism and Grievance Arbitration: Holy Grail, Romance and Real Life." In G. England, ed. *Essays in Labour Relations Law*. Don Mills, Ont.: CCH Canadian Ltd., 1986.

———. "A Role for Criminal Sanctions in Occupational Health and Safety." In *New Developments in Employment Law, 1988 Meredith Memorial Lectures*. Cowansville: Les Éditions Yvon Blais, 1989.

Gorz, André. *Farewell to the Working Class*. London: Pluto Press, 1980.

Grossman, Brian A. *The Executive Firing Line: Wrongful Dismissal and the Law*. Toronto: Carswell/Methuen, 1982.

Guest, Denis. *The Emergence of Social Security in Canada*. Vancouver: University of British Columbia Press, 1980.

Gunderson, M., L. Muszynski, and J. Keck. *Women and Labour Market Poverty*. Ottawa: Canadian Advisory Council on the Status of Women, 1990.

Haiven, Lavery, Stephen McBride, and John Shields eds. *Regulating Labour: The State, Neo Conservatism and Industrial Relations*. Socialist Studies: Winnipeg, 1991.

Harris, David. *Wrongful Dismissal*. Toronto: Richard de Boo, 1978.

Hay, Douglas. "Time, Inequality and Law's Violence." Unpublished paper presented at the Mellon Lecture series, Amherst College, Mass., April 11, 1991.

Heron, Craig. *The Canadian Labour Movement: A Short History*. Toronto: Lorimer, 1989.

Holmes, John. "The Organization and Locational Structure of Production Sub-Contracting." In A.J. Scott and M. Storper, eds. *Production, Work Territory*. London: Allen and Unwin, 1986.

Horowitz, Gad. *Canadian Labour and Politics*. Toronto: University of Toronto Press, 1968.

Hyman, Richard. *Industrial Relations: A Marxist Introduction*. London: Macmillan, 1975.

Innis, Harold. *Essays in Canadian Economic History*. Ed. Mary Q. Innis. Toronto: University of Toronto Press, 1956.

Jamieson, Stuart. *Times of Trouble: Labour Unrest and Industrial Conflict in Canada, 1900–1966*. Study no. 22, Task Force on Labour Relations. Ottawa: Privy Council Office, 1968.

———. *Industrial Relations in Canada*. 2nd ed. Toronto: Macmillan, 1973.

———. "Some Reflections on Violence and Law in Industrial Relations." In D.J. Bercuson, and L.A. Knafla, eds. *Law and Society in Canada in Historical Perspective*. Calgary: University of Calgary, 1979.

———. *Industrial Conflict in Canada 1966–75*. Economic Council of Canada, Centre for the Study of Inflation and Productivity, Discussion Paper No. 142, December, 1979.

Kaplan, L.W. *Everything that Floats: Pat Sullivan, Hal Banks and the Seamen's Unions of Canada.* Toronto: University of Toronto Press, 1987.

Kaplinsky, Raphael. *Automation, Technology and Society.* London: Longman, 1984.

Karlsson, Gosta. *Trade Unions and Collective Capital Formation, European Survey.* European Trade Union Institute, Brussels, 1984.

Kerr, C., J.T. Dunlop, F.H. Harbison, and C.A. Myers. *Industrialism and Industrial Man.* New York: Oxford University Press, 1969.

Kirk Laux, Jean and Maureen Appel Molot. *State Capitalism and Public Enterprise in Canada.* Ithaca: Cornell University Press, 1988.

Krugman, Paul. *The Age of Diminished Expectations U.S. Economic Policy in the 1990s.* Cambridge: MIT Press, 1990.

Lang, John. "A History of Organized Labour in Sudbury, Ontario." M.A. Thesis, Guelph University, Ontario, 1967.

Langille, David I. *From Consultation to Corporation? The Consultative Process between Canadian Business, Labour and Government, 1977–1981.* M.A. thesis, Carleton University, 1982.

Laxer, Gordon ed. *Perspectives on Canadian Economic Development: Class, Staples, Gender and Elites.* Toronto: Oxford U.P., 1991.

Laxer, J. *Rethinking the Economy.* Toronto: New Canada Publications, 1984.

Letourneau, R.S. *Inflation, The Canadian Experience.* Ottawa: Conference Board of Canada, 1980.

Levitt, Kari. *Silent Surrender: The Multinational Corporation in Canada.* Toronto: Macmillan, 1970.

Lewis, Debra J. *Just Give Us the Money: A Discussion of Wage Discrimination and Pay Equity.* Vancouver: Women's Research Centre, 1988.

Lipietz, Alain. "The Globalization of the General Crisis of Fordism." In J. Holmes and C. Leys eds. *Frontyard, Backyard: The Americas in the Global Crisis.* Toronto: Between the Lines, 1987.

Lipsig-Mummé, Carla. "Quebec Labour, Politics, and the Economic Crisis of the 1980's: The Roots of Defensive Accommodation." Unpublished paper, 1990.

Logan, Harold. *State Intervention and Assistance in Collective Bargaining: The Canadian Experience, 1943–54.* Toronto: University of Toronto Press, 1956.

MacAllister, Barbara Heather. "Labour and the State: The Canadian Labour Congress, Consultative Forums, and Incomes Policies 1960–1978." Ph.D thesis, University of Toronto, 1982.

Madison, A. *The World Economy in the 20th Century.* Paris: OECD, 1989.

Magnusson, Warren, William Carroll, Charles Doyle, Monika Langer, and R.B.J. Walker. *The New Reality: The Politics of Restraint in British Columbia.* Vancouver: New Star, 1984.

Mandel, M. *The Charter of Rights and the Legalization of Politics in Canada.* Toronto: Wall & Thompson, 1989.

———. "Rights, Freedoms and Market Power: Canada's Charter of Rights and the New Era of Global Competition." In D. Drache, and M. Gertler, eds. *The New Era of Global Competition.* Montreal: McGill-Queen's U.P., 1991.

Mansell, Jackie. *Workplace Innovation in Canada: Reflections on the Past ... Prospects for the Future, Economic Council of Canada.* Ottawa: Minister of Services and Supply, 1987.

Mathews, John. *Age of Democracy The Politics of Post-Fordism.* Melbourne: Oxford U.P., 1989.

McDermott, Patricia. "Technological Change and the Canada Labour Code." Science Council of Canada, January 1984.

McGrady, L. *A Guide to Organizing Unions.* Toronto: Butterworths, 1989.

McRoberts, Kenneth. *Quebec: Social Change and Political Crisis.* 3rd ed. Toronto: McClelland and Stewart, 1988.

Meltz, N. "Labour Movements in Canada and the U.S.: Are they Really That Different." Centre for Industrial Relations, University of Toronto, July 1983.

———. "Industrial Relations Systems as a Framework for Organizing Contributions to Industrial Relations Theory." Queen's Papers in Industrial Relations, No.1, School of Industrial Relations, Queen's University at Kingston, 1992.

Menzies, H. *Women and the Chip: Case Studies of the Effects of Informatics on Employment in Canada.* Montreal: Institute for Research on Public Policy, 1981.

———. *Fast Forward Out of Control.* Toronto: Macmillan, 1989.

Morin, Claude. *Quebec vs. Ottawa: The Struggle for Self Government 1960–72.* Toronto: University of Toronto Press, 1976.

Morton, Desmond. "Aid to the Civil Power: The Canadian Militia in Support of the Social Order, 1867–1914." In Michiel Horn and Ronald Saborin eds. *Studies in Canadian Social History.* Toronto: McClelland and Stewart, 1974.

Muszynski, L. *Social InfoPact* 1:5 Dec. 1982, Social Planning Council of Metropolitan Toronto, 1982.

———. "The Politics of Labour Market Policy." In Bruce Doern ed. *The Politics of Economic Policy.* Collected Research Studies, Royal Commission on the Economic Union and Development Prospects for Canada, vol. 40. Toronto: University of Toronto Press, 1986.

Muszynski, L. and M. Gunderson. *Women, Poverty and the Labour Market: A Study of the Working Poor in Canada.* Canadian Advisory Council on the Status of Women, February 1989.

Myles, J., G. Picot, and T. Wannell. "Wages and Jobs in the 1980s: Changing Youth Wages and the Declining Middle." *Statistics Canada Analytical Studies.* Branch Research Paper Series no. 17, (October 1988).

Nightingale, D.V. *Workplace Democracy: An Inquiry into Employee Participation in Canadian Work Organizations.* Toronto: University of Toronto Press, 1982.

Niosi, J. *Canadian Multinationals.* Toronto: Between the Lines, 1985.

Noble, David. *The Forces of Production: A Social History of Industrial Automation.* New York: Oxford University Press, 1986.

O'Grady, John. "Beyond the Wagner Act, What Then?" In D. Drache, ed., *Getting on Track: Social Democratic Strategies for Ontario.* Montreal: McGill-Queen's U.P., 1992.

Ohmae, Kenichi. *Triad Power: The Coming Shape of Global Competition.* New York: Free Press, 1986.

Ostry S. and M.A. Zaidi. *Labour Economics in Canada.* 2nd ed. Toronto: Macmillan, 1979.

Pal, Leslie. "Revision and Retreat: Canadian Unemployment Insurance 1971–1981." In J.S. Ismael, ed. *Canadian Social Welfare Policy, Federal and Provincial Dimensions.* Montreal: McGill-Queen's U.P., 1985.

Palmer, Bryan, ed. *The Character of Class Struggle: Essays in Canadian Working Class History, 1850–1985.* Toronto: McClelland and Stewart, 1986.

Panitch, Leo. "Wage and Price Controls." in D. Drache, ed. *Debates and Controversies from This Magazine.* Toronto: McClelland and Stewart, 1979.

Panitch, Leo, and Donald Swartz. *The Assault on Trade Union Freedoms*. Rev. ed. Toronto: Garamond Press, 1988.

Parr, Joy. *The Gender of Breadwinners: Women, Men and Change in Two Industrial Towns, 1889–1950*. Toronto: University of Toronto Press, 1990.

Pentland, Clare H. *A Study of the Changing Social, Economic and Political Background of the Canadian System of Industrial Relations*. Task Force on Labour Relations. Ottawa: Privy Council Office, 1968.

———. *Labour and Capital in Canada, 1650–1860*. Toronto: Lorimer, 1981.

Petit, Pascal. *Slow Growth and the Service Economy*. London: Francis Pinter, 1986.

Piore, M. and C. Sabel. *The Second Industrial Divide*. New York: Basic Books, 1984.

Piotte, Jean-Marc, D. Ethier, and J. Reynolds. *Les travailleurs contre l'état bourgeois*. Montreal: L'Aurore, 1975.

Polanyi, K. *The Great Transformation*. Boston: Beacon Press, 1957.

Quine, T. *How Operation Solidarity Became Operation Sold-out*. Toronto: International Socialists, 1985.

Rand, J. *Ford Motor Company Award 1946*. 1946 Labour Gazette.

Reich, Robert. *The Work of Nations*. New York: Knopf, 1991.

Rhinehart, James W. *The Tyranny of Work: Alienation and the Labour Process*. 2nd ed. Toronto: Harcourt Brace Jovanovich, 1987.

Riddell, Craig W., ed. *Canadian Labour Relations*. Vol. 16, Royal Commission on Economic Union and the Development Prospects for Canada. Toronto: University of Toronto Press, 1986.

Robertson, Dave, and Jeff Wareham. *Technological Change in the Auto Industry*. CAW Technology Project. Toronto: CAW, 1987.

Robinson, Ian. "Organizing Labour: The Moral Economy of Canadian-American Union Density Divergence, 1963–1986." Queen's Papers in Industrial Relations, No. 2, School of Industrial Relations, Queen's University at Kingston, 1992.

Ross, David P. *The Working Poor: Wage Earners and the Failure of Income Security Policies*. Toronto: Lorimer, 1981.

Rotstein, A. *Rebuilding from Within; Remedies for Canada's Ailing Economy*. Toronto: Lorimer, 1984.

Russell, Bob. *Back to Work? Labour, State and Industrial Relations in Canada*. Toronto: Nelson, 1990.

Sabel, Charles. *Work and Politics*. Cambridge: Cambridge University Press.

Sack, J. and M. Mitchell. *Ontario Labour Relations Board Law and Practices*. Toronto: Butterworths, 1985.

Scott, Frank. *Essays on Law and the Constitution*. Toronto: University of Toronto Press, 1980.

Selznick, P. *Law, Society and Industrial Justice*. New York: Basic Books, 1969.

Shaiken, H. *Work Transformed: Automation and Labor in the Computer Age*. Lexington, Mass: D.C. Heath, 1984.

Smiley, Donald V. *Constitutional Adaptation and Canadian Federalism since 1945, Documents of the Royal Commission on Bilingualism and Biculturalism*. Ottawa: Information Canada, 1970.

Stanton, John. *Labour Arbitrations: Boon or Bane for Unions?* Vancouver: Butterworths, 1983.

Strange, Susan. *States and Markets*. New York: Basil Blackwell, 1988.

Swinton, Katherine E. "Enforcement of Occupational Health and Safety Legislation: The Role of the Internal Responsibility System." In Kenneth P. Swan and Katherine E. Swinton, eds. *Studies in Labour Law*. Toronto: Butterworths, 1983.

Swinton, K. "Contract Law and the Employment Relationship. The Proper Forum for Reform." In B. Reiter, and K. Swan, eds. *Studies in Contract Law*. Toronto: Butterworths, 1983.

Taylor, F.W. *Scientific Management*. New York: Harper and Brothers, 1947.

Thompson, M. and E. Swimmer, eds. *Conflict or Compromise: Public Sector Industrial Relations in Canada*. Montreal: IRPP, 1984.

Trudeau, P.E. *The Asbestos Strike*. Trans. James Boake. Toronto: Lorimer, 1974.

Tucker, Eric. "The Persistence of Market Regulation of Occupational Health and Safety: The Stillbirth of Voluntarism." In G. England ed. *Essays in Labour Law*. Don Mills: CCH, 1986.

Tuohy, C. "Decision Trees and Political Thickets: An Approach to Analyzing Regulatory Decision-Making in the Occupational Health Arena." Law and Economics Workshop, Faculty of Law, University of Toronto, 1984.

Waldie, Brennan and Associates. *Labour Standards: An Interjurisdictional Comparison*. A Study Prepared for the Government of Ontario, Ministry of Labour. Toronto: July 31, 1990.

Wallace, Clement, ed. *Class, Power and Property: Essays on Canadian Society* Toronto: Carleton University Press, 1983.

Warrian, P. "Labour is not a Commodity: A Study of the Rights of Labour in the Emergent Postwar Economy in Canada 1944–1948." Ph.D. thesis, Department of History, University of Waterloo, 1986.

Watkins, M.H. "A Staple Theory of Economic Growth." In W.T. Easterbook and M.H. Watkins, eds. *Approaches to Canadian Economic History*. Toronto: McClelland and Stewart, 1967.

Webb, Beatrice, and Sydney Webb. *Industrial Democracy*. London: Longmans, Green and Co., 1926.

Weiler, Paul. *Reconcilable Differences: New Directions in Canadian Labour Law*. Toronto: Carswell, 1980.

Wells, D. *Soft Sell: "Quality of Working Life" Programs and the Productivity Race*. Ottawa: The Canadian Centre for Policy Alternatives, 1986.

White, Julie. *Women and Part-time Work*. Ottawa: Canadian Advisory Council on the Status of Women, 1980.

Wilton, David. "Public Sector Wage Compensation." In Craig W. Riddell, ed. *Canadian Labour Relations*. Vol. 16, Royal Commission on Economic Union and the Development Prospects for Canada. Toronto: University of Toronto Press, 1986.

Wolfe, David. "The Rise and Demise of the Keynesian Era in Canada." in M. Cross and G. Kealey, eds. *Modern Canada 1930–1980s*. Toronto: McClelland and Stewart, 1984.

Wolfe, David, and Armine Yalnizyan. *Target on Training: Meeting Workers' Needs in a Changing Economy*. Toronto: Social Planning Council of Metropolitan Toronto, 1989.

Womack, James P., Daniel T. Jones, and Daniel Roos. *The Machine that Changed the World*. New York: Rawson, 1990.

Women for Economic Survival and the Community Council of Greater Victoria, Women, Poverty and Public Policy. November 1985.

Zohar, U. *Canadian Manufacturing A Study in Productivity and Technological Change*. Toronto: Lorimer, 1982.

Zwelling, Marc, *The Strikebreakers*. Report of the Strikebreaking Committee of the Ontario Federation of Labour and the Labour Council of Metropolitan Toronto, Toronto: New Press, 1972.

Secondary Sources: Articles

Acker, Joan. "Class, Gender and the Relations of Distribution." *Signs* 13:3 (June): 473.

Adams, Roy, J. "The Extent of Collective Bargaining in Canada," *Relations Industrielles* 39:4 (1984).

———. "A Social Charter for European Labour?" *Labour Relations News* (May 1990).

Adler, Paul S. "Managing Flexible Automation," *California Management Review* 30:3 (Spring 1988).

Akeyanpong, E.B. "Working for a minimum wage," *Perspectives on Labour and Income* 1:3 (1989).

Anderson, M. "Shakeout in Detroit: New Technology, New Problems" *Technology Review* 85 (Aug./Sept. 1980).

Andstein, Cliff, and Bryan Palmer In "Solidarity — An Exchange." *New Directions* 3:3 (Jan.-Feb. 1988).

Armstrong, P., and H. Armstrong. "Lessons from Pay Equity." SPE 32 (Summer 1990):29.

Arthurs, H.W. "Developing Industrial Citizenship: A Challenge for Canada's Second Century." (1967), 45 *Can. Bar Rev.* 786.

———. "'The Dullest Bill': Reflections on the Labour code of British Columbia." (1974), 9 *Univ. B.C. L. Rev.* 280.

Backhouse, Constance. "The Fleck Strike: A Case Study in the Need for First Contract Arbitration." (1980), 18 *Osgoode Hall L.J.* 495.

Baigent, J. "Protecting the Right to Organize." In J.J. Weiler and P.A. Gall, eds., *The Labour Code of British Columbia in the 1980's*. Calgary: Carswell, 1984.

Beatty, D. "Secondary Boycotts: A Functional Analysis." (1974), 52 *Can. Bar Rev.* 388.

Boyer, Robert. "Labour Flexibility: Many Forms, Uncertain Effects." *Labour and Society* 12:1 (1987).

Brooks, Neil. "The Changing Structure of the Canadian Tax System: Accommodating the Rich." forthcoming, *Osgoode Hall L. J.*

Brown, Richard H. "The Reform of Bargaining Structure in the Canadian Construction Industry." (1979), 3 *Industrial Relations L. J.* 538.

Bruce, Peter G. "The Processing of Unfair Labour Practice Cases in the United States and Ontario." *Relations Industrielles* 45:3 (1990).

Burke, Mary Anne. "The Growth of Part-Time Work." *Canadian Social Trends* (Autumn 1986).

Clairmonte, Frederick F., and John H. Cavanagh. "Transnational corporations and services: the final frontier." *Trade and Development: An UNCTAD Review* 5 (1984).

Cousineau, Jean-Michel and Elmustopha Najem. "L'effet du développement de la petite entreprise sur l'évolution du syndicalisme au Canada." *Relations Industrielles* 45:3 (1990).

Cox, A. "Rights under a Collective Agreement." (1956), 69 *Harvard L. Rev.* 601.
————. "The Duty to Bargain in Good Faith." (1958), 71 *Harvard L. Rev.* 1401, 1409.
Crispo, J., and H. Arthurs. "Industrial Unrest in Canada: A Diagnosis of Recent Experience." *Relations Industrielles* 23 (1968).
di Carlo, Nick. "The Right to Refuse — Bill 208." *Our Times* (May 1989).
Drache, Daniel. "Harold Innis and Canadian Capitalist Development." *Canadian Journal of Political and Social Theory* 6 (Winter-Spring 1982).
————. "The Formation and Fragmentation of the Canadian Working Class." SPE 16 (November 1984).
Drache, Daniel and John Lang. "Immigrants and Small Factories: The Lessons of Artistic." *This Magazine* 8:1 (January, 1974).
Drache, D., and H.J. Glasbeek. "The New Fordism: Capital's Offensive, Labour's Opportunity." (1989), 27 *Osgoode Hall L.J.* 517.
England, G. "Recent Developments in Wrongful Dismissal Laws and Some Pointers for Reform." (1978), 16 *Alberta L. Rev.* 471.
Evans, J.M. "Jurisdictional Review in the Supreme Court: Realism, Romance and Recidivism." (1991), 48 *Admin. L. Reports* 255.
Feller, D. "A General Theory of the Collective Bargaining Agreement." (1973), 61 *Yale L.J.* 663, 704.
Fisher, E.G., and S. Kushner. "Alberta's Construction Labour Relations during the Recent Downturn." *Relations Industrielles* 41:4 (1986).
Forrest, Anne. "Bargaining Units and Bargaining Power." *Relations Industrielles* 41:4 (1986).
————. "The Rise and Fall of National Bargaining in the Canadian Meat-Packing Industry." *Relations Industrielles* 44:2 (1989).
Freeman, Audrey and William Fulmer. "Last Rites for Pattern Bargaining." *Harvard Business Review* (March-April 1982).
Frenken, Hubert. "Retirement Income Programs in Canada." *Canadian Social Trends.* (Winter 1986).
Giles, Anthony. "The Canadian Labour Congress and Tripartism." *Industrial Relations* 37:1 (1982).
Gindin, Sam. "Breaking Away: The Formation of the Canadian AutoWorkers." SPE 29 (Summer 1989).
Glasbeek, H.J. "A Proposal For a Non-Earnings Related Retirement Income Scheme." *Canadian Taxation* 2:4 (Winter 1980).
————. "TIP: Another Weapon in the Class War Waged Against Workers." *Canadian Taxation* 3 (1981).
————. "The Utility of Model Building — Collins' Capitalist Discipline and Corporatist Law 1984." 13 *Industrial Law Journal* 133.
————. "The Legalization of Politics in Advanced Capitalism: The Canadian Charter of Rights and Freedoms." *Socialist Studies* 2 (1984).
————. "Labour Relations Policy and Law as a Mechanism of Adjustment." (1987), 25 *Osgoode Hall L. J.* 179.
Glasbeek, H.J. and M. Mandel. "The Crime and Punishment of Jean-Claude Parrot." *Canadian Forum* (August 1979).
Gower, David. "Annual Update on Labour Force Trends." *Canadian Social Trends* (Summer 1988).
Gray, Grattan. "Social Policy by Stealth." *Policy Options* (March 1990).

Hasson, R.A. "Tax Evasion and Social Security Abuse: Some Tentative Observations." *Canadian Taxation* 2:2 (1980).

————. "Social Security Abuse." *Canadian Taxation* 3:3 (1981): 121.

————. "Discipline and Punishment in the Law of Unemployment Insurance — A Critical View of Disqualifications and Disentitlement." (1987), 25 *Osgoode Hall L.J.* 615.

Hogg, P. "Proof of Facts in Constitutional Cases." (1976), 26 *University of Toronto L.J.* 386.

Jenson, Jane. "'Different' but not 'Exceptional': Canada's Permeable Fordism." *Canadian Review of Sociology and Anthropology.* 26:1 (1989).

Kilcoyne, John R. "Developments in Employment Law: The 1987–88 Term." (1989), 11 *Supreme Court Law Review.* 241.

Klare, Karl. "Judicial Deradicalization of the Wagner Act." 62 *Minnesota Law Review* 265, (1988).

Kumar, Pradeep. "Estimates of Unionism and Collective Bargaining Coverage in Canada." *Relations Industrielles* 43:1 (1988).

Langille, B. "The Michelin Amendment in Context." (1981), 6 *Dalhousie L.J.* 523.

Laskin, B. "Collective Bargaining and Individual Rights." (1963), 6 *Canadian Bar Journal* 278.

Leaver, E.W. and Brown, J.J. "Machines without Men." *Fortune* magazine, (1946).

Leontief, Wassily. "Technological Advance, Economic Growth, and the Distribution of Income." *Population and Development Review.* 9:3 (1983).

Lindsay, Colin and Craig McKee. "Annual Review of Labour Force Trends." *Social Trends* (Autumn 1986).

Lowe, Graham. "Causes of Unionization in Canadian Banks." *Relations Industrielles* 36:4 (1981).

Manwaring, J. "Legitimacy in Labour Relations: The Courts, The B.C. Labour Board and Secondary Picketing." (1982), 20 *Osgoode Hall L.J.* 274.

McDermott, Patricia. "Pay Equity in Ontario: A Critical Legal Analysis." (1990) *Osgoode Hall L. R.* 381.

McDowell, R.D. "Law and Practice before the Ontario Labour Relations Board." (1977-78). *Advocates Quarterly*, 198.

Moberg, D. "Markets in the casino economy." *Dissent.* (Fall 1990).

Munro, H. and H. Noori. "Reflecting Corporate Strategy in the Decision to Automate: The Case of Canadian Manufacturing Companies." *Business Quarterly.* (March 1986).

Murphy, Rae and Scott Sinclair. "Mission to Mexico." *This Magazine* 24:1 (June 1990).

Muthuchidambaram, S. "Settlement of First Collective Agreement; An Examination of the Canada Labour Code Amendment." *Relations Industrielles* 35:3 (1980).

Nathan, Stephen. "Direct Action at the McDonnell Douglas: The right to refuse unsafe work." *Our Times* 7:1 (February 1988).

Neill, Shirley. "Unionization in Canada." *Canadian Social Trends.* (Spring 1988).

Noel, Alain and Keith Gardner. "The Gainers Strike: Capitalist Offensive, Militancy and the Politics of Industrial Relations in Canada." SPE 31, Spring 1990.

Palmer, Bryan. "A Funny Thing Happened on the Way to Kelowana." *Canadian Dimension* 18:1 (1984).

Palmer, E.E. "The Short Unhappy Life of the 'Aristocratic' Doctrine." (1960), 13 *University of Toronto L.J. 166.*

Panitch, Leo. "Corporatism in Canada." *SPE* 1 (1979).

Pold, Henry and Fred Wong. "The Price of Labour." *Perspectives on Labour Income* 3 (Autumn 1990).

Rohan, Paul C., and Bernard Brody. "Frequency and Costs of Work Accidents in North America, 1971–80." *Labour & Society* 9:2 (April-June 1985).

Rose, J. "Legislative Support For Multi-Employer Bargaining: The Canadian Experience." (1986), 40 *Industrial Labour Relations Review* 3 (1986).

Rose, J.B. and K. Wetzel. "Outcomes of Bargaining Structures in the Ontario and Saskatchewan Construction Industries." *Relations Industrielles* 41:2 (1986).

Rose, Joseph B. and Gary N. Chaison. "New Measures of Union Organizing Effectiveness." *Industrial Relations* 29:3 (1990).

Sack, J., and T. Lee. "The Role of the State in Canadian Labour Relations." *Relations Industrielles* 44:1 (1989).

Sass, Robert. "The Tory Assault on Labour in Saskatchewan." (1987), 7 *Access to Justice* 133.

Shelton Lennon, E.J. "Bank Workers Unionization." *Osgoode Hall L. J.* 18:2 (1980).

Taçon, S. "The Effect of Judicial Review on Grievance Arbitration." (1976), 14 *Osgoode Hall L. J.* 661.

Tolmie, Ellen. "Fleck: Profile of a Strike." *This Magazine* 12:4 (October 1978).

Warskett, Rosemary. "Bank Worker Unionization and the Law." SPE 25 (Spring 1988).

Wolfe, David. "Economic Growth and Foreign Investment." *Journal of Canadian Studies* 13 (Spring 1978).

Woods, H.D. "Canadian Collective Bargaining and Dispute Settlement Policy: An Appraisal." *Canadian Journal of Economics and Political Science* 21:4 (November 1955).

Yates, Charlotte. "CAW Militancy in the 1980s." SPE 31 (Spring 1990).

Zuboff, S. "Problems of Symbolic Toil: How People Fare With Computer-Mediated Work." *Dissent* (Winter 1982).

INDEX